LAWS AND LEGISLATION

THE GLOBAL LAW OF THE SEA

BASELINES AND BOUNDARY DELIMITATION

LAWS AND LEGISLATION

Additional books and e-books in this series can be found on Nova's website under the Series tab.

LAWS AND LEGISLATION

THE GLOBAL LAW OF THE SEA

BASELINES AND BOUNDARY DELIMITATION

GRAEME SCOTT BABER

nova
science publishers
New York

Library of Congress Cataloging-in-Publication Data

Names: Baber, Graeme, author.
Title: The global law of the sea : baselines and boundary delimitation / Graeme Scott Baber.
Description: Hauppauge : Nova Science Publishers, 2020. | Series: Laws and legislation | Includes bibliographical references and index.
Identifiers: LCCN 2020005507 (print) | LCCN 2020005508 (ebook) | ISBN 9781536173604 (hardcover) | ISBN 9781536175059 (adobe pdf)
Subjects: LCSH: Law of the sea. | Maritime boundaries.
Classification: LCC KZA1145 .B33 2020 (print) | LCC KZA1145 (ebook) | DDC 341.4/5--dc23
LC record available at https://lccn.loc.gov/2020005507
LC ebook record available at https://lccn.loc.gov/2020005508

Published by Nova Science Publishers, Inc. † New York

To my Mum for her support, and my Dad for his company,
in the endeavour to research and write this monograph

CONTENTS

PREFACE

Some years ago, when a Senior Lecturer-in-Law at BPP University, one of my Master of Laws' students asked if he could write a dissertation in Maritime Law. He wanted to do a survey of the rules of both Admiralty Law and the Law of the Sea. The department contained no specialist in either of these fields, and I taught neither. As he could not be dissuaded from this plan, I had to undertake a rapid, informal, self-directed learning programme in the subjects in order to gain sufficient professional skill to be able to supervise, and, later, assess, the dissertation. His project was surprisingly good – and I had my first contact with rules concerning territorial seas, contiguous zones, exclusive economic zones, continental shelves and high seas. My interest in these grew and, eventually, flourished in the project of this monograph.

The book covers the laws in the United Nations Convention on the Law of the Sea 1982 that concern baselines and boundary delimitation, together with cases which relate to these topics. There is also a major input to the monograph from procedural matters pertaining to the International Court of Justice, the International Tribunal for the Law of the Sea and arbitration under Annex VII to the Convention, with an example case provided for each of those mechanisms. As States Parties to the Convention may make a Declaration under its Article 287 for the settlement of their disputes by one or more of these methods – together with special arbitration under Annex VIII to the Convention for four issues specified therein – this Article, together with the methods and the remainder of Part XV of the Convention, are core material for a systematic review of the Law of the Sea.

In instances in which it is possible, comparisons are made between: (i) the United Nations Convention on the Law of the Sea and its predecessors, i.e., the Geneva Conventions from 1958, and (ii) the rules of the International Court of Justice and those of the International Tribunal for the Law of the Sea. In essence, the Convention builds upon its precursory instruments – which tend to be simpler than the former, and the procedural rules for the International Tribunal for the Law of the Sea are similar or identical to those of the International Court of Justice – other than a few provisions that are new or materially modified from the terms of the Court, but with the necessary changes from the latter being made.

The cases at this level are fewer than in black-letter subjects of the law, but tend to be complex and, for the legal scholar, very interesting. This is especially true of the *South China Sea Arbitration*, which was a judgment of pioneering brilliance from an Annex VII arbitral tribunal composed of one academic and four experienced judges, to which a substantial literature has – in the short period since this case's resolution – been devoted. The very best of luck with your reading!

Graeme Baber
December 2019

List of Abbreviations

CCS	Convention on the Continental Shelf 1958
CFCLRHS	Convention on Fishing and Conservation of the Living Resources of the High Seas 1958
CHS	Convention on the High Seas 1958
CTSCZ	Convention on the Territorial Sea and Contiguous Zone 1958
FAO	Food and Agriculture Organization of the United Nations
ICAO	International Civil Aviation Organization
ICJ	International Court of Justice
IMO	International Maritime Organization
ITLOS	International Tribunal for the Law of the Sea
ITLOS Statute	Statute of the International Tribunal for the Law of the Sea
M/T	Motor Tanker
M/V	Motor Vessel
nyp	not yet published
PCA	Permanent Court of Arbitration
PHP	Philippine pesos

UK	United Kingdom of Great Britain and Northern Ireland
UN	United Nations
UN Charter	Charter of the United Nations
UNCLOS	United Nations Convention on the Law of the Sea 1982
UNCLOS I	First United Nations Conference on the Law of the Sea
UNCLOS II	Second United Nations Conference on the Law of the Sea
UNCLOS III	Third United Nations Conference on the Law of the Sea
UNSC	Security Council of the United Nations
USA	United States of America
USD	United States Dollars

Chapter 1

An Introduction to the United Nations Convention on the Law of the Sea

Abstract

The UNCLOS is the main international instrument that regulates the Law of the Sea, prevailing, as between States Parties to that Convention, over the CCS, the CFCLRHS, the CHS and the CTSCZ. Subject to international law, a coastal state may exercise sovereignty over an area of sea – its 'territorial sea' – immediately beyond its land territory and internal waters, which includes the territorial sea's bed and subsoil and the airspace over it. Each of these countries has the right to institute the breadth of its territorial sea up to twelve nautical miles, as measured from baselines that are determined in compliance with the UNCLOS. The territorial sea's outer limit is the line every point of which is a distance equal to that sea's width from the baseline's nearest point. Where the coasts of two states are adjacent or opposite to each other, neither is entitled to extend its territorial sea beyond the median line every point of which is equidistant from the closest points on the baselines from which the breadth of the territorial sea of each of these countries is measured, unless they agree otherwise. Subject to the UNCLOS, ships of every state benefit from the right of innocent passage through the territorial sea. In a zone which is contiguous to a coastal state's territorial sea, that country may exert the control necessary to prevent contravention of its customs, fiscal, immigration or sanitary rules within its land territory and territorial sea. The contiguous zone may extend up to 24 nautical miles from the baselines from which the territorial sea's baselines are measured. The exclusive economic zone is an area beyond and adjoining the territorial sea, over which Part V of the UNCLOS confers rights and duties on the coastal state and freedoms and obligations on other countries. This zone may extend up to 200 nautical miles from the baselines from which the breadth of the territorial sea is measured. The delimitation of the exclusive economic zone – and the continental shelf – between countries with opposite or adjacent coasts is to be determined by agreement based upon international law. A coastal state's continental shelf comprises the seabed and subsoil of the submarine places that extend beyond its territorial sea in every part of the natural extension of its land territory to the outer border of the continental margin, or if the latter does not extend to 200 nautical miles from the baselines from which the territorial sea's width is measured – that distance. The coastal state exercises sovereign rights over the continental shelf in order to explore it and use its natural resources. Part XV of, and Annexes V-VIII to, the UNCLOS offer processes for conciliation and the following compulsory dispute-settlement procedures: resolution via the ICJ, the ITLOS, arbitration, and special arbitration for specified categories of dispute. Articles 297 and 298 of the UNCLOS respectively describe limitations on, and optional exceptions to, the applicability of those compulsory procedures. One optional exception concerns disputes regarding sea boundary delimitations or involving historic bays or titles.

Keywords: CCS, CTSCZ, continental, dispute, law, sea, territorial, UNCLOS, zone

INTRODUCTION

'*The Global Law of the Sea*' is a title that engenders idealized images of voyages of discovery, or, in more contemporary times, idyllic cruises that visit picturesque coastal venues in various countries. The reality is different. The subject is similarly packed with rules, cases and precedents to other established areas of law, but is more complex and looser in form than some of these by virtue of being part of public international law rather than a traditional discipline of domestic scope.

Adopted on 10th December 1982 by UNCLOS III and entering into force on 16th November 1994 [1, 2], the UNCLOS is the main international instrument regulating the Law of the Sea. The UNCLOS prevails, as between States Parties to this Convention, over the CCS, the CFCLRHS, the CHS, and the CTSCZ, which were adopted on 29th April 1958 by UNCLOS I – UNCLOS II of 1960 produced no international agreements [3, 4].

This book concerns the maritime zones that the UNCLOS describes, and considers specifically the territorial sea, the contiguous zone, the exclusive economic zone and the continental shelf, together with archipelagic zones and the regime of islands. The high seas and the Area are not discussed. It suffices to say that the former, which "[n]o State may validly purport to subject … to its sovereignty" [5], extends "to all parts of the sea that are not included in the exclusive economic zone, in the territorial sea or in the internal waters of a State, or in the archipelagic waters of an archipelagic State" [6], and that the latter is "the seabed and ocean floor and subsoil thereof, beyond the limits of national jurisdiction" [7] which, together with its resources, comprises "the common heritage of mankind" [8]. Thus, a section is devoted to each of the following Parts of the UNCLOS: (i) Part II – Territorial Sea and Contiguous Zone, (ii) Part IV – Archipelagic States, (iii) Part V – Exclusive Economic Zone, (iv) Part VI – Continental Shelf, (v) Part VIII – Regime of Islands, and (vi) Part XV – Settlement of Disputes, which is relevant to the material which Chapter Two explores.

PART II OF THE UNCLOS: TERRITORIAL SEA AND CONTIGUOUS ZONE

The General Rule

Subject to the UNCLOS and other provisions of international law [9], a coastal state may exercise sovereignty over an area of sea – its 'territorial sea', immediately beyond its land territory and internal waters[1] [10]. This sovereignty includes the territorial sea's bed and subsoil, and the airspace over it [11].

The Limits of the Territorial Sea and the Concept of the Baseline

Each state has the right to institute the breadth of its territorial sea up to, but not in excess of, twelve nautical miles[2] – as measured from baselines that are determined in compliance with the UNCLOS [12]. Unlike the UNCLOS, the CTSCZ does not commit to a specified mileage for the breadth of the territorial sea. The territorial sea's outer limit is the line every point of which is a distance equal to that sea's width from the baseline's nearest point[3] [13].

The Normal Baseline for Coasts and for Islands on or with Reefs

Unless the UNCLOS provides otherwise, the normal baseline for measuring the width of the territorial sea is the low-water line along the coast – as delineated on large-scale charts that the coastal state officially recognizes[4] [14]. The UNCLOS' provisions on the territorial sea apply to islands[5] [15] – thus, islands (at least in the absence of marine territorial

---

[1] Whilst Article 1 of the CTSCZ also contains this statement, Article 2(1) of the UNCLOS differs from the former in that it expressly adds the archipelagic waters of an archipelagic state to the grouping 'land territory and internal waters'.

[2] A nautical mile is one-sixtieth of a degree of latitude, which varies from 6046 feet on the equator to 6092 at a latitude of 60 degrees – the difference being due to the earth being an oblate spheroid; the standard nautical mile is 6080 feet, which is the same length as 1.151 statute miles and as 1853 metres (Royal Museums Greenwich (2019), "What is a nautical mile?," accessed July 19, 2019, <https://www.rmg.co.uk/discover/explore/nautical-mile-0>).

[3] Article 6 of the CTSCZ embodies an identical provision.

[4] The normal baseline: Article 3 of the CTSCZ is identical to Article 5 of the UNCLOS – except that the former specifies 'unless the CTSCZ', rather than the UNCLOS, 'provides otherwise'.

[5] The section below entitled 'Part VIII of the UNCLOS: Regime of Islands' describes the UNCLOS' treatment of islands, in its historical context. An 'island' "is a naturally formed

claims from other states) are surrounded by a territorial sea with a width of twelve nautical miles. Islands that are located on atolls, and those with fringing reefs, use a baseline for measuring the territorial sea's breadth which is the seaward low-water line of the reef – as the charts that the coastal state offically recognizes show by means of the suitable symbol[6] [16].

Straight Baselines

At places at which the coastline is indented deeply and chopped into, or where there is a nearby fringe of islands along the coast, the method of straight baselines may be used in order to draw the baseline from which the territorial sea's width is measured[7] [17]. The drawing of straight baselines must follow the general direction of the coast, and the areas of sea that are inside these baselines must be sufficiently closely-connected to the coastal state's land to be subject to the internal waters' regime[8] [18].

If the presence of a delta and other natural conditions render the coastline very unstable, then the most suitable points may be chosen along the outermost extent of the low-water line, and the straight baselines are to remain effective until the coastal state alters them in conformity with the UNCLOS[9] [19]. Straight baselines are not to be drawn to and from low-tide elevations, unless: (i) installations that are permanently above sea level, such as lighthouses, have been constructed on them, *or* (ii) the drawing of baselines to and from these elevations has been given international recognition[10] [20].

---

area of land, surrounded by water, which is above water at high tide" (United Nations (1982), "United Nations Convention on the Law of the Sea," *United Nations Treaty Series* Registration Number 31363, Article 121(1)).

[6] The CTSCZ lacks this provision.

[7] Article 4(1) of the CTSCZ contains an identical provision. Fn 5 defines 'island'.

[8] Article 4(2) of the CTSCZ embodies an identical rule.

[9] The CTSCZ lacks a corresponding provision.

[10] Article 4(3) of the CTSCZ contains a rule that differs from Article 7(4) of the UNCLOS only in that: (a) it refers to 'baselines' rather than to 'straight baselines', and (b) clause (ii) in the text is absent from it.

In determining particular straight baselines, economic interests specific to the region may be taken into account if the actuality and importance of these are clearly evidenced by lengthy usage[11] [21]. A state may not apply the system of straight baselines in such a way as to sever another country's territorial sea from an exclusive economic zone or the high seas[12] [22].

Internal Waters

Waters that are on the landward side of the territorial sea's baseline are part of the state's internal waters, except as Part IV of the UNCLOS provides[13] [23]. If the delineation of a straight baseline results in areas being enclosed as internal waters that were not previously considered as such, then there shall be a right of innocent passage in those places[14] [24].

The Baseline for a River entering the Sea

The baseline for a river that flows directly into the sea is a straight line across that river's mouth between points on the low-water line of its banks[15] [25].

---

[11] Article 4(4) of the CTSCZ embodies a very similar provision.

[12] The text immediately-preceding '[6]' above defines 'high seas' for the purposes of Part VII of the UNCLOS. Article 4(5) of the CTSCZ contains a very similar rule to Article 7(6) of the UNCLOS, but differs from the latter in omitting reference to 'an exclusive economic zone'. It is submitted that this is because the concept of 'exclusive economic zone' was introduced *after* the adoption of the CTSCZ in April 1958. This phrase was first assumed at UNCLOS III, which lasted from 1973 to 1982 (Organisation for Economic Co-operation and Development (2019), "Glossary of Statistical Terms: Exclusive Economic Zone (EEZ)," accessed July 20, 2019, <https://stats.oecd.org/glossary/detail.asp?ID=884>; Continental Shelf Programme (2019), "Background to UNCLOS," accessed July 20, 2019, <http://www.continentalshelf.org/about/1143.aspx>) The CTSCZ entered into force on 10th September 1964 (fn 771).

[13] Article 5(1) of the CTSCZ contains the same rule, but without the exception. Part IV of the UNCLOS is entitled 'Archipelagic States'. The section below entitled 'Part IV of the UNCLOS: Archipelagic States' considers provisions that Part IV of the UNCLOS includes.

[14] Article 5(2) of the CTSCZ contains a very similar provision. The subsection below titled 'Right of Innocent Passage' outlines the right of innocent passage in the territorial sea.

[15] Article 13 of the CTSCZ embodies an identical provision, except for using the term 'low-tide line' rather than 'low-water line'.

The Baseline for a Bay the Coast of Which Belongs to a Single State

The following provisions relate only to bays whose coasts belong to a single country[16] [26]. They apply to neither 'historic' bays, nor a situation in which the method of straight baselines is applied[17] [27]. A 'bay' comprises "a well-marked indentation whose penetration is in such proportion to the width of its mouth as to contain land-locked waters and constitute more than a mere curvature of the coast"[18] [28].

If the distance between the low-water marks of a bay's natural entrance points is 24 nautical miles or less, then a closing line may be drawn between these marks, and the waters enclosed thereby are considered to be internal waters[19] [29]. If this distance exceeds 24 nautical miles, then a straight baseline of this length is drawn within the bay in such a way as to

---

[16] Article 10(1) of the CTSCZ contains an identical condition.

[17] Article 7(6) of the CTSCZ embodies a very similar provision. The subsection above entitled 'Straight Baselines' describes the method of straight baselines.

[18] An indentation is not considered to be a bay, "unless its area is as large as, or larger than, that of the semi-circle whose diameter is a line drawn across the mouth of that indentation" (United Nations (1982), "United Nations Convention on the Law of the Sea," Article 10(2)). Article 7(2) of the CTSCZ is very similar to Article 10(2) of the UNCLOS. The 'area of an indentation' is "that lying between the low-water mark around the shore of the indentation and a line joining the low-water mark of its natural entrance points" (United Nations (1982), "United Nations Convention on the Law of the Sea," Article 10(3)). If an indentation has at least two mouths due to the presence of islands, then the semi-circle is drawn on a line amounting to the total of the lengths of the lines across these mouths (United Nations (1982), "United Nations Convention on the Law of the Sea," Article 10(3)). Islands that are located within an indentation are included as if they were part of that indentation's area of water (United Nations (1982), "United Nations Convention on the Law of the Sea," Article 10(3)). Article 7(3) of the CTSCZ is the same as Article 10(3) of the UNCLOS. Fn 5 defines 'island'.

[19] Article 7(4) of the CTSCZ contains an identical provision – except for the fact that the distance to which it refers is 24 *miles*, i.e., the word 'nautical' is absent. As fn 2 specifies, a nautical mile is longer than a statute mile. It is submitted that, prior to the adoption of the UNCLOS, the reference to '24 miles' in the CTSCZ could have been ambiguous, because there is an argument towards it referring to nautical miles – which is that it is a measurement over water, and there is also an argument towards it referring to statute miles – which is that references to 'miles' in most situations are implied references to statute miles rather than to nautical miles. On the basis of the ICJ's Judgment in *Fisheries Case (United Kingdom v. Norway)*, in which reference to the 'ten-mile rule' for the closing lines of bays meant ten sea miles, i.e., ten nautical miles (International Court of Justice (1951), *Fisheries Case (United Kingdom v. Norway)*, Judgment of December 18th 1951, *I.C.J. Reports 1951*, 116-144, 131), the phrase '24 miles' in Article 7(4) of the CTSCZ means ten *nautical* miles.

enclose the maximum area of water that is possible with a line of that extent[20] [30].

Ports and Boundary Delimitation

In order to delimit the territorial sea, the outermost permanent works that constitute an integral part of the harbour are considered to form part of the coast; this excludes artificial islands and offshore installations[21] [31].

Roadsteads

Roadsteads that are usually used for anchoring, loading and unloading ships are included in the territorial sea, even if they would otherwise be located entirely or partly outside this sea's outer limit[22] [32].

Low-Tide Elevations

If a low-tide elevation is placed completely or partly at distance less than or equal to the width of the territorial sea from the mainland or an island, then the low-water line on that elevation may be used as the baseline for measuring this sea's breadth[23] [33]. If a low-tide elevation is entirely situated at a distance that exceeds the breadth of the territorial sea

---

[20] Article 7(5) of the CTSCZ embodies an identical rule – other than for the fact that the distance to which it refers is 24 miles, i.e., the word 'nautical' is absent. Fn 19 comments on this matter.

[21] Article 8 of the CTSCZ comprises an identical statement to the first clause; the second clause is absent from this provision. Fn 5 defines 'island'.

[22] Article 9 of the CTSCZ includes an identical rule.

[23] Article 11(1) of the CTSCZ contains an identical provision. Fn 5 defines 'island'. A 'low-tide elevation' "is a naturally formed area of land which is surrounded by and above water at low tide but submerged at high tide" (United Nations (1982), "United Nations Convention on the Law of the Sea," Article 13(1)).

from the mainland or an island, then the elevation is denied its own territorial sea[24] [34].

The Coastal State's Approach to Using Baselines

The coastal state may settle baselines *seriatim* by any of the abovementioned methods, to befit different conditions[25] [35].

Delimitation of the Territorial Sea between States

In situations in which the coasts of two states are adjacent or opposite to each other, neither of these countries is entitled to extend its territorial sea beyond the median line every point of which is equidistant from the closest points on the baselines from which the width of the territorial sea of each of these states is measured, unless they agree otherwise[26] [36].

Charting or Listing the Geographical Co-Ordinates of Baselines

The baselines for measuring the width of the territorial sea (or the limits derived from these) that are determined by the rules concerning: (i)

---

[24] Article 11(2) of the CTSCZ embodies an identical rule.

[25] The CTSCZ does not contain this declaration. '*Seriatim*' is from medieval Latin, meaning "taking one subject after another in regular order; point by point" (Pearsall, J. (editor) (1998), *The New Oxford Dictionary of English* (Oxford: Oxford University Press), 1697). Dr. McFarlane's definition of '*seriatim*' confirms these meanings, i.e., "[t]aking each point in a series one at a time" (McFarlane, G. (1984), *The Layman's Dictionary of English Law* (London: Waterlow Publishers Limited), 260).

[26] This provision is inapplicable in situations in which it is necessary, because of special circumstances – such as historic title, to delimit the territorial sea of each of the two states in a way that is at variance with the median line (United Nations (1982), "United Nations Convention on the Law of the Sea," Article 15). Article 12 of the CTSCZ comprises a statement that is identical to the first sentence of Article 15 of the UNCLOS – which is paraphrased in the text to this footnote, and a statement which is substantially the same as the second sentence of Article 15 of the UNCLOS – which is reworded in this footnote. Fn 625 investigates legal practice and guidance with regard to historic title to waters, as contextual information in respect of China's claim over the preponderance of the South China Sea – which the arbitral tribunal addressed in the *South China Sea arbitration*.

straight baselines[27], (ii) rivers entering the sea[28] and (iii) baselines for bays the coast of which is within a single state[29], and the lines of delimitation which are drawn in conformity with the provision on roadsteads[30] and the law regarding the delimitation of territorial sea between neighbouring states[31], are to be shown on suitable charts or described by a list of geographical co-ordinates [37].

The Right of Innocent Passage through the Territorial Sea

Subject to the UNCLOS, ships of every state benefit from the right of innocent passage via the territorial sea[32] [38]. 'Passage' means navigation through this sea for the purpose of transversing it without entering internal waters or visiting a port or roadstead outside these waters [39], or progressing to or from internal waters or calling at such a port or roadstead[33] [40]. Whilst passage must "be continuous and expeditious,"

---

[27] The subsection above entitled 'Straight Baselines' covers the circumstances under which the straight baselines may be drawn and the way in which these are to be delineated.

[28] The subsection above titled 'The Baseline for a River entering the Sea' specifies how a baseline is drawn at this location.

[29] The subsection above named 'The Baseline for a Bay the Coast of Which Belongs to a Single State' defines a 'bay', states the circumstances under which an indentation is considered to be a bay, and describes how a straight baseline is drawn between the bay's natural entrance points or, if necessary, within the bay.

[30] The subsection above entitled 'Roadsteads' specifies the status of roadsteads with regard to the territorial sea.

[31] The subsection above titled 'Delimitation of the Territorial Sea between States' declares the rule for the delimitation of the territorial sea between countries whose coasts are adjacent or opposite.

[32] Article 14(1) of the CTSCZ contains a very similar provision.

[33] This meaning of 'passage' in the UNCLOS is similar to the meaning of 'passage' in the CTSCZ, which is "navigation through the territorial sea for the purpose either of traversing that sea without entering internal waters, or of proceeding to internal waters, or of making for the high seas from internal waters" (United Nations (1958), "Convention on the Territorial Sea and the Contiguous Zone," *United Nations Treaty Series* Registration Number 7477, Article 14(2)). It is submitted that one reason for changes in this provision from the version of it in the CTSCZ (above in this footnote) to that in the UNCLOS (text to this footnote) is that ports and roadsteads outside the territorial zone are located in the exclusive economic zone, which did not exist at the time of adoption of the CTSCZ (fn 12) – so Article 18(1) of the UNCLOS would need to refer to 'exclusive economic zone and high seas' if this provision was to remain entirely consistent with the version of it in Article 14(2) of the CTSCZ.

"stopping and anchoring" are permitted to the extent that these "are incidental to ordinary navigation or are rendered necessary by *force majeure*[34] or distress or for the purpose of rendering assistance to persons, ships or aircraft in danger or distress"[35] [41].

Passage is 'innocent' as long as it is not detrimental to the coastal state's good order, peace or security, and is to take place in accordance with the rules of international law – including the UNCLOS[36] [42]. A foreign ship's passage is prejudicial in this way if it participates in any of the following: a contravention of the principles of international law that the UN Charter contains [43], the use of, or practice with, any weapon [44], any act whose objective is to collect information that is damaging to the security or defence of the coastal state [45], any act of propaganda whose purpose is to affect this security or defence [46], the emplaning, launching or landing of any aircraft [47] or military device [48], the loading or unshipping of any currency, commodity or person in breach of the coastal state's customs, immigration, sanitary or fiscal laws and regulations [49], any intentional, serious act of pollution that is antithetical to the UNCLOS [50], any activities of fishing [51], the conducting of activities relating to surveys or research [52], any act whose aim is to impede any of the coastal state's installations or facilities [53], and/or any other activity that does not directly support passage[37] [54].

---

[34] Emphasis original.

[35] The corresponding provision in the CTSCZ states: "Passage includes stopping and anchoring, but only insofar as the same are incidental to ordinary navigation or are rendered necessary by force majeure or by distress." (United Nations (1958), "Convention on the Territorial Sea and the Contiguous Zone," Article 14(3)). Thus, the CTSCZ refers to neither 'continuous and expeditious' passage nor 'stopping and anchoring for the purpose of rendering assistance to persons, ships or aircraft in distress'.

[36] Article 14(4) of the CTSCZ comprises an identical provision to that in the text, except that the former refers to the Articles of the CTSCZ and the latter to the UNCLOS.

[37] Whilst there the CTSCZ contains no corresponding provision to this long list of detriments, it includes the following rule: "Passage of foreign fishing vessels shall not be considered innocent if they do not observe such laws and regulations as the coastal State may make and publish in order to prevent these vessels from fishing in the territorial sea." (United Nations (1958), "Convention on the Territorial Sea and the Contiguous Zone," Article 14(5)).

Underwater Vehicles in the Territorial Sea

In the territorial sea, underwater vehicles – including submarines – must navigate on the water's surface and display their flag[38] [55].

Nuclear Presence in the Territorial Sea

Foreign ships with nuclear power, and ships conveying hazardous or poisonous materials, are to carry documents and comply with special, precautionary measures that international agreements institute for these vessels, when using the right of innocent passage through the territorial sea[39] [56].

The Coastal State's Rights Regarding Its Territorial Sea

The Adoption of Laws

The coastal state may enact legislation and introduce regulations that conform to the rules of international law, including the provisions of the UNCLOS, which relate to innocent passage through the territorial sea, as regards all or any of the following: the regulation of maritime traffic and the safety of navigation [57], the protection of installations and[40] facilities [58], the safeguarding of cables and pipelines [59], the conservation of marine flora and fauna [60], the prevention of contravention of the coastal state's laws and regulations on fisheries [61], the preservation of that country's environment and the preclusion, curtailment and control of its pollution [62], hydrographic surveys and thalassic scientific research [63],

---

[38] Article 15(1) of the CTSCZ contains a similar provision, but refers only to 'submarines' and not to 'underwater vehicles'.

[39] The CTSCZ lacks a parallel provision.

[40] Article 21(1)(b) of the UNCLOS reads "or" at this point. It is submitted that the drafters of the UNCLOS meant 'and', as they would have wanted both facilities and installations to be protected. The 'or' may mean that an item to be protected may either be a facility or an installation.

and the prevention of breach of the coastal state's customs, immigration, sanitary or fiscal laws and regulations[41] [64]. These laws and regulations do not apply to the design, building, manning or equipment of foreign ships – unless they are pursuant to generally-accepted international standards or rules[42] [65]. The coastal State must publicize these laws and regulations[43] [66]. Foreign ships employing the right of innocent passage via the territorial sea are to observe all these laws and regulations, and all generally-accepted international rules that concern the prevention of maritime collisions[44] [67].

The Use of Sea Lanes and Traffic Separation Schemes in the Territorial Sea

Respecting the navigational safety where this is necessary, the coastal state may require foreign ships using the right of innocent passage through its territorial sea to utilize such sea lanes and traffic separation schemes as it may allot or impose for the management of the passage of ships[45] [68]. Tankers, ships with nuclear power, and ships conveying unsafe or toxic materials or substances may be required to proceed in these sea lanes[46] [69]. In its designation of sea lanes and instigation of traffic separation schemes, the coastal state shall consider the competent international organization's recommendations [70], any channels that are habitually employed for international navigation [71], the notable features of particular channels and ships [72], and the density of shipping[47] [73]. The

---

41 The CTSCZ lacks a comparable rule.

42 The CTSCZ lacks a corresponding provision.

43 The CTSCZ lacks a parallel rule.

44 The CTSCZ contains a similar provision: "Foreign ships exercising the right of innocent passage shall comply with the laws and regulations enacted by the coastal State in conformity with these articles and other rules of international law and, in particular, with such laws and regulations relating to transport and navigation." (United Nations (1958), "Convention on the Territorial Sea and the Contiguous Zone," Article 17).

45 The CTSCZ lacks a comparable provision.

46 The CTSCZ lacks a corresponding rule.

47 The CTSCZ lacks a parallel provision. Fn 85 specifies the particular 'competent international organization' for this rule, i.e., Article 22(3) of the UNCLOS.

coastal state is to clearly show these sea lanes and traffic separation schemes on publicized charts[48] [74].

Rights of Protection of the Coastal State

The coastal state may take what actions are necessary in its territorial sea to preclude passage that is not innocent[49] [75]. It also has the right to take any necessary steps to prevent any infringement of the conditions to which admission of ships to internal waters, or to a port outside those waters, is subject[50] [76]. The coastal state may, in specified places within its territorial sea, temporarily suspend without discrimination amongst foreign ships the innocent passage of those vessels, if this suspension is crucial to protect its security[51] [77].

---

[48] The CTSCZ lacks a comparable rule.

[49] Article 16(1) of the CTSCZ contains an identical provision.

[50] Article 16(2) of the CTSCZ empowers the coastal state to take the necessary actions to prevent any contravention of the conditions to which admission of ships to internal waters is subject, which mirrors Article 25(2) of the UNCLOS (text to this footnote). Unlike the latter, Article 16(2) of the CTSCZ does not refer to the access of ships to ports outside internal waters.

[51] This suspension only comes into force after its publication (United Nations (1982), "United Nations Convention on the Law of the Sea," Article 25(3)). Article 16(3) of the CTSCZ contains a very similar provision to Article 25(3) of the UNCLOS. Unlike the suspension which the latter sanctions, that which the former permits is subject to the following condition: "There shall be no suspension of the innocent passage of foreign ships through straits which are used for international navigation between one part of the high seas and another part of the high seas or the territorial sea of a foreign State." (United Nations (1958), "Convention on the Territorial Sea and the Contiguous Zone," Article 16(4)). Notwithstanding this, Article 45 of the UNCLOS states: "There shall be no suspension of innocent passage through … straits used for international navigation … excluded from the application of the regime of transit passage under article 38, paragraph 1 [of the UNCLOS – which permits the freedom of navigation and overflight for the sole purpose of continuous, expeditious transit of a strait used for international navigation between an exclusive economic zone or one part of the high seas and another part of the high seas or an exclusive economic zone (United Nations (1982), "United Nations Convention on the Law of the Sea," Article 38(2))]; or … between a part of the high seas or an exclusive economic zone and the territorial sea of a foreign State." Furthermore, there is "no suspension of transit passage" (United Nations (1982), "United Nations Convention on the Law of the Sea," Article 44). Thus, although the UNCLOS lacks a provision that directly corresponds to Article 16(4) of the CTSCZ, it enacts the effect of that rule by means of the combined effect of its Articles 44 and 45.

The Coastal State's Duties Concerning Its Territorial Sea

The coastal state must not hinder the innocent passage of foreign ships via the territorial sea except in compliance with the UNCLOS[52] [78]. In the application of the UNCLOS or of any laws or regulations adopted in accordance with the UNCLOS, the coastal state must not place requirements on foreign ships that effectively deny or harm the right of innocent passage [79], or discriminate against any country's ships or against vessels carrying freight to, from or on behalf of any state[53] [80]. The coastal State must aptly publicize any danger to navigation of which it is aware, within its territorial sea[54] [81].

A coastal state may not levy a charge on foreign ships by reason only of their passage through its territorial sea[55] [82]. It may impose a non-discrimatory charge upon a foreign ship for specific services provided to that vessel[56] [83].

Criminal Jurisdiction on Board Foreign Commercial Ships

The coastal state's criminal jurisdiction regarding a foreign ship passing through its territorial sea may only be exercised if the crime's consequences extend to that country [84], the crime is of a kind which

[52] Article 15(1) of the CTSCZ embodies a similar rule.

[53] The CTSCZ lacks a corresponding provision.

[54] Article 15(2) of the CTSCZ contains an almost identical rule.

[55] Article 18(1) of the CTSCZ embodies an identical provision. Whilst the rule which Article 26(1) of the UNCLOS embodies applies to all ships, that which Article 18(1) of the CTSCZ contains applies to merchant ships, government ships which are operated for commercial purposes (United Nations (1958), "Convention on the Territorial Sea and the Contiguous Zone," Article 21) and government ships that are operated for non-commercial purposes (United Nations (1958), "Convention on the Territorial Sea and the Contiguous Zone," Article 22(1)), but does not expressly apply to warships.

[56] Article 18(2) of the CTSCZ contains an identical rule. Whilst the rule which Article 26(2) of the UNCLOS contains applies to all ships, that which Article 18(2) of the CTSCZ embodies applies to merchant ships, government ships which are operated for commercial purposes (United Nations (1958), "Convention on the Territorial Sea and the Contiguous Zone," Article 21) and government ships that are operated for non-commercial purposes (United Nations (1958), "Convention on the Territorial Sea and the Contiguous Zone," Article 22(1)), but does not expressly apply to warships.

disturbs the state's peace or the territorial sea's good order [85], the ship's master or a consular officer or diplomatic agent of the flag state has requested the help of the local authorities [86], or penal measures are necessary to repress illegal traffic in narcotic or psychotropic drugs[57] [87]. These provisions do not impair the coastal state's right to take any actions that its laws authorize which contribute to an investigation or an arrest on board a foreign ship that is moving through the territorial sea, subsequent to leaving internal waters[58] [88]. Except as Part XII of the UNCLOS[59] provides, or as regards infractions of laws and regulations that are adopted in conformity with Part V of the UNCLOS[60], the coastal state may not proceed to conduct an investigation or arrest anyone on board a foreign ship transversing its territorial sea, in association with any crime commited prior to this vessel's entry into that sea, if the ship advances from a foreign port and is only crossing the territorial sea without entering internal waters[61] [89].

Civil Jurisdiction in Relation to Foreign Commercial Ships

The coastal state *should*[62] not halt or divert a foreign ship travelling through its territorial sea in order to exercise civil jurisdiction upon a

---

[57] Article 19(1) of the CTSCZ contains a very similar provision on the coastal state's criminal jurisdiction on board merchant ships passing through its territorial sea, which Article 22(1) of the CTSCZ extends to its criminal jurisdiction on board government ships other than warships passing through its territorial sea. By contrast, the UNCLOS does not expressly extend this jurisdiction to government ships operated for *non-commercial* purposes passing through its territorial sea.

[58] Article 20(3) of the CTSCZ contains a similar rule.

[59] Part XII of the UNCLOS is entitled 'Protection and Preservation of the Marine Environment', and contains Articles 192-237 of the Convention.

[60] The section below titled 'Part V of the UNCLOS: Exclusive Economic Zone' details provisions in Part V of the UNCLOS.

[61] Article 19(5) of the CTSCZ contains the same rule as Article 27(5) of the UNCLOS, but, unlike the latter, without any constraints.

[62] The use of the word 'should' indicates that Article 28(1) of the UNCLOS does not prohibit the authorities of a coastal state from stopping or redirecting a foreign ship that is moving through its territorial sea, but discourages them from doing so. It is submitted that these authorities would be required to provide a good reason for this action to interested parties who questioned it, in order for the action to be consistent with Article 28(1) of the UNCLOS.

person on board this vessel[63] [90]. This country must not levy execution[64] against, or detain, the foreign ship for the purpose of civil proceedings, except with regard to obligations assumed or liabilities incurred by that vessel in the course, or for the purpose, of its journey through the coastal state's waters[65] [91]. Notwithstanding this, the coastal state may, in concurrence with its laws, levy execution or detain for the purpose of civil proceedings, a foreign ship that is positioned in its territorial sea, or progressing through that sea subsequent to leaving internal waters[66] [92].

Rules Applicable to Governmental Non-Commercial Ships

If a warship[67] breaches a coastal state's laws and regulations that concern passage via the latter's territorial sea, and ignores any request which is made to it for its conformity with these rules, then the coastal state may require it to vacate this territorial sea forthwith[68] [93]. The flag

---

[63] Article 20(1) of the CTSCZ embodies an identical provision.

[64] To 'levy execution' is "to seize goods in payment of a loan, acting under authority of the law" (McFarlane, G. (1984), *The Layman's Dictionary of English Law*, 165).

[65] Article 20(2) of the CTSCZ contains an identical provision.

[66] Article 20(3) of the CTSCZ embodies the same rule. It is submitted that, as the UNCLOS makes the text to this footnote of preferential application to the text to the immediately-preceding footnote, the combination of these provisions enables the coastal state to legislate to impose civil jurisdiction over a foreign ship passing through its territorial waters over and above that embodied in the above phrase 'except with regard to obligations assumed or liabilities incurred by that vessel in the course, or for the purpose, of its journey through the coastal state's waters' – unless this phrase is interpreted in such a way that 'obligations assumed' includes an automatic duty, once the foreign ship enters the coastal state's territorial waters, to comply with every pertinent aspect of its relevant, effective national laws, and that this duty applies continuously until the moment at which that vessel leaves the coastal state's territorial sea to enter its exclusive economic zone.

[67] For the purposes of the UNCLOS, a 'warship' is "a ship belonging to the armed forces of a State bearing the external marks distinguishing such ships of its nationality, under the command of an officer duly commissioned by the government of the State and whose name appears in the appropriate service list or its equivalent, and manned by a crew which is under regular armed forces discipline" (United Nations (1982), "United Nations Convention on the Law of the Sea," Article 29).

[68] Article 23 of the CTSCZ contains the same rule as Article 30 of the UNCLOS, but is weaker in its form than the latter; it refers to the coastal state's regulations – rather than to the coastal state's laws and regulations, and it empowers the coastal state to require the warship to vacate its territorial sea when the two conditions in the 'if' clause are satisfied – but not necessarily immediately.

state of a governmental ship operated for non-commercial purposes is to carry global responsibility for any damage to a coastal state from the contravention by that vessel of this coastal state's laws and regulations concerning transit across its territorial sea, or of the provisions of the UNCLOS or other international laws[69] [94].

The Contiguous Zone

In a zone that is contiguous to a coastal's state's territorial sea – the 'contiguous zone', this country may exert the control necessary to preclude transgression of its customs, immigration, sanitary or fiscal laws and regulations within its dominions or territorial sea [95], and penalize infringements of these laws and regulations which are committed within those areas[70] [96]. The contiguous zone may extend no more than 24 nautical miles from the baselines from which the territorial sea's baselines are measured[71] [97].

PART IV OF THE UNCLOS: ARCHIPELAGIC STATES

Introduction

None of the Conventions adopted on 29th April 1958 by UNCLOS I – the CCS, the CFCLRHS, the CHS and the CTSCZ – mention archipelogos. The matter of mid-ocean archipelagos was discussed at UNCLOS I, but neither this Conference nor UNCLOS II resolved the issues of whether a special regime should be applied to the seas of these archipelogos and, if

[69] The CTSCZ lacks a corresponding rule.

[70] Article 24(1) of the CTSCZ embodies the same provisions as Article 33(1) of the UNCLOS.

[71] The '24 nautical miles' prescribed by Article 33(2) of the UNCLOS as the maximum seaward extent of the contiguous zone contrasts with the twelve miles that Article 24(2) of the CTSCZ specifies for this distance. In view of the use of word 'nautical' in the former, 'twelve miles' in the latter is likely to mean 'twelve nautical miles' rather than 'twelve statute miles' (fn 19).

so, what this system should be [98]. Mid-ocean archipelagos – contrasting with coastal archipelagos which are those located so near to a mainland that they may reasonably be considered to be part of it[72] – are groups of islands that are placed in the ocean at such a distance from landmass as to be deemed to be an independent whole; Indonesia and the Philippines are examples [99]. UNCLOS III has resolved the issue – Part IV of the UNCLOS, entitled 'Archipelagic States' is a special regime that applies to mid-ocean archipelagos, whilst coastal archipelagos receive the treatment which Part II of the UNCLOS accords[73], as part of the state of which they are a territorial component.

Definitions: 'Archipelago' and 'Archipelagic State' in the UNCLOS

An 'archipelago' is "a group of islands, including parts of islands, interconnecting waters and other natural features which are so closely interrelated that such islands, waters and other natural features form an intrinsic geographical, economic and political entity, or which historically have been regarded as such" [100]. An 'archipelagic state' is "a State constituted wholly by one or more archipelagos[,] and may include other islands" [101].

The Drawing of Archipelagic Baselines

An archipelagic state may draw straight archipelagic baselines that join the furthest points of the archipelago's outermost islands and drying

[72] The coastline of Norway is an exemplar of a coastal archipelago (Brock, J. (1966), Archipelago Concept of Limits of Territorial Seas, *Naval War College Review*, 19(4), 34-97, 55).

[73] The section above entitled 'Part II of the UNCLOS: Territorial Sea and Contiguous Zone', describes most of the Articles of Part II of the UNCLOS.

reefs[74], as long as these baselines encompass the main islands and an expanse in which the ratio of the area of the water to the area of the land – including atolls – is between 1:1 and 9:1[75] [102]. These baselines must be no more than 100 nautical miles, except that 3% or less of the total number of baselines surrounding any archipelago may exceed this length, up to a maximum of 125 nautical miles [103]. The baselines are to be drawn so as not to appreciably diverge from the archipelago's general configuration [104].

The straight archipelagic baselines are not to be drawn to and from a low-tide elevation, unless: (i) an installation which is permanently above sea level, such as a lighthouse, has been assembled on that low-tide elevation, or (ii) the low-tide elevation is partly or entirely located at distance of no more than the territorial sea's width from the nearest island[76] [105]. An archipelagic state is not to apply this system of straight archipelagic baselines in a way that isolates the territorial sea of another country from an exclusive economic zone or the high seas[77] [106].

If a part of an archipelagic state's archipelagic waters is situated between two sections of an adjoining country, all legitimate interests that the latter has customarily exercised in these waters and all contractual rights between those states are to continue and be observed [107]. The straight archipelagic baselines that are drawn in compliance with the above

[74] The UNCLOS does not define 'drying reef'. A 'drying reef' may be a low-tide elevation that is part of a reef (Symmons, C. (1995), Some Problems Relating to the Definition of Insular Formations in International Law – Islands and Low-Tide Elevations, *University of Durham Maritime Briefing*, 1(5).6).

[75] In order to calculate the ratio of water to land, "land areas may include water lying within the fringing reefs of islands and atolls, including that part of a steep-sided oceanic plateau which is enclosed or nearly enclosed by a chain of limestone islands and drying reefs lying on the perimeter of the plateau" (United Nations (1982), "United Nations Convention on the Law of the Sea," Article 47(7)). Fn 74 defines 'drying reef'. A 'fringing reef' is "a coral reef that lies close to the shore" (Pearsall, J. (editor) (1998), *The New Oxford Dictionary of English*, 735).

[76] This provision, Article 47(4) of the UNCLOS, applies the same point (i) as that in Article 7(4) of the UNCLOS concerning straight, non-archipelagic baselines, but point (ii) in the former differs from that in the latter (text to fn 10).

[77] This rule, Article 47(5) of the UNCLOS, applies the same prohibition to straight archipelagic baselines as Article 7(6) of the UNCLOS administers to straight, non-archipelagic baselines (text to fn 12).

provisions are to be shown on appropriate charts or described by a list of geographical co-ordinates[78] [108].

Measurements from Archipelagic Baselines

The breadth of an archipelagic state's territorial sea, continuous zone, exclusive economic zone and continental shelf are measured from archipelagic baselines drawn in agreement with Article 47 of the UNCLOS [109], i.e., in accordance with the provisions of the immediately-preceding subsection.

Rules for Ports and for Baselines for Bays and Rivers

Within its archipelagic waters, an archipelagic state may draw closing lines to delimit internal waters in observance of the rules for ports and for the baselines for bays and rivers entering the sea that Part II of the UNCLOS contains[79] [110].

The Legal Status of Archipelagic Waters

An archipelagic state's sovereignty extends to the waters that the archipelagic baselines drawn in fulfilment of Article 47 of the UNCLOS enclose, irrespective of both the depth of those archipelagic waters and their distance from the coast [111]. This sovereignty applies to the airspace over the archipelagic waters, to their seabed and subsoil, and to the

---

[78] This provision, Article 47(8) of the UNCLOS, contains the same treatment for the charting of straight archipelagic baselines as Article 16(1) of the UNCLOS does for the mapping of baselines and lines of delimitation regarding the territorial sea (text to fns 27-31).

[79] The subsections entitled 'The Baselines for a River entering the Sea', 'The Baseline for a Bay the Coast of Which Belongs to a Single State' and 'Ports and Boundary Delimitation', in the section above titled 'Part II of the UNCLOS: Territorial Sea and Contiguous Zone', states these rules.

resources contained within these[80] [112]. This sovereignty is limited by rights that Part IV of the UNCLOS confers on other states [113], which are considered below in this section. Notwithstanding this, the right of archipelagic sea lanes passage that Part IV of the UNCLOS establishes, changes in other ways neither the status of the archipelagic waters nor the archipelagic state's exercise of its sovereignty over these waters and their airspace, seabed and subsoil, and the resources held therein [114].

Rights and Legitimate Activities of Neighbouring States

Without prejudice to an archipelagic state's sovereignty over its archipelagic waters, this country is to observe agreements with other states that are in force, and is to recognize customary fishing rights and other legitimate activities of its adjoining countries in defined areas of these waters[81] [115]. An archipelagic state is to mind submarine cables that other states have laid, and is to allow the maintenance and replacement of these items upon receiving due notice of their whereabouts and the plan to repair or replace them [116].

The Right of Innocent Passage through Archipelagic Waters

Subject to the right of archipelagic sea lanes passage and without prejudice to an archipelagic state's sovereignty over its archipelagic waters, ships of all countries benefit from the right of innocent passage through archipelagic waters in accordance with the provisions of Section 3

---

[80] Likewise, the sovereignty of a coastal state over its territorial sea extends to the airspace above that sea and to its bed and subsoil – but Article 2(2) of the UNCLOS does not refer to the resources contained therein (see the subsection entitled 'The General Rule', in the above section titled 'Part II of the UNCLOS: Territorial Sea and Contiguous Zone').

[81] At the request of any of the relevant states, the terms and conditions for these rights and activities to be exercised shall be regulated by bilateral agreements between them; these rights are not to be transferred to, or shared with, third countries or their nationals (United Nations (1982), "United Nations Convention on the Law of the Sea," Article 51(1)).

of Part II of the UNCLOS[82] [117]. The archipelagic state may, in specified zones within its archipelagic waters, temporarily suspend without discrimination between foreign ships the innocent passage of those vessels, if this suspension is vital for safeguarding that country's security[83] [118].

The Right of Archipelagic Sea Lanes Passage

An archipelagic state may pronounce sea lanes and air routes that are appropriate for the uninterrupted, expeditious passage of foreign ships and aircraft through or over its archipelagic waters and adjoining territorial sea [119]. All ships and aircraft qualify for the right of archipelagic sea lanes passage in these designated sea lanes and air routes [120].

'Archipelagic sea lanes passage' means the exercise in conformity with the UNCLOS of the rights of navigation and overflight in the usual way, entirely for the purpose of unbroken, expeditious, unobstructed transit between an exclusive economic zone or one part of the high seas and another section of the high seas or an exclusive economic zone [121]. These sea lanes and air routes are to cross the archipelagic waters and the vicinal territorial sea, and are to include all courses for normal passage that are used as paths for international navigation (including all standard navigational channels) through, or flight over, archipelagic waters; notwithstanding this, the duplication of routes of similar convenience between the same points for entry and exit will be unnecessary [122]. The sea lanes and air routes are to be specified by a succession of continuous axis lines from the points of entry, to the points of exit, of routes for

[82] The subsections from that entitled 'The Right of Innocent Passage through the Territorial Sea' to that titled 'Rules applicable to Governmental Non-Commercial Ships', inclusive, in the above section entitled 'Part II of the UNCLOS: Territorial Sea and Contiguous Zone', contain provisions of Section 3 of Part II of the UNCLOS.

[83] This provision, Article 52(2) of the UNCLOS, is identical to Article 25(2) of the UNCLOS – except that the former applies to archipelagic waters and the latter to the territorial sea (text to fn 51). As in the case of the territorial sea (fn 51), the suspension of the innocent passage of foreign ships through archipelagic waters only enters into force after its publication (United Nations (1982), "United Nations Convention on the Law of the Sea," Article 52(2)).

transit; subject to one exception[84], ships and aircraft in archipelagic sea lanes passage must not digress more than 25 nautical miles to either side of these axis lines during their passage [123].

An archipelagic state that designates sea lanes thus may also stipulate traffic separation schemes for the safe passage of ships by means of narrow channels in these sea lanes [124]. When circumstances require, and after providing proper publicity, an archipelagic state may replace sea lanes or traffic separation schemes that it has previously specified with others [125]. These sea lanes and traffic separation schemes are to observe generally-accepted international rules [126]. In designating or substituting sea lanes or traffic separation schemes, an archipelagic state is to refer its suggestions "to the competent international organization"[85] in order to secure their adoption; this organization may adopt only the sea lanes and traffic separaton schemes that it has agreed with the archipelagic state, following which that country may specify or substitute them [127].

PART V OF THE UNCLOS: EXCLUSIVE ECONOMIC ZONE

The Exclusive Economic Zone

The phrase 'exclusive economic zone' was first used at UNCLOS III[86]. This expression is absent from the CCS, the CFCLRHS, the CHS and the CTSCZ, which is unsurprising as these Conventions pre-date UNCLOS III.

---

[84] This bilateral limit of 25 nautical miles applies "provided that such ships and aircraft [do] not navigate closer to the coast than 10 per cent of the distance between the nearest points on islands bordering the sea lane" (United Nations (1982), "United Nations Convention on the Law of the Sea," Article 53(5)).

[85] The UNCLOS contains many instances of the phrase 'competent international organization' (or 'competent international organizations') but does not define this expression. In the context of the text to this footnote, the 'competent international organization' is the IMO for the navigation of ships and the ICAO for overflights; for Article 22(3) of the UNCLOS (text to fn 47), the 'competent international organization' is the IMO (Walker, G. (editor) (2012), *Definitions for the Law of the Sea: Terms Not Defined by the 1982 Convention* (Leiden: Martinus Nijhoff Publishers), 138).

[86] Fn 12.

The 'exclusive economic zone' is an area beyond and adjoining the territorial sea, which is subject to the provisions of Part V of the UNCLOS; these rules govern a coastal state's jurisdiction and rights over this zone, and the freedoms and rights of other countries concerning it [128]. The exclusive economic zone must extend no more than 200 nautical miles from the baselines from which the width of the territorial sea is measured [129].

The Coastal State's Jurisdiction, Rights and Duties Therein

In its exclusive economic zone, a coastal state has: (i) sovereign rights that permit it to explore, exploit, conserve and manage the natural resources of the waters overlying the seabed and of the ocean floor and its subsoil, and to pursue other activities that constitute economic exploitation and exploration of the area – for instance, the generation of energy from the water, its currents and winds [130], (ii) jurisdiction in accordance with the pertinent provisions of the UNCLOS regarding the construction and use of artificial islands, structures and installations [131], marine scientific research [132], and the safeguarding and prevention of the thalassic environment [133], and (iii) other rights and obligations that the UNCLOS provides [134]. In exercising these rights and performing these duties, the coastal state is to duly consider the rights and responsibilities of other countries, and is to act in a way that is consistent with the provisions of the UNCLOS [135]. The rights that this paragraph sets out concerning the seabed and its subsoil are to be exercised in conformity with Part VI of the UNCLOS[87] [136].

[87] The section below entitled 'Part VI: Continental Shelf' describes provisions from Part VI of the UNCLOS.

Rights and Duties of Other States in the Exclusive Economic Zone

In the exclusive economic zone, and subject to the relevant provisions of the UNCLOS, all countries enjoy the following freedoms of the high seas that Article 87 of the UNCLOS lays down – the freedoms of navigation, of overflight, and to set down submarine cables and pipelines, and other uses of the sea that are related to these freedoms and which are permitted by international law – for instance, those connected with the operation of aircraft, ships and submarine cables and pipelines and which are consistent with the other rules of the UNCLOS [137]. Articles 88 to 115 of the UNCLOS[88] apply to the exclusive economic zone, to the extent that they are compatible with the provisions of Part V of the UNCLOS [138]. In applying their rights and undertaking their obligations under the UNCLOS in a coastal state's exclusive economic zone, countries must duly consider that state's rights and duties, and are to observe the laws and regulations which the coastal state adopts in compliance with rules of international law including the UNCLOS – in so far as those national rules are consistent with Part V of the UNCLOS [139].

The Equitable Resolution of Interstate Conflicts Therein

If the UNCLOS does not allot jurisdiction or rights to the coastal state or to other countries within the former's exclusive economic zone, and if a conflict occurs between the interests of that state and those of any other country, then the dispute should be settled on the basis of equity and considering all circumstances of relevance, taking into account the significance of the interests involved to the parties and to the global community [140].

---

[88] These Articles contain general provisions of the UNCLOS that apply to the high seas. For example, the high seas are to "be reserved for peaceful purposes" (United Nations (1982), "United Nations Convention on the Law of the Sea," Article 88).

Artificial Islands, Installations and Structures

The coastal state has the sole right in its exclusive economic zone to build, and to authorize and supervise the construction, functioning and use of, artificial islands [141], installations and structures for economic purposes [142], and installations and structures that may interfere with the exercise of its rights in this zone [143]. The coastal state has exclusive jurisdiction over these artificial islands, installations and structures – which includes legal authority over customs, immigration, health, safety and fiscal matters [144]. The coastal state must provide due notice of the construction of artificial islands, installations or structures, and maintain permanent means for warning of their presence[89] [145].

In every instance in which it is necessary, the coastal state may institute reasonable safety zones around these artificial islands, installations and structures; in such places, that country may take suitable measures to ensure the safety both of those objects and of navigation [146]. The coastal state is to determine the breadth of the safety zones, taking applicable international standards into account; it shall design these areas to ensure that they reasonably relate to the nature and function of the artificial islands, installations or structures[90] [147]. All ships are to show due regard for these safety zones, and are to observe generally-accepted worldwide standards concerning navigation in the neighbourhood of artificial islands, installations, structures and safety zones [148].

---

[89] Any abandoned or disused structures must be removed to ensure safe navigation, taking into consideration any generally-accepted worldwide standards that "the competent international organization" (fn 85) has established; this removal must duly consider the rights and obligations of other countries, fishing, and the safeguarding of the marine environment (United Nations (1982), "United Nations Convention on the Law of the Sea," Article 60(3)). The IMO is the 'competent international organization' for Articles 60(3) and 60(5) of the UNCLOS (Walker, G. (2005), Defining Terms in the 1982 Law of the Sea Convention IV: The Last Round of Definitions Proposed By the International Law Association (American Branch) Law of the Sea Committee, *California Western International Law Journal*, 36(1), 133-183, 160).

[90] The safety zones must be no more than 500 metres around the artificial islands, installations or structures, except as "the competent international organization" (fn 85) recommends or generally-accepted global standards authorize (United Nations (1982), "United Nations Convention on the Law of the Sea," Article 60(5)). This 'competent international organization' is the IMO (fn 89).

Artificial islands, installations and structures, and the safety zones around these, may not be set up where there may be resultant interference to the use of recognized sea lanes that are crucial to international navigation [149]. These objects lack the status of islands, thus having no territorial sea of their own; their presence has no effect on the delimitation of the territorial sea, the exclusive economic zone or the continental shelf [150].

Conservation and Utilization of Living Resources

The coastal state is to determine the permissible catch of the living resources in its exclusive economic zone [151]. Taking into consideration the best scientific evidence that is available to it, this country is to ensure through proper measures for conservation and management that the preservation of living resources in its exclusive economic zone is not imperilled by over-exploitation[91] [152]. These measures shall also be designed to maintain or restore populations of harvested species that are able to produce the maximum sustainable yield [153].

In taking these measures, the coastal state is to consider the effects on groups of living organisms that are connected with, or dependent upon, harvested species, with the intention of continuing or restoring populations of the former to levels which are higher than those at which their propagation may be gravely threatened [154]. Data that are relevant to the conservation ot stocks of fish are to be regularly contributed and exchanged, as appropriate[92] [155].

---

[91] As is fitting, "the coastal State and competent international organizations, whether subregional, regional or global, shall cooperate to this end" (United Nations (1982), "United Nations Convention on the Law of the Sea," Article 61(2)). In Articles 61(2) and 61(5) of the UNCLOS, 'competent international organizations, whether subregional, regional or global' means the FAO and regional fishery organizations inside and outside the FAO (Walker, G. (2005), Defining Terms in the 1982 Law of the Sea Convention IV, 161).

[92] This contribution and exchange of data is "through competent international organizations, whether subregional, regional or global … with participation by all States concerned, including States whose nationals are allowed to fish in the exclusive economic zone" (United Nations (1982), "United Nations Convention on the Law of the Sea," Article 61(5)).

Subject to the above provisions concerning the conservation of living resources, the coastal state is to further the aim of optimum utilization of these resources in the exclusive economic zone [156]. Whilst the coastal state is to determine its capacity to gather the living resources of the exclusive economic zone, if it lacks the scope to harvest the whole allowable catch, then it is to allow other countries access to the surplus [157]. In permitting other states to enter its exclusive economic zone in order to utilize natural resources located there, the coastal state is to take factors of relevance into account [158]. Nationals of other countries who are fishing in the coastal state's exclusive economic zone are to observe the terms and conditions that the latter's laws and regulations have laid down – including its measures for conservation [159]. These laws and regulations must be compatible with the UNCLOS and may relate, but are not limited, to the following: the licensing of fishing vessels, fishermen and equipment [160], determining the species that may be caught and fixing quotas of catch [161], regulating areas and seasons of fishing, the types, quantity and sizes of fishing equipment, and the varieties, number and sizes of fishing vessels that may be utilized [162], deciding upon the age and size of species which may be caught [163], stating information that fishing vessels may be required to provide [164], requiring specified fisheries to carry out research programmes, and regulating the conduct of this research [165], the coastal state's placing of trainees or observers on board fishing vessels [166], the landing of any portion, or the whole, of the vessels' catch of fish in the coastal state's ports [167], terms and conditions that concern co-operative arrangements [168], requirements for the training of personnel and the transfer of technology concerning fisheries [169], and procedures for enforcement [170].

Fn 91 defines these 'competent international organizations' for Article 61(5) of the UNCLOS.

Migratory, Anadromous[93], Catadromous[94] and Sedentary[95] Species

The coastal state, and other countries whose nationals fish in the area for the highly migratory species that Annex I to the UNCLOS lists[96], shall co-operate with the aim of ensuring conservation and advancing the objective of optimum use of these stocks of fish throughout the region [171]. Nothing in Part V of the UNCLOS limits the right of a coastal state or the power of an international organization, as the case may be, to ban, restrict or regulate the exploitation of marine mammals more strictly that this Part of the UNCLOS requires[97] [172].

Countries in whose rivers anadromous[98] stocks of fish orginate have the main interest in, and responsibility for, these supplies [173]. The state of origin of anadromous stocks must ensure their conservation by the instituting of suitable regulatory measures for fishing in all waters that are landward of the exclusive economic zone's outer boundary, and for fishing of these stocks by other countries[99] [174]. This state of origin's fisheries for its anadromous stocks are to be placed in waters that are landward of the outer boundary of its exclusive economic zone, except in instances in

---

[93] An 'anadromous' fish is one that "migrat[es] up rivers from the sea to spawn" (Pearsall, J. (editor) (1998), *The New Oxford Dictionary of English*, 58).

[94] A 'catadromous' fish is one that "migrat[es] down rivers to the sea to spawn" (Pearsall, J. (editor) (1998), *The New Oxford Dictionary of English*, 286).

[95] A 'sedentary' fish is one that "inhabit[es] the same locality throughout [its] life" (Pearsall, J. (editor) (1998), *The New Oxford Dictionary of English*, 1681).

[96] The highly migratory species are, or are specified families and/or species of: albacore, bluefin, bigeye, skipjack, yellowfin, blackfin, little and southern bluefin tuna, frigate mackerel, pomfrets, marlins, sail-fishes, swordfish, sauries, dolphin, oceanic sharks and cetaceans (United Nations (1982), "United Nations Convention on the Law of the Sea," Annex I).

[97] States must co-operate with the aim of conserving marine mammals and, with regard to cetaceans in particular, work for their management, conservation and study by means of suitable international organizations (United Nations (1982), "United Nations Convention on the Law of the Sea," Article 65).

[98] Fn 93 defines 'anadromous'.

[99] After consultations with other countries that are affected by the anadromous stocks of the state of their origin, the latter may "establish total allowable catches for stocks originating in its rivers" (United Nations (1982), "United Nations Convention on the Law of the Sea," Article 66(2)).

which this would result in economic difficulties for another country[100] [175]. The state of origin of anadromous stocks must co-operate in reducing as far as possible economic dislocation in other countries that fish these stocks [176]. These countries are to participate by agreement with the state of origin in measures to replenish anadromous stocks; that state is to provide those countries with special consideration in the collecting of such stocks originating in its rivers [177]. The enforcement of regulations concerning anadromous stocks beyond their state of origin's exclusive economic zone is to be by agreement between that country and the other interested states [178]. In instances in which anadromous stocks migrate into or through waters that are landward of the outer limits of the exclusive economic zone of a country other than the state of origin of those stocks, the former is to co-operate with the latter regarding their conservation and management [179].

A coastal state in whose waters catadromous[101] species spend the major part of their life cycle is to bear responsibility for their management and ensure the ingress and egress of migrating fish [180]. Harvesting of catadromous species is to be carried out solely in waters that are landward of the outer limits of exclusive economic zones[102] [181]. If catadromous fish migrate through the exclusive economic zone of a country other than the coastal state in whose waters their species spends the greater part of its life cycle, then the management of these fish is to be regulated by agreement between these two states[103] [182].

---

[100] With regard to fishing for anadromous stocks beyond the outer limits of their state of origin's exclusive economic zone, countries concerned are to continue consultations with the intention of attaining agreement on terms and conditions of fishing for these stocks – giving due consideration to the state of origin's conservation requirements and needs concerning those fish (United Nations (1982), "United Nations Convention on the Law of the Sea," Article 66(3)(a)).

[101] Fn 94 defines 'catadromous'.

[102] When carried out in exclusive economic zones, harvesting of catadromous species is subject to the provisions of the UNCLOS concerning fishing in these areas (United Nations (1982), "United Nations Convention on the Law of the Sea," Article 67(2)).

[103] This agreement is to ensure the rational management of the catadromous species, and take into consideration the responsibility of the coastal state in whose waters it spends the major part of its life cycle for its conservation (United Nations (1982), "United Nations Convention on the Law of the Sea," Article 67(3)).

Part V of the UNCLOS does not apply to sedentary[104] species [183]. 'Living organisms belonging to sedentary species' are "organisms which, at the harvestable stage, either are immobile on under the seabed or are unable to move except in constant physical contact with the seabed or the subsoil" [184].

Rights of Landlocked States as Regards Exclusive Economic Zones

Landlocked states have a right to participate equitably "in the exploitation of an appropriate part of the surplus of the living resources of the exclusive economic zones of the same subregion or region" [185]. The countries concerned are to establish the modes and terms of this participation by means of bilateral, subregional or regional agreements that consider, amongst other things: the need to circumvent effects that are detrimental to the pertinent coastal state's fishing industries or communities [186], the extent to which the relevant landlocked state is participating, or entitled to participate, in the utilization of living resources within the exclusive economic zones of other coastal countries [187], the extent to which other landlocked states and geographically-disadvantaged states are participating in the use of living resources of the coastal state's exclusive economic zone, and the resulting need to avoid a particular burden for any one coastal state or a part of it [188], and the nutritional requirements of the populations of the respective states [189].

As the harvesting capacity of a coastal state nears a point which would enable it to gather the whole permissible catch of the living resources in its exclusive economic zone, that country and other states concerned are to co-operate in the forming of equitable arrangements on a bilateral, subregional or regional basis to accommodate participation of developing landlocked countries within the same subregion or region in the utilization of the living resources of the exclusive economic zones of coastal states of the

[104] Fn 95 defines 'sedentary'.

subregion or region that may be apt in the circumstances, and on terms which all parties consider to be satisfactory[105] [190] Developed landlocked countries are entitled to participate in the use of living resources only in the exclusive economic zones of developed coastal states of the same subregion or region, respecting the extent to which a particular coastal state, in providing access to other countries to the living resources of its exclusive economic zone, has considered the need to minimize the harmful effects on fishing communities and economic disruption, in states whose nationals have customarily fished in that area[106] [191].

Rights of Geographically Disadvantaged States

'Geographically disadvantaged states' are coastal states, including: (i) those that border enclosed or semi-enclosed seas, whose geographical position renders them dependent upon utilization of the living resources of the exclusive economic zones of other countries in the subregion or region for sufficient supplies of fish, in order to nourish their populations or parts of these, and (ii) coastal states that are without an exclusive economic zone [192]. Geographically disadvantaged states have the right to equitably participate in the exploitation of a suitable part of the surplus of the living resources of the exclusive economic zones of coastal countries of the same subregion or region, taking into consideration the pertinent economic and geographical situation of all the states concerned, and in compliance with

---

105 In the implementation of this provision, the factors that Article 69(2) of the UNCLOS mentions – i.e., those stated in the second sentence of the immediately-preceding paragraph – are also to be taken into account (United Nations (1982), "United Nations Convention on the Law of the Sea," Article 69(3)).

106 The provisions within this subsection (entitled 'Rights of Landlocked States as regards Exclusive Economic Zones') "are without prejudice to arrangements agreed upon in subregions or regions where the coastal States may grant to land-locked States of the same subregion or region equal or preferential rights for the exploitation of the living resources in the exclusive economic zones" (United Nations (1982), "United Nations Convention on the Law of the Sea," Article 69(5)).

the provisions of the current Article[107] and that of Articles 61 and 62 of the UNCLOS[108] [193]. The terms and modes of this equitable participation are to be established by the relevant countries by means of bilateral, subregional or regional agreements [194], which take into account, amongst other things, the need to avoid effects that are injurious to the coastal state's fishing industries or communities [195], the degree to which the geographically disadvantaged state is participating, or entitled to take part, under operative bilateral, subregional or regional agreements, in the use of living resources of other coastal countries' exclusive economic zones [196], the extent to which other geographically-disadvantaged states and landlocked countries are participating in the utilization of the living resources of the coastal state's exclusive economic zone, and the consequent necessity of avoiding an especial burden for any one coastal state or a part of it [197], and the nutritional requirements of the respective countries' populations [198].

As the harvesting capacity of a coastal state draws close to a point that would enable it to reap the total permissible catch of the living resources in its exclusive economic zone, this country and other interested states are to co-operate in the instituting of equitable arrangements on a bilateral, subregional or regional basis to provide scope for participation of developing geographically disadvantaged states within the same subregion or region in the use of the living resources of the exclusive economic zones of coastal states of the subregion or region that may be suitable in the circumstances, and on terms which all parties deem to be satisfactory[109] [199]. Developed geographically disadvantaged countries are entitled to take part in the utilization of living resources solely in the exclusive economic zones of developed coastal states of the same subregion or

[107] The 'current Article' is Article 70 of the UNCLOS, which is entitled 'Right of geographically disadvantaged States' and described in the current subsection, i.e., that titled 'Rights of Geographically Disadvantaged States'.

[108] Articles 61 and 62 of the UNCLOS are entitled 'Conservation of the living resources' and 'Utilization of the living resources', respectively, and are described in the subsection above titled 'Conservation and Utilization of Living Resources'.

[109] In the application of this provision, the factors that Article 70(3) of the UNCLOS mentions – i.e., those expressed in the final sentence of the immediately-preceding paragraph – are also to be taken into consideration (United Nations (1982), "United Nations Convention on the Law of the Sea," Article 70(4)).

region, having regard to the degree to which a particular coastal state, in granting access to other countries to the living resources of its exclusive economic zone, has considered the need to minimize the damaging effects on fishing communities and economic disturbance, in states whose nationals have, by way of habit, fished in that area[110] [200].

Non-Applicability and Restrictions on Transfer of These Rights

The above rights of landlocked and geographically disadvantaged states are disapplied in the instance of a coastal state whose economy is heavily dependent upon the utilization of the living resources of its exclusive economic zone [201]. These rights are not to be transferred to third countries or their nationals, unless the states concerned agree[111] [202].

The Coastal State's Powers of Enforcement of Its Laws

In the exercise of its sovereign rights to investigate, use, conserve and manage the living resources in its exclusive economic zone, the coastal state may take the measures that are necessary – including boarding, inspection, arrest and lawsuits – to ensure observance of the laws and regulations that it adopts in compliance with the UNCLOS[112] [203].

---

[110] The provisions within this subsection (entitled 'Rights of Geographically Disadvantaged States') "are without prejudice to arrangements agreed upon in subregions or regions where the coastal States may grant to geographically disadvantaged States of the same subregion or region equal or preferential rights for the exploitation of the living resources in the exclusive economic zones" (United Nations (1982), "United Nations Convention on the Law of the Sea," Article 70(6)).

[111] This prohibition does not prevent the relevant states from acquiring financial or technical help from third countries or international organizations, in order to facilitate the exercise of those rights of landlocked and geographically disadvantaged states, as long as the procurement of this assistance does not have the effect of transferring the rights to third countries or their nationals (United Nations (1982), "United Nations Convention on the Law of the Sea," Article 72(2)).

[112] The coastal state is to swiftly release ships and their crews that it has arrested, upon the posting of reasonable security (United Nations (1982), "United Nations Convention on the Law of the Sea," Article 73(2)).

Penalties that the coastal state imposes for contraventions of laws and regulations concerning fisheries in its exclusive economic zone may not include imprisonment or any other type of physical punishment, unless the countries concerned have agreed to this [204]. If the coastal state has arrested or detained a foreign vessel, then it must promptly inform the flag state – through suitable channels – of the action that it has taken and of any penalties that it has thereafter imposed [205].

Delimitation of the Exclusive Economic Zone between States

The delimitation of the exclusive economic zone between countries with opposite or adjacent coasts is to be accomplished by agreement founded on international law – as mentioned in Article 38 of the Statute of the ICJ[113], in order to reach a just solution[114] [206]. If an agreement cannot be attained "within a reasonable period of time," then the relevant states must pursue the procedures that Part XV of the UNCLOS provides[115] [207]. If such an agreement is in force between these countries, then

[113] Paragraph 1 of this Article states: "The Court, whose function is to decide in accordance with international law such disputes as are submitted to it, shall apply: a. international conventions, whether general or particular, establishing rules expressly recognized by the contesting states; b. international custom, as evidence of a general practice accepted as law; c. the general principles of law recognized by civilized nations; d. subject to the provisions of Article 59 [of the Statute of the ICJ, which declares that the ICJ's decisions are only binding upon the parties in the specific case], judicial decisions and the teachings of the most highly qualified publicists of the various nations, as subsidiary means for the determination of rules of law (United Nations (1945), "Statute of the International Court of Justice," *United Nations Treaty Series* Registration Number N/A, Article 38(1)). However, Article 38(2) of the Statute of the ICJ "shall not prejudice the power of the Court to decide a case *ex aequo et bono*, if the parties agree thereto" (United Nations (1945), "Statute of the International Court of Justice," Article 38(2); emphasis original). The phrase '*ex aequo et bono*' means "[i]n accordance with justice and fairness" (McFarlane, G. (1984), *The Layman's Dictionary of English Law*, 101).

[114] Pending this agreement, "the States concerned, in a spirit of understanding and cooperation, shall make every effort to enter into provisional arrangements of a practical nature and, during this transitional period, not to jeopardize or hamper the reaching of the final agreement[; these provisional] arrangements shall be without prejudice to the final delimitation" of the exclusive economic zone (United Nations (1982), "United Nations Convention on the Law of the Sea," Article 74(3)).

[115] The section below entitled 'Part XV of the UNCLOS: Settlement of Disputes' specifies procedures that states may use for resolving disputes that concern the interpretation or application of the UNCLOS.

problems concerning the delimitation of the exclusive economic zone are to be determined in conformity with its provisions [208].

Charting the Exclusive Economic Zone or Listing Its Co-Ordinates

The exclusive economic zone's outer limit lines, and the lines of delimitation drawn according to Article 74 of the UNCLOS[116], are to be shown on appropriate charts or detailed by a list of geographical co-ordinates[117] [209].

PART VI OF THE UNCLOS: CONTINENTAL SHELF

Definition of the Continental Shelf

A coastal state's continental shelf consists of the seabed and subsoil of the submarine places which extend beyond its territorial sea in every part of the natural extension of its land territory to the outer border of the continental margin, or to a length of 200 nautical miles from the baselines from which the territorial sea's width is measured – in instances in which the continental margin's[118] outer edge does not extend to that distance [210]. Thus, the surface area of a coastal state's continental shelf is equal to or greater than that of the exclusive economic zone – with the two

---

[116] The immediately-preceding subsection, entitled 'Delimitation of the Exclusive Economic Zone between States', relates the provisions of Article 74 of the UNCLOS.

[117] Article 16(1) of the UNCLOS contains a corresponding requirement regarding the baselines for measuring the width of the territorial sea and their associated lines of delimitation. The subsection entitled 'Charting or Listing the Geographical Co-ordinates of Baselines', in the section above titled 'Part II of the UNCLOS: Territorial Sea and Contiguous Zone', states Article 16(1) of the UNCLOS.

[118] The 'continental margin' is "the submerged prolongation of the land mass of the coastal State, and consists of the seabed and subsoil of the [continental] shelf, the [continental] slope and the [continental] rise[; i]t does not include the deep ocean floor with its oceanic ridges or the subsoil thereof" (United Nations (1982), "United Nations Convention on the Law of the Sea," Article 76(3)).

surface areas including the same thalassic ground which constitutes that of the exclusive economic zone[119]. This definition of 'continental shelf' differs considerably from the definition of 'continental shelf' in the CCS[120] – whose adoption and operationalization[121] both precede the introduction of the concept of 'exclusive economic zone'[122]. Furthermore, the definition of 'continental shelf' in the UNCLOS includes the following additional elements – which are absent from the CCS.

A coastal state's continental shelf must not extend beyond the limits that the following provisions[123] specify [211]. For the UNCLOS' purposes, that country is to establish the continental margin's outer edge, wherever this margin reaches beyond 200 nautical miles from the baselines from which the territorial sea's breadth is measured by a line delineated in conformity with Article 76(7) of the UNCLOS by reference to either: (i) each outermost fixed point at each of which the distance through sedimentary rocks is 1% or more of the shortest length from this point to

---

[119] The last sentence of the subsection entitled 'The Exclusive Economic Zone', in the section above titled 'Part V of the UNCLOS: Exclusive Economic Zone', states that the exclusive economic zone is to extend no more than 200 nautical miles from the baselines from which the width of the territorial sea is measured. Thus, the *surface area* of a coastal state's exclusive economic zone is a subset of the surface area of its continental shelf. Notwithstanding this, it would be incorrect to assert that a coastal state's exclusive economic zone is a subset of its continental shelf, because, whilst both include the seabed and its subsoil, *only the exclusive economic zone includes the waters overlying the seabed* (i.e., compare the first sentence of the current subsection entitled 'Definition of the Continental Shelf' with point (i) of the first sentence of the subsection titled 'The Coastal State's Jurisdiction, Rights and Duties Therein' in the section above named 'Part V of the UNCLOS: Exclusive Economic Zone').

[120] "For the purposes of" the Articles in the CCS, the 'continental shelf' refers to "the seabed and subsoil of the submarine areas adjacent to the coast but outside the area of the territorial sea, to a depth of 200 metres or, beyond that limit, to where the depth of the superjacent waters admits of the exploitation of the natural resources of the said areas [, and] "the seabed and subsoil of similar submarine areas adjacent to the coasts of islands" (United Nations (1958), "Convention on the Continental Shelf," *United Nations Treaty Series* Registration Number 7302, Article 1).

[121] The second sentence of the second paragraph of the section above entitled 'Introduction' states that the CCS, the CFCLRHS, the CHS, and the CTSCZ were adopted on 29th April 1958. Fn 771 specifies that the CCS entered into force on 10th June 1964.

[122] Fn 12, and the first paragraph of the subsection entitled 'The Exclusive Economic Zone', in the section above titled 'Part V of the UNCLOS: Exclusive Economic Zone'.

[123] Article 76(2) of the UNCLOS refers to "paragraphs 4 to 6," i.e., Paragraphs 4, 5 and 6 of Article 76 of the UNCLOS.

the continental slope's foot, or[124] (ii) fixed points of up to 60 nautical miles from that foot [212]. Article 76(7) of the UNCLOS reads as follows.

> The coastal State shall delineate the outer limits of its continental shelf, where that shelf extends beyond 200 nautical miles from the baselines from which the breadth of the territorial sea is measured, by straight lines not exceeding 60 nautical miles in length, connecting fixed points, defined by coordinates of latitude and longitude [213].

The foot of the continental slope is considered to be "the point of maximum change in the gradient at its base"[125], unless there is contrary

---

[124] The Commission on the Limits of the Continental Shelf stated that a coastal state could employ either of these two tests, or both of them, to delineate the outer edge of its continental margin: "The use of an inclusive disjunction as a connective between the two formulae implies that the compound is true so long as at least one of the components is true. Thus, the limit of the continental shelf can be extended up to a 1 per cent sediment thickness line delineated by reference to fixed points, or to a line delineated by reference to fixed points at a distance of 60 nautical miles from the foot of the continental slope, or both." (Commission on the Limits of the Continental Shelf (1999), Scientific and Technical Guidelines of the Commission on the Limits of the Continental Shelf: Adopted by the Commission on 13 May 1999 at its fifth session (New York, Commission on the Limits of the Continental Shelf), para.2.1.5).

[125] GNS Science explains: "There are two steps to finding the foot of the continental slope 1. Identify the region of the base of the continental slope 2. Determine the location of the foot of the continental slope within that region. Identification of the region of the base of the continental slope may be on the basis of – morphological evidence – morphological evidence supported by geological and geophysical evidence – geological and geophysical evidence. The complexity of the [continental] margin and availability of data will dictate the choice of evidence to use. In areas where the morphology of the continental margin is clearly divided into [continental] slope, [continental] rise and abyssal plain, and there is no contradicting geological and geophysical evidence, identification of the region of the continental slope and location of the point of maximum change in gradient within this region are based on morphological evidence and are relatively straightforward. ... [A]long some [continental] margins[,] the region of the base of the continental slope may be located within the continent-ocean transition zone. The location of the foot of the continental slope within that region can be determined by the maximum change in sea floor gradient rule, or, if this is inappropriate, by locating the inner edge of the continent-ocean transition. ... In areas where the morphology of the continental margin can be clearly divided into [continental] shelf, [continental] slope, [continental] rise and abyssal plain, the region of the base of the continental slope is where the lower continental slope meets the rise, or where it meets the abyssal plain where a rise is absent. The morphology of the seabed where the continental slope merges with the rise may be an abrupt boundary where gently-dipping rise sediments onlap a smooth, relatively steep slope, or it may be a complex transition where local relief on the ocean floor meets an irregular lower slope. ... Regional gradients less than 1 degree are generally considered representative of the rise and abyssal plain, and regional gradients greater than 2 degrees are generally considered representative of the

evidence[126] [214]. The fixed points that comprise the line of the continental shelf's outer limits on the seabed – drawn in conformity with Paragraphs 4(a)(i) and (ii) of Article 76 of the UNCLOS[127] – are not to exceed 350 nautical miles from the baselines from which the territorial sea's breadth is measured *or* are not to exceed 100 nautical miles from the 2,500 metre

---

slope. There are many exceptions to these values[;] other evidence, such as the erosion effects of deep sea currents, underwater slides, [continental] margin collapse, local volcanic activity and deep-sea canyons, must be considered before finally establishing the region of the base of the continental slope. … Having established the region of the base of the continental slope, the point of maximum change in gradient is determined by computing the second derivative of the bathymetry within that region. The foot of the continental slope has the maximum value of the second derivative of the bathymetry." (GNS Science (2019), "The Foot of the Continental Slope," Accessed August 25, 2019, <https://www.gns.cri.nz/static/unclos/footslope.html>). A 'bathymeter' is "an instrument used to measure the depth of water in seas or lakes" (Pearsall, J. (editor) (1998), *The New Oxford Dictionary of English*, 146). Thus, 'the bathymetry within the region of the base of the continental slope' is the collection of measurements of the depth of water in the relevant sea over that area. Consequently, 'the first derivative of the bathymetry within the region of the base of the continental slope' is the change in the depth of water per unit change in distance over that area, and 'the second derivative of the bathymetry within the region of the base of the continental slope' is the change in that first derivative per unit change in distance over that area.

[126] GNS Science explains: "Analysis of geophysical and geological data can help [to] identify the region of the base of the [continental] slope where the maximum change of sea floor gradient rule [(fn 125)] can be applied. If these data show that the maximum change of sea floor gradient rule does not reliably locate the edge of the continental margin within that region, then they might be used as "evidence to the contrary" in terms of article 76 [of the UNCLOS]. Situations in which the maximum change in sea floor gradient rule might not reliably locate the foot of the continental slope include – continental margins that have a very smooth transition from slope to [continental] rise, and no single point represents a significant maximum change in gradient – continental margins with irregular seafloor morphology, and a point of maximum change in gradient at its base that does not reliably locate the foot of the continental slope." (GNS Science (2019), "The Foot of the Continental Slope," Accessed August 25, 2019, <https://www.gns.cri.nz/static/unclos/footslope.html>). For rifted, non-volcanic and sheared continental margins, the Commission on the Limits of the Continental Shelf proposed the following alternative to the maximum change in sea floor gradient rule: "… If the foot of the continental shelf is very difficult to define on the basis of bathymetric data, [then] the Commission might consider the continental-oceanic transitional (COT) zone … as the place to determine the outer edge of the continental margin. Since the transitional zone can extend over several tens of kilometers, the Commission may consider the landward limit of the transitional zone as an equivalent of the foot of the continental slope in the context of paragraph 4 [i.e., Article 76(4) of the UNCLOS], provided that the submitted geophysical and geological data conclusively demonstrate that the submerged land mass of the coastal State extends to this point." (Scientific and Technical Guidelines of the Commission on the Limits of the Continental Shelf, para.6.3.10).

[127] These are points (i) and (ii) within the second paragraph of the current subsection entitled 'Definition of the Continental Shelf'.

isobath[128] [215]. However, on submarine ridges – excluding submarine elevations that are natural elements of the continental margin (such as its banks, caps, plateaux, rises and spurs), the '2,500 metres isobath' constraint does not apply [216]; i.e., the continental shelf's outer limit is not to exceed 350 nautical miles from the baselines from which the territorial sea's width is measured [217].

The coastal state is to submit information on the limits of its continental shelf beyond 200 nautical miles from the baselines from which the breadth of its territorial sea is measured to the Commission on the Limits of the Continental Shelf, which shall make recommendations to that country on issues concerning the establishment of the outer limits of its continental shelf; the limits that the coastal state establishes on the basis of those recommendations are to be binding and final [218]. The coastal state's submission to the Commission on the Limits of the Continental Slope comprises an executive summary – which includes charts that indicate the continental shelf's outer limits and the relevant baselines relating to the territorial sea, a main body – which contains a detailed account of the data set, maps, technical procedures and scientific methodolgies applied in implementing Article 76 of the UNCLOS, and a copy of all data to which the main body of the submission refers [219].

The Coastal State's Rights over the Continental Shelf

The coastal state exercises sovereign rights over the continental shelf in order to explore it and utilize its natural resources[129] [220]. These rights are exclusive in so far as no-one may perform these activities without the coastal state's express agreement, if the latter does not undertake them[130] [221]. 'Natural resources' comprise non-living resources of the ocean floor

[128] The 2,500 metre isobath "is a line connecting the depth of 2,500 metres" (United Nations (1982), "United Nations Convention on the Law of the Sea," Article 76(6)).

[129] Article 2(1) of the CCS contains an identical provision.

[130] Article 2(2) of the CCS embodies the same rule, with the additional prohibition that no-one may "make a claim to the continental shelf" without the coastal state's assent, if the latter does not undertake the aforementioned activities on its continental shelf.

and its subsoil, and living organisms that are members of sedentary species[131] [184].

The Legal Status of Overlying Waters and Rights of Other States

The coastal State's rights over its continental shelf do not affect the legal position concerning the superjacent waters or the air space over these[132] [222]. That country's exercise of its rights over this continental shelf must not contravene or unjustifiably interfere with rights and freedoms of other states for which the UNCLOS provides[133] [223].

Submarine Cables and Pipelines on the Continental Shelf

All countries are entitled to place submarine cables and pipelines on the continental shelf, in conformity with the following provisions[134] [224]. Whilst the coastal state has a "right to take reasonable measures" to: (i) explore its continental shelf and utilize the "natural resources" that it contains, and (ii) prevent, lower and control pollution from pipelines, this

[131] The second sentence of the last paragraph of the subsection entitled 'Migratory, Anadromous, Catadromous and Sedentary Species', in the section above titled 'Part V of the UNCLOS: Exclusive Economic Zone', defines the term 'sedentary species'. Article 2(4) of the CCS contains an identical provision.

[132] Article 3 of the CCS lays down a provision that is the same as that of Article 78(1) of the UNCLOS, except that the former refers to "the legal status of the superadjacent waters *as high seas*" (emphasis added), whilst the latter does not mention 'high seas'. As the adoption of the CCS precedes the introduction of the concept of 'exclusive economic zone' (text to fn 122), then the waters overlying a continental shelf are high seas under the CCS. By contrast, the waters overlying the continental shelf may be part of a coastal state's exclusive economic zone – if they fall within its exclusive economic zone as defined within Part V of the UNCLOS (above); if these waters are beyond the outer limit of the coastal State's exclusive economic zone, then they are part of the high seas (United Nations (1982), "United Nations Convention on the Law of the Sea," Article 86). Thus, as, under the UNCLOS, the waters overlying a continental shelf may constitute a coastal state's exclusive economic zone *or* the high seas, then the phrase 'as high seas' in Article 3 of the CCS would not be true for all these waters according to the provisions of the UNCLOS.

[133] The CCS lacks this provision.

[134] The CCS lacks this clause.

country may not hinder others from laying or maintaining those conduits or cables[135] [225]. The coastal state's consent is required for the laying of these pipelines on the continental shelf[136] [226].

Nothing in this Part (i.e., Part VI) of the UNCLOS affects the coastal state's right to institute conditions for pipelines or cables to enter its territory or territorial sea, or its jurisdiction over pipelines and cables that are built or used in association with the exploration of its continental shelf or use of the latter's resources or the functioning of artificial islands, structures and installations over which it has jurisdiction[137] [227]. When positioning submarine pipelines or cables, states are to duly respect pipelines or cables that are already *in situ*[138] [228].

Artificial Islands, Installations and Structures; Drilling

Article 60 of the UNCLOS[139] "applies *mutatis mutandis*[140] to artificial islands, installations and structures on the continental shelf" [229]. The coastal state is exclusively entitled to sanction and regulate all drilling on its continental shelf[141] [230].

---

[135] Article 4 of the CCS contains a similar rule to that of Article 78(1) of the UNCLOS, but lacks the 'anti-pollution' phrase in point (ii) of the text.

[136] The CCS lacks this provision.

[137] The CCS lacks this rule.

[138] The CCS lacks this provision.

[139] The subsection entitled 'Artificial Islands, Installations and Structures', in the section above titled 'Part V of the UNCLOS: Exclusive Economic Zone', specifies the provisions of Article 60 of the UNCLOS.

[140] The phrase '*mutatis mutandis*' means "the necessary changes being made" (McFarlane, G. (1984), *The Layman's Dictionary of English Law*, 186). It is submitted that these changes comprise: (i) the replacement in the title of Article 60 of the UNCLOS of 'in the exclusive economic zone' with 'on the continental shelf' – which is present in the title of Article 80 of the UNCLOS, and (ii) the replacement in Paragraph 1 of Article 60 of the UNCLOS of 'In the exclusive economic zone' with 'On the continental shelf' – which is reflected by substituting 'in its exclusive economic zone' in the first line of the first paragraph of the subsection to which fn 139 refers with 'on its continental shelf'.

[141] The CCS lacks this provision.

Payments/Contributions for Use of the Outmost Continental Shelf

The coastal state must make contributions-in-kind or payments regarding its exploitation of the continental shelf beyond 200 nautical miles from the baselines from which the territorial sea's breadth is measured [231]. These payments and contributions are to be made annually in respect of production at a site, after the first five years of such activity there[142] [232]. A developing country that is a net importer of a mineral resource that is extracted from its continental shelf is exempt from making these payments or contributions in connection with that substance [233]. The coastal state shall make these payments to the International Seabed Authority[143], which shall apportion them to States Parties to the UNCLOS based on equitable criteria for sharing – taking into consideration the needs and interest of developing countries[144] [234].

Delimitation of the Continental Shelf between States

The delimitation of the continental shelf between countries with opposite or adjacent coasts shall be achieved by agreement based on international law – as referred to in Article 38 of the Statute of the ICJ[145],

[142] This provision continues thus: "For the sixth year, the rate of payment of contribution shall be 1 per cent of the value or volume of production at the site. The rate shall increase by 1 per cent for each subsequent year until the twelfth year and shall remain at 7 per cent thereafter. Production does not include resources used in connection with exploitation." (United Nations (1982), "United Nations Convention on the Law of the Sea," Article 82(2)).

[143] The UNCLOS establishes an International Seabed Authority, to which all States Parties to the UNCLOS belong, and through which these countries – in conformity with Part XI of the UNCLOS (entitled 'The Area') – organize and direct activities in the Area, especially with the aim of managing the resources of the Area (United Nations (1982), "United Nations Convention on the Law of the Sea," Articles 156(1), 156(2) and 157(1)). Fn 161 defines the 'Area'.

[144] The CCS lacks equivalent provisions to those of Article 82 of the UNCLOS, i.e., those in the current subsection entitled 'Payments/Contributions for Use of the Outmost Continental Shelf'.

[145] Fn 113 quotes Article 38 of the Statute of the ICJ. Pending this agreement, "the States concerned, in a spirit of understanding and cooperation, shall make every effort to enter into provisional arrangements of a practical nature and, during this transitional period, not to

in order to attain a fair solution[146] [235]. If an agreement cannot be attained "within a reasonable period of time," then the relevant countries must adopt the procedures that Part XV of the UNCLOS supplies[147] [236]. If such an agreement is in force between these states, then issues concerning the delimitation of the continental shelf are to be determined in line with its provisions[148] [237].

Charting the Continental Shelf or Listing Its Co-Ordinates

The continental slope's outer limit lines, and the lines of delimitation drawn in compliance with Article 83 of the UNCLOS[149], are to be shown on suitable charts or presented as a list of geographical co-ordinates[150] [238].

---

jeopardize or hamper the reaching of the final agreement[; these provisional] arrangements shall be without prejudice to the final delimitation" of the continental shelf (United Nations (1982), "United Nations Convention on the Law of the Sea," Article 83(3)).

[146] Paragraphs 1 and 2 of Article 6 of the CCS are similar to Article 83(1) of the UNCLOS in that they require the boundary between states with, respectively, opposite and adjacent coasts, to be decided by agreement between these countries. Unlike Article 83(1) of the UNCLOS, neither Paragraph 1 nor Paragraph 2 of Article 6 of the CCS refers to international law or Article 38 of the Statute of the ICJ.

[147] The section below entitled 'Part XV of the UNCLOS: Settlement of Disputes' specifies procedures that states may use for settling disputes that concern the interpretation or application of the UNCLOS. Paragraphs 1 and 2 of Article 6 of the CCS differ from Article 83(2) of the UNCLOS as follows: (i) both of the former require the principle of equidistance to be applied "from the nearest points of the baselines from which the breadth of the territorial sea of each State is measured" to be used to determine the position of the boundary between the continental shelf of each – if there is no agreement, and,(ii) unlike Article 83(2) of the UNCLOS which refers to agreement not being attained "within a reasonable period of time," Paragraphs 1 and 2 of the CCS specify only "[i]n the absence of agreement."

[148] The CCS lacks this rule. The provisions of this subsection (entitled 'Delineation of the Continental Shelf between States') – which Article 83 of the UNCLOS contains – are identical to those of the subsection above titled 'Delimitation of the Exclusive Economic Zone between States' – which Article 74 of the UNCLOS contains, other than the replacement of the term 'exclusive economic zone' in Article 74 with the phrase 'continental shelf' in Article 83.

[149] The immediately-preceding subsection entitled 'Delimitation of the Continental Shelf between States' declares the provisions of Article 83 of the UNCLOS.

[150] Article 16(1) of the UNCLOS contains a corresponding requirement concerning the baselines for measuring the breadth of the territorial sea and their associated lines of delimitation. The subsection entitled 'Charting or Listing the Geographical Co-ordinates of Baselines', in the section above titled 'Part II of the UNCLOS: Territorial Sea and Contiguous Zone', states

Tunnelling in the Subsoil of the Ocean Floor

Nothing in this Part (i.e., Part VI) of the UNCLOS affects the coastal state's right to utilize the subsoil by means of tunnelling[151] [239].

PART VIII OF THE UNCLOS: REGIME OF ISLANDS

Article 121 of the UNCLOS comprises the following provisions.

> 1. An island is a naturally formed area of land, surrounded by water, which is above water at high tide[152] [240].
>
> 2. Except as provided for in paragraph 3 [of Article 121 of the UNCLOS], the territorial sea, the contiguous zone, the exclusive economic zone and the continental shelf of an island are determined in accordance with the provisions of this Convention applicable to other land territory [241].
>
> 3. Rocks which cannot sustain human habitation or economic life of their own shall have no exclusive economic zone or continental shelf [242].

In its Legislative History of Part VIII of the UNCLOS, the Division for Ocean Affairs and the Law of the Sea at the UN Office of Legal Affairs specifies how the content of Article 121 of the UNCLOS was reached.

> 3. The question concerning the status of islands had been raised in a number of international forums. For instance, at the Hague Conference for the regulation of North Sea Fisheries (1881) discussions focused on the types of insular formations which should be accorded fishery zones in

Article 16(1) of the UNCLOS. Article 75(1) of the UNCLOS contains an equivalent requirement regarding the exclusive economic zone's outer limit lines and lines of delimitation between countries with opposite or adjacent coasts. The subsection entitled 'Charting the Exclusive Economic Zone or Listing its Co-ordinates' in the section above titled 'Part V of the UNCLOS: Exclusive Economic Zone', states Article 75(1) of the UNCLOS.

[151] Article 7 of the CCS contains a very similar provision to Article 85 of the UNCLOS. The former refers to "The provisions of these articles," whilst the latter mentions "the Part" of the UNCLOS.

[152] Fn 5 quotes this definition of 'island'.

the North Sea. Attempts were also made at the 1930 Hague Codification Conference to find a definition for an island. It was not however until the First United Nations Conference on the Law of the Sea in 1958 that a major step was taken to clarify the status of islands [243].

4. This matter was dealt with in the Convention on the Territorial Sea and the Contiguous Zone and in the Convention on the Continental Shelf, both signed in 1958. An island is defined therein as "a naturally-formed area of land, surrounded by waters, which is above water at high tide"[153]. An island generates its own territorial sea[154] and continental shelf[155]. Thus, under the régime of islands as reflected in the 1958 Geneva Convention on the Law of the Sea any insular formation which is above water at high tide possesses a territorial sea and a continental shelf [244].

5. The 1982 Convention has retained the definition of an island as "a naturally formed area of land, surrounded by water, which is above water at high tide[156] (article 121, paragraph 1). Islands generate their own territorial seas, contiguous zones, exclusive economic zones and continental shelves just like any other land territory (article 121, paragraph 2). However, rocks which cannot sustain human habitation or economic life of their own shall have no exclusive economic zone or continental shelf (article 121, paragraph 3). This is a significant modification to the régime of islands introduced by the 1982 Convention [245].

Part XV of the UNCLOS: Settlement of Disputes

Disputes Are to Be Settled by Peaceful Means of the Parties' Choice

States Parties to the UNCLOS are to resolve any dispute between them regarding "the interpretation or application of this Convention by peaceful

[153] Article 10(1) of the CTSCZ contains this definition of 'island', which is identical to the definition of 'island' that Article 121(1) of the UNCLOS provides (text to fn 152).

[154] Article 10(2) of the CTSCZ states: "The territorial sea of an island is measured in accordance with the provisions of these articles."

[155] Article 1(b) of the CCS grants a continental shelf to each island (fn 120).

[156] Text to fn 152.

means" in conformity with Article 2(3) of the UN Charter, and, with that goal in mind, shall pursue a solution in accordance with Article 33(1) of the UN Charter [246]. Article 2(3) of the UN Charter requires the UN's Member States to settle their international disagreements "by peaceful means" in a way that preserves global security and peace, and justice [247]. Article 33(1) of the UN Charter directs disputants, the continuation of whose dispute will probably imperil the preservation of worldwide security and peace, to attempt to find a solution by "a peaceful means of their choice" [248]. Article 280 of the UNCLOS reinforces this Paragraph by holding that nothing in Part XV of the UNCLOS diminishes the right of any States Parties to the UNCLOS to agree at whatever time to resolve a dispute between them regarding "the interpretation or application of this Convention by any peaceful means of their own choice" [249].

Circumstances under Which Part XV of the UNCLOS Applies

If the States Parties to the UNCLOS which are disputants regarding "interpretation or application of this Convention" have agreed to pursue resolution of their dispute by a peaceful method that they have chosen, then the procedures for which Part XV of the UNCLOS provides only apply in circumstances under which these parties have not reached a settlement by recourse to this means, any time-limit that those parties have set has expired, *and* the agreement between them does not debar any further course of action [250]. If such States Parties have agreed, by means of a bilateral, regional or general agreement or otherwise, that their dispute – at the request of any disputant – is to be submitted to a process that necessitates a binding decision, then that procedure is to apply in place of the procedures for which Part XV of the UNCLOS provides, unless the disputants agree otherwise [251].

Obligation for the Disputants to Exchange Views

If a dispute occurs between States Parties to the UNCLOS regarding "the interpretation or application of this Convention," then the disputants are to advance expeditiously to an interchange of views concerning its resolution by negotiation or another peaceful method [252]. The parties shall also move expeditiously to an exchange of opinions in the each of the following situations: (i) where a process for the settlement of such a dispute has been concluded unsuccessfully, and (ii) where the circumstances require consultation as to the way of implementing the settlement [253].

Conciliation

A State Party to the UNCLOS that is a disputant regarding "the interpretation or application of this Convention" is permitted to request the other disputant(s) to conciliation – either under the procedure in Section 1 of Annex V to the UNCLOS[157] or another process for conciliation [254]. If

[157] Articles 1-10 of Annex V to the UNCLOS lay down this conciliation procedure. The current footnote quotes aspects of these provisions, in order to summarize this process. *Article 1 (Institution of proceedings)*: "If the parties have agreed, in accordance with [A]rticle 284 [of the UNCLOS – i.e., the reference in the text to this footnote], to submit it to conciliation under this section [i.e., Section 1 of Annex V to the UNCLOS – which is entitled 'Conciliation Procedure Pursuant to Section 1 of Part XV'], any such party may institute the proceedings by written notification addressed to the other party or parties to the dispute."; *Article 2 (List of conciliators)*: "A list of conciliators shall be drawn up and maintained by the Secretary-General of the United Nations. Every State Party [to the UNCLOS] shall be entitled to nominate four conciliators, each of whom shall be a person enjoying the highest reputation for fairness, competence and integrity. ..."; *Article 3 (Constitution of the conciliation commission)*: "The conciliation commission shall, unless the parties otherwise agree, be constituted as follows: [the notifying and receiving disputant each appoint two conciliators, who jointly appoint a fifth conciliator from the above list of conciliators who is to be chairman]"; *Article 4 (Procedure)*: The conciliation commission shall, unless the parties otherwise agree, determine its own procedure. ... Decisions of the commission regarding procedural matters, the report and recommendations shall be made by a majority vote of the members."; *Article 5 (Amicable settlement)*: The commission may draw the attention of the parties to any measure which might facilitate an amicable settlement of the dispute."; *Article 6 (Functions of the commission)*: The commission shall hear the parties, examine their claims and objections, and make proposals to the parties with a view to reaching an amicable settlement."; *Article 7 (Report)*: 1. The commission shall report within

this invitation is accepted, and if the parties agree upon the mechanism for conciliation that they wish to apply, then any party may present the dispute for resolution by using this procedure [255]. If the invitation is rejected, or if the parties disagree as to the process for conciliation to employ, then the conciliation proceedings are deemed to be ended[158] [256].

The Seabed Disputes Chamber of the ITLOS and UNCLOS Part XV

Section 1 of Part XV of the UNCLOS[159] applies to any dispute which, pursuant to Section 5 of Part XI of this Convention[160], is to be resolved in line with procedures for which Part XV provides [257]. Section 5 of Part XI of the UNCLOS concerns the submission of disputes concerning the

---

12 months of its constitution. Its report shall record any agreements reached and, failing agreement, its conclusions on all questions of fact or law relevant to the matter in dispute and such recommendations as the commission may deem appropriate for an amicable settlement. ... 2. The report of the commission, including its conclusion and recommendations, shall not be binding on the parties."; *Article 8 (Termination)*: The conciliation proceedings are terminated when a settlement has been reached, when the parties have accepted or one party has rejected the recommendations of the report ... , or when a period of three months has expired from the date of transmission of the report to the parties."; *Article 9 (Fees and expenses)*: The fees and expenses of the commission shall be borne by the parties to the dispute."; *Article 10 (Rights of parties to modify procedure)*: The parties to the dispute may by agreement applicable solely to that dispute modify any provision of this Annex." (United Nations (1982), "United Nations Convention on the Law of the Sea," Annex V, Section 1). Fn 192 defines 'States Parties'.

[158] Unless the parties agree otherwise, if their dispute has been submitted to conciliation, then the proceedings may be concluded only in conformity with the mechanism for conciliation that they have agreed to use (United Nations (1982), "United Nations Convention on the Law of the Sea," Article 284(4)).

[159] Section 1 of Part XV of the UNCLOS comprises Articles 279-285 of this Convention, which are described in the present and above subsections of the current section entitled 'Part XV of the UNCLOS: The Settlement of Disputes'. Section 1 of Part XV of the UNCLOS is titled 'General Provisions'.

[160] Section 5 of Part XI of the UNCLOS, which consists of Articles 186-191 of this Convention and is entitled 'Settlement of Disputes and Advisory Opinions', provides for the Seabed Disputes Chamber of the ITLOS to exercise its jurisdiction – whose heads Article 187 of the UNCLOS lists – in accordance with "the provisions of this [S]ection, of Part XV and of Annex VI [of the UNCLOS] (United Nations (1982), "United Nations Convention on the Law of the Sea," Article 186). Part XI of the UNCLOS is titled 'The Area' (fn 143). Fn 161 defines the 'Area'. Annex VI is entitled 'Statute of the International Tribunal for the Law of the Sea' – which it duly contains. Fn 195 introduces the contents of Annex VI to the UNCLOS.

Area[161] to settlement processes and the jurisdiction of the Seabed Disputes Chamber of the ITLOS[162].

Compulsory Procedures Entailing Binding Decisions: Applicability

Subject to Section 3 of Part XV of the UNCLOS[163], and where recourse to Section 1 of Part XV of the UNCLOS[164] has not yielded a settlement, any dispute regarding "the interpretation or application of this Convention" may be submitted to the court or tribunal that has jurisdiction under Section 2 of Part XV of the UNCLOS[165] [258]. A dispute that is either excluded under Article 297 of the UNCLOS[166] or excepted by a

[161] The 'Area' is "the seabed and ocean floor and subsoil thereof, beyond the limits of national jurisdiction" (United Nations (1982), "United Nations Convention on the Law of the Sea," Article 1(1)).

[162] Fn 160.

[163] Section 3 of Part XV of the UNCLOS comprises Articles 297-299 of this Convention, and is entitled 'Limitations and Exceptions to Applicability of Section 2'. 'Section 2' is a reference to Section 2 of Part XV of the UNCLOS, which contains Articles 286-296 of this Convention and is titled 'Compulsory Procedures Entailing Binding Decisions'. The current subsection of this book, i.e., that entitled 'Compulsory Procedures Entailing Binding Decisions: Applicability', comprises Articles 286 and 299 of the UNCLOS. The next two subsections respectively contain Articles 297 and 298 of the UNCLOS. The remaining subsections within the present section consist of Articles 287-296 of the UNCLOS.

[164] Fn 159 describes Section 1 of Part XV of the UNCLOS.

[165] Fn 163 describes Sections 2 and 3 of Part XV of the UNCLOS. Article 288 of the UNCLOS is entitled 'Jurisdiction'. Paragraphs 1 and 2 of that Article address this matter with reference to Article 287 of the UNCLOS. Paragraph 3 of Article 288 of the UNCLOS attends to the jurisdiction of the Seabed Disputes Chamber of the ITLOS, and any other arbitral tribunal or chamber to which Section 5 of Part XI of the UNCLOS refers. The subsection entitled 'Compulsory Procedures: Jurisdiction', below in the current section, comprises Article 288 of the UNCLOS. The subsection titled 'Compulsory Procedures: Choice of Procedure', below in the present section, contains Article 287 of the UNCLOS. The immediately-preceding subsection entitled 'The Seabed Disputes Chamber of the ITLOS & UNCLOS Part XV' describes Section 5 of Part XI of the UNCLOS, and states its relationship to Part XV of the UNCLOS – especially to Section 1 of the latter Part.

[166] The next subsection, which is entitled 'Limitations to the Applicability of the Compulsory Procedures', comprises Article 297 of the UNCLOS – which is titled 'Limitations on applicability of section 2'.

declaration made under Article 298 of the UNCLOS[167] from the application of the compulsory procedures for settlement for which Section 2 of Part XV of the UNCLOS provides[168], may be submitted to any of those procedures only by the disputants' agreement [259]. Nothing in Section 3 of Part XV of the UNCLOS[169] weakens the right of these parties to agree to a procedure for the resolution of their dispute that is beyond the scope of Section 2 of Part XV of the UNCLOS, or to come to a friendly settlement [260].

Limitations to the Applicability of the Compulsory Procedures

Subject to two exceptions[170], disputes regarding "the interpretation or application of the provisions of" the UNCLOS in respect of marine

[167] The subsection after the next one, which is entitled 'Optional Exceptions to the Applicability of Compulsory Procedures', consists of Article 298 of the UNCLOS – which is titled 'Optional exceptions to the applicability of section 2'.

[168] Fn 163 describes Sections 2 and 3 of Part XV of the UNCLOS.

[169] Fn 163 describes Sections 2 and 3 of Part XV of the UNCLOS.

[170] These exceptions are as follows: "[T]he coastal State shall not be obliged to accept the submission to such settlement [i.e., in conformity with Section 2 of Part XV of the UNCLOS] of any dispute arising out of: (i) the exercise by the coastal State of a right or discretion in accordance with [A]rticle 246 [of the UNCLOS]; or (ii) a decision by the coastal State to order suspension or cessation of a research project in accordance with [A]rticle 253 [of the UNCLOS]." (United Nations (1982), "United Nations Convention on the Law of the Sea," Article 297(2)(a)). A coastal State's right/discretion to which the first exception refers is as follows: *right* – "Coastal States, in the exercise of their jurisdiction, *have the right to* regulate, authorize and conduct marine scientific research in their exclusive economic zone and on their continental shelf in accordance with the relevant provisions of this Convention (United Nations (1982), "United Nations Convention on the Law of the Sea," Article 246(1); emphasis added); *discretion* – "Coastal States may however *in their discretion* withhold their consent to the conduct of a marine scientific research project of another State or competent international organization in the exclusive economic zone or on the continental shelf of the coastal State if that project: (a) is of direct significance for the exploration and exploitation of natural resources, whether living or non-living; (b) involves drilling into the continental shelf, the use of explosives or the introduction of harmful substances into the marine environment; (c) involves the construction, operation or use of artificial islands, installations and structures … ; (d) contains information … regarding the nature and objectives of the project which is inaccurate or if the researching State or competent international organization has outstanding obligations to the coastal State from a prior research project." (United Nations (1982), "United Nations Convention on the Law of the Sea," Article 246(5); emphasis added). With regard to the second exception, Article 253(1) of the UNCLOS provides two grounds upon which a coastal state may require the *suspension* of its current activities in

scientific research are to be resolved in accordance with Section 2 of Part XV of the UNCLOS[171] [261]. Disputes about "the interpretation or application of" the UNCLOS in connection with the use by a coastal state of its sovereign rights or jurisdiction for which that Convention provides, are to be subject to the procedures that Section 2 of Part XV of the UNCLOS specifies in the following instances: (i) when it is asserted that a coastal state has acted in breach of the provisions of that Convention concerning the rights and freedoms of navigation, overflight or the laying of submarine pipelines and cables, or regarding other uses of the sea that are permitted by international law and specified in Article 58 of the UNCLOS[172] [262], (ii) when it is alleged that a country, in exercising those rights, freedoms or uses, has acted in infraction of the UNCLOS or of laws or regulations that the coastal state adopts in compliance with that Convention and other rules of international law that are compatible with it [263], or (c) when it is claimed that a coastal state has contravened specified worldwide rules and standards for the safeguarding and conservation of the thalassic environment which are applicable to that country – and which the UNCLOS, or a diplomatic conference or competent international organization have established in conformity with the UNCLOS [264].

Disputes regarding "the interpretation or application of the provisions of" the UNCLOS in respect of fisheries are to be resolved in accordance with Section 2 of Part XV of the UNCLOS[173], although the coastal state is not obliged to accept the submission to settlement under Section 2 of any dispute that concerns its sovereign rights as regards the living resources

---

marine scientific research on its continental slope or within its exclusive economic zone, and Paragraphs 2 and 3 of Article 253 of the UNCLOS each supply one ground upon which a coastal state may require the *cessation* of its activities in marine scientific research.

[171] Part XIII of the UNCLOS, which comprises Articles 238-265 of this Convention and is entitled 'Marine Scientific Research', specifies provisions relating to marine scientific research. Article 264 of the UNCLOS states: "Disputes concerning the interpretation or application of the provisions of this Convention with regard to marine scientific research shall be settled in accordance with Part XV [of the UNCLOS], [S]ections 2 and 3." Fn 163 describes Sections 2 and 3 of Part XV of the UNCLOS.

[172] The subsection entitled 'Rights and Duties of Other States in the Exclusive Economic Zone', in the section above titled 'Part V of the UNCLOS: Exclusive Economic Zone', comprises Article 58 of the UNCLOS.

[173] Fn 163 describes Sections 2 and 3 of Part XV of the UNCLOS.

within its exclusivce economic zone or their exercise [265]. Where recourse to Section 1 of Part XV of the UNCLOS[174] has not yielded a settlement, a dispute is to be submitted to conciliation under Section 2 of Annex V to the UNCLOS[175] at the request of any disputant, when it is argued that a coastal state has: (i) clearly failed to abide by its obligations to ensure, by means of appropriate measures for the management and conservation of the living resources in its exclusive economic zone, that the preservation of those resources is not severly endangered, (ii) arbitrarily refused to decide upon, at another country's request, the permissible catch and its capacity to reap living resources concerning stocks which that other state is wishing to fish, or (iii) arbitrarily refused to allot to any country – under Articles 62[176], 69[177] and 70[178] of the UNCLOS

---

[174] Fn 159 describes Section 1 of Part XV of the UNCLOS.

[175] Section 2 of Annex V to the UNCLOS is entitled 'Compulsory Submission to Conciliation Procedure Pursuant to Section 3 of Part XV', and comprises the following provisions: (i) "Any party to a dispute which, in accordance with Part XV [of the UNCLOS], [S]ection 3, may be submitted to conciliation under this [S]ection, may institute the proceedings by written notification addressed to the other party or parties to the dispute." (United Nations (1982), "United Nations Convention on the Law of the Sea," Annex V, Article 11(1)); (ii) "Any party to the dispute, notified under paragraph 1 [i.e., Article 11(1) of Annex V to the UNCLOS], shall be obliged to submit to such proceedings." (United Nations (1982), "United Nations Convention on the Law of the Sea," Annex V, Article 11(2)); (iii) "The failure of a party or parties to the dispute to reply to notification of institution of proceedings or to submit to such proceedings shall not constitute a bar to the proceedings." (United Nations (1982), "United Nations Convention on the Law of the Sea," Annex V, Article 12); (iv) "A disagreement as to whether a conciliation commission acting under this section has competence shall be decided by the [conciliation] commission." (United Nations (1982), "United Nations Convention on the Law of the Sea," Annex V, Article 13); (v) "*Articles 2 to 10 of [S]ection 1 of this Annex* [i.e., Section 1 of Annex V to the UNCLOS] *apply subject to this [S]ection* [i.e., Section 2 of Annex V to the UNCLOS] (United Nations (1982), "United Nations Convention on the Law of the Sea," Annex V, Article 14; emphasis added). Fn 157 summarizes the conciliation procedure that Section 1 of Annex V to the UNCLOS – comprising Articles 1-10 of that Annex – lays down. Fn 163 describes Sections 2 and 3 of Part XV of the UNCLOS.

[176] The third – and final – paragraph of the subsection entitled 'Conservation and Utilization of Living Resources', in the section above titled 'Part V of the UNCLOS: Exclusive Economic Zone', states the provisions of Article 62 of the UNCLOS – which is entitled 'Utilization of living resources'.

[177] The subsection entitled 'Rights of Landlocked States as regards Exclusive Economic Zones', in the section above titled 'Part V of the UNCLOS: Exclusive Economic Zone', comprises the provisions of Article 69 of the UNCLOS – which is entitled 'Rights of land-locked states'.

[178] The subsection entitled 'Rights of Geographically-Disadvantaged States', in the section above titled 'Part V of the UNCLOS: Exclusive Economic Zone', consists of the provisions of

and according to the terms and conditions compatible with this Convention that the coastal state has established, all or part of the surplus that it has proclaimed to exist [266]; the conciliation commission may not replace the coastal state's discretion with that of its own [267].

Optional Exceptions to the Applicability of Compulsory Procedures

Without affecting the obligations imposed on it by Section 1 of Part XV of the UNCLOS[179], a state may asseverate in writing that it does not accept any one or more of the procedures for which Section 2 of Part XV of the UNCLOS[180] provides[181] concerning one or more of the following classes of disputes: (a)(i) *disputes regarding "the interpretation or appliction of [A]rticles 15[182], 74[183] or 83[184] [of the UNCLOS] relating to sea boundary delimitations, or those involving historic bays[185] or titles[186]"[187]* [268], although that country may be required, in any particular

Article 70 of the UNCLOS – which is entitled 'Rights of geographically disadvantaged States'.

179 Fn 159 describes Section 1 of Part XV of the UNCLOS.

180 Fn 163 describes Sections 2 and 3 of Part XV of the UNCLOS.

181 Article 287(1) of the UNCLOS lists these procedures. The first sentence of the next subsection, which is entitled 'Compulsory Procedures: Choice of Procedure', states Article 287(1) of the UNCLOS.

182 The subsection entitled 'Delimitation of the Territorial Sea between States', in the section above titled 'Part II of the UNCLOS: Territorial Sea and Contiguous Zone', comprises Article 15 of the UNCLOS.

183 The subsection entitled 'Delimitation of the Exclusive Economic Zone between States', in the section above titled 'Part V of the UNCLOS: Exclusive Economic Zone', contains the provisions of Article 74 of the UNCLOS.

184 The subsection entitled 'Delimitation of the Continental Shelf between States', in the section above titled 'Part VI of the UNCLOS: Continental Shelf', comprises the provisions of Article 83 of the UNCLOS.

185 Whilst the UNCLOS lacks a rule on historic bays, these make an exception to the rules concerning baselines across bays that Article 10 of the UNCLOS contains. The subsection entitled 'The Baselines for a Bay the Coast of Which Belongs to a Single State', in the section above titled 'Part II of the UNCLOS: Territorial Sea and Contiguous Zone', consists of Article 10 of the UNCLOS.

186 Whilst the UNCLOS contains no rule on historic titles, these form part of an exception to the general rule in Article 15 of the UNCLOS for the delimitation of the territorial sea between states with adjacent or opposite coasts. Fn 26 specifies this exception. The text accompanying that footnote states the general rule in Article 15 of the UNCLOS. Fn 625

dispute of this category to which it is a party, to accept compulsory submission of that dispute to conciliation under Section 2 of Annex V to the UNCLOS[188] – clauses (ii)[189] and (iii)[190] provide further conditions, (b) disputes about military activities, and disputes concerning activities of law enforcement with regard to the exercise of sovereign jurisdiction or rights that are excluded from the purview of a court or tribunal under Paragraph 2 or 3 of Article 297 of the UNCLOS[191] [269], and/or (c) disputes in respect

---

explores legal practice and guidance with regard to historic title to waters, as contextual information in respect of China's claim over the preponderance of the South China Sea – which the arbitral tribunal addressed in the *South China Sea arbitration*.

[187] Emphasis added.

[188] A state's written declaration under this clause, i.e., Article 298(1)(a)(i) of the UNCLOS, is subject to the following condition concerning compulsory submission of any dispute within this provision's ambit to which that country is a party to conciliation under Section 2 of Annex V to the UNCLOS: "provided that a State having made such a declaration shall, when such a dispute arises subsequent to the entry into force of this Convention [(i.e., the UNCLOS)] and where no agreement within a reasonable period of time is reached in negotiations between the parties, at the request of any party to the dispute, accept submission of the matter to conciliation under Annex V [to the UNCLOS], [S]ection 2; and provided further that any dispute that necessarily involves the concurrent consideration of any unsettled dispute concerning sovereignty or other rights over continental or insular land territory shall be excluded from such submission;" (United Nations (1982), "United Nations Convention on the Law of the Sea," Annex V, Article 298(1)(a)(i)). Fn 175 quotes the provisions of Section 2 of Annex V to the UNCLOS, and refers to fn 157 – which summarizes the conciliation procedure that Section 1 of Annex V to the UNCLOS lays down; in particular, Article 14 of Annex V to the UNCLOS – which is within Section 2 of that Annex – applies this conciliation procedure to disputes which may be submitted to conciliation under that Section, subject to the provisions within that Section (fn 175).

[189] Clause (ii), i.e., Article 298(1)(a)(ii) of the UNCLOS, states: "after the conciliation commission has presented its report [pursuant to conciliation under Section 2 of Annex V to the UNCLOS], which shall state the reasons on which it is based, the parties shall negotiate an agreement on the basis of that report; if these negotiations do not result in an agreement, [then] the parties shall, by mutual consent, submit the question to one of the procedures provided for in [S]ection 2 [of Part XV of the UNCLOS], unless the parties otherwise agree." Article 287(1) of the UNCLOS lists these procedures; the first sentence of the next subsection, which is entitled 'Compulsory Procedures: Choice of Procedure', states Article 287(1) of the UNCLOS. Fn 175 quotes the provisions of Section 2 of Annex V to the UNCLOS, and refers to fn 157 – which summarizes the conciliation procedure that Section 1 of Annex V to the UNCLOS lays down; in particular, Article 14 of Annex V to the UNCLOS – which is within Section 2 of that Annex – applies this conciliation procedure to disputes which may be submitted to conciliation under that Section, subject to the provisions within that Section (fn 175).

[190] Clause (iii), i.e., Article 298(1)(a)(iii) of the UNCLOS, declares: "this subparagraph [i.e., Article 298(1)(a) of the UNCLOS] does not apply to any sea boundary dispute finally settled by an arrangement between the parties, or to any such dispute which is to be settled in accordance with a bilateral or multilateral agreement binding upon those parties."

[191] The first sentence of the immediately-preceding subsection entitled 'Limitations to the Applicability of the Compulsory Procedures', together with fn 170, concerns Subparagraph

of which the UNSC is exercising the functions that the UN Charter assigns to it – unless the UNSC decides to delete the issue from its agenda or requests the parties to resolve it by the means which the UNCLOS provides [270]. A State Party[192] that has made an asseveration under Article 298(1) of the UNCLOS[193] may withdraw it at any time or agree to submit a dispute which this declaration excludes to any procedure that the UNCLOS specifies [271], and is not entitled to submit a dispute which falls within the excepted class of disputes to any procedure in the UNCLOS as against another State Party – unless the latter consents to this [272]. If one of the States Parties has made a declaration under Article 298(1)(a) of the UNCLOS[194], then any other State Party may submit a dispute against the declarant party which falls within an excepted category to the procedure that is specified in this asseveration [273].

Compulsory Procedures: Choice of Procedure

At the time of signing, ratifying or acceding to the UNCLOS, or at whatever moment thereafter, a state is free to select, by using a written declaration, one or more of the following modes for the resolution of disputes regarding "the interpretation or application of" the UNCLOS: (a) the ITLOS, established in conformity with Annex VI to the UNCLOS[195],

---

2(a) of Article 297 of the UNCLOS. The second paragraph of that immediately-preceding subsection states Subparagraphs 3(a)-(c) of Article 297 of the UNCLOS.

192 'States Parties' are "States which have consented to be bound by this Convention [(i.e., the UNCLOS)] and for which this Convention is in force" (United Nations (1982), "United Nations Convention on the Law of the Sea," Article 1(2)(1)).

193 The first sentence of the current subsection (entitled 'Optional Exceptions to the Applicability of Compulsory Procedures'), together with fns 188-190, states Article 298(1) of the UNCLOS.

194 This is a declaration made under Clause 298(1)(a)(i) of the UNCLOS – which is italicized in the first sentence of the present subsection (entitled 'Optional Exceptions to the Applicability of Compulsory Procedures'), subject to the conditions that fns 188-190 specify.

195 Annex VI to the UNCLOS is entitled 'Statute of the International Tribunal for the Law of the Sea', and comprises 41 Articles. Article 1 is entitled 'General provisions', the first of which states: "The International Tribunal for the Law of the Sea is constituted and shall function in accordance with the provisions of this Convention and this Statute." (United Nations (1982), "United Nations Convention on the Law of the Sea," Annex VI, Article 1(1)).

(b) the ICJ, (c) an arbitral tribunal that is constituted in conformity with Annex VII to the UNCLOS[196], and/or (d) "a special arbitral tribunal" which is established in line with Annex VIII to the UNCLOS[197] for one or

---

Article 1(4) of Annex VI to the UNCLOS states: "A reference of a dispute to the Tribunal shall be governed by the provisions of Parts XI and XV." Part XI of the UNCLOS is titled 'The Area', and comprises Articles 133-191 of this Convention. Fn 161 defines the 'Area'. Part XV of the UNCLOS is entitled 'Settlement of Disputes', consists of Articles 279-299 of the UNCLOS, and is described in the current section (i.e., that titled 'Part XV of the UNCLOS: Settlement of Disputes'). Section 1 of Annex VI to the UNCLOS is titled 'Organization of the Tribunal', and contains Articles 2-19 of that Annex. Section 2 of Annex VI to the UNCLOS is entitled 'Competence' (i.e., the competence of the tribunal as to the range of disputes that it addresses), and consists of Articles 20-23 of that Annex. Section 3 of Annex VI to the UNCLOS is titled 'Procedure', and comprises Articles 24-34 of that Annex. Section 4 of Annex VI to the UNCLOS is entitled 'Seabed Disputes Chamber', and contains Articles 35-40 of that Annex. The subsection titled 'The Seabed Disputes Chamber of the ITLOS & UNCLOS Part XV', and fn 207 and its accompanying text, the former above and the latter below in the current section entitled 'Part XV of the UNCLOS: Settlement of Disputes', provide information concerning the Seabed Disputes Chamber of the ITLOS. Section 5 of Annex VI to the UNCLOS is titled 'Amendments', and comprises Article 41 of that Annex – which refers to Article 313 of the UNCLOS (entitled 'Amendment by simplified procedure') or a conference convoked in conformity with the UNCLOS for the adoption of amendments to Sections 1-3 and 5 of Annex VI to the UNCLOS (United Nations (1982), "United Nations Convention on the Law of the Sea," Annex VI, Article 41(1)), and to Article 314 of the UNCLOS (titled 'Amendments to the provisions of this Convention relating exclusively to activities in the Area') for the adoption of amendments to Section 4 of Annex VI to the UNCLOS (United Nations (1982), "United Nations Convention on the Law of the Sea," Annex VI, Article 41(2)). The subsection entitled 'A Summary of the ITLOS' Jurisdictional and Procedural Aspects', in the section titled 'The International Tribunal for the Law of the Sea' in Chapter 2, describes provisions within Sections 1, 2 and 3 of Annex VI to the UNCLOS.

[196] Annex VII to the UNCLOS is entitled 'Arbitration', and contains 13 Articles. Article 1 of Annex VII to the UNCLOS is titled 'Institution of proceedings', and states: "Subject to the provisions of Part XV [of the UNCLOS], any party to a dispute may submit the dispute to the arbitral procedure provided for in this Annex by written notification addressed to the other party or parties to the dispute. The notification shall be accompanied by a statement of the claim and the grounds on which it is based." Annex VII to the UNCLOS includes substantial provisions on the list of arbitrators (Article 2) and the constitution of the arbitral tribunal (Article 3), but specifies little about the arbitral tribunal's functions (Article 4) and its procedure (Article 5) – "Unless the parties to the dispute otherwise agree, the arbitral tribunal shall determine its own procedure, assuring to each party a full opportunity to be heard and to present its case." (United Nations (1982), "United Nations Convention on the Law of the Sea," Annex VII, Article 5). The arbitral tribunal's award "shall be confined to the subject-matter of the dispute and state the reasons on which it is based" (United Nations (1982), "United Nations Convention on the Law of the Sea," Annex VII, Article 10). The arbitral award is "final and without appeal, unless the parties to the dispute have agreed in advance to an appellate procedure" and – significantly, especially in the absence of an appellate procedure – "shall be complied with by the parties to the dispute" (United Nations (1982), "United Nations Convention on the Law of the Sea," Annex VII, Article 11).

[197] Annex VIII to the UNCLOS is entitled 'Special Arbitration', and comprises five Articles. Article 1 of Annex VIII to the UNCLOS is titled 'Institution of Proceedings', and declares:

more of the classes of disputes that this Annex specifies[198] [274]. A State Party[199] that is a disputant which is not covered by an effective declaration, is deemed to have accepted arbitration in conformity with Annex VII to the UNCLOS[200] [275].

If the disputants have chosen the same procedure for the resolution of their disagreement, then the dispute may be submitted only to that process – unless the parties agree otherwise [276]. If the disputants have selected different procedures for the settlement of their disagreement, then the dispute may be submitted only to arbitration in line with Annex VII to the UNCLOS – unless the parties agree elsewise [277].

"Subject to Part XV [of the UNCLOS], any party to a dispute concerning the interpretation or application of the [A]rticles of this Convention relating to (1) fisheries, (2) protection and preservation of the marine environment, (3) marine scientific research, or (4) navigation, including pollution from vessels and by dumping, may submit the dispute to the special arbitral procedure provided for in this Annex by written notification addressed to the other party or parties to the dispute. The notification shall be accompanied by a statement of the claim and the ground on which it is based." Annex VIII to the UNCLOS contains sizeable provisions on the list of experts to be set up and maintained for each of these four spheres of activity (Article 2 (fn 221)) and the constitution of the special arbitral tribunal (Article 3). Articles 4-13 of Annex VII to the UNCLOS (fn 196) "apply *mutatis mutandis* to the special arbitration proceedings in accordance with this Annex [i.e., Annex VIII to the UNCLOS] (United Nations (1982), "United Nations Convention on the Law of the Sea," Annex VIII, Article 4). Fn 140 defines '*mutatis mutandis*'. Article 5 of Annex VIII to the UNCLOS contains provisions – for which there are no corresponding rules in Annex VII to the UNCLOS – that empower the special arbitral tribunal to conduct a fact-finding exercise, three of which are as follows: (i) "The parties to a dispute concerning the interpretation of application of the provisions of this Convention relating to (1) fisheries, (2) protection and preservation of the marine environment, (3) marine scientific research, or (4) navigation, including pollution from vessels and by dumping, may at any time agree to request a special arbitral tribunal constituted in accordance with [A]rticle 3 of this Annex to carry out an inquiry and establish the facts giving rise to the dispute." (United Nations (1982), "United Nations Convention on the Law of the Sea," Annex VIII, Article 5(1)); (ii) "Unless the parties otherwise agree, the findings of fact of the special arbitral tribunal acting in accordance with [Article 5(1) of Annex VIII to the UNCLOS], shall be considered as conclusive between the parties." (United Nations (1982), "United Nations Convention on the Law of the Sea," Annex VIII, Article 5(2)); (iii) If all the parties to the dispute so request, the special arbitral tribunal may formulate recommendations which, without having the force of a decision, shall only constitute the basis for a review by the parties of the questions giving rise to the dispute." (United Nations (1982), "United Nations Convention on the Law of the Sea," Annex VIII, Article 5(3)).

[198] Fn 197 quotes Article 1 of Annex VIII to the UNCLOS, which lists the four categories of disputes that may be submitted to the special arbitral procedure for which Annex VIII to the UNCLOS provides.

[199] Fn 192 defines 'States Parties'.

[200] Fn 196 summarizes Annex VII to the UNCLOS.

A declaration that a state makes under Article 287(1) of the UNCLOS[201], remains in force until three months after any notice of its revocation has been been lodged with the Secretary-General of the UN [278]. If a disputant makes a new declaration or provides a notice of revocation, or if the current declaration expires, then proceedings that are pending before a court or arbitral tribunal are unaffected – unless the parties agree otherwise [279]. Declarations and notices to which Article 287 of the UNCLOS[202] refers must be placed with the Secretary-General of the UN, who issues copies thereof to the States Parties[203] [280].

Compulsory Procedures: Jurisdiction

A court or tribunal to which Article 287 of the UNCLOS[204] refers has jurisdiction over any dispute regarding "the interpretation or application of": (i) the UNCLOS, which is submitted to that forum in conformity with this Part (i.e., Part XV) of the UNCLOS [281], and (ii) an international agreement that is connected with the purposes of the UNCLOS, which is submitted to the court or tribunal in line with that agreement[205] [282]. The Seabed Disputes Chamber of the ITLOS, and any other chamber or arbitral tribunal to which Section 5 of Part XI of the UNCLOS[206] refers, has

---

[201] The first sentence of this subsection (entitled 'Compulsory Procedure: Choice of Procedure') lists the means for settling disputes concerning how the UNCLOS is interpreted or applied whose decisions are binding on the disputants, one or more of which a country may select by using a written declaration.

[202] The current subsection (titled 'Compulsory Procedure: Choice of Procedure') comprises Article 287 of the UNCLOS.

[203] Fn 192 defines 'States Parties'.

[204] The immediately-preceding subsection, entitled 'Compulsory Procedure: Choice of Procedure', consists of Article 287 of the UNCLOS. Points (a)-(d) in the first sentence of that subsection specify the court (i.e., the ICJ) and the tribunals to which Article 287 of the UNCLOS refers.

[205] If there is a disagreement as to whether a court or tribunal has jurisdiction over a dispute, then that court or tribunal shall decide the matter (United Nations (1982), "United Nations Convention on the Law of the Sea," Article 288(4)).

[206] Fn 160, and the text to fn 162, provide information concerning Section 5 of Part XI of the UNCLOS.

jursidiction over any matter that is submitted to it in accordance with that Section and Annex VI to the UNCLOS[207] [283].

---

[207] Article 187 of the UNCLOS states: "The Seabed Disputes Chamber [of the ITLOS] shall have jurisdiction under this Part [i.e., Part XI of the UNCLOS] and the Annexes relating thereto in disputes with respect to activities in the Area falling within the following categories: (a) disputes between States Parties concerning the interpretation or application of this Part and the Annexes relating thereto; ... (f) any other disputes for which the jurisdiction of the Chamber is specifically provided for in this Convention [(i.e., the UNCLOS)]." Article 188(1) of the UNCLOS provides for disputes between States Parties to which Article 187(a) of the UNCLOS refers (i.e., point (a) in the immediately-preceding sentence) to be submitted: (a) at the disputants' request, to a special chamber of the ITLOS to be set up in conformity with Articles 15 and 17 of Annex VI to the UNCLOS, or (b) at the request of any disputant, to an *ad hoc* chamber of the Seabed Disputes Chamber of the ITLOS to be launched in compliance with Article 36 of Annex VI to the UNCLOS. The phrase '*ad hoc*' is the Latin for 'to this', and means "formed, arranged or done for a particular purpose only" (Pearsall, J. (editor) (1998), *The New Oxford Dictionary of English*, 21). Similarly, Dr. McFarlane's definition of '*ad hoc*' focuses on the particular, i.e., "[f]or a specific case, in the sense of an arrangement or action taken to deal with a particular situation" (McFarlane, G. (1984), *The Layman's Dictionary of English Law*, 6). Thus, the *ad hoc* chamber is created for a particular purpose or to address a specific situation. Article 36(1) of Annex VI to the UNCLOS states: "The Seabed Disputes Chamber [of the ITLOS] shall form an *ad hoc* chamber, composed of three of its members, for dealing with a particular dispute submitted to it in accordance with [A]rticle 188 [of the UNCLOS], [P]aragraph 1(b). The composition of such a chamber shall be determined by the Seabed Disputes Chamber with the approval of the parties." (emphasis added). Article 188(1)(a) of the UNCLOS refers to Articles 15 and 17 of Annex VI to the UNCLOS; Article 15 of Annex VI to the UNCLOS declares: "1. The Tribunal [i.e., the ITLOS] may form such chambers, composed of three or more of its elected members, as it considers necessary for dealing with particular categories of disputes. 2. The Tribunal shall form a chamber for dealing with a particular dispute submitted to it if the parties so request. The composition of such a chamber shall be determined by the Tribunal with the approval of the parties. ... 4. Disputes shall be heard and determined by the chambers provided for in this [A]rticle if the parties so request. 5. A judgment given by any of the chambers provided for in this [A]rticle and in [A]rticle 14 of this Annex [which establishes the Seabed Disputes Chamber of the ITLOS] shall be considered as rendered by the Tribunal."; Paragraph 4 of Article 17 of Annex VI to the UNCLOS states: "This [A]rticle applies to the chambers referred to in [A]rticles 14 [i.e., the Seabed Disputes Chamber of the ITLOS] and 15 [i.e., special chambers of the ITLOS] of this Annex. In such cases, the President [of the ITLOS], in consultation with the parties, shall request specified members of the Tribunal forming the chamber, as many as necessary, to give place to members of the Tribunal of the nationality of the parties concerned, and failing such, or if they are unable to be present, to the members specially chosen by the parties." Article 21 of Annex VI to the UNCLOS specifies the jurisdiction of the ITLOS (i.e., the whole Tribunal – not just its Seabed Disputes Chamber): "The jurisdiction of the Tribunal comprises all disputes and all applications submitted to it in accordance with this Convention [(i.e., the UNCLOS)] and all matters specifically provided for in any other agreement which confers jurisdiction of the Tribunal."

Compulsory Procedures: Finality and Binding Force of Decisions

Any decision that a court or tribunal having jurisdiction under Section 2 of Part XV of the UNCLOS[208] makes is final, and must be observed by all the disputants [284]. This decision is binding only between those parties and with regard to that particular dispute [285].

Compulsory Procedures: Exhaustion of Local Remedies

Any dispute between States Parties[209] regarding "the interpretation or application of" the UNCLOS may be submitted to the dispute-settlement procedures for which Section 2 of Part XV of the UNCLOS provides[210], solely: (i) after local remedies have been depleted, and (ii) where "international law"[211] requires this [286].

Compulsory Procedures: Preliminary Proceedings[212]

A court or tribunal for which Article 287 of the UNCLOS provides[213], to which an application is made regarding a dispute to which Article 297 of

[208] Fn 165 and the immediately-preceding subsection, which is entitled 'Compulsory Procedures: Jurisdiction', address compulsory jurisdiction under Section 2 of Part XV of the UNCLOS.

[209] Fn 192 defines 'States Parties'.

[210] Article 287(1) of the UNCLOS – which the first sentence of the subsection entitled 'Compulsory Procedures: Choice of Procedure', above in the current section (i.e., that titled 'Part XV of the UNCLOS: Settlement of Disputes'), lays down – identifies these dispute-resolution procedures as the ITLOS, the ICJ, an arbitral tribunal as established in accordance with Annex VII to the UNCLOS (fn 196), and a special arbitral tribunal as founded in observance of Annex VIII to the UNCLOS (fn 197).

[211] Article 295 of the UNCLOS does not specify what the scope of 'international law' is, in this context. It is submitted that this phrase includes, but is not limited to, the UNCLOS and any international agreements that are made pursuant to the UNCLOS.

[212] Article 294(3) of the UNCLOS states: "Nothing in this [A]rticle [i.e., Article 294 of the UNCLOS] affects the right of any party to a dispute to make preliminary objections in accordance with the applicable rules of procedure." The subsection headed by the present subtitle (i.e., 'Compulsory Procedures: Preliminary Proceedings') consists of Article 294 of the UNCLOS.

the UNCLOS[214] refers, is to determine at the request of a disputant, or choose whether or not to decide *proprio motu*[215], whether the claim put before that forum is *prima facie*[216] well-founded or whether it constitutes a misuse of legal procedure; if the court or tribunal finds that this claim is *prima facie* unfounded or that it amounts to an abuse of due process of law, then it does not pursue the case any further [287]. Upon receipt of this application, the court or tribunal is to instantly inform the other disputant(s) of the application, and is to set a reasonable time-limit within which those parties may request it to make a determination in compliance with Article 294(1) of the UNCLOS[217] [288].

Compulsory Procedures: Proceedings

In a dispute which involves issues of science and/or[218] expertise, a court or tribunal that exercises jurisdiction under Section 2 of Part XV of

---

[213] These are the ICJ, the ITLOS, an arbitral tribunal that is constituted in line with Annex VII, and a special arbitral tribunal which is set up in conformity with Annex VIII for one or more of the classes of dispute specified therein (United Nations (1982), "United Nations Convention on the Law of the Sea," Article 287(1)). The first sentence of the subsection entitled 'Compulsory Procedures: Choice of Procedure', above in the current section (i.e., that titled 'Part XV of the UNCLOS: Settlement of Disputes'), comprises Article 287(1) of the UNCLOS.

[214] Article 297 of the UNCLOS places limits on the applicability of the compulsory dispute-resolution procedures (fn 210) that Article 287(1) of the UNCLOS lists. The subsection entitled 'Limitations to the Applicability of the Compulsory Procedures', above in the present section (i.e., that titled 'Part XV of the UNCLOS: Settlement of Disputes'), contains Article 297 of the UNCLOS.

[215] The phrase '*proprio motu*' means "by one's own motion[;] on one's own initiative" (Merriam-Webster (2019), "*proprio motu* adverb," accessed September 23, 2019, <https://www.merriam-webster.com/dictionary/proprio%20motu>).

[216] The term '*prima facie*' is the Latin for 'first face', and means "based on the first impression; accepted as correct until proved otherwise" (Pearsall, J. (editor) (1998), *The New Oxford Dictionary of English*, 1471). Dr. McFarlane's definition of '*prima facie*' reinforces the first of these two meanings, i.e., "[o]n the face of things; at first sight" (McFarlane, G. (1984), *The Layman's Dictionary of English Law*, 221).

[217] The first sentence of the current subsection (entitled 'Compulsory Procedures: Preliminary Proceedings') comprises Article 294(1) of the UNCLOS.

[218] Whilst Article 289 of the UNCLOS reads "or," it is submitted that the drafters of the UNCLOS meant either scientific matters, or technical issues, or both – hence the substitution of 'or' with 'and/or' in the text.

the UNCLOS[219] may, either at a disputant's request or *proprio motu*[220], choose in discussion with the parties at least two scientific or technical specialists who are preferably selected from the relevant list which is prepared in conformity with Article 2 of Annex VIII to the UNCLOS[221], to attend that forum without the right to vote [289]. A court or tribunal having jurisdiction under Section 2 of Part XV of the UNCLOS shall apply the UNCLOS and other provisions of international law that are compatible with this Convention[222] [290].

All the procedures for resolving disputes that this Part (i.e., Part XV) of the UNCLOS specifies, are available to States Parties[223] [291]. These processes are open to entities other than States Parties only as the UNCLOS specifically permits [292].

If a dispute has been put before a court or tribunal which adjudges that *prima facie*[224] it has jurisdiction under this Part (i.e., Part XV), or Section 5 of Part XI, of the UNCLOS[225], then this forum may impose any provisional measures which it considers to be suitable under the circumstances to safeguard the respective rights of the disputants or prevent serious damage to the thalassic environment, whilst awaiting the final decision [293]. Provisional measures may be altered or revoked, once the circumstances that justify them have ended or become different [294]. Provisional

[219] Fn 163 describes Sections 2 and 3 of Part XV of the UNCLOS.

[220] Fn 215 defines '*proprio motu*'.

[221] Article 2(1) of Annex VIII to the UNCLOS requires a list of experts to be constructed and maintained regarding fisheries, preservation and protection of the environment, marine scientific research and navigation (fn 197). Article 2(2) of Annex VIII to the UNCLOS states: "The list of experts shall be drawn up and maintained, in the field of fisheries by the Food and Agriculture Organization of the United Nations, in the field of protection and preservation of the marine environment by the United Nations Environment Programme, in the field of marine scientific research by the Intergovernmental Oceanographic Commission, in the field of navigation, including pollution from vessels and by dumping, by the International Maritime Organization, or in each case by the appropriate subsidiary body concerned to which such organization, programme or commission has delegated this function."

[222] Article 293(1) of the UNCLOS (text to the present footnote) does not impair that forum's power to determine a case *ex aequo et bono*, if the parties agree to this course of action (United Nations (1982), "United Nations Convention on the Law of the Sea," Article 293(2)). Fn 113 defines '*ex aequo et bono*'.

[223] Fn 192 defines 'States Parties'.

[224] Fn 216 defines '*prima facie*'.

[225] Fn 160, and the text to fn 162, supply information regarding Section 5 of Part XI of the UNCLOS.

measures may be specified, adjusted or cancelled only at a disputant's request and after the parties have been granted an opportunity to speak [295]. The court or tribunal must immediately notify the disputants, and other States Parties[226] as it considers to be fitting, of its prescribing, modifying or rescinding of provisional measures[227] [296]. The disputants must promptly act in accordance with any provisional measures that are laid down under Article 290 of the UNCLOS[228] [297].

When a State Party's authorities have detained a vessel which flies the flag of another State Party and it is asserted that the detaining country has not observed the provisions of the UNCLOS for the swift release of the vessel and/or[229] its crew upon the posting of a financial security, the issue of discharge from detention may be submitted to any court or tribunal upon which the parties agree or, in the absence of such agreement within ten days of the moment of detention, to the ITLOS[230] or a court or tribunal that

---

[226] Fn 192 defines 'States Parties'.

[227] Article 290(5) of the UNCLOS concerns actions relating to provisional measures in the time between the submission of a dispute to arbitration and the establishment of an arbitral tribunal: "Pending the constitution of an arbitral tribunal to which a dispute is being submitted under this section [i.e., Section 2 of Part XV of the UNCLOS (fn 163)], any court or tribunal agreed upon by the parties or, failing such agreement within two weeks from the date of the request for provisional measures, the International Tribunal for the Law of the Sea or, with respect to activities in the Area, the Seabed Disputes Chamber [of the ITLOS], may prescribe, modify or revoke provisional measures in accordance with this [A]rticle [i.e., Article 290 of the UNCLOS (fn 228)] if it considers that *prima facie* the tribunal which is to be constituted would have jurisdiction and that the urgency of the situation so requires. Once constituted, the tribunal to which the dispute has been submitted may modify, revoke or affirm those provisional measures, acting in conformity with [P]aragraphs 1 to 4 [of Article 290 of the UNCLOS]." The sentence in the text corresponding to the present footnote, and the former's three immediately-preceding sentences, together comprise Paragraphs 1-4 of Article 290 of the UNCLOS. Fn 195 describes the content of Annex VI to the UNCLOS, which is entitled 'Statute of the International Tribunal for the Law of the Sea'. Fn 161 defines the 'Area'. The subsection titled 'The Seabed Disputes Chamber of the ITLOS & UNCLOS Part XV', and fn 207 and its accompanying text, each above in the current section entitled 'Part XV of the UNCLOS: Settlement of Disputes', provide information concerning the Seabed Disputes Chamber of the ITLOS. Fn 216 defines '*prima facie*'.

[228] The current paragraph in the text, together with fn 227, comprises Article 290 of the UNCLOS.

[229] Whilst Article 292(1) of the UNCLOS reads "or," it is submitted that the drafters of the UNCLOS meant either the vessel, or that ship's crew, or both – hence the substitution of 'or' with 'and/or' in the text.

[230] Fn 195 describes the content of Annex VI to the UNCLOS, which is entitled 'Statute of the International Tribunal for the Law of the Sea'.

the detaining country has accepted under Article 287 of the UNCLOS[231], unless the disputants agree otherwise [298]. The ship's flag state, or a representative of that country, must make the application for release [299]. The court or tribunal is to promptly process this application[232] [300]. Upon the posting of a financial security that the court or tribunal determines, the detaining state's authorities must promptly follow the decision of this forum regarding the release of the vessel and/or[233] its crew [301].

Conclusion

This chapter relates those Parts of the UNCLOS with which the remainder of this monograph is concerned, each of which is allotted a section therein – namely, Parts II (Territorial Sea and Contiguous Zone), IV (Archipelagic States), V (Exclusive Economic Zone), VI (Continental Shelf), VIII (Regime of Islands) and XV (Settlement of Disputes). Where possible, comparisons are made between provisions of the UNCLOS and corresponding rules in the relevant Convention adopted by UNCLOS I – which means that the CCS and the CTSCZ, as the CFCLRHS and the CHS are beyond the scope of this book. Whilst some of these cross-Conventional comparisons reveal identical or similar provisions in the CCS/CTSCZ and the UNCLOS, there has been considerable development from the those Conventions to the UNCLOS over some areas – such as the introduction of the maximum breadth of the territorial sea of twelve

---

[231] Article 287(1) of the UNCLOS – which the first sentence of the subsection entitled 'Compulsory Procedures: Choice of Procedure', above in the present section (i.e., that titled 'Part XV of the UNCLOS: Settlement of Disputes'), sets down – identifies the fora that the detaining country may accept in accordance with Section 3 of Part XV of the UNCLOS (fn 163) as the ITLOS, the ICJ, an arbitral tribunal as established in accordance with Annex VII to the UNCLOS (fn 196), and a special arbitral tribunal as founded in observance of Annex VIII to the UNCLOS (fn 197).

[232] This forum "shall deal only with the question of release, without prejudice to the merits of any case before the appropriate domestic forum against the vessel, its owner or its crew. The authorities of the detaining State remain competent to release the vessel or its crew at any time." (United Nations (1982), "United Nations Convention on the Law of the Sea," Article 292(3)).

[233] Fn 229.

nautical miles from that sea's baselines, the institution of an Exclusive Economic Zone for coastal states, and the development of detailed rules concerning the identification of the continental shelf. Moreover, the extensive provisions on the resolution of disputes that Part XV of, and Annexes V, VI, VII and VIII to, the UNCLOS lays down are a major advance on the specified position for adjudication under the Conventions adopted by UNCLOS I – the CCS, the CTSCZ and the CHS are silent on the matter of dispute resolution, and Articles 9-12 of the CFCLRHS describe the operation of a special commission that is authorized to settle disputes between countries arising under Articles 4-8 of that Convention in the absence of agreement by the disputants to pursue another means of peaceful resolution [302].

Chapter 2 considers the dispute-settlement procedures that are in use for cases over the area of the Law of the Sea. These are the ICJ, the ITLOS, and international arbitrations, for which Annex VII to the UNCLOS[234] contains a procedure.

[234] Fn 196 synopsizes Annex VII to the UNCLOS.

Chapter 2

AN INTRODUCTION TO THE CASES OF THE INTERNATIONAL COURT OF JUSTICE, THE INTERNATIONAL TRIBUNAL FOR THE LAW OF THE SEA, AND INTERNATIONAL ARBITRATIONS

ABSTRACT

Article 287(1) of the UNCLOS empowers states to make a written declaration in order to choose one or more of the following methods for settling disputes regarding that Convention's interpretation or application: the ICJ, the ITLOS, an arbitral tribunal that is constituted in accordance with Annex VII to the UNCLOS, and a special arbitral tribunal which is formed in line with Annex VIII to the UNCLOS for matters that are specified therein. Accordingly, the procedures before the ICJ and the ITLOS are described and compared, with the aid of a case before each. The standard form of the written proceedings for both comprises Memorial, Counter-Memorial, Reply and Rejoinder. These are followed by the oral proceedings, in which witnesses and experts are called and cross-examined. International arbitration under Annex VII to the UNCLOS is explored, with the help of a case of contemporary interest. Due to the absence of a specified arbitral procedure within Annex VII, arbitration may provide a more flexible means of settling disputes than either the ICJ or the ITLOS. Article 298(1)(a) of the UNCLOS provides an optional exemption from one, two, three or all four of the methods for resolving disputes mentioned above, in respect of disputes concerning the interpretation or application of those provisions of the UNCLOS that regulate the delimitation of maritime boundaries between neighbouring states and those involving historic bays or titles. The prevalence of declarations pursuant to Article 298(1)(a) which countries have deposited with the Secretary-General of the UN tends to show that States Parties to the UNCLOS do not favour submitting disputes involving the delimitation of their territorial sea, exclusive economic zone and/or continental shelf versus other coastal states to fora for which the Convention provides that impose a binding decision upon them.

Keywords: arbitral, case, chamber, court, dispute, ICJ, ITLOS, tribunal, UNCLOS

Introduction

Paragraph 1 of Article 287 of the UNCLOS[235] empowers countries that are parties to the UNCLOS to make a written declaration in order to select one or more or the following methods for resolving disputes regarding that Convention's interpretation or application: the ICJ, the ITLOS[236], an arbitral tribunal that is established in compliance with Annex VII to the UNCLOS[237], and, for matters concerning fisheries, safeguarding and conservation of the thalassic environment, scientific research concerning the sea, and navigation, a special arbitral tribunal which is founded in observance of Annex VIII to the UNCLOS[238] [274]. As these matters are beyond the scope of this book, special arbitration in accordance with Annex VIII to the UNCLOS is not considered further. A section below is dedicated to each of: (i) the ICJ, (ii) the ITLOS, and (iii) international

[235] The first sentence of the subsection entitled 'Compulsory Procedures: Choice of Procedure', in the section titled 'Part XV of the UNCLOS: Settlement of Disputes' in Chapter 1, comprises Article 287(1) of the UNCLOS.

[236] The ITLOS is established by Article 1 of Annex VI to the UNCLOS, and functions in accordance with that Annex. Fn 195 introduces Annex VI to the UNCLOS.

[237] Fn 196 summarizes Annex VII to the UNCLOS.

[238] Fn 197 describes Annex VIII to the UNCLOS.

arbitrations – the last of these being focused on, but wider in scope than, arbitration in conformity with Annex VII to the UNCLOS, as countries are free to choose to resolve their dispute by methods other than those which Part XV of the UNCLOS provides[239] – thereby accommodating arbitrations that are conducted independently from Annex VII to the UNCLOS and those which predate the introduction of that Convention[240].

THE INTERNATIONAL COURT OF JUSTICE

The Basis for Determination of UNCLOS Disputes

A State Party[241] to the UNCLOS may, by written declaration, choose the ICJ as the forum, or a forum, for settlement of its dispute regarding "the interpretation or application of this Convention" [303]. If the disputants have accepted the ICJ as the forum for the resolution of their dispute, then this may be submitted only to the ICJ unless they agree elsewise [276]. However, if one (or both) of the parties does not agree to the ICJ as a forum, then their dispute would be submitted to arbitration in line with Annex VII to the UNCLOS[242] in preference to the ICJ – unless they concur otherwise [277]. If an international organization and at least one of its member states are joint parties to a dispute concerning the interpretation or application of the UNCLOS, or disputants in the same interest regarding that disagreement, then if a member state has selected only the ICJ as the forum to resolve the matter, it is deemed to have agreed

---

[239] Disputants are to settle their disagreements concerning the interpretation or application of the UNCLOS by any peaceful means of their choice – the subsection entitled 'Disputes are to be Settled by Peaceful Means of the Parties' Choice', in the section titled 'Part XV of the UNCLOS: Settlement of Disputes' in Chapter 1, details this statement. Pursuant to this declaration, the subsection entitled 'Circumstances under which Part XV of the UNCLOS applies', in the section titled 'Part XV of the UNCLOS: Settlement of Disputes' in Chapter 1, identifies circumstances under which Part XV of the UNCLOS applies.

[240] The first sentence of the second paragraph of the section entitled 'Introduction' in Chapter 1 states that the UNCLOS was adopted on 10th December 1982 and came into force on 16th November 1994.

[241] Fn 192 defines 'States Parties'.

[242] Fn 196 synopsizes Annex VII to the UNCLOS.

to arbitration in conformity with Annex VII to the UNCLOS – unless the disputants agree otherwise [304]. The ICJ's decision is only binding between the disputants and as regards their particular dispute [285, 305].

A Summary of Jurisdictional and Procedural Aspects of the ICJ

The UN Charter establishes the ICJ [306]. Whilst the UNSC is empowered to request parties to resolve a dispute [307] – "the continuance of which is likely to endanger the maintenance of international peace and security" – by "peaceful means of their own choice" [248], it may, at any stage of this dispute, "recommend appropriate procedures or methods of adjustment" [308] – "taking into consideration that legal disputes should as a general rule by referred by the parties to the International Court of Justice in accordance with the provisions of the Statute of the Court" [309]. The ICJ is "the principle judicial organ of the United Nations", which functions in conformity with its Statute [310]. Each Member State of the UN is *ipso facto*[243] a party to the Statute of the ICJ [311], and undertakes to abide by the decision of the Court in any dispute in which it participates [312].

The ICJ comprises fifteen independent judges, each of whom is of a different nationality to the others, ethical, and qualified for senior judicial office or a jurist "of recognized competence in international law" [313]. At every election of judges, the electors – the UNSC and the General Assembly [314] – shall ensure that the judical body as a whole shall represent "the main forms of civilization and ... the principal legal systems of the world"[244] [315]. The members of the ICJ are elected for nine years,

---

[243] The phrase '*ipso facto*' is from Latin, and means "by that very fact or act" (Pearsall, J. (editor) (1998), *The New Oxford Dictionary of English* (Oxford: Oxford University Press), 963). Dr. McFarlane's definition of '*ipso facto*' is similar: "[b]y the very fact itself" (McFarlane, G. (1984), *The Layman's Dictionary of English Law* (London: Waterlow Publishers Limited), 150). Thus, the use of *ipso facto* in the UN Charter can be interpreted as follows: 'By virtue of the fact that any country is a Member State of the UN, it is also a party to the Statute of the ICJ'.

[244] The countries currently represented on the ICJ are Australia, Brazil, China, France, India, Italy, Jamaica, Japan, Lebanon, Morocco, Russia, Slovakia, Somalia, Uganda, and the USA (International Court of Justice (2019), "Current Members," accessed October 4, 2019, <https://www.icj-cij.org/en/current-members>). These countries occupy each of the world's

and may be re-elected [316]. No member may: (i) play any administrative or political role, or pursue any other professional occupation [317], or (ii) act as an advocate, a counsel or an agent in any case [318]. The ICJ remains continuously in session, except during the judicial holidays [319].

Only states may be parties to cases before the ICJ [320]. The Court's jurisdiction comprises all cases that the disputants refer to it, and every issue for which the UN Charter or operative conventions or treaties provide[245] [321]. A country which is a party to the Statute of the ICJ may at any time announce that it recognizes as compulsory – in relation to any other state which makes the same commitment – the jurisdiction of the Court in all legal disputes that concern: (i) the interpretation of a treaty [322], (ii) any matter of international law [323], (iii) the presence of any fact which, if established, would amount to the infringement of an international obligation [324], and (iv) the nature or degree of the reparation to be made for the transgression of an international commitment [325]. These declarations may be made unconditionally, contingent on reciprocity from several or specified countries, or for a stated time [326], and are to be placed with the Secretary-General of the UN – who will convey copies of them to the parties to the Statute of the ICJ and to the Registrar of the Court[246] [327]. The ICJ's function is to resolve, in

---

continents (other than Antarctica) – which, it is submitted, approximately satisfies the requirement for judicial body to represent the principal civilizations. The University of Ottawa categorizes the legal systems of these states as follows: *civil law* – Brazil, France, Italy, Russia, Slovakia; *mixed civil law/customary* – China, Japan; *mixed civil law/Muslim* – Lebanon, Morocco; *mixed civil law/common law/customary/Muslim* – Somalia; *mixed common law/customary/Muslim* – India; *mixed common law/customary* – Uganda; *common law* – Australia, Jamaica, the USA (University of Ottawa (2019), "JuriGlobe: World Legal Systems Research Group – Alphabetical Index of the Political Entities and Corresponding Legal Systems," accessed October 4, 2019, <http://www.juriglobe.ca/eng/sys-juri/index-alpha.php>). Thus, civil, common, customary and Islamic legal systems – at least in part – have representative judges on the judicial body, and together these types form the world's principal legal systems.

245 The UNCLOS is one of these effective conventions. The subsection entitled 'Basis for Determination of UNCLOS Disputes', above in the current section (i.e., that titled 'The International Court of Justice'), describes the circumstances under which the ICJ settles disputes concerning the interpretation or application of the UNCLOS.

246 74 States have made declarations that recognize the jurisdiction of the ICJ as compulsory (International Court of Justice (2019), "Declarations recognizing the jurisdiction of the Court as compulsory," accessed October 5, 2019, <https://www.icj-cij.org/en/declarations>). The fairly-short declaration that Mr. Eamon Gilmore made on behalf of the

compliance with international law, those disputes that are submitted to it[247] [328].

The ICJ's official languages are English and French; if the disputants agree that the judgment of the Court is to be delivered in one of these tongues, then the ICJ will pronounce the judgment in this language [329]. If there is no agreement as to which language the Court is to use, then each party may, in the pleadings[248], use its preferred tongue[249]; the ICJ will deliver its decision in English and French, and shall simultaneously determine which of these two texts is to be considered the authoritative version [330].

A dispute is brought before the ICJ by either notification to the Court's Registrar of a Special Agreement between the disputants[250], or written

---

Government of the Republic of Ireland provides an example: "Ireland 15 December 2011 [i.e., the date of deposition of the declaration with the Secretary-General of the UN] Ireland hereby declares that it recognizes as compulsory *ipso facto* and without special agreement, in relation to any other state accepting the same obligation, the jurisdiction of the International Court of Justice in all legal disputes as specified in Article 36, paragraph 2 [of the Statute of the ICJ], with the exception of any legal dispute with the United Kingdom of Great Britain and Northern Ireland in regard to Northern Ireland. The present Declaration shall take effect from the date of its receipt by the Secretary-General of the United Nations. The Government of Ireland reserves the right at any time, by means of a notification addressed to [the] Secretary-General of the United Nations and with effect from the date of such notification, either to amend or withdraw the present Declaration; or to add to, amend or withdraw the foregoing reservation or any other reservations which may subsequently be made. Dublin, 8 December 2011. (Signed) Eamon Gilmore, T.D. Tánaiste and Minister for Foreign Affairs and Trade of Ireland" (International Court of Justice (2019), "Declarations recognizing the jurisdiction of the Court as compulsory: Ireland," accessed October 5, 2019, <https://www.icj-cij.org/en/declarations/ie>; emphasis added).

[247] Paragraph 1 of Article 38 of the Statute of the ICJ specifies the sources of international law that the ICJ applies to the disputes over which it has jurisdiction (fn 113). The ICJ may also settle a dispute in accordance with justice and fairness, if the disputants agree to this (fn 113).

[248] 'Pleadings' are "formal statement[s] of the cause of an action or defence" (Pearsall, J. (editor) (1998), *The New Oxford Dictionary of English*, 1423). Dr. McFarlane's definition of 'pleadings' is more specific than the above meaning of that word: 'pleadings' are "[w]ritten statements delivered by both sides to a civil case setting out the arguments each will be putting forward at the trial" (McFarlane, G. (1984), *The Layman's Dictionary of English Law*, 214). It is submitted that 'pleadings' in respect of the contentious proceedings before the ICJ means the totality of the *written* part of those proceedings, i.e., the Memorial(s), the Counter-Memorial(s) and, if present, any Reply/Replies and Rejoinder(s). Fn 542 comments further on the use of the word 'pleadings'.

[249] At the request of any disputant, the ICJ shall authorize that party to use a language other than English or French (*United Nations Treaty Series* Registration Number N/A, Article 39(3)).

[250] If proceedings are initiated at the ICJ by the notification to its Registrar of a Special Agreement, then "the notification may be effected by the parties jointly or by any one or

application addressed to the Registrar[251] – indicating in both cases the parties and topic of that dispute [331]. The Registrar promptly forwards the application to everyone concerned[252] [332], and notifies[253] both the

more of them. If the notification is not a joint one, [then] a certified copy of it shall forthwith be communicated by the Registrar to the other party." (International Court of Justice (2019), Rules of Court (1978) adopted on 14 April 1978 and entered into force on 1 July 1978 – amended to 21 October 2019 (The Hague: International Court of Justice), Article 39(1)). The notification must "be accompanied by an original or certified copy of the special agreement," and "indicate the precise subject of the dispute and identify the parties to it" (International Court of Justice (2019), Rules of Court (1978) adopted on 14 April 1978 and entered into force on 1 July 1978 – amended to 21 October 2019, Article 39(2)). As there is neither an 'applicant' state nor a 'respondent' state in a Special Agreement, in the ICJ's publications the names of the disputants are separated by a forward slash at the end of the case's official title, e.g., *Sovereignty over Pulau Ligitan and Pulau Sipadan (Indonesia/Malaysia)* – which is abbreviated from the Special Agreement's Title: 'Special Agreement for Submission to the International Court of Justice of the Dispute between Indonesia and Malaysia concerning Sovereignty over Pulau Ligitan and Pulau Sipadan' (International Court of Justice (2019), "How the Court Works," accessed October 6, 2019, <https://www.icj-cij.org/en/how-the-court-works>; International Court of Justice (2019), "Basis of the Court's jurisdiction," accessed October 6, 2019, <https://www.icj-cij.org/en/basis-of-jurisdiction>; International Court of Justice (1998), Special Agreement for Submission to the International Court of Justice of the Dispute between Indonesia and Malaysia concerning Sovereignty over Pulau Ligitan and Pulau Sipadan – jointly notified to the Court on 2 November 1998: 1998 General List No. 102 (The Hague: International Court of Justice), Title).

[251] If proceedings are brought before the ICJ by means of a written application addressed to its Registrar, then "the application shall indicate the party making it [i.e., the applicant state], the State against which the claim is brought [i.e., the respondent state], and the subject of the dispute" (International Court of Justice (2019), Rules of Court (1978) adopted on 14 April 1978 and entered into force on 1 July 1978 – amended to 21 October 2019, Article 38(1)). This written application is to "specify as far as possible the legal grounds upon which the jurisdiction of the Court is said to be based[,] the precise nature of the claim, [and] a succinct statement of the facts and grounds on which the claim is based" (International Court of Justice (2019), Rules of Court (1978) adopted on 14 April 1978 and entered into force on 1 July 1978 – amended to 21 October 2019, Article 38(2)). In the ICJ's publications, the names of the disputants are separated by a versus sign in the following form: (Applicant State v. Respondent State), which appears after the case's official title, e.g., *Land and Maritime Boundary between Cameroon and Nigeria (Cameroon v. Nigeria: Equatorial Guinea intervening)* (International Court of Justice (2019), "How the Court Works," accessed October 6, 2019, <https://www.icj-cij.org/en/how-the-court-works>; International Court of Justice (2019), "Basis of the Court's jurisdiction," accessed October 6, 2019, <https://www.icj-cij.org/en/basis-of-jurisdiction>; International Court of Justice (2002), *Land and Maritime Boundary between Cameroon and Nigeria (Cameroon v. Nigeria: Equatorial Guinea intervening)*, Judgment of 10 October 2002, *I.C.J. Reports 2002*, 303-458, 303).

[252] When the Registrar receives a written application from the appellant State (fn 251), (s)he "shall forthwith transmit to the respondent [state] a certified copy of the application" (International Court of Justice (2019), Rules of Court (1978) adopted on 14 April 1978 and entered into force on 1 July 1978 – amended to 21 October 2019, Article 38(4)). The current Registrar of the ICJ is Mr. Philippe Gautier (International Court of Justice (2019), Press

Member States of the UN via the Secretary-General and any other countries that are entitled to appear before the ICJ[254] [333]. The parties are represented by agents [334], and may be assisted by advocates or counsel before the Court[255] [335].

The procedure before the ICJ comprises written and oral proceedings [336]. The written proceedings[256] are composed of the communication to

Release Unofficial No. 2019/22: 22 May 2019, Mr. Philippe Gautier elected Registrar of the International Court of Justice (The Hague, International Court of Justice), 1)).

[253] This notification by the Registrar of the ICJ applies to both a written application and a Special Agreement: "The Registrar shall transmit copies of any application or notification of a special agreement instituting proceedings before the Court to: (a) the Secretary-General of the United Nations; (b) the Members of the United Nations; (c) other States entitled to appear before the Court (International Court of Justice (2019), Rules of Court (1978) adopted on 14 April 1978 and entered into force on 1 July 1978 – amended to 21 October 2019, Article 42).

[254] A country that is not a Member State of the UN "may become a party to the Statute of the International Court of Justice on conditions to be determined in each case by the General Assembly upon the recommendation of the Security Council" (United Nations (1945),"Charter of the United Nations," *United Nations Treaty Series* Registration Number N/A, Article 93(2)).

[255] These agents, advocates and counsel "shall enjoy the privileges and immunities necessary to the independent exercise of their duties" (United Nations (1945), "Statute of the International Court of Justice," *United Nations Treaty Series* Registration Number N/A, Article 42(3)).

[256] The written proceedings comprise the pleadings. Fn 248 defines 'pleadings'. From 21st October 2019, Article 79 of the ICJ's Rules of Court – having been recently amended and Articles 79*bis* and 79*ter* having been newly introduced – has provided for the ICJ to decide, with regard to each dispute brought before it for adjudication, whether or not it should rule on issues of its jurisdiction and/or the admissibility of the application prior to its consideration of the merits of the case – such determination of the merits being consequent upon it taking the appropriate decision on these initial matters, i.e., that the dispute is within its jurisdiction and the application is admissible. Article 79*bis*(1) of the ICJ's Rules of Court continues the right – which Article 79(1) of the ICJ's Rules of Court furnished immediately prior to the changes that became effective on 21st October 2019 (see the antepenultimate sentence of this footnote) – of a respondent to raise a preliminary objection, but only when the Court has not taken a decision on whether or not it should rule as described above in this footnote. Article 79(1) of the ICJ's Rules of Court states: "Following the submission of the application and after the President [of the ICJ] has met and consulted with the parties, the Court may decide, if the circumstances so warrant, that questions concerning its jurisdiction or the admissibility of the application shall be determined separately. Article 79(2) of the ICJ's Rules of Court declares: "Where the Court so decides, the parties shall submit pleadings concerning jurisdiction or admissibility within the time-limits fixed, and in the order determined, by the Court. Each pleading shall contain the party's observations and submissions, including any evidence on which it relies, and shall attach copies of supporting documents." Article 79*bis*(1) of the ICJ's Rules of Court proclaims: "When the Court has not taken any decision under Article 79 [of the ICJ's Rules of Court (above in this footnote)], an objection by the respondent to the jurisdiction of the Court or to the admissibility of the application, or other objection the decision upon which is requested

before any further proceedings on the merits, shall be made in writing as soon as possible, and not later than three months after the delivery of the Memorial [fn 257]. Any such objection made by a party other than the respondent shall be filed within the time-limit fixed for the delivery of that party's first pleading." Article 79*bis*(2) of the ICJ's Rules of Court asseverates: "The preliminary objection shall set out the facts and the law on which the objection is based, the submissions and a list of the documents in support; it shall include any evidence on which the party relies. Copies of the supporting documents shall be attached." Article 79*bis*(3) of the ICJ's Rules of Court asserts: "Upon receipt by the Registry of a preliminary objection, the proceedings on the merits shall be suspended and the Court, or the President if the Court is not sitting, shall fix the time-limit for the presentation by the other party of a written statement of its observations and submissions, which shall include any evidence on which the party relies. Copies of the supporting documents shall be attached." Article 79*bis*(4) of the ICJ's Rules of Court states: "The Court shall give effect to any agreement between the parties that an objection submitted under paragraph 1 [i.e., Article 79*bis*(1) of the ICJ's Rules of Court (above in this footnote)] be heard and determined within the framework of the merits." Article 79*ter*(1) of the ICJ's Rules of Court declares: "Pleadings with respect to preliminary questions, or objections filed pursuant to Article 79, paragraph 2 [of the ICJ's Rules of Court (above in this footnote)], or Article 79*bis*, paragraphs 1 and 3 [of the ICJ's Rules of Court (above in this footnote)], shall be confined to those matters that are relevant to the preliminary questions or objections." Article 79*ter*(2) of the ICJ's Rules of Court proclaims: "Unless otherwise decided by the Court, the further proceedings shall be oral." Article 79*ter*(3) of the ICJ's Rules of Court asseverates: "The Court, whenever necessary, may request the parties to argue all questions of law and fact, and to adduce all evidence, which bear on the preliminary questions or objections." Article 79*ter*(4) of the ICJ's Rules of Court asserts: "After hearing the parties, the Court shall decide upon a preliminary question or uphold or reject a preliminary objection. The Court may however declare that, in the circumstances of the case, a question or objection does not possess an exclusively preliminary character." Article 79*ter*(5) of the ICJ's Rules of Court avers: "The Court shall give its decision in the form of a judgment. If the judgment does not dispose of the case, [then] the Court shall fix time-limits for the further proceedings." The case to which fn 251 refers, i.e., *Land and Maritime Boundary between Cameroon and Nigeria (Cameroon v. Nigeria: Equatorial Guinea intervening)*, was preceded by *Land and Maritime Boundary between Cameroon and Nigeria, Preliminary Objections*, in which the Respondent State (i.e., Nigeria) submitted eight preliminary objections, including those questioning the jurisdiction of the ICJ with regard to the dispute and the admissibility of the Applicant State's (i.e., Cameroon's) contentions (*Land and Maritime Boundary between Cameroon and Nigeria, Preliminary Objections*, Judgment of 11 June 1998, *I.C.J. Reports 1998*, 275-327, 275-276). The Court: (i) rejected seven of Nigeria's preliminary objections, (ii) declared the eighth to lack an exclusively preliminary character, (iii) found that, on the basis of Article 36(2) of the Statute of the ICJ, it had jurisdiction to judge the dispute, and (iv) held the written application filed by Cameroon to be admissible (*Land and Maritime Boundary between Cameroon and Nigeria, Preliminary Objections*, Judgment of 11 June 1998, *I.C.J. Reports 1998*, 275-327, 325-326). The third sentence of the third paragraph of the current subsection (i.e., that titled 'A Summary of Jurisdictional and Procedural Aspects of the ICJ') comprises Article 36(2) of the Statute of the ICJ, which specifies the compulsory jurisdiction of the Court. Further to the third sentence of this footnote, prior to 21st October 2019 the operative revision of Article 79(1) of the ICJ's Rules of Court stated: "Any objection by the respondent to the jurisdiction of the Court or to the admissibility of the application, or other objection the decision upon which is requested before any further proceedings on the merits, shall be made in writing as soon as possible, and not later than the ICJ and to the parties of Memorials[257], Counter-Memorials[258] and, as necessary, Replies[259] – together with all ancillary documentation[260] [337]. The form differs between cases opened by written application addressed to the Registrar of the Court[261], and those commenced by notification to the Registrar of a Special Agreement between the parties[262]. The above

---

three months after the delivery of the Memorial. Any such objection made by a party other than the respondent shall be filed within the time-lime fixed for the delivery of that party's first pleading." Before 21st October 2019, the ICJ was empowered to raise preliminary questions – Article 79(2) of the ICJ's Rules of Court then declared: "Notwithstanding paragraph 1 above [i.e., Article 79(1) of the ICJ's Rules of Court – which the immediately-preceding sentence quotes], following the submission of the application and after the President [of the ICJ] has met and consulted with the parties, the Court may decide that any questions of jurisdiction and admissibility shall be determined separately." The revisions to Article 79 of the ICJ's Rules of Court that became effective on 21st October 2019, and Articles 79*bis* and 79*ter* of the ICJ's Rules of Court – which became operative for the first time on that date, co-ordinated the procedures of preliminary questions that the Court might raise and preliminary objections that the respondent or other parties to the case might raise (see above in this footnote).

[257] Article 49(1) of the ICJ's Rules of Court states: "A Memorial shall contain a statement of the relevant facts, a statement of law, and the submissions."

[258] Article 49(2) of the ICJ's Rules of Court declares: "A Counter-Memorial shall contain an admission or denial of the facts stated in the Memorial; any additional facts, if necessary; observations concerning the statement of law in the Memorial; a statement of law in answer thereto; and the submissions."

[259] Article 49(3) of the ICJ's Rules of Court proclaims: "The Reply and Rejoinder, whenever authorized by the Court, shall not merely repeat the parties' contentions, but shall be directed to bringing out the issues that still divide them."

[260] Article 49(4) of the ICJ's Rules of Court asseverates: "Every pleading shall set out the party's submissions at the relevant state of the case, distinctly from the arguments presented, or shall confirm the submissions previously made." Article 50 of the ICJ's Rules of Court asserts: "1. There shall be annexed to the original of every pleading certified copies of any relevant documents adduced in support of the contentions contained in the pleading. 2. If only parts of a document are relevant, [then] only such extracts as are necessary for the purpose of the pleading in question need be annexed. A copy of the whole document shall be deposited in the Registry, unless it has been published and is readily available. 3. A list of all documents annexed to a pleading shall be furnished at the time the pleading is filed."

[261] Article 45(1) of the ICJ's Rules of Court states: "The pleadings in a case begun by means of an application shall consist, in the following order, of: a Memorial by the applicant; a Counter-Memorial by the respondent." Article 45(2) of the ICJ's Rules of Court declares: "The Court may authorize or direct that there shall be a Reply by the applicant and a Rejoinder by the respondent if the parties are so agreed, or if the court decides, *proprio motu* or at the request of one of the parties, that these pleadings are necessary." Fn 215 defines '*proprio motu*'.

[262] Article 46(1) of the ICJ's Rules of Court proclaims: "In a case begun by the notification of a special agreement, the number and order of the pleadings shall be governed by the provisions of the agreement, unless the Court, after ascertaining the views of the parties, decides otherwise." Article 46(2) of the ICJ's Rules of Court asseverates: "If the special agreement contains no such provision [i.e., the 'provisions of the agreement' in Article 46(1) of the Rules of Court], and if the parties have not subsequently agreed on the number

communications are made through the Registrar, in the order and within the time[263] that the ICJ determines [338]. A certified copy of each document that one disputant produces is to be conveyed to the other party [339].

The oral proceedings comprise the hearing by the court of agents, advocates, counsel, witnesses and experts [340]. The hearing takes places after the closure of the written proceedings; the ICJ determines the date upon which the oral proceedings are commenced [341]. Following this cessation, neither disputant may submit any further documents to the Court except with the consent of the other party or, in the absence of that assent, if the ICJ – after hearing the parties – considers the production of the relevant item to be indispensable[264] [342]. In enough time before the oral proceedings are started, each disputant must communicate to the Registrar of the Court – together with a copy for transmission to the other party – information concerning its evidence, including a list of the names, nationalities, descriptions and places of residence of the witnesses and experts whom it intends to call – with general indications as to the point(s) to which their evidence will be aimed [343]. The ICJ determines whether the disputants should present their arguments before or after the evidence is produced[265] [344]. The Court decides the order in which parties are to be heard, the method of managing the evidence and of examining witnesses and experts, and the number of advocates and counsel representing each

---

and order of pleadings, [then] they shall each file a Memorial and a Counter-Memorial, within the same time-limits. The Court shall not authorize the presentation of Replies unless it finds them to be necessary."

[263] Article 48 of the ICJ's Rules of Court asserts: "Time-limits for the completion of steps in the proceedings may be fixed by assigning a specified period but shall always indicate definite dates. Such time-limes shall be as short as the character of the case permits."

[264] The other party is deemed to have granted its consent if it does not register an objection to the document's production (International Court of Justice (2019), Rules of Court (1978) adopted on 14 April 1978 and entered into force on 1 July 1978 – amended to 21 October 2019, Article 56(1)). Article 56(3) of the ICJ's Rules of Court states: "If a new document is produced under paragraph 1 or paragraph 2 of this Article [i.e., in accordance with the text to this footnote], the other party shall have an opportunity of commenting upon it and of submitting documents in support of its comments."

[265] Notwithstanding the Court's decision on this matter, the parties have the right to remark on the evidence that is presented (International Court of Justice (2019), Rules of Court (1978) adopted on 14 April 1978 and entered into force on 1 July 1978 – amended to 21 October 2019, Article 58(1)).

disputant to be heard, after ascertaining the parties' views [345]. The President of the ICJ superintends the hearing, in whose absence the Vice-President of the Court oversees it[266]; if both are non-attending, then the senior judge present supervises it [346]. The hearing at the ICJ is held in public, unless the Court decides otherwise, or unless the disputants require it to be a private sitting[267] [347, 348]. Minutes are made at each hearing, and signed by the President and Registrar of the Court[268] [349]. The ICJ makes orders for how the case is to be conducted, determines the form and time in which each disputant must complete its arguments, and makes all arrangements concerning the adducing of evidence [350]. The Court may call upon agents of the parties to furnish any document or explanations – refusal of which is noted officially [351]. The oral statements that are made on each disputant's behalf must be as concise as possible, given what is necessary for the satisfactory presentation of that party's arguments at the

---

[266] On 6th February 2018, the ICJ elected Judge Abdulqawi Ahmed Yusuf – a Somali – as President, and Judge Xue Hanqin – a Chinese – as Vice-President (International Court of Justice (2019), "Presidency," accessed October 9, 2019, <https://www.icj-cij.org/en/presidency>).

[267] The second sentence of Article 59 of the ICJ's Rules of Court declares: "Such a decision or demand may concern either the whole or part of the hearing, and may be made at any time."

[268] Article 47(2) of the Statute of the ICJ proclaims: "These minutes alone shall be authentic." Article 71(1) of the ICJ's Rules of Court asseverates: "A verbatim record shall be made by the Registrar of every hearing, in the official language of the Court which has been used. ..." Article 71(3) of the ICJ's Rules of Court asserts: "The transcript of the verbatim record shall be preceded by the names of the judges present, and those of the agents, counsel and advocates of the parties." Article 71(4) of the ICJ's Rules of Court states: "Copies of the transcript shall be circulated to the judges sitting in the case, and to the parties. The latter may, under the supervision of the Court, correct the transcripts of speeches and statements made on their behalf, but in no case may such corrections affect the sense and bearing thereof. The judges may likewise make corrections in the transcript of anything they may have said." Article 71(5) of the ICJ's Rules of Court declares: "Witnesses and experts shall be shown that part of the transcript which relates to the evidence given, or the statements made by them, and may correct it in like manner as the parties." Article 71(6) of the ICJ's Rules of Court proclaims: "One certified true copy of the eventual corrected transcript, signed by the President and the Registrar, shall constitute the authentic minutes of the sitting for the purpose of Article 47 of the Statute [of the ICJ, the first Paragraph of which is the text to this footnote and the second Paragraph of which is the first sentence in this footnote]. The minutes of public hearings shall be printed and published by the Court." '*Verbatim*' is from Latin, i.e., from *verbum*, which means 'word'; '*verbatim*' means "in exactly the same words as were used originally" (Pearsall, J. (editor) (1998), *The New Oxford Dictionary of English*, 2053). Dr. McFarlane's definition of '*verbatim*' is essentially the same: "[w]ord for word; applied to a record of something made 'exactly as it was said'" (McFarlane, G. (1984), *The Layman's Dictionary of English Law*, 305).

hearing[269] [352]. At the end of a party's last oral statement, its agent reads its final submissions, signs a copy of the written text of these, communicates them to the ICJ and conveys them to the other disputant [353]. At any time before or during the hearing, the Court may indicate any matters to which it would like the parties to attend or on which it considers that there is no need for further argument [354]. During the hearing, the judges of the ICJ may put questions to, and ask explanations from, the agents, advocates and counsel [355], who may answer either instantly or within a time limit that the President of the Court sets [356]. The ICJ may, at any time, request the parties to provide such evidence or explanations as it deems to be necessary for the clarification of any aspect of the case, or may itself look for other information for this purpose [357], and charge any organization that it may choose with the task of conducting an enquiry or supplying an expert opinion[270] [358]. The disputants may call any witnesses or experts whose names are on the list communicated to the Registrar of the ICJ pursuant to Article 57 of its Rules of Court[271] [359]. A disputant may call a witness or expert who is absent from the list, if either the other party does not object to this or the ICJ is satisfied that the evidence of the witness or expert "seems likely to prove relevant" [360]. The parties' agents, advocates or counsel examine the witnesses and experts, under the direction of the President of the Court – who, together with other judges, may put questions to those witnesses and experts [361]. After the ICJ has received the proofs and evidence within the time stipulated for that purpose, it may refuse to accept any fresh written or oral

---

[269] The second sentence of Article 60(1) of the ICJ's Rules of Court asseverates: "Accordingly, they [i.e., the oral statements made on each disputant's behalf] shall be directed to the issues that still divide the parties, and shall not go over the whole ground covered by the pleadings, or merely repeat the facts and arguments [that] these contain."

[270] Article 67 of the ICJ's Rules of Court asserts: "1. If the Court considers it necessary to arrange for an enquiry or an expert opinion, it shall, after hearing the parties, issue an order to this effect, defining the subject of the enquiry or expert opinion, stating the number and mode of appointment of the persons to hold the enquiry or of the experts, and laying down the procedure to be followed. ... 2. Every report or record of an enquiry and every expert opinion shall be communicated to the parties, which shall be given the opportunity of commenting upon it." Article 62(2) of the ICJ's Rules of Court specifies: "The Court may, if necessary, arrange for the attendance of a witness or expert to give evidence in the proceedings."

[271] The fourth sentence of the current paragraph describes this list.

evidence that one disputant may wish to present – unless the other party consents [362]. If one of the disputants fails to appear before the ICJ, or does not defend its case, then the other party may ask the Court to decide in favour of its lawsuit [363]. Before doing this, the Court must satisfy itself that it has jurisdiction[272] and that the requester's claim is well-founded in both law and fact [364]. After the agents, advocates and counsel have completed their presentations before the ICJ, the President of the Court announces that the hearing is closed [365]. Any written reply from a disputant to a question put by a judge during the hearing – or any evidence or explanation that a party supplies to the ICJ, which the Court receives after the oral proceedings have been closed, is transmitted to the other party, which is granted the opportunity to comment upon it [366]. The oral proceedings are reopened for this purpose, as necessary [367].

Next, the Court withdraws to come to a judgment [368]. The ICJ's deliberations take place in private and are secret [369]. All questions are decided by a preponderance of the judges present[273] [370]. The Court's judgment states the reasons upon which it is based [371]. If the judgment does not represent, in whole or in part, the unanimous view of the judges, then any judge may provide a separate opinion[274] [372]. The judgment is signed by both the President, and the Registrar, of the ICJ, and is read out at a public sitting of the Court[275] – becoming binding on the disputants on the day on which it is read [373, 374]. It is final – no appeal is available [375]. The judgment contains the following items: (i) the date on which that ruling is read, (ii) the names of the judges who have participated in the decision [376], (iii) the names of the disputants, (iv) the names of the parties' agents, advocates and counsel, (v) a synopsis of the proceedings,

---

[272] The third paragraph of the present subsection (i.e., that titled 'A Summary of Jurisdictional and Procedural Aspects of the ICJ') describes the jurisdiction of the ICJ.

[273] Article 55(2) of the Statute of the ICJ states: "In the event of an equality of votes, the President [of the Court] or the judge who acts in his place shall have a casting vote."

[274] Article 95(2) of the ICJ's Rules of Court declares: "Any judge may, if he so desires, attach his individual opinion to the judgment, whether he dissents from the majority or not; a judge who wishes to record his concurrence or dissent without stating his reasons may do so in the form of a declaration. The same shall also apply to orders made by the Court."

[275] Article 94(1) of the ICJ's Rules of Court proclaims: "When the Court has completed its deliberations and adopted its judgment, the parties shall be notified of the date on which it will be read."

(vi) the parties' submissions, (vii) a statement of the facts of the case, (viii) the legal reasoning for arriving at the decision, (ix) the judgment's operative provisions, (x) the decision respecting costs, (xi) the number, and names, of the judges that form the majority, and (xii) an authoritative statement as to the text of the judgment [377]. The disputants, and all Member States of the UN, are entitled to receive a copy of the judgment[276]. When, as a consequence of an agreement that the parties have reached, the written and oral proceedings have been carried out in one of the ICJ's two official languages[277] and, pursuant to Article 39(1) of the Statute of the ICJ[278], the judgment is to be delivered in that tongue, the text of the judgment in that language is to be the authoritative text [378].

A party may apply for the revision of a judgment, when it is founded upon the discovery of a fact that was, when the Court made its decision, unknown to both it and the party claiming revision, and whose nature is such "as to be a decisive factor" – provided that this lack of knowledge was not caused by negligence [379]. A request for this emendation is made by an application which contains the particulars necessary to show that the above conditions are satisfied[279] [380]. The other disputant is entitled to submit written remarks on the admissibility of the application, within a time limit that the ICJ determines – which are transmitted to the party making this request[280] [381]. If the Court adjudges that the application is admissible, then it decides upon the time-limits for further proceedings on that request's merits which it considers to be necessary – after ascertaining

---

[276] Article 94(3) of the ICJ's Rules of Court asseverates: "One copy of the judgment duly signed and sealed, shall be placed in the archives of the Court and another shall be transmitted to each of the parties. Copies shall be sent by the Registrar to: *(a)* the Secretary-General of the United Nations; *(b)* the Members of the United Nations; *(c)* other States entitled to appear before the Court." (emphasis original).

[277] The ICJ's official languages are English and French (first sentence of the fourth paragraph of the current subsection (i.e., that titled 'A Summary of Jurisdictional and Procedural Aspects of the ICJ')).

[278] The first sentence of the fourth paragraph of the present subsection (i.e., that titled 'A Summary of Jurisdictional and Procedural Aspects of the ICJ') comprises Article 39(1) of the Statute of the ICJ.

[279] The second sentence of Article 99(1) of the ICJ's Rules of Court asserts: "Any documents in support of the application shall be annexed to it."

[280] Article 99(3) of the ICJ's Rules of Court states: "The Court, before giving its judgment on the admissibility of the application may afford the parties a further opportunity of presenting their views thereon."

the views of the disputants [382]. The ICJ may require previous observance of the terms of the judgment before it allows proceedings in revision, in which case it makes an order to this effect [383]. The proceedings for revision are commenced by a judgment of the ICJ, which records the existence of a new fact that has such a character as to render the case open to revision and proclaims the application to be admissible on this ground [384]. The application for revision of a judgment must be made within six months of the discovery of the new fact [385] and ten years from the date of the judgment [386]. The decision of the ICJ (or of one of its Chambers[281]) on an application for interpretation[282] or revision of a judgment is given in the form of a judgment [387].

If a state considers that it has a legal interest which may be affected by the judgment, then it may submit a request to the ICJ to be allowed to intervene[283] [388], upon which the Court will decide [389]. The application[284] states the name of an agent and the case to which it relates [390]. It sets out: (i) the legal interest which the country applying to intervene considers may be affected by the decision [391], (ii) "the precise

---

[281] A decision given by a Chamber of the ICJ is deemed to be provided by the Court (United Nations (1945), "Statute of the International Court of Justice," Article 27). Proceedings before a Chamber of the ICJ differ somewhat from those before the Court. Article 92 of the ICJ's Rules of Court avers: "1. Written proceedings in a case before a Chamber shall consist of a single pleading by each side. In proceedings begun by means of an application [in writing], the pleadings shall be delivered within successive time-limits. In proceedings begun by the notification of a special agreement, the pleadings shall be delivered within the same time-limits, unless the parties have agreed on successive delivery of their pleadings. The time-limits referred to in this paragraph shall be fixed by the Court, or by the President [of the ICJ] if the Court is not sitting, in consultation with the Chamber concerned if it is already constituted. 2. The Chamber may authorize or direct that further pleadings be filed if the parties are so agreed, or if the Chamber decides, *proprio motu* or at the request of one of the parties, that such pleadings are necessary. 3. Oral proceedings shall take place unless the parties agree to dispense with them, and the Chamber consents. Even when no oral proceedings take place, the Chamber may call upon the parties to supply information or furnish explanations orally." Fn 248 defines 'pleadings'. Fn 215 defines '*proprio motu*'.

[282] Article 98(1) of the ICJ's Rules of Court declares: "In the event of dispute as to the meaning or scope of a judgment any party make a request for its interpretation, whether the original proceedings were begun by an application or by the notification of a special agreement."

[283] Article 81(1) of the ICJ's Rules of Court proclaims: "An application for permission to intervene under the terms of Article 62 of the Statute [of the ICJ (text to this footnote)] shall be filed as soon as possible, and not later than the closure of the written proceedings. In exceptional circumstances a declaration submitted at a later stage may[,] however[,] be admitted."

[284] Fn 283.

object of the intervention" [392], (iii) "any basis of jurisdiction" that the applicant claims to be present as between it and the disputants [393], and (iv) a list of supporting documents – which are attached [394].

If the interpretation or explanation of a convention to which countries other than the disputants is in question, then the Registrar of the ICJ notifies those states immediately [395]. Each country so notified has the right to intervene in the Court's proceedings for the relevant case, but, if it exercises this right, it is bound by the construction of the convention that the judgment gives[285] [396]. The declaration[286] specifies the name of an agent, the case, and the convention to which it relates [397]. It contains: (i) particulars of the ground upon which the declarant state considers itself to be a party to the convention [398], (ii) identification of those provisions of the convention, the construction of which the declarant deems to be in question [399], (iii) a statement of the construction of the aforementioned provisions for which it argues [400], and (iv) a list of supporting documents – which are attached [401].

Example ICJ Case – El Salvador/Honduras: Nicaragua Intervening

The title to this subsection shows that this case was brought before the ICJ by notification of the Registrar of the Court of a Special Agreement between the disputants – El Salvador and Honduras[287]. The case's full title is *Land, Island and Maritime Frontier Dispute (El Salvador/Honduras: Nicaragua intervening)*. It was initiated by a joint notification[288] from El

---

[285] There is a contradiction between Article 59 of the Statute of the ICJ and the text to this footnote, i.e., Article 63(2) of the Statute of the ICJ, which fn 494 describes.

[286] Article 82(1) of the ICJ's Rules of Court declares: "A State which desires to avail itself of the right of intervention conferred upon it by Article 63 of the Statute [of the ICJ (text to this footnote)] shall file a declaration to that effect ... as soon as possible, and not later than the date fixed for the opening of oral proceedings. In exceptional circumstances a declaration submitted at a later stage may[,] however[,] be admitted."

[287] Fn 250 and accompanying text.

[288] The first sentence of Article 39(1) of the ICJ's Rules of Court provides for the notification to the Registrar of the Court of a Special Agreement by the parties jointly (fn 250).

Salvador and Honduras dated 11th December 1986, which was filed at the Registry of the ICJ on the same day [402, 403]. That notification prompted the initiation of a precursive case before the Court, which took place in order to determine whether Nicaragua had the standing to intervene in the main proceedings and, if so, the issues over which it was permitted to give its views, namely *Land, Island and Maritime Frontier Dispute (El Salvador/Honduras), Application to Intervene*. On 17th November 1989, Nicaragua filed at the Registry of the ICJ an application for permission to intervene in the dispute between El Salvador and Honduras, which was stated therein to be made under Articles 36(1)[289] and 62[290] of the Statute of the ICJ [404]. In a Court Order dated 28th February 1990, the ICJ held that it was for the Chamber formed to adjudicate the current case, i.e., *Land, Island and Maritime Frontier Dispute (El Salvador/Honduras)* – whose Chamber comprised Judges Jennings[291], Oda[292] and Sette-Camera[293] and Judges *ad hoc*[294] Torres Bernárdes[295] and Valticos[296] [405], to decide

---

289 The text to fn 245 contains Article 36(1) of the Statute of the ICJ, which concerns the jurisdiction of the Court. In this instance, the parties, i.e., El Salvador and Honduras, have jointly referred their dispute to the ICJ, and so, by virtue of this Paragraph, their case is within the Court's jurisdiction.

290 The first sentence of the penultimate paragraph of the subsection entitled 'A Summary of Jurisdictional and Procedural Aspects of the ICJ', above in the current section (i.e., that titled 'The International Court of Justice'), comprises Article 62 of the Statute of the ICJ.

291 Judge Sir Robert Yewdall Jennings – a Brit – was a judge of the ICJ from 1982-1995, and the President of the Court from 1991-1994 (International Court of Justice (2019), "All Members," accessed October 18, 2019, <https://www.icj-cij.org/en/all-members>).

292 Judge Shigeru Oda – a Japanese – was a judge of the ICJ from 1976-2003, and the Vice-President of the Court from 1991-1994 (International Court of Justice (2019), "All Members," accessed October 18, 2019, <https://www.icj-cij.org/en/all-members>).

293 Judge José Sette-Camara – a Brazilian – was a judge of the ICJ from 1979-1988, and the President of the Court from 1982-1985 (International Court of Justice (2019), "All Members," accessed October 18, 2019, <https://www.icj-cij.org/en/all-members>).

294 Fn 207 defines '*ad hoc*'. Article 31(2) of the Statute of the ICJ states: "If the Court includes upon the Bench a judge of the nationality of one of the parties, any other party may choose a person to sit as judge. ..." Article 31(3) of the Statute of the ICJ declares: "If the court includes upon the Bench no judge of the nationality of the parties, each of these parties may proceed to choose a judge ..." In accordance with these Paragraphs, a party to a case before the Court which lacks a judge of its nationality on the Bench, may select a judge *ad hoc* in that particular case under the conditions which Articles 35-37 of the ICJ's Rules of Court prescribe (International Court of Justice (2019), "Judges *ad hoc*," accessed October 18, 2019, <https://www.icj-cij.org/en/judges-ad-hoc>).

295 Judge *ad hoc* Santiago Torres Bernárdes – a Spaniard – participated as a judge in the following ICJ cases: *Land, Island and Maritime Frontier Dispute (El Salvador/Honduras: Nicaragua intervening)*, *Maritime Delimation and Territorial Questions between Qatar and*

whether Nicaragua's request for permission to intervene pursuant to Article 62 of the Statute of the ICJ should be granted [406].

Article 81(1) of the ICJ's Rules of Court requires an application for permission to intervene under Article 62 of the Statute of the ICJ to be filed, in normal circumstances, before the conclusion of written proceedings[297]. Nicaragua filed its application for permission to intervene in the dispute between El Salvador and Honduras "two months before the time-limit fixed for the filing of the Parties' Replies" [407]. El Salvador contended that, given Nicaragua's requests in this application for the Chamber's reformation and the rearranging of the written proceedings, it should not have postponed its application for permission to intervene for almost three years after being informed of the proceedings [408]. In view of Nicaragua's attempts in its application to limit the scope of the proceedings for consideration of its entreaty to intervene [409], the Chamber concluded that this country's requests in its application as outlined in the immediately-preceding sentence did not invalidate that

Bahrain (Qatar v. Bahrain), Fisheries Jurisdiction (Spain v. Canada), Legality of Use of Force (Yugoslavia v. Spain), Territorial and Maritime Dispute between Nicaragua and Honduras in the Caribbean Sea (Nicaragua v. Honduras), Application for Revision of the Judgment of 11 September 1992 in the Case concerning the Land, Island and Maritime Frontier Dispute (El Salvador/Honduras: Nicaragua intervening) *(El Salvador v. Honduras)*, and *Pulp Mills on the River Uruguay (Argentina v. Uruguay)* (International Court of Justice (2019), "All Judges *ad hoc,*" accessed October 18, 2019, <https://www.icj-cij.org/en/all-judges-ad-hoc>).

[296] Judge *ad hoc* Nicolas Valticos – a Greek – participated as a judge in the following ICJ cases: *Continental Shelf (Libyan Arab Jamahiriya/Malta), Land, Island and Maritime Frontier Dispute (El Salvador/Honduras: Nicaragua intervening)*, and *Maritime Delimation and Territorial Questions between Qatar and Bahrain (Qatar v. Bahrain)* (International Court of Justice (2019), "All Judges *ad hoc,*" accessed October 18, 2019, <https://www.icj-cij.org/en/all-judges-ad-hoc>).

[297] Fn 283.

application as a whole[298] and, therefore, there was no basis for it to reject the application *in limine*[299] [410].

Pursuant to Subparagraph 2(a) of Article 81 of the ICJ's Rules of Court[300], the ICJ considered whether Nicaragua had shown the existence of a legal interest that may be affected by the decision [411]. In its application for permission to intervene in the dispute between El Salvador and Honduras, Nicaragua listed considerations which supported its claim of an interest of a legal nature that may be affected by the Chamber's decision, but specified neither such interest(s) nor the manner in which that decision might affect it/them [412]. Furthermore, a state's legal interest(s) may be affected by the Chamber's decision on one aspect of the case but not by the latter's decisions over others – "the Chamber has to consider the matter of the islands [within the Gulf of Fonseca], the situation of the waters within the Gulf, the possible delimitation of the waters within the Gulf, the situation of the waters outside the Gulf, and the possible delimitation of the waters outside the Gulf" [413]. The Chamber commented on the burden of proof in respect of establishing an interest of a legal nature that may be affected by the Chamber's decision, as follows.

> [I]t is for a State seeking to intervene to demonstrate convincingly what it asserts, and thus to bear the burden of proof; ... it has only to show that its interest "may" be affected, not that it will or must be affected. What needs to be shown by a State seeking permission to intervene can only be judged *in concreto*[301] and in relation to all the

---

[298] At Paragraph 49 of its judgment, the Chamber stated: "A rejection of the Application on these grounds would only be appropriate if the Chamber were to conclude that the inclusion of the requests in paragraphs 23 and 24 of the original Application invalidated the entire Application. The Chamber does not however consider that this is the case." (International Court of Justice (1990), *Land, Island and Maritime Frontier Dispute (El Salvador/Honduras), Application to Intervene*, Judgment of 13 September 1990, *I.C.J. Reports 1990*, 92-137, 113).

[299] The phrase '*in limine*' is from Latin, and means "[a]t the edge; at the beginning" (McFarlane, G. (1984), *The Layman's Dictionary of English Law*, 142).

[300] Point (i) of the last sentence of the penultimate paragraph of the subsection entitled 'A Summary of Jurisdictional and Procedural Aspects of the ICJ', above in the present section (i.e., that titled 'The International Court of Justice'), comprises this Subparagraph.

[301] Emphasis original. The phrase '*in concreto*' is from Latin – literally 'in the concrete'; it means "[c]oncretely or palpably thinking or speaking[; w]ith reference to actual, verifiable facts rather than theoretically" (Oxford Reference (2019), "*In concreto,*" accessed October 20,

circumstances of a particular case. It is for the State seeking to intervene to identify the interest of a legal nature which it considers may be affected by the decision in the case, and to show in what way that interest may be affected ... [414].

The Chamber holds that it should not grant permission for intervention by Nicaragua with regard to sovereignty over the islands in the Gulf of Fonseca, unless a Nicaraguan legal interest is directly affected by a decision on this matter; any effects of the islands as pertinent circumstances for maritime delimitation is to be considered as part of the question as to whether Nicaragua should be allowed to intervene on the basis of a legal interest that may be affected by a decision concerning the Gulf's waters[302] [415]. Nicaragua argues that, if the Chamber, pursuant to the judgment of the Central American Court of Justice in *El Salvador v. Nicaragua*[303], declares the waters of the Gulf of Fonseca to be a

---

2019, <https://www.oxfordreference.com/view/10.1093/acref/9780195369380.001.0001/acref-9780195369380-e-897>).

302 The text to fn 305 answers this query with regard to any requirement for the Chamber to effect delimitation of the waters of the western part of the Gulf of Fonseca between El Salvador and Honduras. If, in contrast, the Chamber declares the waters to be a condominium of the coastal states bordering the Gulf, then it would still need to determine the sovereignty of the islands within the Gulf of Fonseca whose status was in dispute between El Salvador and Honduras – "the islands dispute is not a conflict of delimitation but of attribution of sovereignty over a detached territory" (International Court of Justice (1992), *Land, Island and Maritime Frontier Dispute (El Salvador/Honduras: Nicaragua intervening)*, Judgment of 11 September 1992, *I.C.J. Reports 1992*, 351-618, 583). This 'attribution of sovereignty' is not a matter with regard to which Nicaragua has a legal interest and consequently for which the Chamber would allow that country to intervene in the dispute between El Salvador and Honduras.

303 The Central American Court of Justice ruled as follows: "Whereas: The legal status of the Gulf of Fonseca having been recognized by this Court to be that of a historic bay possessed of the characteristics of a closed sea, *the three riparian States of El Salvador, Honduras and Nicaragua are, therefore, recognized as coöwners of its waters*, except as to the littoral marine league which is the exclusive property of each, and with regard to the coöwnership existing between the States here litigant, the Court ... took into account the fact that as to a portion of the non-littoral waters of the Gulf there was an overlapping or confusion of jurisdiction in matters pertaining to inspection for police and fiscal purposes and purposes of national security, and that, as to another portion thereof, it is possible that no such overlapping and confusion takes place. *The Court, therefore, has decided that as between El Salvador and Nicaragua coöwnership exists with respect to both portions, since they are both within the Gulf, with the express proviso, however, that the rights pertaining to Honduras as coparcener in those portions are not affected by that decision*. (Central American Court of Justice (1917), *El Salvador v. Nicaragua*, Judgment of 9 March 1917, *American Journal of International Law*, 11(3), 674-730, 716; emphasis added). A

condominium of the coastal states bordering the Gulf, then this arrangement would unquestionably include Nicaragua; the Chamber considers that "this is a sufficient demonstration by Nicaragua that it has an interest of a legal nature in the determination whether or not this is the régime governing the waters of the Gulf" [416]. However, as the following passage shows, the Chamber did not consider that Nicaragua had a legal interest in the execution of any delimitation that it was required to make in the current dispute between El Salvador and Honduras over the contested areas of the Gulf.

> *The Chamber does not however consider that an interest of a third State* [i.e., Nicaragua] *in the general legal rules and principles likely to be applied by the decision can justify an intervention.* ... The contention [of Nicaragua in its application to intervene in the dispute between El Salvador and Honduras] that in the Gulf of Fonseca "it would be impossible to carry out a delimitation which took into account only the coasts in the Gulf of two of the three riparian States" would be more convincing were it not for the fact that in 1900 a maritime boundary was defined in the Gulf between Nicaragua and Honduras. In any event, *the question is whether a legal interest of Nicaragua would be "affected" by such maritime delimitation.* [T]he taking into account of all the coasts and coastal relationships within the Gulf as a geographical fact for the purpose of effecting an eventual delimitation as between two riparian States [as argued by Nicaragua] – El Salvador and Honduras in the instant case – in no way signifies that *by such an operation itself* the legal interest of a third riparian State of the Gulf, Nicaragua, may be affected. In any case, *it is for the Applicant State in the present proceedings to demonstrate to the satisfaction of the Chamber that this would actually be the case in the present instance.* This Nicaragua has failed to do. ... *[T]he essential difficulty in which the Chamber finds itself, on this matter of a possible delimitation within the waters of the Gulf, is that Nicaragua did not in its Application indicate any maritime spaces in which Nicaragua might have a legal interest which could be said to be affected by a*

'coparcener' is "a person who shares equally with others in the inheritance of an undivided estate or in the rights to it (in the UK now as equitable interests)" (Pearsall, J. (editor) (1998), *The New Oxford Dictionary of English*, 405).

possible delimitation line between El Salvador and Honduras. The area in which such maritime spaces could exist is in any event limited, in view of the delimitation effected in 1900 with Honduras. ... The Agent of Nicaragua also suggested that the Chamber might, in making any delimitation within the Gulf between El Salvador and Honduras, have to take account of "navigation routes in a Gulf whose mouth is less than 20 miles wide and the reasonable security of the riparians," but *this consideration is too general to justify intervention in relation to a decision on delimitation in the present case*. Accordingly, *the Chamber is not satisfied that a decision in the present case either as to the law applicable to a delimitation, or effecting a delimitation, between Honduras and El Salvador, of the waters of the Gulf (except as regards the alleged "community of interests"), would affect Nicaragua's interests*. The Chamber therefore considers that *although Nicaragua has, for purposes of Article 62 of the Statute*[304]*, shown an interest of a legal nature which may be affected by the Chamber's decision on the question of the existence or nature of a régime of condominium or community of interests within the Gulf of Fonseca, it has not shown such an interest which might be affected by the Chamber's decision on any question of delimitation within the Gulf*. This finding also disposes of the question ... of the possible relevance of a decision in the island dispute[305] [417].

Next, the Chamber determined the possible impact on Nicaragua's legal interests of its future decision concerning the waters beyond the Gulf of Fonseca [418]. It found that Nicaragua failed to show how the delimitation of these waters proposed by Honduras, or any other delimitation that Nicaragua considered to be a possible one, would affect an actual Nicaraguan legal interest; it could not therefore grant Nicaragua permission to intervene over the delimitation of the waters outwith the closing line of the Gulf [419].

---

304 The first sentence of the penultimate paragraph of the subsection entitled 'A Summary of Jurisdictional and Procedural Aspects of the ICJ', above in the present section (i.e., that titled 'The International Court of Justice'), contains Article 62 of the Statute of the ICJ. The remainder of that paragraph comprises the operational requirements for an application for permission to intervene under Article 62 of the Statute of the ICJ – which are contained in Article 81(2)-(3) of the ICJ's Rules of Court.

305 Emphasis added. Fn 302 and its accompanying text refer to the situation concerning the islands in the Gulf of Fonseca whose sovereignty is in dispute between El Salvador and Nicaragua, with regard to whether Nicaragua has an interest of a legal nature that might be affected by the Chamber's decision on this aspect of the case.

> Having found that Nicaragua has shown a legal interest that may be affected by part of the Chamber's judgment on the merits of the current case, the Chamber must now consider 'the precise object of the intervention', as required by the Article 81(2)(b) of the ICJ's Rules of Court[306] [420]. Nicaragua's application for permission to intervene in the dispute between El Salvador and Honduras states the following.
>
> The intervention for which permission is requested has the following objects: *First*, generally to protect the legal rights of the Republic of Nicaragua in the Gulf of Fonseca and the adjacent maritime areas by all legal means available. *Secondly*, to intervene in the proceedings in order to inform the Court of the nature of the legal rights of Nicaragua which are in issue in the dispute. This form of intervention would have the conservative purpose of seeking to ensure that the determination of the Chamber did not trench upon the legal rights and interests of the Republic of Nicaragua ...[307] [421].

The Chamber held that the second object, i.e., 'to inform the Court of the nature of the legal rights of Nicaragua which are in issue in the dispute', is a proper one which accords with the role of intervention, notwithstanding the use of the strong wording, i.e., 'trench upon the legal rights and interests' [422]. It considered that Nicaragua's first object, i.e., 'generally to protect the legal rights of the Republic of Nicaragua in the Gulf of Fonseca and the adjacent maritime areas by all legal means available', was not to be interpreted – in the light of this country's statements – as involving the pursuit a judicial pronouncement on its own claims, and that, for this object to be deemed proper, the 'legal means available' are to "be those afforded by the institution of intervention for the protection of a third State's legal interests" [423].

In respect of Article 81(2)(c) of the ICJ's Rules of Court[308], Nicaragua argues in its application for permission to intervene in the dispute between

---

[306] Point (ii) in the second sentence of the penultimate paragraph of the subsection entitled 'A Summary of Jurisdictional and Procedural Aspects of the ICJ', above in the current section (i.e., that titled 'The International Court of Justice'), comprises Article 81(2)(b) of the ICJ's Rules of Court.

[307] Emphasis original.

[308] Point (iii) in the second sentence of the penultimate paragraph of the subsection entitled 'A Summary of Jurisdictional and Procedural Aspects of the ICJ', above in the present section

El Salvador and Honduras that Article 62 of the Statute of the ICJ[309] does not necessitate a separate title of jurisdiction, and does not claim the existence of any basis of jurisdiction save the Statute [424]. The question – unresolved from previous ICJ cases[310] – is whether any valid connection of jurisdiction with the disputants, i.e., "a basis of jurisdiction which could be invoked, by a State seeking to intervene, in order to institute proceedings against either or both of the parties," is a necessary condition for the according of permission to intervene pursuant to Article 62 of the Statute of the ICJ[311] [425]. The Chamber held that no jurisdictional link between the applicant and the disputants was necessary in order for it to grant

---

(i.e., that titled 'The International Court of Justice'), contains Article 81(2)(c) of the ICJ's Rules of Court.

309 The first sentence of the penultimate paragraph of the subsection entitled 'A Summary of Jurisdictional and Procedural Aspects of the ICJ', above in the current section (i.e., that titled 'The International Court of Justice'), comprises Article 62 of the Statute of the ICJ.

310 The cases to which the Chamber refers are *Continental Shelf (Tunisia/Libyan Arab Jamahiriya), Application to Intervene* and *Continental Shelf (Libyan Arab Jamahiriya/ Malta) Application to Intervene* (International Court of Justice (1990), *Land, Island and Maritime Frontier Dispute (El Salvador/Honduras), Application to Intervene*, Judgment of 13 September 1990, *I.C.J. Reports 1990*, 92-137, 132). In the former, the Court states the following: "Having reached the conclusion ... that Malta's request for permission to intervene is ... not one to which it can accede, the Court finds it unnecessary to decide in the present case the question whether the existence of a valid link of jurisdiction with the parties to the case is an essential condition for the granting of permission to intervene under Article 62 of the Statute [of the ICJ]" (International Court of Justice (1981), *Continental Shelf (Tunisia/Libyan Arab Jamahiriya), Application to Intervene*, Judgment of 14 April 1981, *I.C.J. Reports 1981*, 3-21, 20). In the latter, the Court declares thus: "Since the Court finds it possible ... to reach a decision on the present Application [for Italy to intervene in the dispute between Libya and Malta] without generally resolving the vexed question of the "valid link of jurisdiction," no more need be said than that the Court is convinced of the wisdom of the conclusion reached by its predecessor [i.e., the Permanent Court of International Justice] in 1922, that it should not attempt to resolve in the Rules of Court the various questions which have been raised, but leave them to be decided as and when they occur in practice and in the light of the circumstances of each particular case." (International Court of Justice (1984), *Continental Shelf (Libyan Arab Jamahiriya/Malta), Application to Intervene*, Judgment of 21 March 1984, *I.C.J. Reports 1984*, 3-30, 28).

311 The Chamber summarizes to this juncture in its judgment as follows: "Since in the present case the Chamber has reached the conclusion that Nicaragua has shown the existence of an interest of a legal nature which may be affected by the decision, and that the intervention of Nicaragua has a proper object, the only remaining question is whether a jurisdictional link is required; and since it is conceded that no such link exists [between the party seeking to intervene (i.e., Nicaragua) and the disputants (i.e., El Salvador and Honduras)], the Chamber is obliged to decide the point." (International Court of Justice (1990), *Land, Island and Maritime Frontier Dispute (El Salvador/Honduras), Application to Intervene*, Judgment of 13 September 1990, *I.C.J. Reports 1990*, 92-137, 132).

permission to intervene under Article 62 of the Statute, reasoning as follows.

> [P]rocedures for a "third" State to intervene in a case are provided in Articles 62[312] and 63[313] of the Court's Statute. The competence of the Court in this matter of intervention is not, like its competence to hear and determine the dispute referred to it, derived from the consent of the parties to the case, but from the consent given by them, in becoming parties to the Court's Statute, to the Court's exercise of its powers conferred by the Statute. ... [A]cceptance of the Statute entails acceptance of the competence conferred on the Court by Article 62. Thus the Court has the competence to permit an intervention even though it be opposed by one or both of the parties to the case [426].
>
> [A] State which is allowed to intervene in a case does not, *by reason only of being an intervener*, become also a party to the case. [C]onversely, ... *provided that there be the necessary consent by the parties to the case*, the intervener is not prevented by reason of that status from itself becoming a party to the case. ... [T]here is furthermore in international law no process for joinder of a new party, or parties, whether as appellant or respondent, *by move of the Court itself*. ... It thus follows also from the juridical nature and from the purposes of intervention that the existence of a valid link of jurisdiction between the would-be intervener and the parties is not a requirement for the success of the application. On the contrary, *the procedure of intervention is to ensure that a State with possibly affected interests may be permitted to intervene even though there is no jurisdictional link and it therefore cannot become a party*. ... [T]he use of the words "any basis" [in Article 81(2)(c) of the ICJ's Rules of Court[314]] (and in French the formula "toute base de compétence qui ... existerait") shows that a valid link of jurisdiction is not treated as a *sine qua non*[315] for intervention[316]. The

[312] Fn 309.

[313] The first and second sentences of the final paragraph of the subsection entitled 'A Summary of Jurisdictional and Procedural Aspects of the ICJ', above in the present section (i.e., that titled 'The International Court of Justice'), contain Article 63 of the Statute of the ICJ.

[314] Fn 308.

[315] The phrase '*sine qua non*' is from Latin – literally '(cause) without which not'; it means "an essential condition; a thing that is absolutely necessary" (Pearsall, J. (editor) (1998), *The New Oxford Dictionary of English*, 1737).

Chamber therefore concludes that *the absence of a jurisdictional link between Nicaragua and the Parties to this case is no bar to permission being given for intervention*[317] [427].

With regard to the procedural rights of an intervening state: (i) it does not become party to the legal proceedings, and receives neither the rights nor the duties that attach to the status of a disputant under "the general principles of procedural law" or the ICJ's Statute and Rules of Court, (ii) it has a right to be heard by the Chamber – according to Article 85 of the

---

[316] At this point, the Chamber references Paragraph 27 of the ICJ's judgment in *Continental Shelf (Tunisia/Libyan Arab Jamahiriya), Application to Intervene*, which states: "In 1974 ... the question whether or not a link of jurisdiction with the parties to the case is necessary – was directly raised when Fiji applied for permission to intervene in the *Nuclear Tests* cases. [T]he court did not itself make any pronouncement on that aspect of Fiji's application for permission to intervene under Article 62 [of the Statute of the ICJ]. ... [O]n the completion in 1978 of the revision of the [ICJ's] Rules [of Court], the Court introduced, in Article 81, paragraph 2 thereof, a new subparagraph *(c)* requiring an application for permission to intervene under Article 62 of the Statute [of the ICJ] to specify: "any basis of jurisdiction which is claimed to exist as between the State applying to intervene and the parties to the case." This it did in order to ensure that, when the question did arise in a concrete case, it would be in possession of all the elements which might be necessary for its decision. [T]he court left any question with which it might in future be confronted in regard to intervention to be decided on the basis of the Statute and in the light of the particular circumstances of each case. ..." (International Court of Justice (1981), *Continental Shelf (Tunisia/Libyan Arab Jamahiriya), Application to Intervene*, Judgment of 14 April 1981, *I.C.J. Reports 1981*, 3-21, 20; italic emphasis original; bold emphasis added). It is submitted that the reference to 'the *Nuclear Tests* cases' is one to the ICJ's judgment in *Nuclear Tests Case (Australia v. France)*, which is dated 20th December 1974 and reported in the ICJ's Reports of Judgments, Advisory Opinions and Orders (i.e., the '*I.C.J. Reports*') for 1974 at pages 253-274. Although Fiji filed a request on 17th May 1973 at the Registry of the Court for permission under Article 62 of the Statute of the ICJ to intervene in the dispute between Australia and France, the ICJ decided, by an Order dated 12th July 1973, to defer its consideration of Fiji's application to intervene until it had adjudicated, pursuant to an Order dated 22nd June 1973, on the questions of its jurisdiction to judge this dispute and the admissibility of Australia's written application (International Court of Justice (1974), *Nuclear Tests (Australia v. France)*, Judgment of 20 December 1974, *I.C.J. Reports 1974*, 253-274, 255). In the event, the ICJ did not entertain Fiji's application to intervene, because it deemed at this preliminary stage of the proceedings that it did not need to examine the merits of the case due to its determination that Australia's object in initiating legal action – to require France to cease performing nuclear tests in the atmosphere of the South Pacific Ocean – had been accomplished (International Court of Justice (1974), *Nuclear Tests (Australia v. France)*, Judgment of 20 December 1974, *I.C.J. Reports 1974*, 253-274, 263 and 270-272).

[317] Emphasis added, except for the phrase '*sine qua non*' – in respect of which the emphasis is in original document.

ICJ's Rules of Court[318], and (iii) there may be restrictions on the right of the intervener to be heard in the specific case – as in the current proceedings in which it is not for Nicaragua to participate in argument before the Chamber on the Special Agreement to which El Salvador and Honduras are the parties[319], because for Nicaragua this is *res inter alios acta*[320] [428].

In the penultimate Paragraph[321] of its judgment in *Land, Island and Maritime Frontier Dispute (El Salvador/Honduras), Application to Intervene*, the Chamber summarizes the decisions that it has arrived at, in respect of Nicaragua's application under Article 62 of the Statute of the ICJ[322] and Article 81 of the ICJ's Rules of Court[323] for permission to

---

[318] Article 85 of the ICJ's Rules of Court states: "1. If an application for permission to intervene under Article 62 [of the Statute of the ICJ] is granted, the intervening State shall be supplied with copies of the pleadings and documents annexed and shall be entitled to submit a written statement within a time-limit to be fixed by the Court. A further time-limit shall be fixed within which the parties may, if they so desire, furnish their written observations on that statement prior to the oral proceedings. If the Court is not sitting, these time-limits shall be fixed by the President [of the Court]. 2. The time-limits fixed according to the preceding paragraph shall, so far as possible, coincide with those already fixed for the pleadings in the case. 3. The intervening State shall be entitled, in the course of the oral proceedings, to submit its observations with respect to the subject-matter of the intervention." Article 86 of the ICJ's Rules of Court provides a similar procedure to Article 85 of these Rules in respect of Article 63 of the Statute of the ICJ (fn 313).

[319] Paragraph 4 of the Chamber's judgment reads: "The Special Agreement was … signed in the City of Esquipulas, Republic of Guatemala, on 24 May 1986; its preamble refers to the conclusion on 30 October 1980, in Lima, Peru, of a General Peace Treaty between the two States [i.e., El Salvador and Honduras] whereby, *inter alia*, they delimited certain sections of their common land frontier; and the Special Agreement records that no direct settlement had been achieved in respect of the remaining land areas, or as regards "the legal situation of the islands and maritime spaces." (International Court of Justice (1990), *Land, Island and Maritime Frontier Dispute (El Salvador/Honduras), Application to Intervene*, Judgment of 13 September 1990, *I.C.J. Reports 1990*, 92-137, 97). The phrase '*inter alia*' is from Latin, and means "among other things" (Pearsall, J. (editor) (1998), *The New Oxford Dictionary of English*, 950).

[320] The phrase '*res inter alios acta*' is from Latin – literally 'thing done among others'; it means "something transacted between other parties" (Merriam-Webster (2019), "*res inter alios acta* noun," accessed October 25, 2019, <https://www.merriam-webster.com/legal/res%20 inter%20alios%20acta>).

[321] Paragraph 104.

[322] The first sentence of the penultimate paragraph of the subsection entitled 'A Summary of Jurisdictional and Procedural Aspects of the ICJ', above in the current section (i.e., that titled 'The International Court of Justice'), comprises Article 62 of the Statute of the ICJ.

[323] Fn 283 contains Paragraph 1 of Article 81 of the ICJ's Rules of Court. The remainder of the paragraph to which fn 304 refers, states the operational requirements for an application for

intervene in the dispute between El Salvador and Honduras concerning the delimitation of their boundary in the Gulf of Fonseca, thus.

> ... Nicaragua has not shown the existence of any interest of a legal nature which may be affected by its decision on "the legal situation of the islands." As regards the decision required of the Chamber concerning the legal situation of the maritime spaces within the Gulf [of Fonseca], the Chamber has indicated ... that Nicaragua has a legal interest that may be affected by a decision as to the legal régime of those waters ... . Nicaragua has not demonstrated to the satisfaction of the Chamber the existence of an interest of a legal nature which may be affected by any decision of the Chamber delimiting the waters of the Gulf of Fonseca between El Salvador and Honduras, or by any decision as to the legal situation of the maritime spaces outside the Gulf ... and intervention in those respects has not been justified. *The Chamber therefore finds that Nicaragua should be permitted to intervene but solely in respect of the Chamber's consideration of the legal régime of the maritime spaces within the Gulf of Fonseca*, and to participate in the proceedings in the case in accordance with Article 85 of the [ICJ's] Rules of Court[324] [429].

The last Paragraph[325] of the Chamber's judgment in *Land, Island and Maritime Frontier Dispute (El Salvador/Honduras), Application to Intervene* contains its findings, as follows.

> For these reasons, THE CHAMBER, Unanimously, 1. *Finds* that the Republic of Nicaragua has shown that it has an interest of a legal nature which may be affected by part of the judgment of the Chamber on the merits in the present case, namely its decision on the legal régime of the waters of the Gulf of Fonseca, but has not shown such an interest which may be affected by any decision which the Chamber may be required to make concerning the delimitation of those waters, or any decision as to the legal situation of the maritime spaces outside the Gulf, or any decision as to the legal situation of the islands in the Gulf; 2. *Decides*

---

permission to intervene under Article 62 of the Statute of the ICJ – which Paragraphs 2 and 3 of Article 81 of the ICJ's Rules of Court specify.

[324] Emphasis added. Fn 318 contains Article 85 of the ICJ's Rules of Court.

[325] Paragraph 105.

accordingly that the Republic of Nicaragua is permitted to intervene in the case, pursuant to Article 62 of the Statute [of the ICJ], to the extent, in the manner and for the purposes set out in the present Judgment, but not further or otherwise[326] [430].

The main proceedings, i.e., *Land, Island and Maritime Frontier Dispute (El Salvador/Honduras: Nicaragua intervening)*, which Chapter 3 covers, was determined by the same Chamber – comprising Judges Jennings, Oda, Sette-Camera and Judges *ad hoc* Torres Bernárdes and Valticos – that considered Nicaragua's application to intervene in the dispute, i.e., *Land, Island and Maritime Frontier Dispute (El Salvador/Honduras), Application to Intervene*, which this subsection

[326] Emphasis original. Pursuant to Article 95(2) of the ICJ's Rules of Court (fn 274), Judge Oda (fn 292 and accompanying text) attached an individual opinion to the Chamber's judgment, which is found in the *I.C.J. Reports* for 1990 at pages 138-144. As the opinion concludes, Judge Oda would have preferred the Chamber to permit Nicaragua to intervene more extensively in the dispute between El Salvador and Honduras than it did: "In short, I take the view that (i) Nicaragua, having now been permitted to intervene in respect of the legal régime within the waters of the Gulf [of Fonseca], should not have been excluded from expressing its views in due course on any delimitation between El Salvador and Honduras within the Gulf which may fall to be effected by the Chamber; and that (ii) Nicaragua should not have been excluded from expressing its views in due course with respect to any delimitation which may fall to be effected outside the Gulf in the event that some title may have been established in favour of Honduras." (International Court of Justice (1990), *Land, Island and Maritime Frontier Dispute (El Salvador/Honduras), Application to Intervene*, Separate Opinion of Judge Oda, *I.C.J. Reports 1990*, 138-144, 144) Judge Oda considered that the applicant did not need to prove as much as the Chamber specified in order to establish a legal interest that may be affected by the decisions in the case: "The Judgment [of the Chamber] finds … that the degree of imprecision in respect of parts of Nicaragua's claim to a legal interest is excessive and must result in a denial of such permission in relation to certain areas. This distinction I do not find wholly justified. I find it … difficult on the evidence to state that Nicaragua, while having *sufficiently* shown interest of a legal nature which may be affected by the decision of the Chamber in the case of the legal régime of the maritime spaces within the Gulf [of Fonseca], has *not* done so as concerns the delimitation of the maritime boundaries there and outside the Gulf. The Applicant, after all, although required to show an interest of a legal nature which *may* (but not *will* or *must*) be affected, does not at this stage need to indicate those positions and considerations which it can be expected to draw to the Chamber's attention in its eventual declaration and any subsequent oral observations. Nor is it required, as the Judgment contends, "to show *in what way* that interest may be affected" (para. 61, emphasis added)." (International Court of Justice (1990), *Land, Island and Maritime Frontier Dispute (El Salvador/Honduras), Application to Intervene*, Separate Opinion of Judge Oda, *I.C.J. Reports 1990*, 138-144, 140-141; emphasis original). The relevant excerpt from Paragraph 61 of the Chamber's judgment is in the first quoted passage, above in the current subsection (i.e., that titled 'Example ICJ Case – El Salvador/Honduras: Nicaragua intervening').

describes above. Whilst much of the judgment in *Land, Island and Maritime Frontier Dispute (El Salvador/Honduras: Nicaragua intervening)* – Paragraphs 40 to 322 inclusive – concerns determination of the land boundary between El Salvador and Honduras, there are also sections on the islands whose sovereignty is in dispute – Paragraphs 323 to 368 inclusive, and the legal status of the waters both inside and beyond the Gulf of Fonseca – Paragraphs 369 to 420 inclusive. In the following extract from *Land, Island and Maritime Frontier Dispute (El Salvador/Honduras: Nicaragua intervening),* the judgment confirmed that, unlike the parties to the case (El Salvador and Honduras), Nicaragua – an intervening state but not a disputant – is not bound by the judgment of the Chamber[327].

> The terms on which intervention was granted, as stated in paragraph 102 of the 1990 Judgment[328], were that Nicaragua would not, as an intervening State, become party to the proceedings. The binding force of the present Judgment for the Parties, as contemplated by Article 59 of the Statute of the Court[329], does not therefore extend to Nicaragua as intervener [431].

The Chamber expressed this view in a different way in the next-but-one Paragraph of its judgment, as follows.

327 Both Article 59 of the Statute of the ICJ, and Paragraph 2 of Article 296 of the UNCLOS, hold that the ICJ's decision is only binding between the parties and as regards their particular dispute (last sentence of the subsection entitled 'Basis for Determination of UNCLOS Disputes', above in the current section (i.e., that titled 'International Court of Justice'); second sentence of the subsection entitled 'Compulsory Procedures: Finality and Binding Force of Decisions', in the section titled 'Part XV of the UNCLOS: Settlement of Disputes' in Chapter 1).

328 Points (i) and (ii) of the text to fn 318 are from Paragraph 102 of the Chamber's judgment in *Land, Island and Maritime Frontier Dispute (El Salvador/Honduras), Application to Intervene*.

329 Fn 327. The final sentence of the subsection entitled 'Basis for Determination of UNCLOS Disputes', above in the present section (i.e., that titled 'International Court of Justice'), states Article 59 of the Statute of the ICJ.

> The Chamber considers that it is correct that a State permitted to intervene under Article 62 of the Statute[330], but which does not acquire the status of a party to the case, is not bound by the Judgment given in the proceedings in which it has intervened. ... In these circumstances, the right to be heard, which the intervener does acquire, does not carry with it the obligation of being bound by the decision [432].

Next, the Chamber ruled when the principle of *res judicata*[331] applied to an intervening state, concluding that it only did so when that country was also a disputant in the case in which the ICJ had permitted the intervention.

> In the Chamber's Judgment of 13 September 1990, emphasis was laid on the need, if an intervener is to become a party, for the consent of the existing parties to the case, either consent *ad hoc*[332] or in the form of a pre-existing link of jurisdiction. This is essential because the force of *res judicata*[333] does not operate in one direction only: if an intervener becomes a party, and is thus bound by the judgment, it becomes entitled equally to assert the binding force of the judgment against the other parties. A non-party to a case before the Court, whether or not admitted to intervene, cannot by its own unilateral act place itself in the position of a party, and claim to be entitled to rely on the judgment against the original

---

[330] The first sentence of the penultimate paragraph of the subsection entitled 'A Summary of Jurisdictional and Procedural Aspects of the ICJ', above in the present section (i.e., that titled 'The International Court of Justice'), comprises Article 62 of the Statute of the ICJ.

[331] The phrase '*res judicata*' is from Latin – literally 'judged matter'; it means "a matter that has been adjudicated by a competent court and may not be pursued further by the same parties" (Pearsall, J. (editor) (1998), *The New Oxford Dictionary of English*, 1579). In relation to the above definition, Dr. McFarlane's definition of '*res judicata*' reverses in the sentence the order of the adjudication of the matter and the extent of its pursuit, and, on the latter, is less specific than the earlier definition, i.e., '*res judicata*' means "[t]he principle that a matter can no longer be questioned once a court has given its decision on it" (McFarlane, G. (1984), *The Layman's Dictionary of English Law*, 246). It is submitted that the wider scope of the latter definition is because Dr. McFarlane is assuming the application of the doctrine of precedent – i.e., as the Law of England and Wales is a common law stream, and as this doctrine applies in systems of common law, the court's decision can only be quashed by a higher court whose rulings apply in the same jurisdiction, whilst the definition from the *New Oxford Dictionary* is in accordance with the principle contained in Article 59 of the Statute of the ICJ (fn 329).

[332] Fn 207 defines '*ad hoc*'.

[333] Fn 331 defines '*res judicata*'.

> parties. In the present case, El Salvador requested the Chamber to deny the permission to intervene sought by Nicaragua; and neither Party has given any indication of consent to Nicaragua's being recognized to have any status which would enable it to rely on the Judgment. The Chamber therefore concludes that in the circumstances of the present case, this Judgment is not *res judicata* for Nicaragua[334] [433].

Three judges attached individual opinions to the Chamber's judgment in *Land, Island and Maritime Frontier Dispute (El Salvador/Honduras: Nicaragua intervening)*, in accordance with Article 95(2) of the ICJ's Rules of Court[335]. Judges *ad hoc* Torres Bernárdes[336] and Valticos[337] each included a separate opinion[338], and Judge Oda[339] both a declaration[340] and a dissenting opinion[341].

Judge Oda's declaration queries the last clause of the immediately-preceding quoted passage, both sentences of the extract directly above this, and the second sentence of the excerpt closely-preceding the latter [434]. It then asks whether these statements from the judgment of the Chamber in *Land, Island and Maritime Frontier Dispute (El Salvador/Honduras: Nicaragua intervening)* mean that Nicaragua is not bound to observe the following findings: (i) the waters of the Gulf of Fonseca were, from 1821 when Spanish control of the area ceased, and continue to be, held in joint sovereignty by El Salvador, Honduras and Nicaragua[342], (ii) the waters at the closing line of the Gulf's central portion are liable to the joint entitlement of those three states[343], and (iii) the Chamber's conclusions as

---

334 Emphasis original.
335 Fn 274 states Article 95(2) of the ICJ's Rules of Court.
336 Fn 295 and accompanying text.
337 Fn 296 and accompanying text.
338 Judge *ad hoc* Torres Bernárdes' individual opinion is found in the *I.C.J. Reports* for 1992 at pages 629-731, and that of judge *ad hoc* Valticos in these Reports at pages 621-628.
339 Fn 292 and accompanying text.
340 Judge Oda's declaration is located in the *I.C.J. Reports* for 1992 at pages 619-620.
341 Judge Oda's dissenting opinion is situated in the *I.C.J. Reports* for 1992 at pages 732-761.
342 This finding is from Subparagraph 432(1) of the Chamber's judgment in *Land, Island and Maritime Frontier Dispute (El Salvador/Honduras: Nicaragua intervening)*.
343 Fn 342.

to the legal situation of the waters immediately beyond the Gulf[344] [435]. Judge Oda states: "Nicaragua, as a non-party intervener, will certainly be bound by this Judgment in so far as it relates to the legal situation of the maritime spaces of the Gulf [of Fonseca]" [436].

Judge *ad hoc* Torres Bernárdes' individual opinion in *Land, Island and Maritime Frontier Dispute (El Salvador/Honduras: Nicaragua intervening)*, amongst other things, gives a partial endorsement to Judge Oda's view in his declaration in the same case[345] – whilst backing the Chamber's statement that its judgment in this lawsuit does not bind Nicaragua.

> I agree with the finding of the [Chamber's] Judgment [in *Land, Island and Maritime Frontier Dispute (El Salvador/Honduras: Nicaragua intervening)*] that "in the circumstances of the present case, this judgment is not *res judicata* for Nicaragua" [346] (paragraph 424 of the reasoning). There remains, however, the question of the effects of the Judgment other than that of *res judicata* (Art.59 of the Statute [of the ICJ][347]) on a non-party State intervening under Article 62 of the Statute[348]. In this respect, I concur with the statement contained in the

[344] By four votes to one (Judge Oda dissenting), the Chamber, at Subparagraph 432(3), held that "the legal situation of the waters of the Gulf [of Fonseca] is that, the Gulf of Fonseca being an historic bay with three coastal States [i.e., El Salvador, Honduras and Nicaragua], the closing line of the Gulf constitutes the baseline of the territorial sea; the territorial sea, continental shelf and exclusive economic zone of El Salvador and those of Nicaragua off the coasts of those two States are also to be measured outwards from a section of the closing line extending 3 miles (1 marine league) along that line from Punta Amapala (in El Salvador) and 3 miles (1 marine league) from Punta Cosigüina (in Nicaragua) respectively; but entitlement to territorial sea, continental shelf and exclusive economic zone seaward of the central portion of the closing line appertains to the three States of the Gulf, El Salvador, Honduras and Nicaragua; and that any delimitation of the relevant maritime areas is to be effected by agreement on the basis of international law" (International Court of Justice (1992), *Land, Island and Maritime Frontier Dispute (El Salvador/Honduras: Nicaragua intervening)*, Judgment of 11 September 1992, *I.C.J. Reports 1992*, 351-618, 617).

[345] The immediately-preceding paragraph summarize the declaration of Judge Oda.

[346] The final sentence of the immediately-preceding quoted passage contains this statement. Fn 331 defines '*res judicata*'.

[347] The last sentence of the subsection entitled 'Basis for Determination of UNCLOS Disputes', above in the current section (i.e., that titled 'International Court of Justice'), states Article 59 of the Statute of the ICJ.

[348] The first sentence of the penultimate paragraph of the subsection entitled 'A Summary of Jurisdictional and Procedural Aspects of the ICJ', above in the present section (i.e., that titled 'The International Court of Justice'), comprises Article 62 of the Statute of the ICJ.

declaration of Vice-President Oda appended to the Judgment. My position is based upon the fact that I cannot ... conceive of rights without obligations as well as upon the general economy of the institution of intervention as embodied in Articles 62 and 63[349] of the Statute of the Court. Interventions under Article 63, for example, are non-party interventions and nevertheless the intervening State is under the obligation set forth in that Article[350]. *Mutatis mutandis*[351], an obligation of that kind also exists ... for a non-party State intervening under Article 62, notwithstanding the fact that that Article does not say so in plain words[352] [437].

In *Application for Revision of the Judgment of 11 September 1992 in the Case concerning the* Land, Island and Maritime Frontier Dispute (El

---

349 The first and second sentences of the final paragraph of the subsection entitled 'A Summary of Jurisdictional and Procedural Aspects of the ICJ', above in the current section (i.e., that titled 'The International Court of Justice'), contain Article 63 of the Statute of the ICJ.

350 This is the obligation to observe the construction of the convention that the ICJ places on the latter, which corresponds to the right to intervene under Article 63 of the Statute of the ICJ (text to fn 285).

351 The phrase '*mutatis mutandis*' means 'the necessary changes being made' (fn 140). It is submitted that Judge Torres Bernárdes means that there is an implicit obligation for a state that the Court or Chamber permits to intervene under Article 62 of the Statute of the ICJ to comply with that part of the judgment which relates to the granted intervention. The 'necessary changes' comprise the substitution of the relevant provisions of the pertinent convention that the Court or Chamber needs to construct under Article 63 of the Statute of the ICJ with the scope of the intervention that the Court or Chamber allows under Article 62 of the Statute of the ICJ. Thus, in *Land, Island and Maritime Frontier Dispute (El Salvador/Honduras: Nicaragua intervening)*, Nicaragua would be bound by that part of the judgment that related to the Chamber's determination of the form of the sovereignty over the waters of the Gulf of Fonseca (for which the Chamber granted Nicaragua permission to intervene in *Land, Island and Maritime Frontier Dispute (El Salvador/Honduras), Application to Intervene*, but not to other aspects of the case – including: (i) the Chamber's determination of land boundaries between El Salvador and Honduras, and (ii) the sovereignty over those islands in that Gulf whose territory was in dispute between those latter two countries (i.e., El Tigre, Meanguera and Meanguerita). It is also submitted that, if the Chamber in *Land, Island and Maritime Frontier Dispute (El Salvador/Honduras: Nicaragua intervening)* had taken this approach, then the effect would be similar or identical to the view of Judge Oda that 'Nicaragua will be bound by the judgment in so far as it relates to the legal structure of the maritime spaces of the Gulf of Fonseca' (see the last sentence of the paragraph immediately preceding the sentence that the current quote follows). However, Judge Oda's view differs from that of Judge Torres Bernárdes in that the former queries the Chamber's finding in *Land, Island and Maritime Frontier Dispute (El Salvador/Honduras: Nicaragua intervening)* that its judgment is not *res judicata* for Nicaragua, whilst the latter concurs with the Chamber in this aspect of its decision.

352 Emphasis original. Fn 351 explains how such an obligation might work in respect of Article 62 of the Statute of the ICJ.

Salvador/Honduras: Nicaragua intervening) *(El Salvador v. Honduras)*, El Salvador, on 10th September 2002, made a written request to the ICJ under Articles 61 of the Statute of the ICJ and 99 of ICJ's Rules of Court[353], for revision of the judgment that the Chamber of the Court delivered on 11th September 2002 in *Land, Island and Maritime Frontier Dispute (El Salvador/Honduras: Nicaragua intervening)* [438]. Paragraphs 15 and 16 of the Chamber's judgment in the revisory case[354] introduce the part of the earlier decision[355] to which the request for revision relates, as follows.

> By a Judgment of 11 September 1992, the Chamber of the Court formed to deal with the case concerning the *Land, Island and Maritime Frontier Dispute (El Salvador/Honduras: Nicaragua intervening)* decided the course of the land boundary between El Salvador and Honduras in six disputed sectors of that boundary. By the same Judgment the Chamber settled the dispute between the Parties over the legal status of various islands in the Gulf of Fonseca and the legal status of waters in the Gulf and outside it.
>
> El Salvador has submitted an Application to the Court for revision of the 1992 Judgment in respect of the sixth sector of the land boundary lying between Los Amates and the Gulf of Fonseca. During the original proceedings, it was the contention of Honduras that in that sector "the boundary … follows the present stream [of the River Goascorán], flowing into the Gulf north-west of the Islas Ramaditas in the Bay of La Unión." El Salvador however claimed that the boundary was defined by "a previous course followed by the river … and that this course, since abandoned by the stream, can be traced, and it reaches the Gulf at Estero La Cutú" (Judgment, para. 306). In the Judgment revision of which is

---

353 The antepenultimate paragraph of the subsection entitled 'A Summary of Jurisdictional and Procedural Aspects of the ICJ', above in the present section (i.e., that titled 'The International Court of Justice') includes Paragraphs 1, 2, 4 and 5 of Article 61 of the Statute of the ICJ, and all five Paragraphs of Article 99 of the ICJ's Rules of Court.

354 International Court of Justice (2003), *Application for Revision of the Judgment of 11 September 1992 in the Case concerning the* Land, Island and Maritime Frontier Dispute (El Salvador/Honduras: Nicaragua intervening) *(El Salvador v. Honduras)*, Judgment of 18 December 2003, *I.C.J. Reports 2003*, 392-412.

355 International Court of Justice (1992), *Land, Island and Maritime Frontier Dispute (El Salvador/Honduras: Nicaragua intervening)*, Judgment of 11 September 1992, *I.C.J. Reports 1992*, 351-618.

now sought, the Chamber unanimously upheld the submissions of Honduras (Judgment, paras. 321, 322 and 430)[356] [439].

In *Application for Revision of the Judgment of 11 September 1992 in the Case concerning the* Land, Island and Maritime Frontier Dispute (El Salvador/Honduras: Nicaragua intervening) *(El Salvador v. Honduras)*, the counsel for El Salvador attempted to present their arguments as 'new facts' for the purposes of Paragraphs 1 and 2 of Article 61 of the Statute of the ICJ, as follows.

> El Salvador first claims to possess scientific, technical and historical evidence showing ... that the [River] Goascorán did in the past change its bed, and that the change was abrupt, probably as the result of a cyclone in 1762. ... El Salvador argues that evidence can constitute "new facts" for purposes of Article 61 of the Statute, [relying] on the *travaux préparatoires*[357] of the provision of the Statute of the Permanent Court of International Justice, on which Article 61 is modelled, which are said to confirm that a document can be considered to be a "new fact." ... El Salvador further contends that the evidence it is now offering establishes the existence of an old bed of the Goascorán debouching in the Estero La Cutú, and the avulsion of the river in the mid-eighteenth century ... . These are said to be "new facts" for the purposes of Article 61 [440].

The counsel for El Salvador argued that these facts are decisive (as Article 61(1) of the Statute of the ICJ requires), maintaining that the Chamber's rejection in *Land, Island and Maritime Frontier Dispute (El Salvador/Honduras: Nicaragua intervening)* of that country's claimed

---

[356] Emphasis original.

[357] Emphasis original. The phrase '*travaux préparatoires*' is from French, and means "[p]reparatory drafts and discussions relating to legislation which may be considered in interpreting [the] law"; in this definition, Dr. McFarlane states that these items may be used in interpreting European Economic Community law (now European Union law) but not Acts of the UK's Parliament (McFarlane, G. (1984), *The Layman's Dictionary of English Law*, 293). In international law, Article 32 of the Vienna Convention on the Law of Treaties declares that *travaux préparatoires* of a treaty may be used as a "supplementary means of interpretation of that treaty" in three circumstances specified therein (United Nations (1969), "Vienna Convention on the Law of Treaties," *United Nations Treaty Series* Registration Number 18232, Article 32).

avulsion of the River Goascorán as its boundary with Honduras should be overturned, now that this fact had been proved [441]. The Chamber in *Application for Revision of the Judgment of 11 September 1992 in the Case concerning the* Land, Island and Maritime Frontier Dispute (El Salvador/Honduras: Nicaragua intervening) *(El Salvador v. Honduras)*[358] rejected this contention, as follows.

> [W]hile the Chamber in 1992 rejected El Salvador's claims that the 1821 [i.e., when Central America gained its independence from Spain] boundary [between El Salvador and Honduras] did not follow the course of the river [Goascorán] at that date, it did so on the basis of that State's conduct during the nineteenth century. ... Even if avulsion [of the Goascorán] were now proved, and even if its legal consequences were those inferred by El Salvador, findings to that effect would provide no basis for calling into question the decision taken by the Chamber in 1992 on wholly different grounds. The facts asserted in this connection by El Salvador are not "decisive factors" in respect of the Judgment which it seeks to have revised. In the light of the 1992 Judgment, the Chamber cannot but reach such a conclusion, independently of the positions taken by the Parties on this point in the course of the present proceedings [442].

[358] The Chamber in *Application for Revision of the Judgment of 11 September 1992 in the Case concerning the* Land, Island and Maritime Frontier Dispute (El Salvador/Honduras: Nicaragua intervening) *(El Salvador v. Honduras)* comprised Judges Buergenthal, Guillaume and Rezek, and Judges *ad hoc* Paolillo and Torres Bernárdes (International Court of Justice (2003), *Application for Revision of the Judgment of 11 September 1992 in the Case concerning the* Land, Island and Maritime Frontier Dispute (El Salvador/Honduras: Nicaragua intervening) *(El Salvador v. Honduras)*, Judgment of 18 December 2003, *I.C.J. Reports 2003*, 392-412, 392). Judge Thomas Buergenthal – an American – was a judge of the ICJ from 2000-2010; Judge Gilbert Guillaume – a Frenchman – was a judge of the ICJ from 1987-2005, and President of the Court from 2000-2003; Judge Francisco Rezek – a Brazilian – was a judge of the ICJ from 1996-2006 (International Court of Justice (2019), "All Members," accessed November 5, 2019, <https://www.icj-cij.org/en/all-members>). Fn 294 provides information concerning the appointment of Judges *ad hoc* to the ICJ. Judge *ad hoc* Felipe Paolillo – a Uruguayan – participated as a judge in *Application for Revision of the Judgment of 11 September 1992 in the Case concerning the* Land, Island and Maritime Frontier Dispute (El Salvador/Honduras: Nicaragua intervening) *(El Salvador v. Honduras)*, but in no other cases of the ICJ (International Court of Justice (2019), "All Judges *ad hoc*," accessed November 5, 2019, <https://www.icj-cij.org/en/all-judges-ad-hoc>). Fn 295 lists the cases of the ICJ in which Judge *ad hoc* Torres Bernárdes participated.

The Chamber noted at Paragraph 22 of its judgment in *Application for Revision of the Judgment of 11 September 1992 in the Case concerning the* Land, Island and Maritime Frontier Dispute (El Salvador/Honduras: Nicaragua intervening) *(El Salvador v. Honduras)* that it is for the Court to find out whether the admissibility requirements which Article 61 of the Statute of the ICJ[359] lays down have been satisfied [443]. In Paragraph 20 of this ruling, the Chamber repeats the Court's statement from an earlier application for revision of a judgment under Article 61 of the Statute, as follows.

> The Court observes that an application for revision is admissible only if each of the conditions laid down in Article 61 [of the Statute of the ICJ] is satisfied. If one of them is not met, the application must be dismissed [444].

Having determined that the items which El Salvador presented to the Chamber in *Application for Revision of the Judgment of 11 September 1992 in the Case concerning the* Land, Island and Maritime Frontier Dispute (El Salvador/Honduras: Nicaragua intervening) *(El Salvador v. Honduras)* were not decisive factors with regard to the Chamber's judgment in *Land, Island and Maritime Frontier Dispute (El Salvador/Honduras: Nicaragua intervening)*[360], then the first-mentioned

---

359 Paragraphs 1, 4 and 5 of Article 61 of the Statute of the ICJ contain the admissibility requirements for an application for revision of a judgment of the Court or one of its Chambers. The first and seventh sentences of the antepenultimate paragraph of the subsection entitled 'A Summary of Jurisdictional and Procedural Aspects of the ICJ', above in the current section (i.e., that titled 'The International Court of Justice'), comprise these provisions.

360 The previous-but-one quoted section concludes this, as does Paragraph 55 of the Chamber's judgment in relation to additional documents that El Salvador discovers after 1992 in the Newberry Library in Chicago (International Court of Justice (2003), *Application for Revision of the Judgment of 11 September 1992 in the Case concerning the* Land, Island and Maritime Frontier Dispute (El Salvador/Honduras: Nicaragua intervening) *(El Salvador v. Honduras)*, Judgment of 18 December 2003, *I.C.J. Reports 2003*, 392-412, 407), stating: "The Chamber concludes from the foregoing that the new facts alleged by El Salvador in respect of the "Carta Esférica" and the report of the *El Activo* expedition are not "decisive factors" in respect of the Judgment whose revision it seeks." (International Court of Justice (2003), *Application for Revision of the Judgment of 11 September 1992 in the Case concerning the* Land, Island and Maritime Frontier Dispute (El Salvador/Honduras:

Chamber concludes that, pursuant to Article 61(1) of the Statute of the ICJ[361] – whose wording it quoted at this point in the judgment, it "cannot find admissible an application for revision on the basis of facts *which El Salvador itself does not allege to be new facts within the meaning of Article 61* [of the Statute][362]" [445]. On first reading, this seems to be a confusing statement from the Chamber; as stated above[363], El Salvador claims that it is presenting new facts in the current case[364] – whilst the Chamber therein holds that this country does *not* assert these to be new facts *within the meaning of Article 61*. Article 61(1) of the Statute of the ICJ describes a new fact as one "unknown to the Court and also to the party claiming revision." Thus, the Chamber in the current case is declaring that both El Salvador and the Chamber in the earlier case to which it relates[365] knew at the time of that previous case the facts which that country is putting forward as 'new facts' in the present lawsuit, and, therefore, El Salvador is not putting those facts forward as 'new facts' as defined in Article 61(1) of the Statute.

As not all the conditions which Article 61 of the Statute of the ICJ lays down are satisfied, El Salvador's application in *Application for Revision of the Judgment of 11 September 1992 in the Case concerning the* Land, Island and Maritime Frontier Dispute (El Salvador/Honduras: Nicaragua intervening) *(El Salvador v. Honduras)* for revision of the Chamber's judgment in *Land, Island and Maritime Frontier Dispute (El Salvador/Honduras: Nicaragua intervening)* is inadmissible. The Chamber

---

Nicaragua intervening) *(El Salvador v. Honduras)*, Judgment of 18 December 2003, *I.C.J. Reports 2003*, 392-412, 410; emphasis original).

361 The first sentence of antepenultimate paragraph of the subsection entitled 'A Summary of Jurisdictional and Procedural Aspects of the ICJ', above in the present section (i.e., that titled 'The International Court of Justice'), comprise these provisions.

362 Emphasis added.

363 See the previous-but-two quoted section and the sentence immediately preceding that passage, and also fn 360.

364 The 'current case' is *Application for Revision of the Judgment of 11 September 1992 in the Case concerning the* Land, Island and Maritime Frontier Dispute (El Salvador/Honduras: Nicaragua intervening) *(El Salvador v. Honduras)*.

365 This 'earlier case' is *Land, Island and Maritime Frontier Dispute (El Salvador/Honduras: Nicaragua intervening)*.

concluded this by four votes to one, Judge *ad hoc* Paolillo[366] dissenting[367] [445].

---

[366] Fn 358.

[367] Judge *ad hoc* Paolillo's dissenting opinion is found in the *I.C.J. Reports* for 2003 at pages 413-426. Judge Paolillo considered that the Chamber's claim in the current case that its predecessor in *Land, Island and Maritime Frontier Dispute (El Salvador/Honduras: Nicaragua intervening)* rejected El Salvador's claim 'on the basis of that State's conduct during the nineteenth century' (see the first sentence of the previous-but-one quoted section in the text) was not the real reason for the latter's rejection of the claim – that being (as stated in Paragraphs 308 and 309 of the Chamber's judgment in *Land, Island and Maritime Frontier Dispute (El Salvador/Honduras: Nicaragua intervening)* that there was neither record nor scientific evidence of an avulsion of the River Goascorán (International Court of Justice (2003), *Application for Revision of the Judgment of 11 September 1992 in the Case concerning the* Land, Island and Maritime Frontier Dispute (El Salvador/Honduras: Nicaragua intervening) *(El Salvador v. Honduras)*, Dissenting Opinion of Judge Paolillo, *I.C.J. Reports 2003*, 413-426, 417; International Court of Justice (1992), *Land, Island and Maritime Frontier Dispute (El Salvador/Honduras: Nicaragua intervening)*, Judgment of 11 September 1992, *I.C.J. Reports 1992*, 351-618, 546). Judge Paolillo proceeded to determine that the items which El Salvador produced in the present case amounted to new facts that might constitute a decisive factor under Article 61 of the Statute of the ICJ, stating at Paragraphs 35 and 36 of his dissenting opinion: "[T]aken overall, the material and information that El Salvador presented in these proceedings as "new facts" largely satisfy the conditions laid down in Article 61 of the Statute of the Court. Given the *ratio decidendi* of the 1992 Judgment in respect of the sixth sector of the land boundary [between El Salvador and Honduras] is … explained in paragraphs 308, 309 and 321 of that decision (no evidence of an abrupt change of course of the river; lack of scientific evidence that the previous course of the river was such that it debouched in the Estero La Cutú), any evidence demonstrating the fact of the Goascorán avulsion may be of such a nature as to be a decisive factor. During the present proceedings, El Salvador produced technical evidence that irrefutably demonstrates, in its view, the existence of the old bed [of the river], which the Goascorán allegedly left following an avulsion and which debouched into the Cutú inlet. El Salvador also produced scientific evidence contained in an expert report which states categorically that an abrupt change in the course of the river occurred after the Spanish colonial authorities had defined the boundary between the Alcadía Mayor de Tegucigalpa and the municipality of San Miguel as following the river-bed, and that the Cutú inlet and its distributory channels were the primary outlets of the Goascorán at the time when the old course was abandoned" (International Court of Justice (2003), *Application for Revision of the Judgment of 11 September 1992 in the Case concerning the* Land, Island and Maritime Frontier Dispute (El Salvador/Honduras: Nicaragua intervening) *(El Salvador v. Honduras)*, Dissenting Opinion of Judge Paolillo, *I.C.J. Reports 2003*, 413-426, 424). This difference in emphasis from the Chamber's approach to the additional material produced by El Salvador enabled Judge Paolillo to conclude as follows: "[T]he conditions [that Article 61 of the Statute of the ICJ lays down] were satisfied and the Application for revision was therefore admissible. Having concluded, erroneously … , that the *ratio decidendi* of the 1992 Judgment in respect of the sixth sector of the land boundary was not related to the substance of the dispute but to its previous history, and that the new facts presented during the proceedings were therefore not of such a nature as to be a decisive factor, the Chamber decided that the Application for revision filed by El Salvador was inadmissible. … A new decision on the merits, relating to the sixth sector [of the land boundary between El Salvador and Honduras], might have better served the cause of justice than the 1992

Judgment, inasmuch as the better informed a court is, the greater are its chances of adopting correct decisions. [Regrettably,] I [disagree] with the present decision holding inadmissible the Application for revision filed by El Salvador." (International Court of Justice (2003), *Application for Revision of the Judgment of 11 September 1992 in the Case concerning the* Land, Island and Maritime Frontier Dispute (El Salvador/Honduras: Nicaragua intervening) *(El Salvador v. Honduras)*, Dissenting Opinion of Judge Paolillo, *I.C.J. Reports 2003*, 413-426, 425-426). The phrase '*ratio decidendi*' is from Latin – literally 'reason for deciding'; it means "the rule of law on which a judicial decision is based" (Pearsall, J. (editor) (1998), *The New Oxford Dictionary of English*, 1539). Dr. McFarlane's definition of '*ratio decidendi*' is similar: "[t]he fundamental principle underlying a judgement or decision given by a judge" (McFarlane, G. (1984), *The Layman's Dictionary of English Law*, 236). The application of the principle of '*uti possidetis juris*' is worthy of elucidation in the context of Judge *ad hoc* Paolillo's dissenting opinion in *Application for Revision of the Judgment of 11 September 1992 in the Case concerning the* Land, Island and Maritime Frontier Dispute (El Salvador/Honduras: Nicaragua intervening) *(El Salvador v. Honduras)*. The Chamber in *Frontier Dispute (Burkina Faso/Mali)* explored this term in the context of the transformation of African dependencies to independent states in the 20th century: "[T]he principle of *uti possidetis* seems to have been first invoked and applied in Spanish America, inasmuch as this was the continent which first witnessed the phenomenon of decolonization involving the formation of a number of sovereign States on territory formerly belonging to a single metropolitan State. Nevertheless the principle is not a special rule which pertains solely to one specific system of international law. It is a general principle, which is logically connected with the phenomenon of the obtaining of independence, wherever it occurs. Its obvious purpose is to prevent the independence and stability of new States being endangered by fratricical struggles provoked by the challenging of frontiers following the withdrawal of the administering power. It was for that reason that, as soon as the phenomenon of decolonization characteristic of the situation in Spanish America in the 19th century subsequently appeared in Africa in the 20th century, the principle of *uti possidetis* ... fell to be applied. The fact that the new African States have respected the administrative boundaries and frontiers established by the colonial powers must be seen not as a mere practice contributing to the gradual emergence of a principle of customary international law, limited in its impact to the African continent as it had previously been to Spanish America, but as the application in Africa of a rule of general scope. ... There are several different aspects to this principle, in its well-known application in Spanish America. The first aspect, emphasized by the Latin genetive *juris*, is found in the pre-eminance accorded to legal title over effective possession as a basis of sovereignty. ... The essence of the principle lies in its primary aim of securing respect for the territorial boundaries at the moment when independence is achieved. Such territorial boundaries might be no more than delimitations between different administrative divisions or colonies all subject to the same sovereign. In that case, the application of the principle of *uti possidetis* resulted in administrative boundaries being transformed into international frontiers ... . This is true both of the States which took shape in the regions of South America which were dependent on the Spanish Crown, and of the States Parties to the present case, which took shape within the vast territories of French West Africa. *Uti possidetis*, as a principle which upgraded former administrative delimitations, established during the colonial period, to international frontiers, is therefore a principle of a general kind which is logically connected with this form of decolonization wherever it occurs." (International Court of Justice (1986), *Frontier Dispute (Burkina Faso/Mali)*, Judgment of 22 December 1986, *I.C.J. Reports 1986*, 554-651, 565-566). In *Land, Island and Maritime Frontier Dispute (El Salvador/Honduras: Nicaragua intervening)*, both Honduras and El Salvador agree that the main principle to be applied to determine the land frontier between them is *uti possidetis juris*, which Honduras accepts as the norm of international law relevant to the dispute whilst El Salvador also invokes *effectivités* (i.e., human arguments – considered below in this footnote) (International Court of Justice (1992), *Land, Island and Maritime Frontier Dispute (El Salvador/Honduras: Nicaragua intervening)*, Judgment of 11 September 1992, *I.C.J. Reports 1992*, 351-618, 386). Both Honduras and El Salvador recognize that the source of their international rights is that of their succession to the Spanish Crown concerning its colonial lands – the ambit of territory to which each of these countries is entitled being decided by the *uti possidetis juris* of 1821 (International Court of Justice (1992), *Land, Island and Maritime Frontier Dispute (El Salvador/Honduras: Nicaragua intervening)*, Judgment of 11 September 1992, *I.C.J. Reports 1992*, 351-618, 389) – which was the year that Central America attained its independence from Spain. At paragraph 62 of *Land, Island and Maritime Frontier Dispute (El Salvador/Honduras: Nicaragua intervening)*, the Chamber states: "What the Chamber has to do in respect of the land frontier is to arrive at a conclusion as to the position of the 1821 *uti possidetis juris* boundary; to this end it cannot but take into account ... the colonial *effectivités* as reflected in the documentary evidence of the colonial period submitted by the Parties. The Chamber may have regard also, in certain instances, to documentary evidence of post-independence *effectivités* when it considers that they afford indications in respect of the 1821 *uti possidetis juris* boundary, providing a relationship exists between the *effectivités* concerned and the determination of that boundary." (International Court of Justice (1992), *Land, Island and Maritime Frontier Dispute (El Salvador/Honduras: Nicaragua intervening)*, Judgment of 11 September 1992, *I.C.J. Reports 1992*, 351-618, 399). The Max Planck Encyclopedia of International Law makes the following comment: "[I]n a territorial dispute, the legal value of *effectivités* is to be assessed according to the existence or not of a legal title. When there is no title of sovereignty over a territory, or that title cannot be determined by other means, *effectivités* can create a territorial title. Whenever a title of sovereignty exists, it has primacy over contradictory *effectivités* of another State." (Kohen, M.G., and Hébié, M. (2011), Territory, Acquisition, *Max Planck Encyclopedia of Public International Law*, para.36). It is submitted on the basis of the foregoing that, with regard to El Salvador's application under Article 61 of the Statute of the ICJ in *Application for Revision of the Judgment of 11 September 1992 in the Case concerning the* Land, Island and Maritime Frontier Dispute (El Salvador/Honduras: Nicaragua intervening) *(El Salvador v. Honduras)*, the Chamber should be determining the land boundary between El Salvador and Honduras on the basis of the *uti possessidis juris* rule, taking into account any relevant *effectivités* where the outcome based on the rule is uncertain. With regard to the relevant (i.e., in the text of the judgment in *Land, Island and Maritime Frontier Dispute (El Salvador/Honduras: Nicaragua intervening)*, the 'sixth') land sector, the Chamber states: "[T]he reference to the "Goascorán river" [in a text dated 1884 submitted to this Chamber] might conceivably be interpreted to have meant the 1821 course of the river; but in the first place, the 1880 record ... refers to the boundary following the river from its mouth "upstream in a north-easterly direction," i.e., the direction taken by the present course, not the hypothetical old course, of the river. Secondly, an interpretation of these texts as referring to the old course of the river [Goascorán] becomes untenable in the light of the cartographic material of the period, which was presumably available to the delegates, and pointed overwhelmingly to the river being then in its present course, and forming the international boundary. ... In its pleadings, El Salvador has placed reliance on the *effectivités* or "arguments of a human nature" of the same kind as it has invoked in other sectors of the land boundary. However, at the hearings, the Agent and counsel for El Salvador stated that, since a large part of the disputed area in this sector is uninhabited, it appeared that neither side could adduce convincing arguments of a human nature. Since the Chamber has found that the boundary follows the present course of the Goascorán, as claimed by Honduras, there is no need to enquire into any claims of *effectivités* put forward by Honduras. (International Court of Justice (1992), *Land, Island and Maritime Frontier Dispute (El Salvador/Honduras: Nicaragua intervening)*, Judgment of 11 September 1992, *I.C.J. Reports 1992*, 351-618, 551-552).” Thus, the Chamber in *Land, Island and Maritime Frontier Dispute (El Salvador/Honduras: Nicaragua intervening)* has determined the boundary between El Salvador and Honduras in the sixth land sector to follow the course of the River Goascorán as it considered, from the arguments and evidence present to it, that course to be in 1821 following the *uti possessidis juris* rule, which is the same as the current course of the river. Therefore, for the Chamber in *Application for Revision of the Judgment of 11 September 1992 in the Case concerning the* Land, Island and Maritime Frontier Dispute (El Salvador/Honduras: Nicaragua intervening) *(El Salvador v. Honduras)* to accept that El Salvador’s application for revision of the judgment in *Land, Island and Maritime Frontier Dispute (El Salvador/Honduras: Nicaragua intervening)* “is based upon the discovery of some fact of such a nature as to be a decisive factor, which was, when the judgment was given, unknown to the Court and also to the party claiming revision” (International Court of Justice (2019), Rules of Court (1978) adopted on 14 April 1978 and entered into force on 1 July 1978 – amended to 21 October 2019, Article 61(1)), then the evidence produced by El Salvador in *Application for Revision of the Judgment of 11 September 1992 in the Case concerning the* Land, Island and Maritime Frontier Dispute (El Salvador/Honduras: Nicaragua intervening) *(El Salvador v. Honduras)* should be such as to convince the Chamber in this latter case that the boundary between El Salvador and Honduras in the sixth land sector in 1821 may not have been that of the present course of the River Goascorán. This Chamber stated: “In its Application for revision, El Salvador, acting under Article 61 of the Statute [of the ICJ] relies on facts which it considers to be new within the meaning of that Article; those facts relate, on the one hand, to the avulsion of the river Goascorán and, on the other, to the “Carta Esférica and the report of the 1794 *El Activo* expedition. El Salvador first claims to possess scientific, technical and historical evidence showing … that the Goascorán did in the past change its bed, and that the change was abrupt, probably as a result of a cyclone in 1762. In support of this contention El Salvador submits to the Chamber a report dated 5 August 2002 entitled *Geologic, Hydrologic and Historic Aspects of the Goascorán Delta – A Basis for Boundary Determination*. It also produces a study it conducted in 2002 “to check for the presence of vestiges of the Goascorán’s original riverbed and additional information about its hydrographic behavior.” … El Salvador relies on a second “new fact,” that is, the discovery in the Ayer Collection of the Newberry Library in Chicago of a further copy of the “Carta Esférica” and of a further copy of the report of the expedition of the *El Activo*, thereby supplementing the copies from the Madrid Naval Museum to which the Chamber makes reference [in *Land, Island and Maritime Frontier Dispute (El Salvador/Honduras: Nicaragua intervening)*]. … [T]he Estero La Cutú and the mouth of the Rio Goascorán are shown on the copy [of the “Carta Esférica”], just as on the copies from Madrid, at the present-day location. … [T]he body of the text [of] the new version of the report of the *El Activo* expedition found in Chicago … is the same [as] the Madrid version … in particular in the identification of the mouth of the Goascorán.” (International Court of Justice (2003), *Application for Revision of the Judgment of 11 September 1992 in the Case concerning the* Land, Island and Maritime Frontier Dispute (El Salvador/Honduras: Nicaragua intervening) *(El Salvador v. Honduras)*, Judgment of 18 December 2003, *I.C.J. Reports 2003*, 392-412, 401, 407 and 410; emphasis original). These items, which El Salvador produced to the Chamber in *Application for Revision of the Judgment of 11 September 1992 in the Case concerning the* Land, Island and Maritime Frontier Dispute (El Salvador/Honduras: Nicaragua intervening) *(El Salvador v. Honduras)*, support the Chamber’s view in *Land, Island and Maritime Frontier Dispute (El Salvador/Honduras: Nicaragua intervening)* that, in 1821, i.e., when Central America gained independence from Spain – the moment at

The International Tribunal for the Law of the Sea

The Basis for Determination of UNCLOS Disputes

A State Party[368] to the UNCLOS may, by written declaration, select the ITLOS as the forum, or a forum, for resolution of its dispute respecting "the interpretation or application of this Convention"[369] [303]. The decision of the ITLOS is final, and is to be observed by all the disputants[370] [284, 446]. This determination is only binding between the parties and with reference to their particular dispute [285, 447].

A Summary of the ITLOS' Jurisdictional and Procedural Aspects

The UNCLOS constituted the ITLOS[371] [448], which was set up following the entry into force of the UNCLOS in November 1994[372] [449].

---

which the *uti possessidis juris* rule applies, the boundary between El Salvador and Honduras in the sixth land sector followed the current course of the River Goascorán. Therefore, they did not constitute "some fact of such of nature as to be a decisive factor" (International Court of Justice (2019), Rules of Court (1978) adopted on 14 April 1978 and entered into force on 1 July 1978 – amended to 21 October 2019, Article 61(1)), and so the conditions for an application for revision to proceed under Article 61 of the Statute of the ICJ were not all satisfied. Consequently, El Salvador's application for revision of the Chamber's judgment in *Land, Island and Maritime Frontier Dispute (El Salvador/Honduras: Nicaragua intervening)* should, on the basis of this analysis, have been held to be inadmissible.

368 Fn 192 defines 'States Parties'.

369 The second and third sentences of the subsection entitled 'Basis for Determination of UNCLOS Disputes', in the section above titled 'The International Court of Justice', apply to the ITLOS – please read those sentences in the current context with 'ITLOS' replacing 'ICJ'.

370 This rule is essentially the same as the corresponding provision for the ICJ (seventh sentence of the eighth paragraph of the subsection entitled 'A Summary of the Jurisdictional and Procedural Aspects of the ICJ', in the section above titled 'The International Court of Justice').

371 Article 1(1) of Annex VI to the UNCLOS declares the ITLOS to be constituted, and states that the ITLOS is to function in observance of the UNCLOS and the ITLOS Statute – which Annex VI to the UNCLOS comprises (fn 195).

The jurisdiction of the ITLOS comprises: (i) all disputes and all applications that states (or other specified parties[373]) submit to it in conformity with the UNCLOS [450], (ii) all issues that any other agreement which confers jurisdiction upon the ITLOS specify [451], and (iii) "the interpretation or application of [a] treaty or convention" that is effective and includes the topic that the UNCLOS covers – if all of the parties to that agreement so concur [452]. The Seabed Disputes Chamber of the ITLOS judges disputes relating to activities within the Area[374] [453], and is not considered further here.

The ITLOS comprises 21 independent members, who are "elected from among persons enjoying the highest reputation for fairness and integrity and of recognized competence in the field of the law of the sea" [454]. It is to represent "the principle legal systems of the world" and a fair distribution of members geographically[375] [455]. There are to be at least

---

[372] The election of the first judges of the ITLOS, the commencement of its work, and its official inauguration, took place on 1st August, 1st October, and 18th October, 1996, respectively (International Tribunal for the Law of the Sea (2019), "General Information," accessed November 10, 2019, <https://www.itlos.org/general-information/>).

[373] Article 20 of the UNCLOS declares: "1. The Tribunal shall be open to States Parties. 2. The Tribunal shall be open to entities other than States Parties in any case expressly provided for in Part XI or in any case submitted pursuant to any other agreement conferring jurisdiction on the Tribunal which is accepted by all parties to that case. Fn 192 defines 'States Parties'. Part XI of the UNCLOS is entitled 'The Area', and comprises Articles 133-191 of this Convention. Fn 161 defines 'The Area'. Articles 187 of the UNCLOS defines the jurisdiction of Seabed Disputes Chamber of the ITLOS with regard to activities within the Area. Article 188 of the UNCLOS permits specified categories of dispute that Article 187 of the UNCLOS describes to be submitted to a special chamber of the ITLOS, to an *ad hoc* chamber of the Seabed Disputes Chamber, or to binding commercial arbitration. Fn 207 states Paragraphs (a) and (f) of Article 187 of the UNCLOS and Paragraph 1 of Article 188 of the UNCLOS, and defines '*ad hoc*'. Article 189 of the UNCLOS places specified restrictions on the jurisdiction of the Seabed Disputes Chamber of the ITLOS.

[374] The subsection titled 'The Seabed Disputes Chamber of the ITLOS & UNCLOS Part XV', and fn 207 and its accompanying text, in the section entitled 'Part XV of the UNCLOS: Settlement of Disputes' in Chapter 1, provide information concerning the Seabed Disputes Chamber of the ITLOS.

[375] The countries presently represented on the ITLOS are Algeria, Argentina, Cabo Verde, China, France, Iceland, India, Japan, Malta, Mexico, the Netherlands, Paraguay, Poland, the Republic of Korea, Russia, Senegal, South Africa, Tanzania, Thailand, Trinidad and Tobago, and Ukraine (International Tribunal for the Law of the Sea (2019), "Members," accessed November 11, 2019, <https://www.itlos.org/the-tribunal/members/>). Fn 376 describes the geographical distribution of these countries. The University of Ottawa categorizes the legal systems of each of these states as follows: *civil law* – Argentina, Cabo Verde, France, Iceland, Mexico, the Netherlands, Paraguay, Poland, Russia, Thailand, Ukraine; *mixed civil law/customary* – China, Japan, the Republic of Korea, Senegal; *mixed*

three members from each geographic group as determined by the General Assembly of the UN[376] [456]. No two members of the ITLOS may be nationals of the same country [457].

---

civil law/Muslim – Algeria; *mixed civil law/common law* – Malta, South Africa; *mixed common law/customary/Muslim* – India; *mixed common law/customary* – Tanzania; *common law* – Trinidad and Tobago (University of Ottawa (2019), "JuriGlobe: World Legal Systems Research Group – Alphabetical Index of the Political Entities and Corresponding Legal Systems," accessed November 11, 2019, <http://www.juriglobe.ca/eng/sys-juri/index-alpha.php>). Thus, civil, common, customary and Islamic legal systems – at least in part – have representative members on the ITLOS, although the representation from pure civil law systems – at 11 out of 21 countries – forms the largest portion, with the representation from mixed civil law systems – at 7 out of 21 countries – also being significant.

[376] The UN's Regional Groups of Member States are: (i) *African Group*, comprising the following 54 Member States of the UN – Algeria, Angola, Benin, Botswana, Burkina Faso, Burundi, Cabo Verde, Cameroon, Central African Republic, Chad, Comoros, Congo, Côte D'Ivoire, the Democratic Republic of the Congo, Djibouti, Egypt, Equatorial Guinea, Eritrea, Eswatini (formerly Swaziland), Ethiopia, Gabon, Gambia, Ghana, Guinea, Guinea-Bissau, Kenya, Lesotho, Liberia, Libya, Madagascar, Malawi, Mali, Mauritania, Mauritius, Morocco, Mozambique, Namibia, Niger, Nigeria, Rwanda, São Tomé and Principe, Senegal, Seychelles, Sierra Leone, Somalia, South Africa, South Sudan, Sudan, Tanzania, Togo, Tunisia, Uganda, Zambia, and Zimbabwe; (ii) *Asia-Pacific Group*, comprising the following 54 Member States of the UN (including Kiribati, which is a Member State of the UN but does not delegate a permanent representative to that organization) – Afghanistan, Bahrain, Bangladesh, Bhutan, Brunei Darussalam, Cambodia, China, Cyprus, the Democratic People's Republic of Korea, Fiji, India, Indonesia, Iran, Iraq, Japan, Jordon, Kazakhstan, Kiribati, Kuwait, Kyrgyzstan, Laos, Lebanon, Malaysia, the Maldives, the Marshall Islands, Micronesia, Mongolia, Myanmar, Nauru, Nepal, Oman, Pakistan, Palau, Papua New Guinea, the Philippines, Qatar, the Republic of Korea, Samoa, Saudi Arabia, Singapore, the Solomon Islands, Sri Lanka, Syria, Tajikistan, Thailand, Timor-Leste, Tonga, Turkmenistan, Tuvalu, the United Arab Emirates, Uzbekistan, Vanuatu, Vietnam, and Yemen; (iii) *Eastern European Group*, comprising the following 23 Member States of the UN – Albania, Armenia, Azerbaijan, Belarus, Bosnia and Herzegovina, Bulgaria, Croatia, the Czech Republic, Estonia, Georgia, Hungary, Latvia, Lithuania, Moldova, Montenegro, North Macedonia (formerly the Republic of Macedonia), Poland, Romania, Russia, Serbia, Slovakia, Slovenia, and Ukraine; (iv) *Latin American and Caribbean Group*, comprising the following 33 Member States of the UN – Antigua and Barbuda, Argentina, the Bahamas, Barbados, Belize, Bolivia, Brazil, Chile, Colombia, Costa Rica, Cuba, Dominica, the Dominican Republic, Ecuador, El Salvador, Grenada, Guatemala, Guyana, Haiti, Honduras, Jamaica, Mexico, Nicaragua, Panama, Paraguay, Peru, Saint Kitts and Nevis, Saint Lucia, Saint Vincent and the Grenadines, Suriname, Trinidad and Tobago, Uruguay, and Venezuela; (v) *Western European and Others Group*, comprising the following 29 Member States of the United Nations – Andorra, Australia, Austria, Belgium, Canada, Denmark, Finland, France, Germany, Greece, Iceland, Ireland, Israel, Italy, Liechtenstein, Luxembourg, Malta, Monaco, the Netherlands, New Zealand, Norway, Portugal, San Marino, Spain, Sweden, Switzerland, Turkey, the UK, and the USA (United Nations (2019), "Department for General Assembly and Conference Management: United Nations Regional Groups of Member States," accessed November 11, 2019, <https://www.un.org/depts/DGACM/RegionalGroups.shtml>). From this list, the 21 states represented on the ITLOS can be allocated to the corresponding Regional Group, as follows: African Group – Algeria, Cabo Verde, Senegal, South Africa, Tanzania; Asia-

Each State Party[377] to the UNCLOS may nominate one or two individuals with the qualities mentioned above[378]; the members of the ITLOS are elected from the list of nominees [458]. Three months or more before the election of members to the Tribunal, the Registrar of the ITLOS[379] invites the States Parties to submit their nominations within two months; the Registrar prepares a list of the nominees and their nominating country, and provides this to the States Parties "before the seventh day of the last month before the date of each election" [459]. The Tribunal's members are "elected by secret ballot"[380] [460]. These members hold office for nine years – seven are replaced by an election every three years[381] [461]. No member may: (i) play any political or administrative role, or actively associate with or show financial interest in any of the

Pacific Group – China, India, Japan, the Republic of Korea, Thailand; Eastern European Group – Poland, Russia, Ukraine; Latin American and Caribbean Group – Argentina, Mexico, Paraguay, Trinidad and Tobago; Western European and Others Group – France, Iceland, Malta and the Netherlands. It is submitted that this representation on the ITLOS amounts to a fair distribution of members geographically – although: (i) no country from South-East Europe or South-West Asia is currently represented on the ITLOS, (ii) Paraguay – a landlocked country – is represented on the ITLOS, (iii) no state from Central Asia is presently represented on the ITLOS – which is unsurprising as all five of these countries, i.e., Kazakhstan, Kyrgyzstan, Tajikistan, Turkmenistan and Uzbekistan, are landlocked states, and (iv) no Oceanic state is currently represented on the ITLOS, even though all these countries – except Papua New Guinea – are surrounded by sea. The states in Oceania are Australia, Fiji, Kiribati, the Marshall Islands, Micronesia, Nauru, New Zealand, Palau, Papua New Guinea, Samoa, the Solomon Islands, Tonga, Tuvalu, and Vanuatu.

[377] Fn 192 defines 'States Parties'.

[378] These qualities are an excellent reputation for fairness and integrity, and recognized competence regarding the law of the sea (first sentence of the immediately-preceding paragraph in the text).

[379] The current Registrar of the ITLOS is Dr. Ximena Hinrichs Oyarce (International Tribunal for the Law of the Sea (2019), "The Registrar," accessed November 13, 2019, <https://www.itlos.org/the-registry/the-registrar/the-registrar//>).

[380] The members-elect are "those nominees who obtain the largest number of votes and a two-thirds majority of the States Parties present and voting, provided that such majority includes a majority of the States Parties" (United Nations (1982), "United Nations Convention on the Law of the Sea," Annex VI, Article 4(4)).

[381] The Tribunal's members "continue to discharge their duties until their places have been filled," and "finish any proceedings which they may have begun before the date of their replacement" (United Nations (1982), "United Nations Convention on the Law of the Sea," Annex VI, Article 5(3)). The term of office of each member of the ITLOS elected at a triennial election runs from 1st October following the date of that election (International Tribunal for the Law of the Sea (2009), Rules of the Tribunal adopted on 28 October 1997 – amended to 25 September 2018 (ITLOS/8, 17 March 2009) (Hamburg: International Tribunal for the Law of the Sea), Article 2(1)).

activities of any business concerned with commercial usage of the seabed or the sea [462], (ii) act as an advocate, a counsel or an agent in any dispute [463], or (iii) take part in the judgment of any case in which (s)he has previously participated in any other capacity [464].

All available members of the ITLOS sit on the full Tribunal (in constrast to its chambers) in hearing any case; a quorum of eleven elected members consitutes the Tribunal[382] [465]. The Tribunal hears and decides all applications and disputes submitted to the ITLOS, unless these fall within the ambit of the Seabed Disputes Chamber of the ITLOS[383] or the parties request that a special chamber be formed [466].

The ITLOS may set up a chamber, comprising at least three of its elected members, as it deems to be necessary for judging a particular class of disputes [467]. The Tribunal determines the specific category of disputes for which this standing special chamber is created, the number of its members, the time for which these are to serve, the date on which they will commence their duties, and the quorum for meetings [468]. The President of the ITLOS[384] proposes the members of the standing special chamber, which the Tribunal selects – taking into consideration the special knowledge, expertise or experience which any of these individuals have concerning the class of disputes that the chamber addresses [469]. The ITLOS may decide to discontinue a standing special chamber, which completes any cases that are pending [470]. The standing special chambers

---

382 The ITLOS determines which of its members are available to constitute the full Tribunal for the determination of a particular dispute, taking into account the working of its chambers (United Nations (1982), "United Nations Convention on the Law of the Sea," Annex VI, Article 13(2)).

383 The subsection titled 'The Seabed Disputes Chamber of the ITLOS & UNCLOS Part XV', and fn 207 and its accompanying text, in the section entitled 'Part XV of the UNCLOS: Settlement of Disputes' in Chapter 1, supply information regarding the Seabed Disputes Chamber of the ITLOS.

384 The current President of the Tribunal is Dr. Jin-Hyun Paik (International Tribunal for the Law of the Sea (2019), "President Jin-Hyun Paik," accessed November 13, 2019, <https://www.itlos.org/the-tribunal/members/president-jin-hyun-paik/>). Article 45 of the Rules of the ITLOS states: "In every case submitted to the Tribunal, the President [of the ITLOS] shall ascertain the views of the parties with regard to questions of procedure. For this purpose, he may summon the agents of the parties to meet him as soon as possible after their appointment and whenever necessary thereafter, or use other appropriate means of communication."

of the ITLOS are the Chamber for Fisheries Disputes[385], the Chamber for Marine Environment Disputes[386] and the Chamber for Maritime Delimitation Disputes[387] [471].

The ITLOS may institute a chamber for resolving a particular dispute that the parties submit to it, if they request this; the Tribunal determines the composition of the chamber, subject to the approval of these disputants [472]. The parties must make this request within two months of the date on which proceedings are initiated; when receiving this request from one party, the President of the ITLOS ascertains whether the other disputant assents to the creation of the chamber [473]. Once the parties have agreed to form the chamber, the President discovers their views concerning its constitution and duly reports to the Tribunal [474]. Then, the ITLOS, with the parties' approval, decides the members who are to form the chamber – and determines the quorum for the latter's meetings [475]. If a member is replaced following the expiration of that judge's term of office, then (s)he continues to hear all remaining phases of the case [476]. One example of a chamber set up to settle a particular dispute is the Special Chamber formed to adjudicate *Delimitation of the maritime boundary between Ghana and Côte D'Ivoire in the Atlantic Ocean (Ghana/Côte D'Ivoire)*[388] [477, 478], which was constituted in January 2015 [479] and disbanded after it pronounced judgment in September 2017[389] [477].

---

[385] Comprising nine judges, the Chamber for Fisheries Disputes hears cases regarding the conservation and administration of marine life that parties agree to submit to it (International Tribunal for the Law of the Sea (2019), "Chambers," accessed November 13, 2019, <https://www.itlos.org/en/the-tribunal/chambers/>).

[386] Comprising nine judges, the Chamber for Marine Environment Disputes adjudicates cases concerning the safeguarding and conservation of the thalassic environment which parties agree to submit to it (International Tribunal for the Law of the Sea (2019), "Chambers," accessed November 13, 2019, <https://www.itlos.org/en/the-tribunal/chambers/>).

[387] Comprising eleven judges, the Chamber for Maritime Delimitation Disputes tries cases on maritime delimitation that parties agree to submit to it (International Tribunal for the Law of the Sea (2019), "Chambers," accessed November 13, 2019, <https://www.itlos.org/en/the-tribunal/chambers/>).

[388], Case No. 23. Judgment of 23 September 2017, *ITLOS Reports 2017*, 4.

[389] This Special Chamber comprised five judges – i.e., three members of the ITLOS and two judges *ad hoc* (International Tribunal for the Law of the Sea (2017), *Delimitation of the maritime boundary between Ghana and Côte D'Ivoire in the Atlantic Ocean (Ghana/Côte D'Ivoire)*, Judgment of 23 September 2017, *ITLOS Reports 2017*, 4, para.4). Fn 207 defines '*ad hoc*'.

In order to conduct its business quickly, the ITLOS annually establishes a chamber that comprises five of its elected members to hear and resolve disputes by summary procedure[390] [480]. This chamber, named the Chamber of Summary Procedure[391], consists of the President[392] and

---

[390] Two alternative members are selected, in order to replace members who are unable to take part in a particular case (United Nations (1982), "United Nations Convention on the Law of the Sea," Annex VI, Article 15(3); International Tribunal for the Law of the Sea (2009), Rules of the Tribunal adopted on 28 October 1997 – amended to 25 September 2018, Article 28(1)).

[391] The ITLOS' Chamber of Summary Procedure is yet to hear a case (e-mail from Ms. Julia Ritter, Press Officer at the ITLOS, to Dr. Graeme Baber, 16th November 2019). The ICJ also has a Chamber of Summary Procedure (International Court of Justice (2019), "Chambers and Committees," accessed November 15, 2019, <https://www.icj-cij.org/en/chambers-and-committees>). The Statute of the ICJ provides: "With a view to the speedy dispatch of business, the Court shall form annually a chamber composed of five judges which, at the request of the parties, may hear and determine cases by summary procedure. In addition, two judges shall be selected for the purpose of replacing judges who find it impossible to sit." (United Nations (1945), "Statute of the International Court of Justice," Article 29). The ICJ's Chamber of Summary Procedure is established annually, and comprises the President of the Court (Judge Yusuf (fn 266)), the Vice-President of the Court (Judge Hanqin (fn 266)), and three further members elected by secret ballot (International Court of Justice (2019), Rules of Court (1978) adopted on 14 April 1978 and entered into force on 1 July 1978 – amended to 21 October 2019, Articles 15(1) and 18(1)). These members are currently Judges Antônio Augusto Cançado Trindade, Julia Sebutinde and Kirill Gevorgian, who have been members of the ICJ since 6th February 2009, 6th February 2012, and 6th February 2015, respectively (International Court of Justice (2019), "Chambers and Committees," accessed November 15, 2019, <https://www.icj-cij.org/en/chambers-and-committees>; International Court of Justice (2019), "Current Members," accessed November 15, 2019, <https://www.icj-cij.org/en/current-members>). Like the ITLOS' Chamber for Fisheries Disputes, Chamber for Marine Environmental Disputes and Chamber for Maritime Delimitation Disputes (fns 385-387 and accompanying text), the ICJ is empowered to establish chambers to judge specific classes of disputes: "The Court may from time to time form one or more chambers composed of three or more judges as the Court may determine, for dealing with particular categories of cases; for example, labour cases and cases relating to transit and communications." (United Nations (1945), "Statute of the International Court of Justice," Article 26(1)). In 1993, the ICJ formed a Chamber for Environmental Matters, which was regularly reconstituted until 2006; as no state requested that any case to which it was a party be adjudicated by the Chamber for Environmental Matters, the Court decided in 2006 to cancel elections for a Bench for this judicial unit (International Court of Justice (2019), "Chambers and Committees," accessed November 15, 2019, <https://www.icj-cij.org/en/chambers-and-committees>). Whilst, to date, no case has been heard by either the ICJ's Chamber of Summary Procedure or any standing chamber of the ICJ for hearing particular classes of dispute, six cases have been decided by *ad hoc* chambers of the ICJ – three of which are referred to in the subsection entitled 'Example ICJ Case – El Salvador/Honduras: Nicaragua intervening', in the section above titled 'The International Court of Justice', i.e., *Frontier Dispute (Burkina Faso/Mali)* (fn 367), *Land, Island and Maritime Frontier Dispute (El Salvador/Honduras: Nicaragua intervening)*, and *Application for Revision of the Judgment of 11 September 1992 in the Case concerning the* Land, Island and Maritime Frontier Dispute (El Salvador/Honduras:

Vice-President[393] of the Tribunal and three further members of the ITLOS. The President proposes, and the Tribunal then selects, these members[394], and two alternates[395] [481]. The choosing of judges for the Chamber of Summary Procedure is made promptly after 1st October each year, and these people serve from that date until 30th September of the next year[396] [482]. If a member of the Chamber is unable to sit in a particular case, then (s)he is replaced in this legal action by the senior in precedence of the alternates[397] [483]. If the tenure of a member of the Chamber ceases, then

---

Nicaragua intervening) *(El Salvador v. Honduras)*; all six of the ICJ's *ad hoc* chambers comprised five judges, and the three cases listed above in this footnote were decided by three members of the Court and two judges *ad hoc* – one judge *ad hoc* chosen by each of the disputants (International Court of Justice (2019), "Chambers and Committees," accessed November 15, 2019, <https://www.icj-cij.org/en/chambers-and-committees>). Fn 207 defines '*ad hoc*'. Fn 294 furnishes information concerning the appointment of Judges *ad hoc* to the ICJ. Article 26(2) of the Statute of the ICJ states: "The Court may at any time form a chamber for dealing with a particular case. The number of judges to constitute such a chamber shall be determined by the Court with the approval of the parties."

[392] At the moment, the President of the Tribunal is Dr. Paik (fn 384).

[393] The current Vice-President of the Tribunal is Dr. David Joseph Attard (International Tribunal for the Law of the Sea (2019), "Vice-President David Joseph Attard," accessed November 14, 2019, <https://www.itlos.org/the-tribunal/members/vice-president-david-joseph-attard />).

[394] These judges are Dr. Tafsir Malick Ndiaye, Dr. Jean-Pierre Cot, and Ms. Elsa Kelly (International Tribunal for the Law of the Sea (2019), "Chambers," accessed November 14, 2019, <https://www.itlos.org/en/the-tribunal/chambers/>; International Tribunal for the Law of the Sea (2019), "Judge Tafsir Malick Ndiaye," accessed November 14, 2019, <https://www.itlos.org/the-tribunal/members/judge-tafsir-malick-ndiaye/>; International Tribunal for the Law of the Sea (2019), "Judge Jean-Pierre Cot," accessed November 14, 2019, <https://www.itlos.org/the-tribunal/members/judge-jean-pierre-cot/>; International Tribunal for the Law of the Sea (2019), "Judge Elsa Kelly," accessed November 14, 2019, <https://www.itlos.org/the-tribunal/members/judge-elsa-kelly/>).

[395] Fn 390. The alternative members are Mr. Roman A. Kolodkin and Dr. Liesbeth Lijnzaad (International Tribunal for the Law of the Sea (2019), "Chambers," accessed November 14, 2019, <https://www.itlos.org/en/the-tribunal/chambers/>; International Tribunal for the Law of the Sea (2019), "Judge Roman A. Kolodkin," accessed November 14, 2019, <https://www.itlos.org/the-tribunal/members/judge-roman-a-kolodkin/>; International Tribunal for the Law of the Sea (2019), "Judge Liesbeth Lijnzaad," accessed November 14, 2019, <https://www.itlos.org/the-tribunal/members/judge-liesbeth-lijnzaad/>).

[396] Members and alternative members of the Chamber of Summary Procedure who remain on the ITLOS after 30th September continue their respective roles on the Chamber until the immediately-succeeding selection (International Tribunal for the Law of the Sea (2009), Rules of the Tribunal adopted on 28 October 1997 – amended to 25 September 2018 (ITLOS/8, 17 March 2009), Article 28(3)).

[397] The precedence of members of the ITLOS is as follows: "The President and the Vice-President of the Tribunal, while holding these offices, shall take precedence over the other Members. A Member who is re-elected to a new term of office which is continuous with his previous term shall retain his precedence. [Apart from that, t]he Members shall ... take

the place of that judge is taken by the senior in precedence of the alternates[398], who thereupon becomes a full member of the Chamber and is replaced by the choice of a new alternate [484]. The quorum for the Chamber's meetings is three members [485].

If the ITLOS includes on the Bench a member of the nationality of one of the disputants[399], then any other party may select an individual to take part as a member of the Tribunal[400] [486]. If the ITLOS does not include upon the Bench a member of such nationality, then each party may choose a person to so participate[401] [487]. The ITLOS' official languages are English and French[402] [488].

---

precedence according to the date on which their respective terms of office began. Members whose terms of office began on the same date shall take precedence in relation to one another according to seniority of age." (International Tribunal for the Law of the Sea (2009), Rules of the Tribunal adopted on 28 October 1997 – amended to 25 September 2018 (ITLOS/8, 17 March 2009), Article 4(1)-(4)). Thus, the senior in precedence of the alternates for the Chamber of Summary Procedure is Judge Kolodkin – whilst both he and Judge Lijnzaad acceded to membership of the ITLOS on 1st October 2017, the former is 65 days older than the latter (fn 395; International Tribunal for the Law of the Sea (2019), "Judge Roman A. Kolodkin," accessed November 14, 2019, <https://www.itlos.org/the-tribunal/members/judge-roman-a-kolodkin/>; International Tribunal for the Law of the Sea (2019), "Judge Liesbeth Lijnzaad," accessed November 14, 2019, <https://www.itlos.org/the-tribunal/members/judge-liesbeth-lijnzaad/>). The precedence of members of the Tribunal does not affect their roles – "The Members, in the exercise of their functions, are of equal status, irrespective of age, priority of election or length of service." (International Tribunal for the Law of the Sea (2009), Rules of the Tribunal adopted on 28 October 1997 – amended to 25 September 2018 (ITLOS/8, 17 March 2009), Article 3).

398 This would be Judge Kolodkin (fn 397).

399 Article 17(1) of Annex VI to the UNCLOS states: "Members of the Tribunal of the nationality of any of the parties to a dispute shall retain their right to participate as members of the Tribunal."

400 Judges *ad hoc* participate in the case in which they sit on equal terms to the other judges, and take precedence after the members of the ITLOS "and in order of seniority of age" (fn 397) (International Tribunal for the Law of the Sea (2009), Rules of the Tribunal adopted on 28 October 1997 – amended to 25 September 2018 (ITLOS/8, 17 March 2009), Article 8(1)-(2)). Fn 207 defines '*ad hoc*'.

401 Article 17(5) of Annex VI to the UNCLOS declares: "Should there be several parties in the same interest, they shall, for the purpose of the preceding provisions [i.e., Paragraphs 1-4 of Article 17 of Annex VI to the UNCLOS] be considered as one party only. Any doubt on this point shall be settled by the decision of the Tribunal." Article 17(4) of Annex VI to the UNCLOS proclaims: "This article [i.e., Article 17 of Annex VI to the UNCLOS] applies to the chambers referred to in articles 14 and 15 of this Annex [i.e., the Seabed Disputes Chamber (fn 383), standing special chambers – such as the Chamber for Maritime Delimitation Disputes (fn 387), chambers formed to settle a particular dispute, and the Chamber of Summary Procedure (text to fn 390)]. In such cases, the President [of the ITLOS], in consultation with the parties, shall request specified members of the Tribunal forming the chamber ... to give place to the members of the Tribunal of the nationality of

Correspondingly to the ICJ[403], a dispute is submitted to the ITLOS by either notification to the Registrar of the Tribunal of a special agreement between the disputants[404], or written application addressed to the Registrar[405], indicating in both cases the parties and the theme of that

---

the parties concerned, and, failing such, or if they are unable to be present, to the members specially chosen by the parties." Throughout the history of the ITLOS, judges *ad hoc* have been appointed in the following cases: (i) *Southern Bluefin Tuna Cases (New Zealand v. Japan; Australia v. Japan), Provisional Measures* – one appointee, (ii) *Case concerning the Conservation and Sustainable Exploitation of Swordfish Stocks in the South-Eastern Pacific Ocean (Chile/European Union)* – one appointee, (iii) *The "Grand Prince" Case (Belize v. France), Prompt Release* – one appointee, (iv) *The MOX Plant Case (Ireland v. United Kingdom), Provisional Measures* – one appointee, (v) *The "Volga" Case (Russian Federation v. Australia), Prompt Release* – one appointee, (vi) *Case concerning Land Reclamation by Singapore in and around the Straits of Johor (Malaysia v. Singapore), Provisional Measures* – two appointees, (vii) *Dispute concerning delimitation of the maritime boundary between Bangladesh and Myanmar in the Bay of Bengal (Bangladesh/Myanmar)* – two appointees, (viii) *The M/V "Virginia G" Case (Panama/Guinea-Bissau)* – two appointees, (ix) *The "ARA Libertad" Case (Argentina v. Ghana), Provisional Measures* – one appointee, (x) *The "Arctic Sunrise" Case (Kingdom of the Netherlands v. Russian Federation), Provisional Measures* – one appointee, (xi) *Dispute concerning delimitation of the maritime boundary between Ghana and Côte d'Ivoire in the Atlantic Ocean (Ghana/Côte d'Ivoire)* – two appointees, (xii) *The "Enrica Lexie" Incident (Italy v. India)* – one appointee, (xiii) *The M/V "Norstar" Case (Panama v. Italy)* – two appointees, (xiv) *The M/T "San Padre Pio" Case (Switzerland v. Nigeria), Provisional Measures* – two appointees, and (xv) *Dispute concerning delimitation of the maritime boundary between Mauritius and Maldives in the Indian Ocean (Mauritius/Maldives)* – two appointees (International Tribunal for the Law of the Sea (2019), "Judges *ad hoc*," accessed November 15, 2019, <https://www.itlos.org/the-tribunal/judges-ad-hoc/>).

[402] These official languages are identical to those of the ICJ (first line of the fourth paragraph of the subsection entitled 'A Summary of Jurisdictional and Procedural Aspects of the ICJ', in the section above titled 'The International Court of Justice').

[403] Fns 250-251 and accompanying text.

[404] As there is neither an 'applicant' state nor a 'respondent' state in a case commenced by the notification to the Tribunal's Registrar of a special agreement between the parties, in the publications of the ITLOS the names of the disputants are separated by a forward slash at the end of the case's official title, e.g., *Dispute concerning delimitation of the maritime boundary between Mauritius and Maldives in the Indian Ocean (Mauritius/Maldives)* (International Tribunal for the Law of the Sea (2019), Order: Constitution of Chamber for the dispute concerning delimitation of the maritime boundary between Mauritius and Maldives in the Indian Ocean (Mauritius/Maldives) (Case No. 28, Order 2019/4, 27 September 2019) (Hamburg: International Tribunal for the Law of the Sea), 1). The notification of a special agreement to the Registrar of the ITLOS "may be effected by the parties jointly or by any one or more of them" (International Tribunal for the Law of the Sea (2009), Rules of the Tribunal adopted on 28 October 1997 – amended to 25 September 2018 (ITLOS/8, 17 March 2009), Article 55(1)).

[405] For a case initiated by a written application addressed to the Registrar of the ITLOS, in the publications of the Tribunal the names of the disputants are separated by a versus sign in the following form: (Applicant State v. Respondent State), which appears after the case's official title, e.g., *The M/T "San Padre Pio" Case (Switzerland v. Nigeria)* (International

dispute[406] [489]. The Registrar notifies the written application or the special agreement "to all concerned"[407] [490], and "also notif[ies] all States Parties"[408] [491].

The ITLOS has the power to impose provisional measures [492]. The hearing is overseen by the President, *in absentia*[409] by the Vice-President, and both *in absentia* by the most senior judge present[410] [493]. Like the ICJ[411], the hearing before the ITLOS is open to the public, unless either the Tribunal decides otherwise or the disputants request that the public are to

Tribunal for the Law of the Sea (2019), Order: Request for the prescription of provisional measures regarding the M/T "San Padre Pio" Case (Switzerland v. Nigeria) (Case No. 27, 6 July 2019) (Hamburg: International Tribunal for the Law of the Sea), 1). The written application must "specify as far as possible the legal grounds upon which the jurisdiction of the Tribunal is said to be based; it shall also specify the precise nature of the claim, together with a succinct statement of the facts and grounds on which the claim is based" (International Tribunal for the Law of the Sea (2009), Rules of the Tribunal adopted on 28 October 1997 – amended to 25 September 2018 (ITLOS/8, 17 March 2009), Article 54(2)). Article 54(5) of the Rules of the ITLOS states an additional requirement for the written application concerning the Tribunal's jurisdiction: "When the applicant proposes to found the jurisdiction of the Tribunal upon a consent thereto yet to be given or manifested by the party against which the application is made, the application shall be transmitted to that party. It shall not however be entered in the List of cases, nor any action be taken in the proceedings, unless and until the party against which such application is made consents to the jurisdiction of the Tribunal for the purposes of the case."

406 The Rules of the ITLOS reaffirm the need for both a written application and the notification of a special agreement to provide this information. Article 54(1) of the Rules of the Tribunal states: "When proceedings before the Tribunal are instituted by means of an application, the application shall indicate the party making it, the party against which the claim is brought and the subject of the dispute." The second sentence of Article 55(2) of the Rules of the Tribunal declares: "The notification [of a special agreement to the Registrar of the ITLOS] shall also, insofar as this is not already apparent from the agreement, indicate the precise subject of the dispute and identify the parties to it."

407 The Rules of the ITLOS provide particulars for both the written application and the notification of a special agreement, as follows. Article 54(4) of the Rules of the Tribunal proclaims: "The Registrar [of the ITLOS] shall forthwith transmit to the respondent a certified copy of the [written] application." The second sentence of Article 55(1) of the Rules of the ITLOS asseverates: "If the notification [of a special agreement to the Registrar of the Tribunal] is not a joint one [i.e., made by both disputants, then] a certified copy of it shall forthwith be communicated by the Registrar to any other party."

408 Fn 192 defines 'States Parties'.

409 The phrase '*in absentia*' is from Latin – literally 'in absence'; it means "while not present at the event being referred to" (Pearsall, J. (editor) (1998), *The New Oxford Dictionary of English*, 920).

410 This provision is substantially the same as the equivalent rule for the ICJ (text to fn 266).

411 Text to fn 267.

be excluded[412] [494, 495]. The ITLOS decides whether it has jurisdiction to adjudicate the dispute, if this is in question [496].

Like the procedure before the ICJ[413], the procedure at the ITLOS comprises written and oral proceedings[414]. The ITLOS provides orders for

---

412 The second sentence of Article 74 of the Rules of the ITLOS specifies: "Such a decision or request may concern either the whole or part of the hearing, and may be made at any time." This statement is identical to the second sentence of Article 59 of the ICJ's Rules of Court (fn 267), except that former uses the word 'request' in the place that the latter employs the word 'demand'.

413 The first sentence of the sixth paragraph of the subsection entitled 'A Summary of Jurisdictional and Procedural Aspects of the ICJ', in the section above titled 'The International Court of Justice' states this.

414 The written proceedings comprise the pleadings. Fn 248 defines 'pleadings' – please read the final sentence of fn 248 in the current context with 'ITLOS' replacing 'ICJ'. Whilst the ICJ's Rules of Court provide for the ICJ to decide whether or not to determine questions regarding its jurisdiction and/or the admissibility of the application prior to any judgment that it is to make on the merits of the case (fn 256), the Rules of the ITLOS contains an Article – Article 96 – which lays down preliminary proceedings in which the ITLOS judges whether the claim is an abuse of legal process or is well-founded pursuant to Article 294 of the UNCLOS; the subsection entitled 'Compulsory Procedures: Preliminary Proceedings', in the section titled 'Part XV of the UNCLOS: Settlement of Disputes' in Chapter 1, comprises Article 294 of the UNCLOS. Article 96 of the Rules of the ITLOS states: "1. When an application is made in respect of a dispute referred to in article 297 of the Convention [the subsection entitled 'Limitations to the Applicability of the Compulsory Procedures', in the section titled 'Part XV of the UNCLOS: Settlement of Disputes' in Chapter 1, consists of Article 297 of the UNCLOS], the Tribunal shall determine at the request of the respondent or may determine *proprio motu* [fn 215 defines '*proprio motu*'], in accordance with article 294 of the Convention, whether the claim constitutes an abuse of legal process or whether *prima facie* [fn 216 defines '*prima facie*'] it is well founded. ... 4. The request by the respondent for a determination under article 294 of the Convention shall be in writing and shall indicate the grounds for a determination by the Tribunal that: (a) the application is made in respect of a dispute referred to in article 297 of the Convention; and (b) the claim constitutes an abuse of legal process or is *prima facie* unfounded. 5. Upon receipt of such a receipt or *proprio motu*, the Tribunal, or the President [of the ITLOS] if the Tribunal is not sitting, shall fix a time-limit not exceeding 60 days within which the parties may present their written observations and submissions. The proceedings on the merits shall be suspended. 6. Unless the Tribunal decides otherwise, the further proceedings shall be oral. 7. The written observations and submissions referred to in paragraph 5 [above in this quote], and the statements and evidence presented at the hearings contemplated by paragraph 6 [above in this quote], shall be confined to those matters which are relevant to the determination of whether the claim constitutes an abuse of legal process or is *prima facie* unfounded, and of whether the application is made in respect of a dispute referred to in article 297 of the Convention. The Tribunal may, however, request the parties to argue all questions of law and fact, and to adduce all evidence, bearing on the issue. 8. The Tribunal shall make its determination in the form of a judgment." Article 294(3) of the UNCLOS (fn 212) separates the procedure for preliminary proceedings under Paragraphs 1 and 2 of Article 294 of the UNCLOS (the subsection entitled 'Compulsory Procedures: Preliminary Proceedings', in the section titled 'Part XV of the UNCLOS: Settlement of Disputes' in Chapter 1) from that for preliminary objections. Pursuant to Article 294(3) of the UNCLOS,

Article 97 of the Rules of the ITLOS specifies the following procedure for a party to lodge preliminary objections before the Tribunal: "1. Any objection to the jurisdiction of the Tribunal or to the admissibility of the application, or other objection the decision upon which is requested before any further proceedings on the merits, shall be made in writing within 90 days from the institution of proceedings. 2. The preliminary objection shall set out the facts and the law on which the objection is based as well as the submissions. 3. Upon receipt by the Registry of a preliminary objection, the proceedings on the merits shall be suspended and the Tribunal, or the President [of the ITLOS] if the Tribunal is not sitting, shall fix a time-limit not exceeding 60 days within which the other party may present its written observations and submissions. It shall fix a further time-limit not exceeding 60 days from the receipt of such observations and submissions within which the objecting party may present its written observations and submissions in reply. Copies of documents in support shall be annexed to such statements[,] and evidence which it is proposed to produce shall be mentioned. 4. Unless the Tribunal decides otherwise, the further proceedings shall be oral. 5. The written observations and submissions referred to in paragraph 3 [above in this quote], and the statements and evidence at the hearings contemplated by paragraph 4 [above in this quote], shall be confined to those matters which are relevant to the objection. Whenever necessary, however, the Tribunal may request the parties to argue all questions of law and fact and to adduce all evidence bearing on this issue. 6. The Tribunal shall give its decision in the form of a judgment, by which it shall uphold the objection or reject it or declare that the objection does not possess, in the circumstances of the case, an exclusively preliminary character. If the Tribunal rejects the objection or declares that it does not possess an exclusively preliminary character, [then] it shall fix time-limits for further proceedings. 7. The Tribunal shall give effect to any agreement between the parties that an objection submitted under paragraph 1 [above in this quote] be heard and determined within the framework of the merits." The main difference between preliminary proceedings under Article 96 of the Rules of the ITLOS and preliminary objections under Article 97 of the Rules of the ITLOS (both quoted above in this footnote) is that the former relates to a determination of whether the application amounts to an abuse of legal process or is *prima facie* unfounded, whilst the latter concerns: (i) whether the case is within the Tribunal's jurisdiction, (ii) whether the application is admissible, or (iii) any other issue upon which a decision is requested before the ITLOS judges the merits of the dispute. Another difference between preliminary proceedings before the ITLOS and preliminary objections regarding the Tribunal, is that the ITLOS may determine the first on its own initiative (i.e., *proprio motu*, which fn 215 defines), but not the second. Similarities between preliminary proceedings under Article 96 of the Rules of the ITLOS and preliminary objections under Article 97 of the Rules of the Tribunal include: (i) the proceedings on the merits are suspended in both cases, (ii) the further proceedings are oral, unless the ITLOS decides otherwise, (iii) the written observations and submissions, and the statements and evidence at the hearings, are limited to the matters that relate to subject of the preliminary proceedings, or to the preliminary objection, and (iv) in both of these preliminary procedures, the Tribunal takes its decision in the form of a judgment. The main difference between preliminary objections at the ITLOS under Article 97 of the Rules of the Tribunal (above in this footnote) and preliminary objections at the ICJ under Articles 79, 79*bis* and 79*ter* of the ICJ's Rules of Court (fn 256) is that, in the former, one of the parties must make the objection, whereas, in the latter, the ICJ may choose to decide whether or not questions regarding its jurisdiction and/or the admissibility of the application are to be determined before any proceedings on the merits are commenced and, only if the Court does not take this decision, may one of the parties lodge a preliminary objection there. Similarities between the procedure for preliminary objections at the ITLOS and that at the ICJ include: (i) in both, the party making the objection must put this into writing, (ii) the time period within which the party lodging the objection must do so is 90 days from the initiation of proceedings at the ITLOS, and three months after the submission of the Memorial (if the respondent makes the objection) or first pleading (if a party other than the respondent lodges the objection) at the ICJ, (iii) each preliminary objection is to lay down the law and facts on which it is based and the submissions, (iv) at both the ITLOS and the ICJ, the further proceedings are oral – unless the Tribunal or the Court (as appropriate) decides otherwise, (v) in respect of the procedure for preliminary objection(s), for the ITLOS the written observations and submissions, and the statements and evidence at the hearings, and for the ICJ the pleadings, are restricted to the matters that concern the preliminary objection(s), (vi) whenever requisite, both the ITLOS and the ICJ may ask the disputants to argue all issues of law and fact, and to adduce all the evidence, that affects the preliminary objection(s), and (vii) both the ITLOS and the ICJ give the decision in the form of a judgment. In *The M/V "Norstar" Case (Panama v. Italy)*, Italy made the following written preliminary objections: (i) it contended that the ITLOS had no jurisdiction over the current case because: (a) there was no dispute between Italy and Panama relating to the issues raised in the application, (b) Italy was not the proper respondent in the present case, and, anyhow, Panama's claim would inevitably necessitate the determination of rights and duties of a third country in the latter's absence from the current proceedings and without its consent, and (c) Panama had not suitably pursued the resolution of the dispute by negotiation or other peaceful means, as required by Article 283(1) of the UNCLOS (the first sentence of the subsection entitled 'Obligation for the Disputants to Exchange Views', in the section titled 'Part IV of the UNCLOS: Settlement of Disputes' in Chapter 1, comprises Article 283(1) of the UNCLOS); (ii) Italy argued that, were the ITLOS to hold that it had jurisdiction over the present case, notwithstanding the arguments in (i)(a)-(c) above, the claim of the applicant (i.e., Panama) was inadmissible because: (a) whilst Panama was preponderantly attempting to exercise diplomatic protection for the private persons affected by the alleged internationally-illegal conduct, the valid exercise of diplomatic protection does not apply as those entities neither possess Panamanian nationality nor have exhausted the local remedies that are available in the respondent state (i.e., Italy), and (ii) since Panama has neither filed an application for the swift release of the M/V Norstar nor meaningfully sought compensation for damages in the succeeding ten years in a legally-proper way, it is time-barred and estopped from validly laying the current case before the ITLOS due to the passing of eighteen years from the seizure of the ship and Panama's antithetical view all through that time (International Tribunal for the Law of the Sea (2016), Written Preliminary Objections under Article 294, Paragraph 3, of the United Nations Convention on the Law of the Sea: The M/V "Norstar" Case (Panama v. Italy) (Case No. 25, 10 March 2016) (Hamburg: International Tribunal for the Law of the Sea), 1-2). After following the procedure that Article 97 of the Rules of the Tribunal specifies (above in this footnote), the Tribunal ruled in favour of Panama, i.e., it found, by 21 votes to 1, that it had jurisdiction to settle the dispute, and, by 20 votes to 2, that Panama's application is admissible (International Tribunal for the Law of the Sea (2016), *The M/V "Norstar" Case (Panama v. Italy), Preliminary Objections*, Judgment of 4 November 2016, *ITLOS Reports 2016*, 44, para.316). In the judgment on the merits of the case, i.e., *The M/V "Norstar" Case (Panama v. Italy)*, dated 10th April 2019, the Tribunal found, by 15 votes to 7, that Italy was in breach of Article 87(1) of the UNCLOS, i.e., that the Decrees of Seizure against the M/V "Norstar", the Request for its implementation, and the arrest and detention of the ship were contrary to Panama's right to the freedom of the high seas, and, consequently, decided to award Panama compensation for the loss of this vessel to the amount of USD 285,000 with 2.7182% interest compounded annually and payable from 25th September 1998 until 10th April 2019; the seven judges who disagreed with these findings gave a joint dissenting opinion (International Tribunal for the Law of the Sea (2019), *The M/V*

the management of the case, determines the time and form in which each party is to wind up its arguments, and makes all arrangements associated with the collecting of evidence[415] [497].

The Written Proceedings

In the light of the disputants' opinions – as the President of the ITLOS ascertains, the Tribunal makes the orders that are necessary to determine: (i) the number, and the order of filing, of the pleadings, and (ii) the time-limits within which these are to be filed[416] [498]. Every pleading of each party must include the party's submissions at the relevant point in the case – separately from the arguments presented, or confirm the submissions made hitherto[417] [499]. The types of pleadings – i.e., memorial[418], counter-memorial[419], reply and rejoinder[420], the description of each type of

---

"Norstar" Case (Panama v. Italy), Judgment of 10 April 2019, *ITLOS Reports 2019*, nyp, paras.230 and 469). The subsection below entitled 'Example ITLOS Case – The M/V "Norstar" Case (Panama v. Italy)' provides information concerning the written and oral proceedings in *The M/V "Norstar" Case (Panama v. Italy)*.

415 This provision is almost identical to the corresponding rule for the ICJ, which is Article 48 of Annex VI to the UNCLOS (which the tenth sentence of the seventh paragraph of the subsection entitled 'A Summary of the Jurisdictional and Procedural Aspects of the ICJ', in the section above titled 'The International Court of Justice', rephrases).

416 The second sentence of Article 59(1) of the Rules of the ITLOS asserts: "The time-limits for each pleading shall not exceed six months." Article 59(2) of the Rules of the ITLOS states: "The Tribunal may at the request of a party extend any time-limit or decide that any step taken after the expiration of the time-limit fixed therefor shall be considered as valid. It may not do so, however, unless it is satisfied that there is adequate justification for the request. In either case the other party shall be given an opportunity to state its views within a time-limit to be fixed by the Tribunal." Article 59(3) of the Rules of the ITLOS declares: "If the Tribunal is not sitting, [then] its powers under this article [i.e., Article 59 of the Rules of the Tribunal – which this footnote and its accompanying text specify] may be exercised by the President of the Tribunal, but without prejudice to any subsequent decision of the Tribunal."

417 This provision – Article 62(4) of the Rules of the ITLOS – is identical to Article 49(4) of the ICJ's Rules of Court (fn 260).

418 Article 62(1) of the Rules of the ITLOS proclaims: "A memorial shall contain: a statement of the relevant facts, a statement of law and the submissions." Article 49(1) of the ICJ's Rules of Court (fn 257) comprises substantially the same statement as Article 62(1) of the Rules of the Tribunal.

419 Article 62(2) of the Rules of the ITLOS asseverates: "A counter-memorial shall contain: an admission or denial of the facts stated in the memorial; any additional facts, if necessary; observations concerning the statement of law in the memorial; a statement of law in answer thereto; and the submissions." Article 49(2) of the ICJ's Rules of Court (fn 258) contains essentially the same statement as Article 62(2) of the Rules of the Tribunal.

420 Article 62(3) of the Rules of the ITLOS asserts: "A reply and rejoinder shall not merely repeat the parties' contentions, but shall be directed to bringing out the issues that still divide

pleading[421], and the order of the pleadings[422], for the ITLOS are identical to those attributes of the pleadings for the ICJ[423], and – also like, and in a similar way to, the Court – the form of the pleadings for the Tribunal differs between cases begun by written application addressed to the Registrar of the ITLOS[424] and those started by notification to the Registrar of a special agreement between the parties[425]. Unless readily available,

them." Article 49(3) of the ICJ's Rules of Court (fn 259) consists of a very similar statement to that in Article 62(3) of the Rules of the Tribunal. The main difference between these provisions is the inclusion in former of the phrase 'whenever authorized by the Court', whose equivalent (i.e., 'whenever authorized by the Tribunal') is absent from the latter. However, as the ITLOS is required to authorize (or direct) the presentation of any reply/replies and rejoinder(s) (as fns 424-425 specify), the omission of this statement from Article 62(3) of the Rules of the Tribunal does not render that Paragraph significantly different to Article 49(3) of the ICJ's Rules of Court.

[421] Fns 418-420.

[422] A rejoinder (if authorized by the ITLOS) follows a reply (if authorized by the Tribunal), which follows a counter-memorial, which follows a memorial. Fns 257-259 and their accompanying text point to this ordering of pleadings before the ICJ.

[423] Fns 421-422.

[424] Article 60(1) of the Rules of the ITLOS states: "The pleadings in a case begun by means of an application shall consist, in the following order, of: a memorial by the applicant and a counter-memorial by the respondent." Article 45(1) of the ICJ's Rules of Court (fn 261) contains a statement which is almost identical to that in Article 60(1) of the Rules of the Tribunal. Article 60(2) of the Rules of the ITLOS declares: "The Tribunal may authorize or direct that there shall be a reply by the applicant and a rejoinder by the respondent if the parties are so agreed or if the Tribunal decides, at the request of a party or *propio motu*, that these pleadings are necessary." Fn 215 defines '*propio motu*'. Article 45(2) of the ICJ's Rules of Court (fn 261) comprises a statement which is very similar to that in Article 60(2) of the Rules of the ITLOS. The latter provision replaces the word 'Court' in the former Paragraph with the word 'Tribunal'.

[425] Article 61(1) of the Rules of the ITLOS proclaims: "In a case begun by the notification of a special agreement, the number and order of the pleadings shall be governed by the provisions of the agreement, unless the Tribunal, after ascertaining the views of the parties, decides otherwise." Article 46(1) of the ICJ's Rules of Court (fn 262) contains a statement that is identical to that in Article 61(1) of the Rules of the Tribunal – bar the substitution of the word 'Court' in the former provision with the word 'Tribunal' in the latter Paragraph. Article 61(2) of the Rules of the ITLOS asseverates: "If the special agreement contains no such provision [i.e., the 'provisions of the agreement' in Article 61(1) of the Rules of the Tribunal], and if the parties have not subsequently agreed on the number and order of pleadings, [then] they shall each file a memorial and counter-memorial, within the same time-limits." The first sentence of Article 46(2) of the ICJ's Rules of Court (fn 262) comprises a statement that is identical (save its capitalization of the first letter of the word 'memorial', and of the first and eighth letters of the hyphenated word 'counter-memorial') to that in Article 61(2) of the Rules of the ITLOS. Article 61(3) of the Rules of the Tribunal asserts: "The Tribunal shall not authorize the presentation of replies and rejoinders unless it finds them to be necessary." This statement is similar, but not identical, to that in the second sentence of Article 46(2) of the ICJ's Rules of Court (fn 262). The differences between Article 61(3) of the Rules of the ITLOS and the second sentence of Article 46(2) of the

relevant ancillary documentation must be attached to each pleading[426]. Upon receipt of each pleading and all documents annexed to it from one party, the Registrar of the ITLOS relays a certified copy of these items to the other disputant [500]. Copies of the pleadings and the documents attached thereto are made available to the public at the commencement of the oral proceedings – or earlier if the Tribunal (or the President of the ITLOS if the Tribunal is not sitting) so decides after consulting the parties [501]. After the written proceedings are concluded, and before the oral proceedings are initiated, the Tribunal convenes in private to enable judges to exchange opinions regarding the pleadings and the conduct of the litigation [502].

The Oral Proceedings

The ITLOS (or the President of the Tribunal if the ITLOS is not sitting) decides the date on which the oral proceedings are to begin, upon the cessation of the written proceedings[427] [503]. Following this closure,

---

ICJ's Rules of Court are: (i) the latter capitalizes the letter 'r' in the word 'replies', whilst the former does not capitalize that letter; (ii) the latter refers to 'the presentation of Replies', whilst the former mentions 'the presentation of replies *and rejoinders*', and (iii) the latter starts with the words 'The *Court*', whilst the former commences with the words 'The *Tribunal*'. It is submitted that, notwithstanding these differences, the working of these two provisions at the ITLOS and the ICJ, respectively, is substantially the same.

426 Article 63 of the Rules of the ITLOS states: "1. There shall be annexed to the original of every pleading certified copies of any relevant documents adduced in support of the contentions contained in the pleading. Parties need not annex or certify copies of documents which have been published and are readily available to the Tribunal and the other party. 2. If only parts of a document are relevant, [then] only such extracts as are necessary for the purpose of the pleading in question or for identifying the document need be annexed. A copy of the whole document shall be filed in the Registry, unless it has been published and is readily available to the Tribunal and the other party. 3. A list of all documents annexed to a pleading shall be furnished at the time the pleading is filed." Article 63 of the Rules of the ITLOS is very similar to Article 50 of the ICJ's Rules of Court (fn 260), the differences being: (i) the second sentence of Paragraph 1 of the former is absent from Paragraph 1 of the latter, (ii) the phrase 'or for identifying the document' in the first sentence Paragraph 2 of the former is missing from the first sentence of Paragraph 2 of the latter, (iii) in the second sentence of Paragraph 2 of the former, the document is to be *filed* in the Registry – whereas in the second sentence of Paragraph 2 of the latter, the document is to be *deposited* in the Registry, and (iv) the phrase 'to the Tribunal and the other party' in the second sentence of Paragraph 2 of the former is wanting from the second sentence of Paragraph 2 of the latter.

427 The date on which the oral proceedings are to commence "shall fall within a period of six months from the closure of the written proceedings unless the Tribunal is satisfied that there is adequate justification for deciding otherwise" (International Tribunal for the Law of the

neither disputant may submit any additional documents to the Tribunal except with the other party's consent or, if there is no such assent, if the ITLOS – after hearing the parties – authorizes the production of these items on deeming this to be necessary[428] [504]. In adequate time before the oral proceedings are initiated, each disputant must convey to the Registrar of the Court – together with a copy for communication to the other party – information about its evidence, including a list of the names, nationalities, descriptions and locations of residence of the witnesses and experts whom it intends to call – with signs as to the point(s) to which their evidence will be targeted[429] [505]. The Tribunal decides whether the disputants should present their arguments before or after the evidence is produced[430] [506]. After ascertaining the parties' views, the ITLOS determines the order in which they will present their arguments, the method of dealing with the evidence and of questioning the witnesses and experts, and the number of advocates and counsel representing each disputant to be heard[431] [507]. The oral statements that are made on each party's behalf must be as crisp

Sea (2009), Rules of the Tribunal adopted on 28 October 1997 – amended to 25 September 2018 (ITLOS/8, 17 March 2009), Article 69(1)).

[428] These rules are essentially the same as those applying to the ICJ (text to fn 264). The other party is held to have provided its consent if it does not put forward an objection to the document's production within 15 days of receiving this item (International Tribunal for the Law of the Sea (2009), Rules of the Tribunal adopted on 28 October 1997 – amended to 25 September 2018 (ITLOS/8, 17 March 2009), Article 71(1)). This provision differs from the corresponding rule for the ICJ (first sentence of fn 264) solely in the fact that the former adds to the latter a time limit of 15 days after which the other disputant is considered to have given consent to the production of the document if it has lodged no objection to that item being presented by this time.

[429] This provision is identical to the corresponding rule for the ICJ (which the fourth sentence of the seventh paragraph of the subsection entitled 'A Summary of the Jurisdictional and Procedural Aspects of the ICJ', in the section above titled 'The International Court of Justice', rephrases), save: (i) the replacement of the word 'Court' in the latter by the word 'Tribunal' in the former and, (ii) omission of the phrase 'in general terms' – present in the latter and rephrased in the text referred to above in this footnote as the adjective 'general' – from the former.

[430] This provision is the same – other than the substitution of the word 'Tribunal' for the word 'Court' – as its equivalent rule for the ICJ (text to fn 265). Furthermore, the second sentence of Article 73(1) of the Rules of the ITLOS, which states: "[T]he parties shall, however, retain the right to comment on the evidence given." is identical to the second sentence of Article 58(1) of the ICJ's Rules of Court (fn 265).

[431] This rule is fundamentally the same as that applying to the ICJ (sixth sentence of the seventh paragraph of the subsection entitled 'A Summary of the Jurisdictional and Procedural Aspects of the ICJ', in the section above titled 'The International Court of Justice').

as possible, given what is vital for the passable presentation of that disputant's arguments at the hearing[432] [508]. At the close of a party's final oral statement, its agent reads its last submissions, signs a copy of the written text of these, transmits them to the Tribunal and conveys them to the other disputant[433] [509]. At any time before or during the hearing, the Tribunal may indicate any matters to which it would like the parties to attend or on which it regards that there is no necessity for further argument[434] [510]. In the course of the hearing, the judges of the ITLOS may put questions to, and request explanations from, the agents, advocates and counsel[435] [511], who may answer either at once or within a time limit that the President of the Tribunal determines[436] [512]. The Tribunal may, at any time, request the parties to supply such evidence or explanations as it deems to be necessary for the clarification of any facet of the case, or may

---

[432] The second sentence of Article 75(1) of the Rules of the ITLOS declares: "Accordingly, they [i.e., the oral statements made on each disputant's behalf] shall be directed to the issues that still divide the parties, and shall not go over the whole ground covered by the pleadings or merely repeat the facts and arguments [that] these contain." This provision is identical to the corresponding rule for the ICJ (fn 269), bar the omission of a comma after the word 'pleadings'.

[433] This provision is indistinguishable from the equivalent rule for the ICJ (which the thirteenth sentence of the seventh paragraph of the subsection entitled 'A Summary of the Jurisdictional and Procedural Aspects of the ICJ', in the section above titled 'The International Court of Justice', rephrases), except for the replacement of the word 'Court' in the latter by the word 'Tribunal' in the former.

[434] This rule is substantially the same as the equivalent provision for the ICJ (which the fourteenth sentence of the seventh paragraph of the subsection entitled 'A Summary of the Jurisdictional and Procedural Aspects of the ICJ', in the section above titled 'The International Court of Justice', rephrases).

[435] This provision is identical to the corresponding rule for the ICJ (which the first part of the fifteenth sentence of the seventh paragraph of the subsection entitled 'A Summary of the Jurisdictional and Procedural Aspects of the ICJ', in the section above titled 'The International Court of Justice', rephrases), save the substitution of the word 'Court' in the latter with the word 'Tribunal' in the former. Article 76(3) of the Rules of the ITLOS proclaims: "Each judge has a similar right to put questions, but before exercising it he should make his intention known to the President of the Tribunal." This right also applies to judges at the ICJ, but with the President of the Court in the place of the President of the Tribunal in Article 76(3) of the Rules of the ITLOS (International Court of Justice (2019), Rules of Court (1978) adopted on 14 April 1978 and entered into force on 1 July 1978 – amended to 21 October 2019, Article 61(3)).

[436] This rule is the same as the corresponding provision for the ICJ (which the second part of the fifteenth sentence of the seventh paragraph of the subsection entitled 'A Summary of the Jurisdictional and Procedural Aspects of the ICJ', in the section above titled 'The International Court of Justice', rephrases), bar the addition of the words 'of the Tribunal' – which are absent from the latter – to the end of the former.

itself search for other information for this purpose[437] [513]. The disputants may call any witnesses or experts whose names are on the list conveyed to the Registrar of the ITLOS pursuant to Article 72 of its Rules[438] [514]. A disputant may call a witness or expert who is missing from the list, if either the other party does not object to this or the Tribunal authorizes that disputant to do so having heard the other party[439] [515]. Starting with the disputant calling each particular witness or expert, the parties' agents, advocates or counsel examine these witnesses and experts under the direction of the President of the Tribunal – who, together with other judges, may put questions to those witnesses and experts[440] [516]. At any time before concluding the oral proceedings, the ITLOS may, either at a party's request or *proprio motu*[441], ask "an appropriate intergovernmental organization" to produce information that is material to a case before it[442]

---

[437] This provision and its equivalent rule for ICJ (which the first part of the sixteenth sentence of the seventh paragraph of the subsection entitled 'A Summary of the Jurisdictional and Procedural Aspects of the ICJ', in the section above titled 'The International Court of Justice', rephrases) are exactly alike, except for the replacement of two occurrences of the word 'Court' in the latter by the word 'Tribunal' in the former. Article 77(2) of the Rules of the ITLOS states: "The Tribunal may, if necessary, arrange for the attendance of a witness or expert to give evidence in the proceedings." This statement is identical to that in Article 62(2) of the ICJ's Rules of Court (fn 270), save the replacement of the word 'Court' in the latter by the word 'Tribunal' in the former. Article 82 of the Rules of the Tribunal comprises two Paragraphs that are the same as the two Paragraphs of Article 67 of the ICJ's Rules of Court (fn 270), save the following differences between Article 82(1) of the Rules of the ITLOS and Article 67(1) of the ICJ's Rules of Court: (i) the word 'Court' in the latter is substituted with the word 'Tribunal' in the former, (ii) the word 'enquiry' in the latter is replaced by the word 'inquiry', and (iii) the former omits the comma that is placed immediately after the word 'experts' in the latter.

[438] The text to fn 429 describes this list. This rule is fundamentally the same as the corresponding provision for the ICJ (text to fn 271).

[439] This provision is similar – but not identical – to the corresponding rule for the ICJ (eighteenth sentence of the seventh paragraph of the subsection entitled 'A Summary of the Jurisdictional and Procedural Aspects of the ICJ', in the section above titled 'The International Court of Justice').

[440] This rule is similar to, and slightly more detailed than, the equivalent provision for the ICJ (nineteenth sentence of the seventh paragraph of the subsection entitled 'A Summary of the Jurisdictional and Procedural Aspects of the ICJ', in the section above titled 'The International Court of Justice').

[441] Fn 215 defines '*proprio motu*'.

[442] The second sentence of Article 84(1) of the Rules of the ITLOS states: "The Tribunal, after consulting the chief administrative officer of the organization concerned, shall decide whether such information shall be presented to it orally or in writing and fix the time-limits for its presentation." Article 84(1) of the Rules of the Tribunal is similar – but not identical – to Article 69(1) of the ICJ's Rules of Court, which, for instance, refers to "a public

[517]. Unless the ITLOS elects otherwise, all statements and speeches made, and evidence provided, at the hearing in one of the Tribunal's official languages are translated into the other official language[443] [518]. Minutes are made of every hearing; accordingly, the Registrar of the ITLOS makes a *verbatim*[444] record of each hearing, in the official language(s) of the Tribunal used throughout the oral proceedings[445] [519].

---

international organization" rather than "an appropriate intergovernmental organization" – which the former uses. Article 84(4) of the Rules of the ITLOS proclaims: "In the foregoing paragraphs [i.e., Paragraphs 1, 2 and 3 of Article 84 of the ITLOS], "intergovernmental organization" means an intergovernmental organization other than any organization which is a party or intervenes in the case concerned." This contrasts with Article 69(4) of the ICJ's Rules of Court, which declares: "In the foregoing paragraph, the term "public international organization" denotes an international organization of States." It is submitted that, given that the term 'public international organization' is present in Article 69(1) of the ICJ's Rules of Court – *as well as* in Article 69(3) of the ICJ's Rules of Court, Article 69(4) of the ICJ's Rules of Court *should* read: 'In the foregoing paragraph*s*, the term ...' (emphasis added). It is also submitted that the drafters of the Rules of the ITLOS must have noticed this mistake, when creating Article 84 of the Rules of the Tribunal, which they have adapted from Article 69 of the ICJ's Rules of Court; consequently, Article 84(4) of the Rules of the ITLOS begins: "In the foregoing paragraphs. ..."

443 The official languages of the ITLOS are English and French (text to fn 402). If these statements and speeches are made, and evidence furnished, in any other tongue, then they are translated into the Tribunal's official languages (International Tribunal for the Law of the Sea (2009), Rules of the Tribunal adopted on 28 October 1997 – amended to 25 September 2018 (ITLOS/8, 17 March 2009), Article 85(1)). Article 85(2) of the Rules of the ITLOS regulates the arrangements to be made for undertaking and verifying this translation: "Whenever a language other than an official language is used, the necessary arrangements for interpretation into one of the official languages shall be made by the party concerned. The Registrar [of the Tribunal] shall make arrangements for the verification of the interpretation provided by a party at the expense of that party. In the case of witnesses or experts who appear at the instance of the Tribunal, arrangements for interpretation shall be made by the Registrar."

444 Fn 268 defines '*verbatim*'.

445 Article 71(1) of the ICJ's Rules of Court contains a very similar statement, as applied to the ICJ (fn 268). Article 86(3) of the Rules of the ITLOS states: "The transcript of the verbatim record shall be preceded by the names of the judges present, and those of the agents, counsel and advocates of the parties."; this statement is identical to Article 71(3) of the ICJ's Rules of Court. Article 86(4) of the Rules of the ITLOS declares: "Copies of the transcript shall be circulated to the judges sitting in the case and to the parties. The latter may, under the supervision of the Tribunal, correct the transcripts of speeches and statements made on their behalf, but in no case may such corrections affect the meaning and scope thereof. The judges may likewise make corrections in the transcript of anything they have said."; this provision is essentially the same as Article 71(4) of the ICJ's Rules of Court (fn 268), differing from the latter only in the following respects: (i) the comma after the phrase 'sitting in the case' is omitted, (ii) the word 'Court' is replaced by the word 'Tribunal', (iii) the phrase 'the sense and bearing thereof' is substituted with the phrase 'the meaning and scope thereof', and (iv) the word 'may' is deleted in the last phrase, i.e., 'anything they may have said' becomes 'anything they have said'. Article 86(5) of the

If one of the disputants fails to appear before the ITLOS, or does not defend its case, then the other party may ask the Tribunal to persist with the proceedings and come to a decision[446]; before making this decision, the ITLOS must assure itself that its jurisdiction covers the dispute[447] and that the requester's claim is well-founded in both law and fact[448] [520]. All questions are decided by a majority of the Tribunal's sitting members[449] [521]. After the agents, advocates and counsel have finished their presentations before the ITLOS, the President of the Tribunal proclaims the hearing to be concluded[450] [522], at which point the Tribunal withdraws to deliberate over the judgment that it is to reach[451] [523].

Rules of the ITLOS proclaims: "Witnesses and experts shall be shown that part of the transcript which relates to the evidence given or the statements made by them, and may correct it in like manner as the parties."; this rule and Article 71(5) of the ICJ's Rules of Court (fn 268) are exactly alike, save the omission from the former of the comma after the word 'given' in the latter. Article 86(6) of the Rules of the ITLOS asseverates: "One certified copy of the corrected transcript, signed by the President of the Tribunal and the Registrar, shall constitute the authentic minutes of the hearing. The minutes of public hearings shall be printed and published by the Tribunal." This statement is substantially the same as its equivalent provision for the ICJ, which is Article 71(6) of the ICJ's Rules of Court (fn 268).

446 The second sentence of Article 28 of Annex VI to the UNCLOS asserts: "Absence of a party or failure of a party to defend its case shall not constitute a bar to the proceedings." Thus, *unlike* their equivalent provision for the ICJ (i.e., Article 53(1) of the Statute of the ICJ) – in which, when a disputant does not appear before the Court, the other party may request the ICJ to judge in favour of its legal claim (21st sentence of the seventh paragraph of the subsection entitled 'A Summary of the Jurisdictional and Procedural Aspects of the ICJ', in the section above titled 'The International Court of Justice'), the first and second sentences of Article 28 of Annex VI to the UNCLOS do *not* permit the solitary party to appear before the ITLOS or defend its case to ask the Tribunal to decide in favour of its lawsuit.

447 The second sentence of the first paragraph of the current subsection (i.e., that titled 'A Summary of the ITLOS' Jurisdictional and Procedural Aspects') specifies the jurisdiction of the Tribunal.

448 This provision (i.e., the third sentence of Article 28 of Annex VI to the UNCLOS) is essentially the same as its corresponding rule for the ICJ – which is Article 53(2) of the Statute of the ICJ (which the preantepenultimate sentence of the seventh paragraph of the subsection entitled 'A Summary of the Jurisdictional and Procedural Aspects of the ICJ', in the section above titled 'The International Court of Justice', rephrases).

449 This provision is substantially the same as the equivalent rule for the ICJ (text to fn 273). Article 29(2) of Annex VI to the UNCLOS states: "In the event of an equality of votes, the President or member of the Tribunal who acts in his place shall have a casting vote," which is essentially the same as the corresponding statement for the ICJ (fn 273).

450 This rule is almost identical to the corresponding provision for the ICJ (antepenultimate sentence of the seventh paragraph of the subsection entitled 'A Summary of the Jurisdictional and Procedural Aspects of the ICJ', in the section above titled 'The International Court of Justice'). The second sentence of Article 88(1) of the Rules of the

The Judgment Contains

(i) the names of the members of the ITLOS who have participated in the decision[452] [524, 525], (ii) the date on which that ruling is read[453] [526], (iii) the names of the disputants[454] [527], (iv) the names of the parties' agents, advocates and counsel[455] [528]. (v) the names of the experts, if any, who are appointed pursuant to Article 289 of the UNCLOS[456] [529], (vi) a synopsis of the proceedings[457] [530], (vii) the parties' submissions[458] [531], (viii) a statement of the facts of the case[459] [532], (ix) the reasons in law on which the decision is based[460] [533, 534], (x) the judgment's operative

---

ITLOS declares: "The agents shall remain at the disposal of the Tribunal," which has no equivalent in the provisions for the ICJ.

451 This provision is the same as the corresponding rule for the ICJ (first sentence of the eighth paragraph of the subsection entitled 'A Summary of the Jurisdictional and Procedural Aspects of the ICJ', in the section above titled 'The International Court of Justice'), except that the word 'Court' in the latter is replaced by the word 'Tribunal' in the former.

452 This provision is present in both Annex VI to the UNCLOS and the Rules of the ITLOS. It is essentially the same as the equivalent rule for the ICJ – which is contained in both the Statute of the ICJ and the ICJ's Rules of Court (point (ii) in the eighth sentence of the eighth paragraph of the subsection entitled 'A Summary of the Jurisdictional and Procedural Aspects of the ICJ', in the section above titled 'The International Court of Justice').

453 This provision is identical to its equivalent for the ICJ (point (i) in the eighth sentence of the eighth paragraph of the subsection entitled 'A Summary of the Jurisdictional and Procedural Aspects of the ICJ', in the section above titled 'The International Court of Justice').

454 This provision is identical to its equivalent for the ICJ (point (iii) in the eighth sentence of the eighth paragraph of the subsection entitled 'A Summary of the Jurisdictional and Procedural Aspects of the ICJ', in the section above titled 'The International Court of Justice').

455 This provision is identical to its equivalent for the ICJ (point (iv) in the eighth sentence of the eighth paragraph of the subsection entitled 'A Summary of the Jurisdictional and Procedural Aspects of the ICJ', in the section above titled 'The International Court of Justice').

456 This provision is unique to the ITLOS, i.e., it has no equivalent rule for the ICJ in either the Statute of the ICJ or the ICJ's Rules of Court. The first sentence of the subsection entitled 'Compulsory Procedure: Proceedings', in the section titled 'Part XV of the UNCLOS: Settlement of Disputes' in Chapter 1, comprises Article 289 of the UNCLOS.

457 This provision is identical to its equivalent for the ICJ (point (v) in the eighth sentence of the eighth paragraph of the subsection entitled 'A Summary of the Jurisdictional and Procedural Aspects of the ICJ', in the section above titled 'The International Court of Justice').

458 This provision is identical to its equivalent for the ICJ (point (vi) in the eighth sentence of the eighth paragraph of the subsection entitled 'A Summary of the Jurisdictional and Procedural Aspects of the ICJ', in the section above titled 'The International Court of Justice').

459 This provision is identical to its equivalent for the ICJ (point (vii) in the eighth sentence of the eighth paragraph of the subsection entitled 'A Summary of the Jurisdictional and Procedural Aspects of the ICJ', in the section above titled 'The International Court of Justice').

460 This provision is a combination of similar rules in Annex VI to the UNCLOS and the Rules of the ITLOS, both of which are referenced. It is essentially the same as an equivalent rule for the ICJ – which is an amalgamation of two provisions – one in the Statute of the ICJ and the other in the ICJ's Rules of Court (the fourth sentence, and point (viii) in the eighth sentence,

provisions[461] [535], (xi) the decision respecting costs[462] [536], (xii) "the number and names of the judges constituting the majority and those constituting the minority, on each operative provision"[463] [537], and (xiii)

---

respectively, of the eighth paragraph of the subsection entitled 'A Summary of the Jurisdictional and Procedural Aspects of the ICJ', in the section above titled 'The International Court of Justice').

[461] This provision is identical to its equivalent for the ICJ (point (ix) in the eighth sentence of the eighth paragraph of the subsection entitled 'A Summary of the Jurisdictional and Procedural Aspects of the ICJ', in the section above titled 'The International Court of Justice').

[462] This provision is identical to its equivalent for the ICJ (point (x) in the eighth sentence of the eighth paragraph of the subsection entitled 'A Summary of the Jurisdictional and Procedural Aspects of the ICJ', in the section above titled 'The International Court of Justice').

[463] This provision (i.e., Article 125(1)(m) of the Rules of the ITLOS) is more meticulous than the corresponding rule for the ICJ (point (xi) in the eighth sentence of the eighth paragraph of the subsection entitled 'A Summary of the Jurisdictional and Procedural Aspects of the ICJ', in the section above titled 'The International Court of Justice'), which only requires the listing of the judges in favour of the Court's primary decision in the case. It is submitted that the drafters of the Rules of the ITLOS were wise to develop this statement within the ICJ's Rules of Court for the particular circumstances of cases comprising matters relating to the Law of the Sea, as the Tribunal may be required to resolve multiple issues. For example, in *Delimitation of the maritime boundary in the Bay of Bengal (Bangladesh/Myanmar)*, the Tribunal determined six concerns, including an initial decision as to whether it had jurisdiction to delimit the maritime boundary between Bangladesh and Myanmar; the operative provision of the judgment – Paragraph 506 – listed, for the each of the five decisions in which there was at least one dissenting judge, a summary description of the determination reached by the majority of the members of the Tribunal (i.e., the judges present – of which there were 22 including two judges *ad hoc*), the number of judges who voted in favour of the view of the majority, the number of judges who voted against that view, the names of the concurring judges, and the name(s) of the dissenting judge(s) (International Tribunal for the Law of the Sea (2012), *Delimitation of the maritime boundary in the Bay of Bengal (Bangladesh/Myanmar)*, Judgment of 14 March 2012, *ITLOS Reports 2012*, 4, para.506). This comprises all the information that Article 125(1)(m) of the Rules of the ITLOS requires. It is also submitted that the ICJ should modify Article 95(1) of its Rules of Court in such a way that the judgments of the Court and of its chambers are – like those of the ITLOS and its chambers – required to publish 'the number and names of the judges constituting the majority, and those constituting the minority, on each operative provision'. In *Land, Island and Maritime Frontier Dispute (El Salvador/Honduras: Nicaragua intervening)*, considered in the subsection entitled 'Example ICJ Case – El Salvador/Honduras: Nicaragua intervening' in the section above titled 'The International Court of Justice', the operative part of the judgment – Paragraphs 425-432 – listed for each decision in which there a dissenting judge, the same information that Paragraph 506 of *Delimitation of the maritime boundary in the Bay of Bengal (Bangladesh/Myanmar)* provided for each decision that was not reached unanimously (see the third sentence of this footnote) (International Court of Justice (1992), *Land, Island and Maritime Frontier Dispute (El Salvador/Honduras: Nicaragua intervening)*, Judgment of 11 September 1992, *I.C.J. Reports 1992*, 351-618, 610-617).

an authoritative statement as to the text of the judgment[464] [538]. If the ruling does not represent, in whole or in part, the unanimous view of the Tribunal's members, then any member may supply a separate opinion[465] [539]. The judgment is signed by both the President and the Registrar, of the ITLOS, and is read out at a public sitting of the ITLOS – becoming binding on the disputants on the day on which it is read[466] [540, 541].

A disputant may make ask for the revision of a judgment only when this request is grounded upon the discovery of a fact that was, when the ITLOS made its decision, unknown to both it and the party claiming revision, and whose nature is such "as to be a decisive factor" – as long as this nescience was not caused by negligence[467]; the request must be made within six months of the learning of the new fact and ten years from the time of the judgment[468] [542]. The proceedings for revision are commenced by a judgment of the ITLOS, which records the existence of a new fact that has such a character as to render the case open to revision and

---

464 This provision is identical to its equivalent for the ICJ (point (xii) in the eighth sentence of the eighth paragraph of the subsection entitled 'A Summary of the Jurisdictional and Procedural Aspects of the ICJ', in the section above titled 'The International Court of Justice').

465 This rule is identical to the corresponding provision for the ICJ, save: (i) the replacement of the word 'judges' in the latter by the phrase 'members of the Tribunal' in the former, and (ii) the substitution of the word 'judge' in the latter with the word 'member' in the former. Article 125(2) of the Rules of the ITLOS states: "Any judge may attach a separate or dissenting opinion to the judgment; a judge may record concurrency or dissent without stating reasons in the form of a declaration. The same applies to orders." This provision is essentially the same as Article 95(2) of the ICJ (fn 274).

466 These rules are substantially the same as the corresponding provisions for the ICJ (seventh sentence of the eighth paragraph of the subsection entitled 'A Summary of the Jurisdictional and Procedural Aspects of the ICJ', in the section above titled 'The International Court of Justice'). As for each decision of the Court in cases before the ICJ (final sentence of the subsection entitled 'Basis for Determination of UNCLOS Disputes', in the section above titled 'The International Court of Justice'), each judgment of the ITLOS is only binding between the parties and with reference to their particular dispute (last sentence of the subsection entitled 'Basis for Determination of UNCLOS Disputes', above in the current section (i.e., that titled 'The International Tribunal for the Law of the Sea')).

467 This statement is almost identical to the corresponding provision for the ICJ (first sentence of the antepenultimate paragraph of the subsection entitled 'A Summary of Jurisdictional and Procedural Aspects of the ICJ', in the section above titled 'The International Court of Justice').

468 This statement is almost the same as the equivalent rule for the ICJ (penultimate sentence of the antepenultimate paragraph of the subsection entitled 'A Summary of Jurisdictional and Procedural Aspects of the ICJ', in the section above titled 'The International Court of Justice').

announces the application to be admissible on this basis[469] [543]. A request for this correction is made by an application which contains the details necessary to show that the above conditions are met[470] [544]. The other disputant is entitled to submit written comments on the admissibility of the application, within a time limit upon which the ITLOS decides – which are conveyed to the party making this request[471] [545]. If the Tribunal holds the application to be admissible, then it determines the time-limits for further proceedings on that request's merits which it considers to be necessary – after discovering the opinions of the disputants[472] [546]. If the ITLOS decides to render the admission of the proceedings for the revision of a judgment dependent on prior conformity with that ruling, then it makes and order to this effect[473] [547]. The decision on an application for

---

469 This provision is nearly identical to the corresponding rule for the ICJ (antepenultimate sentence of the antepenultimate paragraph of the subsection entitled 'A Summary of Jurisdictional and Procedural Aspects of the ICJ', in the section above titled 'The International Court of Justice').

470 This statement is almost the same as the equivalent rule for the ICJ (second sentence of the antepenultimate paragraph of the subsection entitled 'A Summary of Jurisdictional and Procedural Aspects of the ICJ', in the section above titled 'The International Court of Justice'). The second sentence of Article 128(1) of the Rules of the ITLOS states: "Any documents in support of the application shall be annexed to it," which is indistinguishable from the second sentence of Article 99(1) of the ICJ's Rules of Court (fn 279).

471 This provision is nearly identical to the corresponding rule for the ICJ (third sentence of the antepenultimate paragraph of the subsection entitled 'A Summary of Jurisdictional and Procedural Aspects of the ICJ', in the section above titled 'The International Court of Justice'). Article 128(3) of the Rules of the ITLOS declares: "The Tribunal, before giving its judgment on the admissibility of the application, may afford the parties a further opportunity of presenting their views thereon," which is the same as Article 99(3) of the ICJ's Rules of Court (fn 280), bar: (i) the replacement of the word 'Court' in the latter by the word 'Tribunal' in the former, and (ii) the addition of a comma to the former after the word 'application', which is absent from the latter.

472 This rule is almost identical to the equivalent provision for the ICJ (fourth sentence of the antepenultimate paragraph of the subsection entitled 'A Summary of Jurisdictional and Procedural Aspects of the ICJ', in the section above titled 'The International Court of Justice').

473 This provision is almost indistinguishable from the corresponding rule for the ICJ (fifth sentence of the antepenultimate paragraph of the subsection entitled 'A Summary of Jurisdictional and Procedural Aspects of the ICJ', in the section above titled 'The International Court of Justice').

interpretation[474] or revision of a judgment is provided in the form of a judgment[475] [548].

If a State Party[476] considers that it has a legal interest which may be affected by the judgment in any dispute before the ITLOS, then it may submit a request to the Tribunal to be allowed to intervene[477] [549], upon which the Tribunal will decide[478] [550]. If the ITLOS grants that State Party's request to intervene, then the Tribunal's decision regarding the dispute is binding upon the intervening State Party to the extent that it concerns issues in respect of which that country intervened[479] [551]. The

---

[474] Article 126(1) of the Rules of the ITLOS proclaims: "In the event of dispute as to the meaning or scope of a judgment, any party may make a request for its interpretation."

[475] This rule is essentially the same as the corresponding provision for the ICJ (final sentence of the antepenultimate paragraph of the subsection entitled 'A Summary of Jurisdictional and Procedural Aspects of the ICJ', in the section above titled 'The International Court of Justice').

[476] Fn 192 defines 'States Parties'.

[477] This provision is substantially the same as the equivalent provision for the ICJ (first two lines of the penultimate paragraph of the subsection entitled 'A Summary of Jurisdictional and Procedural Aspects of the ICJ', in the section above titled 'The International Court of Justice'). Article 99(1) of the Rules of the Tribunal asseverates: "An application for permission to intervene under the terms of Article 31 of the [ITLOS] Statute [i.e., Annex VI to the UNCLOS, Article 31(1) of which the text to this footnote specifies] shall be not later than 30 days after the counter-memorial becomes available under article 67, paragraph 1, of these Rules. In exceptional circumstances, an application submitted at a later stage may[,] however[,] be admitted." Article 67(1) of the Rules of the ITLOS asserts: "Copies of the pleadings and documents annexed thereto shall, as soon as possible after their filing, be made available by the Tribunal to a State or other entity entitled to appear before the Tribunal and which has asked to be furnished with such copies. However, if the party submitting the memorial so requests, the Tribunal shall make the memorial available at the same time as the counter-memorial." Article 99(1) of the Rules of the ITLOS is very similar to Article 81(1) of the ICJ's Rules of Court (fn 283), save the following difference: the latter places the time-limit for the application for permission to intervene at the conclusion of the written proceedings, whilst the former sets this time-limit at 30 days after the counter-memorial becomes available.

[478] This rule is identical to the corresponding provision for the ICJ (last six words of the first sentence of the penultimate paragraph of the subsection entitled 'A Summary of Jurisdictional and Procedural Aspects of the ICJ', in the section above titled 'The International Court of Justice'), except for the substitution of the word 'Court' in the latter with the word 'Tribunal' in the former.

[479] This provision (i.e., Article 31(3) of Annex VI to the UNCLOS) has no equivalent in the rules that concern the ICJ – in particular Article 62 of the Statute of the ICJ and Article 81 of the ICJ's Rules of Court. Notwithstanding this, Article 31(3) of the ITLOS Statute is similar to Article 63(2) of the Statute of the ICJ (text to fn 285). In *Land, Island and Maritime Frontier Dispute (El Salvador/Honduras: Nicaragua intervening)*, the Chamber of the ICJ held that the intervening state – Nicaragua – was not bound by the judgment given in the proceedings in which that Chamber, in *Land, Island and Maritime Frontier Dispute (El*

Salvador/Honduras), Application to Intervene, had permitted that country to intervene (quoted passages containing fns 328-330). Then, it ruled that the principle of *res judicata* (fn 331) only applied to an intervening state when that country was also a party to the case in which the ICJ had allowed the intervention (text to fn 331). Judge Oda's declaration in *Land, Island and Maritime Frontier Dispute (El Salvador/Honduras: Nicaragua intervening)* queries these findings of the Chamber in the same case, and states in specific terms that Nicaragua, as an intervening state which is not a party to the proceedings, is nevertheless bound by the judgment in so far as this decision directly affects that country (paragraph containing fns 342-344). Judge *ad hoc* Torres Bernárdes' individual opinion in *Land, Island and Maritime Frontier Dispute (El Salvador/Honduras: Nicaragua intervening)* endorses the Chamber's view in the same case that the judgment is not *res judicata* for Nicaragua, and proceeds to extend the principle within Article 63(2) of the Statute of the ICJ (text to fn 285) into Article 62 of the Statute of the ICJ *mutatis mutandis* (quoted passage containing fns 346-352). Fn 351 elucidates the effect of this expansion, referring to *Land, Island and Maritime Frontier Dispute (El Salvador/Honduras: Nicaragua intervening)*, and indicates that, had the Chamber giving judgment therein taken the approach to intervention that Judge Torres Bernárdes suggested, the result in respect of the binding effect of the relevant parts of the Chamber's judgment for Nicaragua would be similar to that which Judge Oda posited in his declaration – even though these two judges differed in their views as to whether this judgment was *res judicata* for the intervening state. It is submitted that Article 31(3) of Annex VI to the UNCLOS (text to this footnote) disregards the issue of *res judicata*, addressing specifically the extent to which the relevant decision of the ITLOS *should* be binding upon an intervening state – which produces a textual outcome that is consistent with the opinions expressed in Judge Oda's declaration *and* Judge Torres Bernárdes' individual opinion in *Land, Island and Maritime Frontier Dispute (El Salvador/Honduras: Nicaragua intervening)*. It is further submitted that this omission by the drafters of the ITLOS Statute (i.e., Annex VI to the UNCLOS) has led to a constructive contradiction between two provisions of that Statute as to the extent that a decision of the Tribunal is binding upon an intervening state. Whilst Article 33(1) of Annex VI to the UNCLOS states that a judgment of the Tribunal "ha[s] no binding force except between *the parties* in respect of that particular dispute" (emphasis added), Article 31(3) of Annex VI to the UNCLOS specifies that this decision is "binding upon the intervening State Party in so far as it relates to matters in respect of which that State Party intervened." In *Land, Island and Maritime Frontier Dispute (El Salvador/Honduras), Application to Intervene*, the Chamber held that an intervening state does *not* become a party to the legal proceedings (point (i) of the text to fn 318). Thus, *to the extent that this judgment of the ICJ is precedent for cases before the ITLOS*, Article 33(1) of the ITLOS Statute implies that any judgment of the Tribunal is *not* binding upon an intervening state in the proceedings on which that decision is based, because such a country is not a party to those proceedings. *This construction of Article 33(1) of the ITLOS Statute* is contradictory to Article 31(3) of the ITLOS Statute. To address this difficulty, if Article 31(3) of the ITLOS Statute were to be made an exception to Article 33(1) of the ITLOS Statute, then there would be no contradiction between these two provisions. To achieve this result, Article 33(1) of the Annex VI to the UNCLOS should be altered to read the following (emphasis added to show the changes): "*Without prejudice to paragraph 3 of article 31 of this Annex, t*he decision *of the Tribunal* shall have no binding force except between the parties in respect of that particular dispute."

application for permission to intervene states an agent's name and address, and indicates the case to which it relates[480] [552]. It specifies: (i) the legal interest which the State Party applying to intervene considers may be affected by the decision[481] [553], (ii) "the precise object of the intervention"[482] [554], and (iii) a list of supporting documents – copies of which are attached[483] [555]. The Tribunal may grant an applicant State Party "[p]ermission to intervene under the terms of [A]rticle 31 of the [ITLOS] Statute," regardless of whether the applicant has selected the ITLOS, the ICJ[484], an arbitral tribunal established in line with Annex VII to the UNCLOS[485], and/or a special arbitral tribunal founded in conformity

---

[480] These requirements are similar to those for the ICJ (second sentence of the penultimate paragraph of the subsection entitled 'A Summary of Jurisdictional and Procedural Aspects of the ICJ', in the section above titled 'The International Court of Justice'), differing in that the former call for the application to provide the agent's address whilst the latter omit this item.

[481] This provision is almost identical to the equivalent term for the ICJ (point (i) of the final sentence of the penultimate paragraph of the subsection entitled 'A Summary of Jurisdictional and Procedural Aspects of the ICJ', in the section above titled 'The International Court of Justice').

[482] This provision – Article 99(2)(b) of the Rules of the ITLOS – is identical to the corresponding term for the ICJ (Article 81(2)(b) of the ICJ's Rules of Court, i.e., point (ii) of the final sentence of the penultimate paragraph of the subsection entitled 'A Summary of Jurisdictional and Procedural Aspects of the ICJ', in the section above titled 'The International Court of Justice'), except that the semi-colon at the end of the latter Subparagraph is replaced by a full stop in the former Subparagraph – which is due to the non-replication of Article 81(2)(c) of the ICJ's Rules of Court (point (iii) of the final sentence of the penultimate paragraph of the subsection entitled 'A Summary of Jurisdictional and Procedural Aspects of the ICJ', in the section above titled 'The International Court of Justice') as Article 99(2)(c) of the Rules of the ITLOS, the latter consequently being non-existent.

[483] This provision is essentially the same as the equivalent term for the ICJ (point (iv) of the final sentence of the penultimate paragraph of the subsection entitled 'A Summary of Jurisdictional and Procedural Aspects of the ICJ', in the section above titled 'The International Court of Justice').

[484] It is submitted that, if the ICJ hears the subsequent dispute, then the Court's rules would regulate any implications with regard to an intervening state. Thus, pursuant to its judgment in *Land, Island and Maritime Frontier Dispute (El Salvador/Honduras: Nicaragua intervening)*, the decision of the ICJ on the merits of the case would not be binding on the intervening state (third sentence of fn 479).

[485] It is submitted that, if an arbitral tribunal constituted in accordance with Annex VII to the UNCLOS (fn 196) adjudicates the subsequent dispute, then the rules that this Annex contains – and decrees of the arbitral tribunal pursuant to those rules – would direct any implications in respect of an intervening state. As Article 11 of Annex VII to the UNCLOS (last sentence of fn 196) is silent as to whether or not an intervening party is required to comply with the award of the arbitral tribunal, and as the first sentence of Article 12(1) of Annex VII to the UNCLOS states: "Any controversy which may arise between the parties to

with Annex VIII to the UNCLOS[486], to settle its disputes concerning the interpretation or application of the UNCLOS [556, 274].

If the interpretation or application of the UNCLOS is in question, then the Registrar of the ITLOS notifies all States Parties[487] immediately[488] [557]. If, pursuant to Article 21[489] or 22[490] of Annex VI to the UNCLOS, the interpretation or application of an international agreement (other than the UNCLOS[491]) is in question, then the Registrar of the Tribunal informs

---

the dispute as regards the interpretation or manner of implementation of the award may be submitted by either party for decision to the arbitral tribunal which made the award," it is submitted that, *unless all the disputants agree otherwise* (in line with Article 12(2) of Annex VII to the UNCLOS, which declares: "Any such controversy may be submitted to another court or tribunal under article 287 [of the UNCLOS] by agreement of all the parties to the dispute."), *the arbitral tribunal should decide issues concerning the intervening state* – including, if necessary, the extent to which the constituent elements of the award are binding upon that country.

[486] It is submitted that, if a special arbitral tribunal founded in compliance with Annex VIII to the UNCLOS (fn 197) tries the subsequent dispute, then the rules which that Annex contains – and orders of the special arbitral tribunal pursuant to those rules – would govern any implications in connection with an intervening state. As Articles 4-13 of Annex VII to the UNCLOS "apply *mutatis mutandis* to the special arbitration proceedings in accordance with this Annex [i.e., Annex VIII to the UNCLOS]" (United Nations (1982), "United Nations Convention on the Law of the Sea," Annex VIII, Article 4), pursuant to the second sentence of fn 485 *the special arbitral tribunal should determine matters concerning the intervening state unless all the disputants agree elsewise*. Fn 140 defines '*mutatis mutandis*'.

[487] Fn 192 defines 'States Parties'.

[488] Whilst this provision is similar to the corresponding rule for the ICJ (first sentence of the final paragraph of the subsection entitled 'A Summary of Jurisdictional and Procedural Aspects of the ICJ', in the section above titled 'The International Court of Justice'), there are the following differences: (i) the former concerns the interpretation or application of the UNCLOS, whilst the latter relates to the construction of a multilateral convention to which both disputants in the current case are parties, (ii) the former involves the Registrar of the ITLOS, whilst the latter includes the Registrar of the ICJ, and (iii) the former requires all States Parties to the UNCLOS to be notified, whilst the latter necessitates all states that are parties to the multilateral convention whose construction is in question, other than the disputants in the present case, to be notified.

[489] Points (i) and (ii) of the second sentence of the first paragraph of the current subsection (i.e., that titled 'A Summary of the ITLOS' Jurisdictional and Procedural Aspects') comprise Article 21 of Annex VI to the UNCLOS. It is point (ii) only that is relevant to the sentence (in the text) of which this footnote is part, as point (i) refers to the UNCLOS – which the text to fn 488 covers.

[490] Point (iii) of the second sentence of the first paragraph of the present subsection (i.e., that titled 'A Summary of the ITLOS' Jurisdictional and Procedural Aspects') consists of Article 22 of Annex VI to the UNCLOS.

[491] Whilst this provision, i.e., Article 32(2) of Annex VI to the UNCLOS, does not refer to the UNCLOS, the rule in the immediately-preceding sentence, i.e., Article 32(1) of Annex VI to the UNCLOS, covers that Convention.

all the parties to that agreement[492] [558]. Whilst each of these parties[493] is entitled to intervene in the legal proceedings at the ITLOS, if it utilizes this right then the interpretation that the judgment provides is equally binding on it[494] [559]. The declaration[495] states an agent's name and address, and

---

[492] Similarly to Article 32(1) of Annex VI to the UNCLOS (text to fn 488), the current provision (i.e., Article 32(2) of Annex VI to the UNCLOS) corresponds to Article 63(1) of the Statute of the ICJ (first sentence of the final paragraph of the subsection entitled 'A Summary of Jurisdictional and Procedural Aspects of the ICJ', in the section above titled 'The International Court of Justice'). Whilst Article 32(2) of the ITLOS Statute and Article 63(1) of the Statute of the ICJ are similar in that they both concern the interpretation of international agreements, they differ in the following respects: (i) the former includes the Registrar of the ITLOS, whilst the latter involves the Registrar of the ICJ, (ii) the former requires *all* parties to the international agreement whose interpretation or application is in question to be notified, whilst the latter necessitates all states that are parties to the multilateral convention whose construction is in question, *other than the disputants in the present case*, to be informed, and (iii) the former does *not* require the parties to the international agreement to be notified without delay, whilst the latter *does* so require.

[493] Article 32(3) of Annex VI to the UNCLOS specifies: "Every party referred to in paragraphs 1 and 2," i.e., Article 32(1) and Article 32(2) of Annex VI to the UNCLOS, which the first sentence, and the second sentence, respectively, of the present paragraph in the text, contain.

[494] This rule is essentially the same as the equivalent provision for the ICJ (text to fn 285). Similarly to the constructive contradiction that fn 479 identifies between Article 33(1) of Annex VI to the UNCLOS and Article 31(3) of Annex VI to the UNCLOS, there is a constructive contradiction between the former and Article 32(3) to the UNCLOS (text to the current footnote). In order to ensure that there is no contradiction between the former (i.e., Article 33(1) of the ITLOS Statute) and the latter (i.e., Article 32(3) of the ITLOS Statute), the latter should be made an exception to the former. Thus, the modified version of Article 33(1) of Annex VI to the UNCLOS in the last sentence of fn 479 should be altered further to read the following (emphasis added to show the *additional* changes): "Without prejudice to paragraph 3 of article 31 of this Annex *and paragraph 3 of article 32 of this Annex,* the decision of the Tribunal shall have no binding force except between the parties in respect of that particular dispute." There is also a contradiction between Article 59 of the Statute of the ICJ (final sentence of the subsection entitled 'Basis for Determination of UNCLOS Disputes', in the section above titled 'The International Court of Justice') and Article 63(2) of the Statute of the ICJ (text to fn 285). Article 59 of the Statute of the ICJ states that the Court's judgment in any case binds *the parties only* and as regards that specific case. Article 63(2) of the Statute of the ICJ holds that *states which intervene in a case* that involves the construction of a convention to which they are party *are bound by the construction of that convention which the judgment in this case provides*. In *Land, Island and Maritime Frontier Dispute (El Salvador/Honduras), Application to Intervene*, the Chamber held, at Paragraph 102 of its judgment, that *an intervening state does not become party to the proceedings* (point (i) of the text to fn 318; International Court of Justice (1990), *Land, Island and Maritime Frontier Dispute (El Salvador/Honduras), Application to Intervene*, Judgment of 13 September 1990, *I.C.J. Reports 1990*, 92-137, 135-136). However, this statement of the Chamber in *Land, Island and Maritime Frontier Dispute (El Salvador/Honduras), Application to Intervene* is pursuant to an intervention under Article 62 of the Statute of the ICJ, rather than an intervention pursuant to Article 63 of the Statute of the ICJ – which concerns the construction by the Court (or a Chamber of the Court) of a convention. To

explore whether that statement is likely to apply in the case of an intervention under Article 63 of the Statute of the ICJ, it is advisable to inspect the ground(s) on which the Chamber in *Land, Island and Maritime Frontier Dispute (El Salvador/Honduras), Application to Intervene* made it, i.e., on which the Chamber held that an intervening state does not become party to the proceedings. In the quoted passage containing fns 312-317, the Chamber mentions procedures for intervention under Articles 62 *and 63* of the Statute of the ICJ, but then proceeds to discuss intervention in the context of the jurisdictional link mentioned by Article 81(2)(c) of the ICJ's Rules of Court – which corresponds to intervention under *Article 62* of the Statute of the ICJ *only* (point (iii) of the last sentence of the penultimate paragraph of the subsection entitled 'A Summary of Jurisdictional and Procedural Aspects of the ICJ', in the section above titled 'The International Court of Justice'); notwithstanding this, the Chamber – in that quoted passage – makes the following points concerning intervention that *may be considered to be of a general nature*, i.e., *broader* than the scope of intervention under Article 62 of the Statute of the ICJ: (i) the ICJ's competence in the matter of intervention is derived from the consent given by the disputants, in becoming parties to the Statute of the ICJ, to the Court's exercise of its powers conferred on it by that Statute – including those conferred on the ICJ by Article 62 of the Statute of the ICJ – *and (it is now submitted) by inference, the powers conferred on the Court by Article 63 of the Statute of the ICJ*; (ii) a state that is permitted to intervene in a case does *not*, by reason only of being an intervener, *become also a party to that case* – but is *not prevented* by this status from so becoming *if the disputants provide the necessary consent*; (iii) the procedure of intervention is to make sure that a state with possibly-affected interests may be allowed to intervene *even though there is no jurisdictional link between that country and the disputants and, therefore, it cannot become a party to the case*. It is submitted, *on the basis of these points*, that the statement of the Chamber of the ICJ in Paragraph 102 of its judgment in *Land, Island and Maritime Frontier Dispute (El Salvador/Honduras), Application to Intervene* that an intervening state does not become party to the proceedings (above in this footnote), applies to an intervention under Article 63 of the Statute of the ICJ. Thus, *pursuant to the ICJ's case law* – in the form of the above interpretation of the Chamber's judgment in *Land, Island and Maritime Frontier Dispute (El Salvador/Honduras), Application to Intervene*, there exists a contradiction between Article 59 of the Statute of the ICJ and Article 63(2) of the Statute of the ICJ – which, like the constructive contradictions present in the ITLOS Statute (i.e., Annex VI to the UNCLOS) that are identified in fn 479 and above in the current footnote (i.e., fn 494), may be addressed by making Article 63(2) of the Statute of the ICJ an exception to Article 59 of the Statute of the ICJ. To accomplish this result, Article 59 of the Statute of the ICJ should be amended to read the following (emphasis added to show the modifications): "*Without prejudice to Paragraph 2 of Article 63, t*he decision of the Court has no binding force except between the parties in respect of that particular case."

[495] Article 100(1) of the Rules of the ITLOS states: "A State Party or [other] entity ... referred to in article 32, paragraphs 1 and 2, of the [ITLOS] Statute [i.e., Annex VI to the UNCLOS (text to fns 488 and 492)] which desires to avail itself of the right of intervention conferred upon it by article 32, paragraph 3, of the Statute [(text to fn 494)] shall file a declaration to that effect ... not later than 30 days after the counter-memorial becomes available under article 67, paragraph 1, of these Rules [(fn 477)]. In exceptional circumstances, a declaration submitted at a later stage may, however, be admitted." Whilst Article 100(1) of the Rules of the ITLOS is analogous to Article 82(1) of the ICJ's Rules of Court (fn 286), there are the following differences between these provisions: (i) the latter refers to 'states', whereas the former makes reference to 'States Parties' (fn 487), (ii) the latter mentions Article 63 of the Statute of the ICJ (first and second sentences of the last paragraph of the subsection entitled 'A Summary of Jurisdictional and Procedural Aspects of the ICJ', in the

the case to which it relates[496] [560]. It identifies the specific provisions of the international agreement, the interpretation or application of which the declarant deems to be in question[497] [561], presents the particular interpretation or application of those rules for which it contends[498] [562], and lists the supporting documents – copies of which are attached[499] [563].

Proceedings before the Chamber for Fisheries Disputes[500], the Chamber for Marine Environment Disputes[501], the Chamber for Maritime Delimitation Disputes[502], any other standing special chamber of the ITLOS[503], any *ad hoc* special chamber of the Tribunal[504], and the Chamber

---

section above titled 'The International Court of Justice'), whilst the former refers separately to each Paragraph of Article 32 of Annex VI to the UNCLOS (text to fns 488, 492 and 494), and (iii) the latter places the time-limit for the application for permission to intervene at the start of the oral proceedings, whilst the former puts this time-limit at 30 days after the counter-memorial becomes available.

[496] These requirements overlap with the corresponding specifications for the ICJ (third sentence of the final paragraph of the subsection entitled 'A Summary of Jurisdictional and Procedural Aspects of the ICJ', in the section above titled 'The International Court of Justice') – whilst the latter but not the former include the title of the convention to which the declaration relates, the former but not the latter include the address of the agent. It is submitted that it is unnecessary for the declaration to separately state the title of the relevant convention, because both the ICJ's Rules of Court and the Rules of the ITLOS require the declarant to identify the provisions of that agreement whose construction it considers to be in question (fn 497 and accompanying text).

[497] This rule is essentially the same as the equivalent provision for the ICJ (point (ii) of the final sentence of the last paragraph of the subsection entitled 'A Summary of Jurisdictional and Procedural Aspects of the ICJ', in the section above titled 'The International Court of Justice'). Unlike a declaration made under Article 63 of the Statute of the ICJ and Article 82 of the ICJ's Rules of Court (point (i) of the final sentence of the last paragraph of the subsection entitled 'A Summary of Jurisdictional and Procedural Aspects of the ICJ', in the section above titled 'The International Court of Justice'), a declaration made under Article 32 of Annex VI to the UNCLOS and Article 100 of the Rules of the ITLOS does *not* require a statement of the particulars of the ground upon which the declarant considers itself to be a party to the international agreement to which the declaration relates.

[498] This provision is very similar to the corresponding rule for the ICJ (point (iii) of the final sentence of the last paragraph of the subsection entitled 'A Summary of Jurisdictional and Procedural Aspects of the ICJ', in the section above titled 'The International Court of Justice').

[499] This rule is almost identical to the equivalent provision for the ICJ (point (iv) of the final sentence of the last paragraph of the subsection entitled 'A Summary of Jurisdictional and Procedural Aspects of the ICJ', in the section above titled 'The International Court of Justice').

[500] Fn 385 describes the Chamber for Fisheries Disputes.

[501] Fn 386 describes the Chamber for Marine Environment Disputes.

[502] Fn 387 describes the Chamber for Maritime Delimitation Disputes.

[503] Article 15(1) of Annex VI to the UNCLOS empowers the ITLOS to form standing special chambers to address particular classes of disputes (first sentence of the fifth paragraph of

of Summary Procedure[505], are governed by those Rules of the Tribunal that apply in contentious cases before the ITLOS – subject to the provisions of the UNCLOS[506] and of the Rules[507] that specifically concern these special chambers [564]. If "it is desired that" a particular standing special chamber of the ITLOS or the Chamber of Summary Procedure should hear a case, then the document initiating the proceedings or an accompanying paper should contain this request – which should be granted if the disputants so concur[508] [565]. A request that a dispute be brought before an *ad hoc* special chamber of the ITLOS is effected promptly after this chamber has been established in conformity with Article 30 of the Rules of the Tribunal[509] [566]. The President of the ITLOS convokes the *ad hoc* special

---

the current subsection (i.e., that entitled 'A Summary of the ITLOS' Jurisdictional and Procedural Aspects')).

[504] Article 15(2) of Annex VI to the UNCLOS authorizes the ITLOS to establish a chamber to adjudicate a particular dispute (i.e., an *ad hoc* special chamber), if its disputants request this (first sentence of the sixth paragraph of the present subsection (i.e., that entitled 'A Summary of the ITLOS' Jurisdictional and Procedural Aspects')). Fn 207 defines '*ad hoc*', and states that an *ad hoc* chamber is founded for a particular purpose or to address a specific situation.

[505] Article 15(3) of Annex VI to the UNCLOS requires the Tribunal to establish every year a chamber to hear and settle disputes by summary procedure (text to fn 390). This chamber is named the Chamber of Summary Procedure (text to fn 391).

[506] Article 107 of the Rules of the ITLOS refers here to "provisions of the Convention [(i.e., the UNCLOS)], the Statute and these Rules." As Annex VI to the UNCLOS comprises the ITLOS Statute, express referral to the latter at this point in the text is unnecessary. Therefore, the term 'the ITLOS Statute' is omitted.

[507] Articles 108 and 109 of the Rules of the Tribunal concern proceedings before the special chambers of the ITLOS to which the current sentence in the text refers. Paragraphs 1, 3 and 4 of Article 108 of the Rules of the ITLOS respectively form the subject-matter of the three succeeding statements in the present paragraph of the text. Fn 508 contains Paragraph 2 of the last-mentioned Article. Fn 510 comprises Article 109 of the Rules of the Tribunal, and observations on the extent of the similarity of each of its constituent Paragraphs to the equivalent Paragraph in Article 92 of the ICJ's Rules of Court (fn 281).

[508] Article 108(2) of the Rules of the ITLOS states: "Upon receipt by the Registry [of the ITLOS] of this request, the President of the Tribunal shall communicate it to the members of the chamber concerned."

[509] Article 30 of the Rules of the Tribunal contains the following four Paragraphs: "1. A request for the formation of a special chamber to deal with a particular dispute, as provided for in article 15, paragraph 2, of the [ITLOS] Statute [i.e., Annex VI to the UNCLOS (fn 504)], shall be made within two months from the date of the institution of proceedings. Upon receipt of a request made by one party, the President of the Tribunal shall ascertain whether the other party assents. 2. When the parties have agreed, the President of the Tribunal shall ascertain their views regarding the composition of the chamber and shall report to the Tribunal accordingly. 3. The Tribunal shall determine, with the approval of the parties, the Members who are to constitute the chamber [and] the quorum for meetings of the chamber.

chamber at the soonest date that is consistent with the procedural requirements[510] [567].

Example ITLOS Case – The M/V "Norstar" Case (Panama v. Italy)

The Written Proceedings

On 17th December 2015, Panama filed a written application (dated 16th November 2015) with the Registry of the ITLOS, instituting proceedings against Italy in connection with Italy's arrest and detention of the M/V Norstar, an oil tanker owned by the Norwegian-registered company *Inter Marine & Co AS*, and flying the Panamanian flag [568]. In its application, Panama: (i) invoked the declarations that the disputants made in

4. Members of a chamber formed under this article who have been replaced … following the expiration of their terms of office, shall continue to sit in all phases of the case, whatever the stage it has then reached."

[510] Article 109 of the Rules of the Tribunal contains the following procedural requirements for special chambers of the ITLOS: "1. Written proceedings in a case before a chamber shall consist of a single pleading by each party. The time-limits concerning the filing of written pleadings shall be fixed by the chamber, or its President if the chamber is not sitting. 2. The chamber may authorize or direct the filing of further pleadings if the parties are so agreed, or if the chamber decides, *proprio motu* or at the request of one of the parties, that such pleadings are necessary. 3. Oral proceedings shall take place unless the parties agree to dispense with them and the chamber consents. Even when no oral proceedings take place, the chamber may call upon the parties to supply information or furnish explanations orally." Fn 248 defines 'pleadings'. Fn 215 defines '*proprio motu*'. Fn 281 includes Article 92 of the ICJ's Rules of Court, which (regarding the ICJ) corresponds to Article 109 of the Rules of the ITLOS (above in this footnote). Whilst resembling Article 92(1) of the ICJ's Rules of Court in form, Article 109(1) of the Rules of the Tribunal differs from the former in the following respects: (i) Article 92(1) differentiates between the time-limits for the parties' pleadings for proceedings commenced by written application and those started by the notification of a special agreement, whilst Article 109(1) does not pronounce on this matter, (ii) Article 92(1) requires the Court (or its President) to set the time-limits for these pleadings, whilst Article 109(1) calls for the relevant special chamber of the ITLOS (or its President) to fix those time-limits. Article 109(2) of the Rules of the ITLOS is almost identical to Article 92(2) of the ICJ's Rules of Court. Article 109(3) of the Rules of the Tribunal is distinguishable from Article 92(3) of the ICJ's Rules of Court only in the following ways: (i) the comma in the former that is placed immediately-after the word 'them', is deleted from the latter, and (ii) both occurrences of the word 'Chamber' in the former are replaced by the non-capitalized version of this word, i.e., 'chamber', in the latter.

conformity with Article 287 of the UNCLOS[511] as the basis for the Tribunal's jursidiction [569], and (ii) requested that the case be referred to the ITLOS' Chamber of Summary Procedure[512], pursuant to Article 15(3) of Annex VI to the UNCLOS[513] [570]. By *note verbale*[514] dated 21st December 2015, the Registrar of the Tribunal notified the States Parties to the UNCLOS of Panama's application in compliance with Article 24(3) of Annex VI to the UNCLOS [571]. In observance of Article 45 of the Rules of the ITLOS[515], the President of the Tribunal[516] held consultations with the parties' representatives in order to discover their views regarding questions of procedure for the case; in the course of these discussions, the President informed the disputants that, taking Article 108(1) of the Rules of the ITLOS into consideration[517], the full Tribunal would hear the lawsuit [572]. As the ITLOS includes neither an Italian judge nor a Panamanian judge upon its Bench, both Italy and Panama exercised its right under Article 17(3) of Annex VI to the UNCLOS to select a judge *ad hoc*[518] [573]. Italy chose Dr. Tullio Treves[519], and Panama picked Mr.

---

[511] The subsection entitled 'Compulsory Procedures: Choice of Procedure', in the section titled 'Part XV of the UNCLOS: Settlement of Disputes' in Chapter 1, contains Paragraphs 1 and 3-8, of Article 287 of the UNCLOS.

[512] The seventh paragraph of the subsection entitled 'A Summary of the ITLOS' Jurisdictional and Procedural Aspects', above in the current section (i.e., that titled 'The International Tribunal for the Law of the Sea'), describes the ITLOS' Chamber of Summary Procedure.

[513] Fn 390 and its accompanying text contain Article 15(3) of Annex VI to the UNCLOS.

[514] A '*note verbale*' is "a diplomatic note that is more formal than an *aide-mémoire* and less formal than a note, [which] is drafted in the third person, and [which] is never signed" (Merriam-Webster (2019), "*note verbale* noun," accessed December 5, 2019, <https://www.merriam-webster.com/dictionary/note%20verbale>; emphasis added).

[515] Fn 384 contains Article 45 of the Rules of the Tribunal.

[516] The President of the ITLOS at this time was Dr. Vladimir Golitsyn (Bluebird Marine Systems (2019), "Vladimir Golitsyn," accessed December 5, 2019. <http://www.bluebird-electric.net/oceanography/Global_Ocean_Commisioners/Vladimir_Golitsyn.htm>). Dr. Paik (fn 384) replaced Dr. Golitsyn as President of the Tribunal on 2nd October 2017 (International Tribunal for the Law of the Sea (2019), "President Jin-Hyun Paik," accessed December 5, 2019, <https://www.itlos.org/the-tribunal/members/president-jin-hyun-paik/>).

[517] The text to note 274 comprises Article 108(1) of the Rules of the Tribunal.

[518] The text to note 167 consists of Article 17(3) of Annex VI to the UNCLOS.

[519] Dr. Tullio Treves – an Italian – has been selected as a judge *ad hoc* of the ITLOS in the following cases: (i) *The M/V "Virginia G" Case (Panama/Guinea-Bissau)*, in which Panama chose Dr. Treves as a judge *ad hoc*, and (ii) *The M/V "Norstar" Case (Panama v. Italy)*, in which Italy picked Dr. Treves as a judge *ad hoc* (International Tribunal for the Law of the Sea (2019), "Judges *ad hoc*," accessed December 5, 2019, <https://www.itlos.org/the-tribunal/judges-ad-hoc/>). Dr. Treves was a member of the

Gudmundur Eiriksson[520], to sit as a judge *ad hoc* in the case – both of whom were admitted in line with Article 19(3) of the Rules of the ITLOS, as neither the other disputant nor the Tribunal opposed the choice of either appointee[521] [574]. On 11th March 2016, within the time-limit that Article 97(1) of the Rules of the Tribunal sets[522], Italy filed written preliminary objections under Article 294(3) of the UNCLOS[523], in which it challenged the Tribunal's jurisdiction and the admissibility of Panama's claim[524]; upon

---

ITLOS from 1996-2011, graduating with a Doctor of Law degree from the University of Milan in 1964 and holding the post of Professor of International Law at the University of Sassari from 1969-1973, the University of Turin from 1974-1980, and the University of Milan from 1980-2012 at which he remains a Professor ì Emeritus of International Law (Consiglio Nazionale delle Ricerche (2019), "Tullio Treves," accessed December 26, 2019, <https://www.cnr.it/sigla/genericdownload/CV%20Tullio_Treves%20Prot.0000321%20del%2025.09.18.pdf?nodeRef=f0253ea3-10b0-4440-9cab-ff8859d6d142;1.0>; Berkeley Law University of California (2019), "Judge Tullio Treves," accessed December 26, 2019, <https://www.law.berkeley.edu/wp-content/uploads/2015/04/treves-bio.pdf>; Curtis, Mallet-Prevost, Colt & Mosle LLP (2019), "Tullio Treves Consultant," accessed December 26, 2019, https://www.curtis.com/our-people/tullio-treves/experience).

520 Mr. Gudmundur Eiriksson – an Icelander – has only be chosen as a judge *ad hoc* in one case that the ITLOS has heard, i.e., *The M/V "Norstar" Case (Panama v. Italy)*, in which Panama selected him as a judge *ad hoc* (International Tribunal for the Law of the Sea (2019), "Judges *ad hoc*," accessed November 15, 2019, <https://www.itlos.org/the-tribunal/judges-ad-hoc/>). Fn 401 lists the cases before the ITLOS in which judges *ad hoc* have been appointed.

521 Article 19(3) of the Rules of the ITLOS states: "A copy of any notification relating to the choice of a judge *ad hoc* shall be communicated by the Registrar [of the Tribunal] to the other party, which shall be requested to furnish, within a time-limit not exceeding 30 days to be fixed by the President of the Tribunal, such observations as it may wish to make. If within the said time-limit no objection is raised by the other party, and if non appears to the Tribunal itself, [then] the parties shall be so informed. In the event of any objection or doubt, the matter shall be decided by the Tribunal, if necessary after hearing the parties."

522 This time-limit is 90 days from the date on which proceedings were launched (fn 414). As Panama filed its written application with the Registry of the Tribunal on 17th December 2015 (first sentence of the current paragraph, i.e., that headed by the phrase 'The written proceedings'), Article 97(1) of the Rules of the ITLOS requires preliminary objections to be made in writing within 90 days of that time (fn 414), which is by 16th March 2016.

523 Fn 212 contains Article 294(3) of the UNCLOS. Fn 414 includes Article 97 of the Rules of the ITLOS, which specifies the procedure for the consideration of preliminary objections submitted to the Tribunal.

524 The preantepenultimate sentence of fn 414 lists the preliminary objections which Italy files against Panama in *The M/V "Norstar" Case (Panama v. Italy)*. Although Paragraph 17 of the Tribunal's Judgment in *The M/V "Norstar" Case (Panama v. Italy)* states that Italy filed written preliminary objections on 11th March 2016 (text to fn 522), the document containing these preliminary objections is dated 10th March 2016 (preantepenultimate sentence of fn 414; (International Tribunal for the Law of the Sea (2016), Written Preliminary Objections under Article 294, Paragraph 3, of the United Nations Convention on the Law of the Sea: The M/V "Norstar" Case (Panama v. Italy) (Case No. 25, 10 March 2016), i; International Tribunal for the Law of the Sea (2019), "Case No. 25 Preliminary Objections," accessed

the receipt of these preliminary objections by the Registry of the ITLOS, the proceedings on the merits of the case were suspended pursuant to Article 97(3) of the Rules of the Tribunal[525] [575]. At a public sitting on 4th November 2016, the Tribunal rejected Italy's preliminary objections[526] [576]. Further to Article 45 of the Rules of the ITLOS[527], at the request of the Tribunal's President its Registrar sent a letter dated 4th November 2016 to each of the disputants to find out their views regarding the further procedure concerning the merits of the case, which both Panama and Italy expressed in communications returned to the Registrar – the former on 15th November 2016 and the latter on 12th and 21st November 2016 [577]. In fulfilment of Article 59 of the Rules of the ITLOS[528], the President – having ascertained the parties' views – set the following time-limits (by means of an order dated 29th November 2016[529]) for the filing of pleadings in *The M/V "Norstar" Case (Panama v. Italy)*: 11th April 2017 for Panama's Memorial, and 11th October 2017; on 29th November 2016, the Registrar conveyed a copy of the order to each disputant [578]. Panama filed its Memorial on 11th April 2017, and transmitted a copy thereof to Italy on that date [579]. Within its Memorial, Panama had filed a document entitled 'Request for Evidence', in which it asked the Tribunal, *inter*

December 6, 2019, <https://www.itlos.org/en/cases/list-of-cases/case-no-25/case-no-25-preliminary-objections/>).

[525] Fn 414 quotes Article 97(3) of the Rules of the ITLOS.

[526] The Tribunal's Judgment of 4 November 2016 on Preliminary Objections in *The M/V "Norstar" Case (Panama v. Italy)* is recorded at page 44 of the *ITLOS Reports 2016* as *The M/V "Norstar" Case (Panama v. Italy), Preliminary Objections* (International Tribunal for the Law of the Sea (2019), *The M/V "Norstar" Case (Panama v. Italy)*, Judgment of 10 April 2019, *ITLOS Reports 2019*, nyp, para.19). The *ITLOS Reports* are reports of the Tribunal's Judgments, Advisory Opinions and Orders, in both English and French (International Tribunal for the Law of the Sea (2019), "Publications," accessed December 6, 2019, <https://www.itlos.org/publications/>). The antepenultimate sentence of fn 414 provides the operative provisions of the Tribunal's Judgment of 4 November 2016 on Preliminary Objections, which Paragraph 316 of *The M/V "Norstar" Case (Panama v. Italy), Preliminary Objections* comprises.

[527] Fn 384 includes Article 45 of the Rules of the ITLOS.

[528] Fn 416 and its accompanying text comprise Article 59 of the Rules of the Tribunal.

[529] This is Order 2016/6 entitled 'The M/V "Norstar" Case (Panama v. Italy)' (International Tribunal for the Law of the Sea (2016), Order: The M/V "Norstar" Case (Panama v. Italy) (Case No. 25, Order 2016/6, 29 November 2016) (Hamburg: International Tribunal for the Law of the Sea), 1).

alia[530], to order Italy and Spain to furnish certified copies of files regarding the M/V Norstar which were allegedly held by separate authorities within those countries [580]. Italy filed its Counter-Memorial on 11th October 2017, and conveyed a copy thereof to Panama on that date [581]. On 6th November 2017, the President of the ITLOS held telephone conversations with the parties' representatives, in which he[531]: (i) informed them that the Tribunal would consider the status of Panama's 'Request for Evidence' in March 2018 [582], and (ii) ascertained the disputants' views concerning the necessity for them to submit additional pleadings [583]. In concurrence with Article 60 of the Rules of the ITLOS[532], the Tribunal – having discovered the parties' opinions[533] – authorized (by means of an order dated 15th November 2017[534]) Panama to submit a Reply by 28th February 2018 and Italy to present a Rejoinder by 13th June 2018 [584]. Panama filed its Reply on 28th February 2018, and conveyed a copy thereof to Italy on 1st March 2018 [585]. On 15th March 2018, the Tribunal met to discuss the Panamanian document entitled 'Request for Evidence', the contents of which it rejected in a letter dated 28th March 2018 and sent by the Registrar of the ITLOS to the disputants – but therein encouraged Italy and Panama to continue their co-operation regarding evidence [586]. Further to this letter, Panama on 9th April 2018[535], and Italy on 4th May 2018[536], informed

---

530 The last sentence of fn 319 defines '*inter alia*'.

531 This President of the Tribunal was Dr. Paik (fn 384), who succeeded Dr. Golitsyn in this post on 2nd October 2017 (fn 516), continuing therein for the remainder of the case entitled *The M/V "Norstar" Case (Panama v. Italy)*.

532 Article 60 of the Rules of the Tribunal applies to cases commenced by way of a written application addressed to the Registrar of the ITLOS, such as *The M/V "Norstar" Case (Panama v. Italy)* and *The M/T "San Padre Pio" Case (Switzerland v. Nigeria)* (fn 405 and accompanying text). Fn 424 contains Article 60 of the Rules of the ITLOS; Paragraph 2 of that Article is the relevant provision.

533 Panama stated that a second round of pleadings was required, whilst Italy declared that it did not consider a second round of pleadings to be necessary, but would acquiesce in a decision of the Tribunal that authorized this (International Tribunal for the Law of the Sea (2019), *The M/V "Norstar" Case (Panama v. Italy)*, Judgment of 10 April 2019, *ITLOS Reports 2019*, nyp, para.34).

534 This is Order 2017/1 entitled 'The M/V "Norstar" Case (Panama v. Italy)' (International Tribunal for the Law of the Sea (2017), Order: The M/V "Norstar" Case (Panama v. Italy) (Case No. 25, Order 2017/1, 15 November 2017) (Hamburg: International Tribunal for the Law of the Sea), 1).

535 Panama's *note verbale* was addressed to the Tribunal and issued by the Ministry of Foreign Affairs of Panama and (International Tribunal for the Law of the Sea (2019), *The M/V*

the Registrar of the documents possessed concerning *The M/V "Norstar" Case (Panama v. Italy)*, and the M/V Norstar, respectively [587]. Italy filed its Rejoinder on 13th June 2018, and transmitted a copy thereof to Italy on that date [588]. On 26th June 2018, the President of the ITLOS held telephone consultations with the parties' agents[537] to find out their opinions concerning the conduct of the proceedings and the arrangements for the hearing [589]. The President (by means of an order dated 20th July 2018[538]) set the date for the start of the oral proceedings as 10th September 2018 [590]. On 7th September 2018, the Agent of Italy[539] and the Agent of Panama[540] each submitted materials that the Paragraph 14[541] of the Guidelines Concerning the Preparation and Presentation of Cases before

"Norstar" Case (Panama v. Italy), Judgment of 10 April 2019, *ITLOS Reports 2019*, nyp, para.39). Fn 514 defines '*note verbale*'.

536 Italy's communication to the Registrar of the Tribunal was a copy of a letter addressed by the Agent of Italy to the Agent of Panama, which stated that Italy was not willing to share its listed documents unconditionally – but would only consider specific, reasoned Panamanian requests (International Tribunal for the Law of the Sea (2019), *The M/V "Norstar" Case (Panama v. Italy)*, Judgment of 10 April 2019, *ITLOS Reports 2019*, nyp, para.39).

537 The Agent of Panama in *The M/V "Norstar" Case (Panama v. Italy)* was Dr. Nelson Carreyó Collazos (International Tribunal for the Law of the Sea (2019), *The M/V "Norstar" Case (Panama v. Italy)*, Judgment of 10 April 2019, *ITLOS Reports 2019*, nyp, para.2; International Tribunal for the Law of the Sea (2019), "Case No. 25," accessed December 7, 2019, <https://www.itlos.org/cases/list-of-cases/case-no-25/>). The Agent of Italy in *The M/V "Norstar" Case (Panama v. Italy)* was Ms. Gabriella Palmieri, Deputy Attorney General (International Tribunal for the Law of the Sea (2019), *The M/V "Norstar" Case (Panama v. Italy)*, Judgment of 10 April 2019, *ITLOS Reports 2019*, nyp, para.10). On 17th August 2018, the Italian Embassy in Berlin informed the Tribunal by *note verbale* (fn 514) of the appointment of the State Attorney, Mr. Giacomo Aiello, as Co-Agent of Italy in *The M/V "Norstar" Case (Panama v. Italy)* (International Tribunal for the Law of the Sea (2019), *The M/V "Norstar" Case (Panama v. Italy)*, Judgment of 10 April 2019, *ITLOS Reports 2019*, nyp, para.45).

538 This is Order 2018/1 entitled 'The M/V "Norstar" Case (Panama v. Italy)' (International Tribunal for the Law of the Sea (2018), Order: The M/V "Norstar" Case (Panama v. Italy) (Case No. 25, Order 2018/1, 20 July 2018) (Hamburg: International Tribunal for the Law of the Sea), 1).

539 Ms. Palmieri (fn 537).

540 Dr. Carreyó (fn 537).

541 Paragraph 14 of the ITLOS' Guidelines Concerning the Preparation and Presentation of Cases before the Tribunal states: "Each party should submit to the Tribunal, prior to the opening of the oral proceedings, (a) a brief note on the points which in its opinion constitute the issues that still divide the parties; (b) a brief outline of the arguments that it wishes to make in its oral statement; and (c) a list of authorities, including, where appropriate, relevant extracts from such authorities, proposed to be relied upon in its oral statement. None of these materials will be treated as documents or parts of the pleadings."

the Tribunal[542] required [591]. In line with Article 68 of the Rules of the ITLOS[543], the Tribunal held initial discussions on 6th and 7th September 2018 [592]. On 9th September 2018, the President of the ITLOS held consultations with the disputants' representatives to address some procedural issues relating to the oral proceedings, during which he transmitted to the parties the following questions in accordance with the Tribunal's wishes under Article 76(1) of the Rules of the ITLOS[544]:

> 1. Could the Parties provide further information on the cargo on board the *M/V "Norstar"*[545] at the time of seizure?
>
> 2. Could the Parties provide further information on the monitoring and maintenance works of the *M/V "Norstar"*[546] after its seizure? [593].

The Agent of Panama and the Agent of Italy each provided a written response to these questions by 21st September 2018; the Registrar of the Tribunal conveyed these communications to the other disputant by 27th

---

[542] On 28th October 1997, the ITLOS issued its 'Guidelines Concerning the Preparation and Presentation of Cases before the Tribunal', acting pursuant to Article 50 of the Rules of the ITLOS (International Tribunal for the Law of the Sea (2006), Guidelines Concerning the Preparation and Presentation of Cases before the Tribunal (ITLOS/9, 14 November 2006) (Hamburg: International Tribunal for the Law of the Sea), 2). Article 50 of the Rules of the Tribunal declares: "The Tribunal may issue guidelines consistent with these Rules concerning any aspect of its proceedings, including the length, format and presentation of written and oral pleadings and the use of electronic means of communication." The second sentence of fn 248 opines that the word 'pleadings' equates with the *written* part of the contentious proceedings (before the ICJ – but this also applies to the ITLOS), thereby indicating that the term 'pleadings' is used more narrowly in this monograph than it is in Article 50 of the Rules of the Tribunal. Whilst the latter is the *sole* occurrence of the phrase 'oral pleadings' *within the Rules of the ITLOS*, this expression is also found once in the Tribunal's Judgment in *The M/V "Norstar" Case (Panama v. Italy)* (International Tribunal for the Law of the Sea (2019), *The M/V "Norstar" Case (Panama v. Italy)*, Judgment of 10 April 2019, *ITLOS Reports 2019*, nyp, para.144). If the author's view of the meaning of the word 'pleadings' (fn 248) is accepted, then the use of the phrase 'written pleadings' – as, for instance, in Article 109(1) of the Rules of the Tribunal (fn 510) – is tautologous and, consequently, the word 'written' could be omitted from this expression without changing its meaning.

[543] The last sentence of the twelfth paragraph, i.e., that headed by the phrase 'The written proceedings', in the subsection entitled 'A Summary of the ITLOS' Jurisdictional and Procedural Aspects', above in the current section (i.e., that titled 'The International Tribunal for the Law of the Sea'), comprises Article 68 of the Rules of the Tribunal.

[544] The text to fn 434 comprises Article 76(1) of the Rules of the Tribunal.

[545] Emphasis original.

[546] Emphasis original.

September 2018, on which date each recipient commented on the answers that the other party supplied [594]. Pursuant to Article 67(2) of the Rules of the ITLOS[547], copies of the pleadings and the documents annexed to them were made available to the public at the commencement of the oral proceedings [595].

The Oral Proceedings

The ITLOS held ten public sittings from 10th to 15th September 2018, at which it was addressed by agents, counsel and advocates of Panama and Italy [596]. At the sittings on 10th and 11th September 2018, Panama called three witness – Messrs. Silvio Rossi[548], Arve Morch[549] and Tore Husefest[550], and one expert – Mr. Horacio Estribi[551], who were examined, cross-examined, and (except for Mr. Husefest) re-examined [597]. At the sittings on 13th September 2018, Italy called two experts – Messrs. Vitaliano Esposito[552] and Guido Matteini[553], who were examined and

---

[547] The penultimate sentence of the twelfth paragraph, i.e., that headed by the phrase 'The written proceedings', in the subsection entitled 'A Summary of the ITLOS' Jurisdictional and Procedural Aspects', above in the present section (i.e., that titled 'The International Tribunal for the Law of the Sea'), consists of Article 67(2) of the Rules of the Tribunal.

[548] Mr. Rossi was the manager of *Rossmare International S.A.S.*, which acted as the bunkering broker for the M/V Norstar (International Tribunal for the Law of the Sea (2019), *The M/V "Norstar" Case (Panama v. Italy)*, Judgment of 10 April 2019, *ITLOS Reports 2019*, nyp, paras.55 and 69). 'Bunkering' means "supplying a ship with fuel, lubricating oil, or potable water" (Rotterdam Mainport University of Applied Sciences (2015), Maritime Symposium: Bunkering at sea – March 12th 2015 (Rotterdam: Rotterdam Mainport University of Applied Sciences), 6). The word 'potable' means "safe to drink; drinkable" (Pearsall, J. (editor) (1998), *The New Oxford Dictionary of English*, 1451).

[549] Mr. Morch was the president of the board of directors at *Inter Marine & Co AS* (International Tribunal for the Law of the Sea (2019), *The M/V "Norstar" Case (Panama v. Italy)*, Judgment of 10 April 2019, *ITLOS Reports 2019*, nyp, para.55). This company owned the M/V Norstar (first sentence of the immediately-preceding paragraph, i.e., that headed by the phrase 'The written proceedings').

[550] Mr. Husefest is a former captain of the M/V Norstar (International Tribunal for the Law of the Sea (2019), *The M/V "Norstar" Case (Panama v. Italy)*, Judgment of 10 April 2019, *ITLOS Reports 2019*, nyp, para.55).

[551] Mr. Estribi was an economic adviser to the Ministry of Finance of Panama (International Tribunal for the Law of the Sea (2019), *The M/V "Norstar" Case (Panama v. Italy)*, Judgment of 10 April 2019, *ITLOS Reports 2019*, nyp, para.55).

[552] Mr. Esposito is a retired judge and a former Chief Public Prosecutor at the Supreme Court of Italy (International Tribunal for the Law of the Sea (2019), *The M/V "Norstar" Case (Panama v. Italy)*, Judgment of 10 April 2019, *ITLOS Reports 2019*, nyp, para.56).

[553] Mr. Matteini was a shipmaster, a consultant in the field of commercial navigation, and a member of the national register for experts in naval evaluation (International Tribunal for

cross-examined; further to Article 85 of the Rules of the ITLOS, the requisite arrangements were made for the evidence provided by these two gentlemen to be intepreted from Italian into both English and French[554] [598]. Pursuant to Article 76(3) of the Rules of the Tribunal[555], four, three, two and one judge(s) put questions to Messrs. Esposito, Morch, Rossi and Estribi, respectively, during their testimony [599]. Following on from consultations held between the President of the ITLOS and the disputants on 14th September 2018, the next day Panama submitted two further documents to the Tribunal, which the Registrar forwarded to the Agent of Italy – in conformity with Article 71(1) of the Rules of the ITLOS[556]; this agent, by means of letter dated 21st September 2018, informed the Tribunal that Italy would not be taking issue with the production of these new items [600]. The Registry of the ITLOS prepared the transcript of the *verbatim*[557] records of each of the Tribunal's ten public sittings[558] in the official languages that the latter used during the oral proceedings – in line with Article 86(1) of the Rules of the ITLOS[559]; in observance of Article 86(4) of the Rules of the Tribunal[560], copies of the transcripts of these records were provided to the judges partaking in the case and to the disputants[561] [601].

---

the Law of the Sea (2019), *The M/V "Norstar" Case (Panama v. Italy)*, Judgment of 10 April 2019, *ITLOS Reports 2019*, nyp, paras.56 and 405). A 'shipmaster' is the captain of a ship (Pearsall, J. (editor) (1998), *The New Oxford Dictionary of English*, 1717).

554 Fn 443 contains Paragraphs 1 and 2 of Article 85 of the Rules of the Tribunal. Further to Article 85(2) of these Rules, Italy was responsible for: (i) making the necessary arrangements for interpreting the statements that Messrs. Esposito and Matteini provided at the hearing in *The M/V "Norstar" Case (Panama v. Italy)* into English and French, and (ii) reimbursing the Registrar of the ITLOS the cost of verifying the interpretation which that disputant supplied therein.

555 The second sentence of fn 435 comprises Article 76(3) of the Rules of the ITLOS.

556 Fn 428 and its accompanying text include Article 71(1) of the Rules of the Tribunal.

557 Fn 268 defines '*verbatim*'.

558 The first sentence of the current paragraph, i.e., that headed by the phrase 'The oral proceedings', refers to these ten public sittings of the Tribunal in *The M/V "Norstar" Case (Panama v. Italy)*.

559 The text to fn 445 comprises the first two sentences of Article 86(1) of the Rules of the Tribunal, which contain the rules that are relevant to the statement in the text to this footnote.

560 Fn 445 includes Article 86(4) of the Rules of the ITLOS.

561 These transcripts were made available to the public electronically (International Tribunal for the Law of the Sea (2019), *The M/V "Norstar" Case (Panama v. Italy)*, Judgment of 10 April 2019, *ITLOS Reports 2019*, nyp, para.62).

The Outcome

The Tribunal held Italy to be in breach of Article 87(1) of the UNCLOS, and awarded Panama compensation of USD 285,000 plus annually-compounded interest payable from 25th September 1998 until the date of the Judgment in *The M/V "Norstar" Case (Panama v. Italy)*, i.e., 10th April 2019[562]. In addition to the dissenting opinion that the seven judges who disagreed with these findings gave collectively[563], five judges each made a declaration[564] and two judges each delivered a separate opinion[565], which resulted in eight opinions being appended to the judgment [602, 603].

INTERNATIONAL ARBITRATIONS

The Basis for Determination of UNCLOS Disputes

A State Party[566] to the UNCLOS may, by way of a written declaration, select as the forum, or a forum, for resolution of its dispute regarding "the interpretation or application of this Convention" [303] an arbitral tribunal that is founded in conformity with Annex VII to the UNCLOS[567] [604] and/or a special arbitral tribunal which is established in compliance with Annex VIII to the UNCLOS[568] for one or more of the classes of disputes

---

562 The penultimate sentence of fn 414 states this judgment, with more particulars provided.

563 The penultimate sentence of fn 414 notes the presence of this dissenting opinion, which the seven judges who provided it did so pursuant to Article 30(3) of Annex VI to the UNCLOS (International Tribunal for the Law of the Sea (2019), *The M/V "Norstar" Case (Panama v. Italy)*, Judgment of 10 April 2019, *ITLOS Reports 2019*, nyp, postface). The text to fn 465 comprises Article 30(3) of Annex VI to the UNCLOS.

564 Each of five judges who made a declaration did so pursuant to Article 125(2) of the Rules of the ITLOS (International Tribunal for the Law of the Sea (2019), *The M/V "Norstar" Case (Panama v. Italy)*, Judgment of 10 April 2019, *ITLOS Reports 2019*, nyp, postface). Fn 465 contains Article 125(2) of the Rules of the Tribunal.

565 Each of the two judges who gave a separate opinion did so pursuant to Article 30(3) of Annex VI to the UNCLOS (International Tribunal for the Law of the Sea (2019), *The M/V "Norstar" Case (Panama v. Italy)*, Judgment of 10 April 2019, *ITLOS Reports 2019*, nyp, postface). The text to fn 465 consists of Article 30(3) of Annex VI to the UNCLOS.

566 Fn 192 defines 'States Parties'.

567 Fn 196 synopsizes Annex VII to the UNCLOS.

568 Fn 197 details Annex VIII to the UNCLOS.

listed therein[569] [605]. If the disputants have assented to arbitration in accordance with Annex VII to the UNCLOS for the settlement of their dispute, then this may be resolved only by that means, unless they agree elsewise [276]. Furthermore, if the parties have *not* consented to the same procedure for the resolution of their dispute, then it may be submitted solely to arbitration in line with Annex VII to the UNCLOS – unless they concur otherwise [277]. A State Party that is a disputant not covered by an effective written declaration[570] is deemed to have agreed to arbitration in concurrence with Annex VII to the UNCLOS [275]. If an international organization and at least one of its member states are joint parties to a dispute regarding the interpretation or application of the UNCLOS, or disputants in the same interest concerning that disagreement, then if a member state has selected only the ICJ as the forum to settle the matter, it is deemed to have agreed to arbitration in conformity with Annex VII to the UNCLOS – unless the disputants agree elsewise [304]. The arbitral tribunal's decision is binding merely between the parties and as concerns their specific dispute [285]. The arbitral award is final and not subject to appeal – unless the disputants have agreed beforehand to an appellate process, and is to be observed by all these parties [284, 606].

Example Arbitration Case – The South China Sea Arbitration

Some arbitrations concerning baselines and/or boundary delimitation preceded the entering into force of the UNCLOS – including its Annex VII[571], such as *Delimitation of the Continental Shelf between the United Kingdom of Great Britain and Northern Ireland, and the French*

[569] Special arbitration pursuant to Annex VIII to the UNCLOS is not discussed further, because the matters on which it adjudicates (text to fn 238) are beyond the scope of this monograph (second sentence of the section above entitled 'Introduction').

[570] The first sentence of the current paragraph refers to a State Party's written declaration.

[571] The UNCLOS was adopted on 10th December 1982, and entered into force on 16th November 1994 (fn 240).

Republic[572], and *Delimitation of Maritime Areas between Canada and France*[573]. The *South China Sea Arbitration* was conducted by the Permanent Court of Arbitration[574] according to the terms of the UNCLOS – with Annex VII to this Convention regulating the arbitral procedure, and is used to exemplify an arbitration concerning the Law of the Sea.

By written notification and accompanying statement of claim in fulfilment of Article 1 of Annex VII to the UNCLOS[575], and pursuant to Articles 286[576] and 287[577] of the UNCLOS, the Philippines commenced arbitral proceedings against China [607]. On the day that the Department of Foreign Affairs of the Philippines gave this notification and statement of claim to the Chinese Ambassador to the Philippines, 22nd January 2013, the Secretary of Foreign Affairs of the Philippines, Mr. Albert del Rosaro[578], made (*inter alia*[579]) the following comments.

---

[572] This case's arbitral decisions of 30th June 1977 and 14th March 1978 are reported at pages 3-270 and 271-413, respectively, of Volume XVIII of the *Reports of International Arbitral Awards*, published in 2006 by the UN.

[573] This arbitral judgment dated 10th June 1992 is reported in French at pages 265-341 of Volume XXI of the *Reports of International Arbitral Awards*, published in 2006 by the UN.

[574] With 122 Contracting Parties that have acceded to one or both of its founding conventions (i.e., the Conventions for the Pacific Settlement of International Disputes of 1899 and 1907), the PCA was established in 1899 to facilitate dispute resolution between states (Permanent Court of Arbitration (2019), "About us," accessed December 15, 2019, <https://pca-cpa.org/en/about/>; Permanent Court of Arbitration (2019), "Contracting Parties," accessed December 15, 2019, <https://pca-cpa.org/en/about/introduction/contracting-parties/>; Permanent Court of Arbitration (2019), "Documents and Resources: PCA Rules & Conventions," accessed December 15, 2019, <https://pca-cpa.org/en/documents/pca-conventions-and-rules/pca-founding-conventions-and-internal-rules/>).

[575] Fn 196 specifies Article 1 of Annex VII to the UNCLOS.

[576] The text to fn 165 comprises Article 286 to the UNCLOS.

[577] The subsection entitled 'Compulsory Procedures: Choice of Procedure', in the section titled 'Part XV of the UNCLOS: Settlement of Disputes' in Chapter 1, contains Paragraphs 1 and 3-8, of Article 287 of the UNCLOS.

[578] Mr. Albert del Rosario is a former Secretary of Foreign Affairs of the Philippines and a former Philippine Ambassador to the USA, who has also held many positions in the private sector during his career (Philippine Embassy in Madrid (2019), "Albert F. Del Rosario," accessed December 16, 2019, https://www.philembassymadrid.com/albert-f-del-rosario; South China Morning Post (2019), "Former Philippine diplomat Albert Del Rosario, who criticized China, back in Manila after Hong Kong deportation," accessed December 16, 2019, https://www.scmp.com/week-asia/politics/article/3015470/philippines-del-rosario-held-hong-kong-airport-after-anti-china).

[579] The final sentence of fn 319 defines '*inter alia*'.

... This Notification initiates the arbitral proceedings under Article 287 and Annex VII of UNCLOS. The initiation of Arbitral Proceedings against China on the nine-dash line is an operationalization of President Aquino's policy for a peaceful and rules-based resolution of disputes in the WPS [West Philippine Sea] in accordance with international law specifically UNCLOS. *The Philippines has exhausted almost all political and diplomatic avenues for a peaceful negotiated settlement of its maritime dispute with China*[580]. ... The Philippines asserts that China's so-called nine-dash line claim[581] that encompasses virtually the entire South China Sea/West Philippine Sea is contrary to UNCLOS and thus unlawful. ... Within the maritime area encompassed by the 9-dash line, China has also laid claim to, occupied and built structures on certain submerged banks, reefs and low tide elevations that do not qualify as islands under UNCLOS, but are parts of the Philippine continental shelf, or the international seabed. In addition, China has occupied certain small, uninhabitable coral projections that are barely above water at high tide, and which are "rocks" under Article 121(3) of UNCLOS[582]. ... China has interfered with the lawful exercise by the Philippines of its rights within its legitimate maritime zones, as well as to the aforementioned features and their surrounding waters. ... The Philippines is conscious of China's Declaration of August 25, 2006 under Article 298 of UNCLOS

[580] Emphasis added. This sentence is important, because a disputant may only invoke Article 286 of the UNCLOS (fn 576 and accompanying text) when no settlement has been attained by peaceful means under Section 1 of Part XV of the UNCLOS (fn 159 describes Section 1 of Part XV of the UNCLOS).

[581] The 'nine-dash line' claim refers to a map accompanying each of two *notes verbales* dated 7th May 2009, which the Permanent Mission of the People's Republic of China presented to the then Secretary-General of the UN, Mr. Ban Ki-moon, in which nine black-and-mauve dashes separated Vietnam to the west, Borneo to the south, and the Philippines to the east, from the South China Sea, and to which both of these *notes verbales* referred as follows: "China has indisputable sovereignty over the islands in the South China Sea and the adjacent waters, and enjoys sovereign rights and jurisdiction over the relevant waters as well as the seabed and subsoil thereof (see attached map). The above position is consistently held by the Chinese Government, and is widely known by the international community." (Permanent Mission of the People's Republic of China to the United Nations (2009), *Note verbale* to Mr. Ban Ki-moon, Secretary-General of the United Nations, CML/17/2009, New York, 7th May 2009; Permanent Mission of the People's Republic of China to the United Nations (2009), *Note verbale* to Mr. Ban Ki-moon, Secretary-General of the United Nations, CML/18/2009, New York, 7th May 2009). Fn 514 defines '*note verbale*'.

[582] Point 3 within the first quoted passage in the section entitled 'Part VIII of the UNCLOS: Regime of Islands', in Chapter 1, comprises Article 121(3) of the UNCLOS.

(regarding optional exceptions to the compulsory proceedings)[583], and has avoided raising subjects or making claims that China has, by virtue of that Declaration, excluded from arbitral jurisdiction. In this context, the Philippines is requesting the Arbitral Tribunal to issue an award that, among others: – Declares that China's rights in regard to maritime areas in the South China Sea, like the rights of the Philippines, are those that are established by UNCLOS, and consist of its rights to a Territorial Sea and Contiguous Zone under Part II of UNCLOS[584], to an EEZ [(i.e., exclusive economic zone)] under Part V [of the UNCLOS][585], and to a Continental Shelf under Part VI [of the UNCLOS][586]; – Declares that China's maritime claims in the SCS [South China Sea] based on its so-called nine-dash line are contrary to UNCLOS and invalid; – Requires China to bring its domestic legislation into conformity with its obligation under UNCLOS; and – Requires that China desist from activities that violate the rights of the Philippines in its maritime domain in the West Philippine Sea. The Philippines asserts that the Arbitral Tribunal has jurisdiction to hear and make an award based on its Notification and Statement of Claim because the dispute is about the interpretation and application by States Parties of the obligations under the UNCLOS. Article 287(1) of UNCLOS provides that "settlement of disputes concerning the interpretation and application of this Convention" may be

---

583 China's Declaration under Article 298 of the UNCLOS states: "The Government of the People's Republic of China does not accept any of the procedures provided for in Section 2 of Part XV of the Convention [i.e., dispute resolution via the ICJ, the ITLOS, an arbitral tribunal constituted under Annex VII to the UNCLOS, and a special arbitral tribunal established under Annex VIII to the UNCLOS] with respect to all the categories of disputes referred to in paragraphs 1 (a) (b) and (c) of Article 298 of the Convention." (United Nations Treaty Collection (2019), "Chapter XXI Law of the Sea: 6. United Nations Convention on the Law of the Sea," accessed December 15, 2019, <https://treaties.un.org/Pages/ViewDetailsIII.aspx?src=TREATY&mtdsg_no=XXI-6&chapter=21&Temp=mtdsg3&clang=_en>). The subsection entitled 'Optional Exceptions to the Applicability of Compulsory Procedures', in the section titled 'Part XV of the UNCLOS: Settlement of Disputes' in Chapter 1, comprises Article 298 of the UNCLOS. The section below entitled 'Article 298(1)(a) of the UNCLOS' discusses the operation of Article 298(1)(a) of the UNCLOS. Fn 163 describes Sections 2 and 3 of Part XV of the UNCLOS.

584 The section entitled 'Part II of the UNCLOS: Territorial Sea and Contiguous Zone', in Chapter 1, comprises Part II of the UNCLOS.

585 The section titled 'Part V of the UNCLOS: Exclusive Economic Zone', in Chapter 1, consists of Part V of the UNCLOS.

586 The section headed 'Part VI of the UNCLOS: Continental Shelf', in Chapter 1, contains Part VI of the UNCLOS.

referred by the Parties for resolution under Part XV of UNCLOS. ..."[587] [608].

On 19th February 2013, the Government of China gave a *note verbale*[588] to the Department of Foreign Affairs of the Philippines, which rejected the initiation by the Government of the Philippines of arbitration under Annex VII to the UNCLOS and returned the notification and statement of claim [609, 610]. On 7th December 2014, the Ministry of Foreign Affairs of the People's Republic of China published a paper explaining its position with regard to the dispute, the core of which is as follows.

> This Position Paper will elaborate on the following positions: – The essence of the subject-matter of the arbitration is the territorial sovereignty over several maritime features in the South China Sea, which is beyond the scope of the Convention [(i.e., the UNCLOS)] and does not concern the interpretation or application of the Convention [as required by Articles 286 and 287(1) of the UNCLOS upon which, together with Annex VII to the UNCLOS, the notification and statement of claim are based[589]]; – China and the Philippines have agreed, through bilateral instruments and the Declaration on the Conduct of the Parties in the South China Sea, to settle their relevant disputes through negotiations[590].

---

[587] The first sentence of the subsection entitled 'Compulsory Procedures: Choice of Procedure', in the section titled 'Part XV of the UNCLOS: Settlement of Disputes' in Chapter 1, comprises Article 287(1) of the UNCLOS. That section contains the provisions of Part XV of the UNCLOS.

[588] Fn 514 defines '*note verbale*'.

[589] The first sentence of the first paragraph of the current subsection (i.e., that titled 'Example Arbitration Case – The South China Sea Arbitration') states: "By written notification and accompanying statement of claim in fulfilment of Article 1 of Annex VII to the UNCLOS, and pursuant to Articles 286 and 287 of the UNCLOS, the Philippines commenced arbitral proceedings against China."

[590] The Declaration states: "The Parties concerned [i.e., the Governments of the Member States of the Association of Southeast Asian Nations and the Government of the People's Republic of China] undertake to resolve their territorial and jurisdictional disputes by peaceful means, without resorting to the threat or use of force, through friendly consultations and negotiations by sovereign states directly concerned, in accordance with universally recognized principles of international law, including the 1982 UN Convention on the Law of the Sea;" (Association of Southeast Asian Nations/Government of the People's Republic of China (2012), Declaration on the Conduct of Parties in the South China Sea (Phnom Penh, 4th November 2012), Article 4). The Member States of the Association of Southeast

By unilaterally initiating the present arbitration, the Philippines has breached its obligation under international law; – Even assuming, *arguendo*[591], that the subject-matter of the arbitration were concerned with the interpretation and application of the Convention, that subject-matter would constitute an integral part of maritime delimitation between the two countries, thus falling within the scope of the declaration filed by China in 2006 in accordance with the Convention[592], which excludes, *inter alia*[593], disputes concerning maritime delimitation from compulsory arbitration and other compulsory dispute settlement procedures; – Consequently, the Arbitral Tribunal manifestly has no jurisdiction over the present arbitration. Based on the foregoing positions and by virtue of

---

Asian Nations are Brunei Darussalam, Cambodia, Indonesia, Laos, Malaysia, Myanmar, the Philippines, Singapore, Thailand and Vietnam (Association of Southeast Asian Nations (2019), "ASEAN Member States," accessed December 16, 2019, <https://asean.org/asean/asean-member-states/>).

[591] Emphasis added. The word '*arguendo*' means "for the sake of argument" (Merriam-Webster (2019), "*arguendo* adverb," accessed December 16, 2019, <https://www.merriam-webster.com/legal/arguendo>).

[592] This is the Declaration that the Government of China made under Article 298 of the UNCLOS, which the first sentence of fn 583 quotes. On 25th August 2006, the Government of China also made the following Declaration: "1. In accordance with the provisions of the United Nations Convention on the Law of the Sea, the People's Republic of China shall enjoy sovereign rights and jurisdiction over an exclusive economic zone of 200 nautical miles and the continental shelf. 2. The People's Republic of China will effect, through consultations, the delimitation of boundary of the maritime jurisdiction with the states with coasts opposite or adjacent to China respectively on the basis of international law and in accordance with the equitable principle. 3. The People's Republic of China reaffirms its sovereignty over all its archipelagoes and islands as listed in article 2 of the Law of the People's Republic of China on the Territorial Sea and Contiguous Zone which was promulgated on 25 February 1992. 4. The People's Republic of China reaffirms that the provisions of the United Nations Convention on the Law of the Sea concerning innocent passage through the territorial sea shall not prejudice the right of a coastal state to request, in accordance with its laws and regulations, a foreign state to obtain advance approval from or give prior notification to the coastal state for the passage of its warships through the territorial sea of the coastal state." (United Nations Treaty Collection (2019), "Chapter XXI Law of the Sea: 6. United Nations Convention on the Law of the Sea," accessed December 16, 2019, <https://treaties.un.org/Pages/ViewDetailsIII.aspx?src=TREATY&mtdsg_no=XXI-6&chapter=21&Temp=mtdsg3&clang=_en>). Article 2 of the Law of the People's Republic of China on the Territorial Sea and Contiguous Zone declares: "The PRC's [i.e., the People's Republic of China's] territorial sea refers to the waters adjacent to its territorial land. The PRC's territorial land includes the mainland and its offshore islands, Taiwan and the various affiliated islands including Diaoyu Island, Penghu Islands, Dongsha Islands, Xisha Islands, Nansha (Spratly) Islands and other islands that belong to the People's Republic of China. The PRC's internal waters refer to the waters along the baseline of the territorial sea facing the land."

[593] Emphasis added. The last sentence of fn 319 defines '*inter alia*'.

the freedom of every State to choose the means of dispute settlement, China's rejection of and non-participation in the present arbitration stands on solid ground in international law [611].

In its Award on Jurisdiction and Admissibility, the arbitral tribunal – whose members comprised former/current ITLOS Judges Thomas Mensah (President of the Tribunal), Rüdiger Wolfrum, Stanislaw Pawlak and Jean-Pierre Cot, and Professor Alfred Soons, all five of whom were appointed in accordance with Article 3 of Annex VII to the UNCLOS[594] – unanimously held that: (i) the arbitral tribunal was properly constituted in conformity with Annex VII to the UNCLOS [612], (ii) China's non-appearance before the arbitral tribunal did not divest the latter of jurisdiction over the dispute[595] [613], (iii) the Philippines' deed of instituting this arbitration pursuant to Articles 286 and 287 of the UNCLOS and in compliance with Annex VII to the UNCLOS[596] did not amount to an abuse of process [614],

[594] Permanent Court of Arbitration (2015), *PCA Case No 2013-19 in the matter of an arbitration before an arbitral tribunal constituted under Annex VII to the 1982 United Nations Convention on the Law of the Sea between the Republic of the Philippines and the People's Republic of China: Award on Jurisdiction and Admissibility*, 29 October 2015 (The Hague: Permanent Court of Arbitration), paras.28-31. Article 3 of Annex VII to the UNCLOS comprises detailed rules on the constitution of the arbitral tribunal. Fn 196 summarizes Annex VII to the UNCLOS.

[595] Article 9 of Annex VII to the UNCLOS is unequivocal about the intentional absence of one of the disputants from the hearings – or its failure to submit the requisite pleadings – not being inhibitory to the progression and completion of the arbitral proceedings: "If one of the parties to the dispute does not appear before the arbitral tribunal or fails to defend its case, [then] the other party may request the tribunal to continue the proceedings and to make its award. Absence of a party or failure of a party to defend its case shall not constitute a bar to the proceedings. ..." In its Memorial in the *South China Sea Arbitration*, the Government of the Philippines noted the non-attendance of the Government of China at the arbitral proceedings for this case, and requested that, notwithstanding the latter party's non-appearance before the tribunal, the proceedings continue (Government of the Republic of the Philippines (2014), Arbitration under Annex VII of the United Nations Convention on the Law of the Sea (Republic of the Philippines v. People's Republic of China): Memorial of the Philippines Volume 1, 30 March 2014, paras.1.21 and 7.39). Thus, the Government of China's decision to boycott these proceedings (to which it refers in Paragraph 3 of its Position Paper dated 7th December 2014 (final sentence of the immediately-preceding quoted passage in the text)) neither prevented the proceedings from taking place nor precluded the tribunal from making its arbitral awards of 29th October 2015 and 12th July 2016.

[596] The text to fns 575, 576 and 577 notes the initiation by the Philippines of arbitral proceedings against China. These footnotes specify the location of Article 1 of Annex VII to, Article 286 of, and Article 287 of, the UNCLOS, respectively, within Chapter 1 of this monograph.

(iv) there is no essential third party whose absence removes the arbitral tribunal's jurisdiction [615], (v) the Declaration on the Conduct of the Parties in the South China Sea[597] and other relevant international instruments do not debar, under Article 281[598] or 282[599] of the UNCLOS, recourse to the compulsory procedures for dispute resolution that Section 2 of Part XV of that Convention[600] provides[601] [616], and (vi) the disputants have exchanged views, as Article 283 of the UNCLOS[602] requires [617]. In its Award on Jurisdiction and Admissibility, the arbitral tribunal unanimously ruled that it has jurisdiction to appraise Submissions 3, 4, 6, 7, 10, 11 and 13 of the Philippines, subject to the conditions that Paragraphs 400, 401, 403, 404, 407, 408 and 410 of this Award specify [618] – which the next paragraph covers. In this Award, the tribunal unanimously held that a jurisdictional determination of Philippine Submissions 1[603], 2[604], 5[605], 8[606], 9[607], 12[608] and 14[609] involved

[597] The first sentence of note 356 quotes Article 4 of the Declaration on the Conduct of Parties in the South China Sea.

[598] The first sentence of the subsection entitled 'Circumstances under which Part XV of the UNCLOS applies', in the section titled 'Part XV of the UNCLOS: Settlement of Disputes' in Chapter 1, comprises Article 281 of the UNCLOS.

[599] The last sentence of the subsection entitled 'Circumstances under which Part XV of the UNCLOS applies', in the section titled 'Part XV of the UNCLOS: Settlement of Disputes' in Chapter 1, consists of Article 282 of the UNCLOS.

[600] Fn 163 describes Sections 2 and 3 of Part XV of the UNCLOS.

[601] These compulsory procedures for dispute resolution are the ICJ, the ITLOS, arbitration pursuant to Annex VII to the UNCLOS, and special arbitration under Annex VIII to the UNCLOS (first sentence of the first paragraph of the subsection entitled 'Compulsory Procedures: Choice of Procedure', in the section titled 'Part XV of the UNCLOS: Settlement of Disputes' in Chapter 1).

[602] The subsection entitled 'Obligation for the Disputants to Exchange Views', in the section titled 'Part XV of the UNCLOS: Settlement of Disputes' in Chapter 1, comprises Article 283 of the UNCLOS.

[603] Philippine Submission 1 states: "China's maritime entitlements in the South China Sea, like those of the Philippines, may not extend beyond those permitted by the [UNCLOS];" (Government of the Republic of the Philippines (2014), Memorial of the Philippines Volume 1, 30 March 2014, 271).

[604] Philippine Submission 2 declares: "China's claims to sovereign rights and jurisdiction, and to "historic rights," with respect to the maritime areas of the South China Sea encompassed by the so-called "nine-dash line" are contrary to the Convention [(i.e., the UNCLOS)] and without lawful effect to the extent that they exceed the geographic and substantive limits of China's maritime entitlements under UNCLOS;" (Government of the Republic of the Philippines (2014), Memorial of the Philippines Volume 1, 30 March 2014, 271).

[605] Philippine Submission 5 proclaims: "Mischief Reef and Second Thomas Shoal are part of the exclusive economic zone and continental shelf of the Philippines;" (Government of the

"consideration of issues that do not possess an exclusively preliminary character," and postponed this to the merits phase of the arbitral proceedings [619]. The tribunal instructed the Philippines to clarify the content and reduce the ambit of its Submission 15[610], and reserved deliberation on whether it has jurisdiction over this matter to the merits phase of the proceedings [620].

Republic of the Philippines (2014), Memorial of the Philippines Volume 1, 30 March 2014, 271).

[606] Philippine Submission 8 asseverates: "China has unlawfully interfered with the enjoyment and exercise of the sovereign rights of the Philippines with respect to the living and non-living resources of its exclusive economic zone and continental shelf;" (Government of the Republic of the Philippines (2014), Memorial of the Philippines Volume 1, 30 March 2014, 271).

[607] Philippine Submission 9 avers: "China has unlawfully failed to prevent its nationals and vessels from exploiting the living resources in the exclusive economic zone of the Philippines;" (Government of the Republic of the Philippines (2014), Memorial of the Philippines Volume 1, 30 March 2014, 272).

[608] Philippine Submission 12 states: "China's occupation of and construction activities on Mischief Reef (a) violate the provisions of the Convention concerning artificial islands, installations and structures; (b) violate China's duties to protect and preserve the marine environment under the Convention [(i.e., the UNCLOS)]; and (c) constitute unlawful acts of attempted appropriation in violation of the Convention;" (Government of the Republic of the Philippines (2014), Memorial of the Philippines Volume 1, 30 March 2014, 272).

[609] Philippine Submission 14 declares: "Since the commencement of this arbitration in January 2013, China has unlawfully aggravated and extended the dispute by, among other things: (a) interfering with the Philippines' rights of navigation in the waters at, and adjacent to, Second Thomas Shoal; (b) preventing the rotation and resupply of Philippine personnel stationed at Second Thomas Shoal; and (c) endangering the health and well-being of Philippine personnel stationed at Second Thomas Shoal;" (Government of the Republic of the Philippines (2014), Memorial of the Philippines Volume 1, 30 March 2014, 272). When presenting its final Submissions at the conclusion to the hearing on the merits of the case, the Philippines sought to add a part (d) to its Submission 14, which the arbitral tribunal accepted on 16th December 2015, having invited China to comment on the change, as follows "and (d) conducting dredging, artificial island-building and construction activities at Mischief Reef, Cuarteron Reef, Fiery Cross Reef, Gaven Reef, Johnson Reef, Hughes Reef and Subi Reef;" (Permanent Court of Arbitration (2016), *PCA Case No 2013-19 in the matter of an arbitration before an arbitral tribunal constituted under Annex VII to the 1982 United Nations Convention on the Law of the Sea between the Republic of the Philippines and the People's Republic of China: Award*, 12 July 2016 (The Hague: Permanent Court of Arbitration), paras.1110 and 1111).

[610] Philippine Submission 15 proclaims: "China shall desist from further unlawful claims and activities." (Government of the Republic of the Philippines (2014), Memorial of the Philippines Volume 1, 30 March 2014, 272).

With regard to Philippine Submission 3[611], the arbitral tribunal held that: (i) this statement indicates a dispute regarding the status of Scarborough Shoal as an 'island' or 'rock' as described by Article 121 of the UNCLOS[612], which the requirements of Section 1 of Part XV of the UNCLOS[613] do not prevent the tribunal from addressing, and (ii) this is a dispute regarding neither sovereignty nor delimitation of a sea boundary, therefore (iii) Article 298 of the UNCLOS[614] does not restrict the tribunal's jurisdiction, and (iv) no other exception or limitation in Article 297[615] or 298 of the UNCLOS potentially applies to the Scarborough Shoal's status, and so (v) the tribunal has jurisdiction to attend to the issues raised in Philippine Submission 3 [621]. The tribunal applied similar reasoning to that in Paragraph 400 of its Award on Jurisdiction and Admissibility[616] in Paragraphs 401, 403, 404, 407, 408 and 410 of this Award, which held it to have jurisdiction to address the matters raised in Philippine Submissions 4[617], 6[618], 7[619], 10[620], 11[621] and 13[622], respectively – subject to: (i) the

---

611 Philippine Submission 3 declares: "Scarborough Shoal generates no entitlement to an exclusive economic zone or continental shelf." (Government of the Republic of the Philippines (2014), Memorial of the Philippines Volume 1, 30 March 2014, 271).

612 The first paragraph of the section entitled 'Part VIII of the UNCLOS: Regime of Islands', in Chapter 1, quotes Article 121 of the UNCLOS.

613 Fn 159 describes Section 1 of Part XV of the UNCLOS.

614 The subsection entitled 'Optional Exceptions to the Applicability of Compulsory Procedures', in the section titled 'Part XV of the UNCLOS: Settlement of Disputes' in Chapter 1, contains Article 298 of the UNCLOS. The section below entitled 'Article 298(1)(a) of the UNCLOS' considers the working of Article 298(1)(a) of the UNCLOS.

615 The subsection entitled 'Limitations to the Applicability of the Compulsory Procedures', in the section titled 'Part XV of the UNCLOS: Settlement of Disputes' in Chapter 1, comprises most of the provisions of Article 297 of the UNCLOS.

616 The immediately-preceding sentence in the text synopsizes Paragraph 400 of the arbitral tribunal's Award on Jurisdiction and Admissibility in the *South China Sea Arbitration*.

617 Philippine Submission 4 proclaims: "Mischief Reef, Second Thomas Shoal and Subi Reef are low-tide elevations that do not generate entitlement to a territorial sea, exclusive economic zone or continental shelf, and are not features that are capable of appropriation by occupation or otherwise;" (Government of the Republic of the Philippines (2014), Memorial of the Philippines Volume 1, 30 March 2014, 271).

618 Philippine Submission 6 asseverates: "Gaven Reef and McKennan Reef (including Hughes Reef) are low-tide elevations that do not generate entitlement to a territorial sea, exclusive economic zone or continental shelf, but their low-water tide line may be used to determine the baseline from which the breadth of the territorial sea of Namyit and Sin Cowe, respectively, is measured;" (Government of the Republic of the Philippines (2014), Memorial of the Philippines Volume 1, 30 March 2014, 271).

619 Philippine Submission 7 avers: "Johnson Reef, Cuarteron Reef and Fiery Cross Reef generate no entitlement to an exclusive economic zone or continental shelf;" (Government of the

proviso in each of Paragraphs 401 and 403 of the possible effects of any overlapping Chinese and Philippine entitlements to an exclusive economic zone or continental shelf in the relevant area[623], and (ii) the condition in each of Paragraphs 407 and 410 that the claimed rights and alleged breach of those took place within Scarborough Shoal's territorial sea[624].

Republic of the Philippines (2014), Memorial of the Philippines Volume 1, 30 March 2014, 271).

620 Philippine Submission 10 states: "China has unlawfully prevented Philippine fishermen from pursuing their livelihoods by interfering with traditional fishing activities at Scarborough Shoal;" (Government of the Republic of the Philippines (2014), Memorial of the Philippines Volume 1, 30 March 2014, 272).

621 Philippine Submission 11 declares: "China has violated its obligations under the Convention [(i.e., the UNCLOS)] to protect and preserve the marine environment at Scarborough Shoal and Second Thomas Shoal;" (Government of the Republic of the Philippines (2014), Memorial of the Philippines Volume 1, 30 March 2014, 272).

622 Philippine Submission 13 affirms: "China has breached its obligations under the Convention [(i.e., the UNCLOS)] by operating its law enforcement vessels in a dangerous manner causing serious risk of collision to Philippine vessels navigating in the vicinity of Scarborough Shoal;" (Government of the Republic of the Philippines (2014), Memorial of the Philippines Volume 1, 30 March 2014, 272).

623 Paragraph 401 of the arbitral tribunal's Award on Jurisdiction and Admissibility reasons: "The Philippines' Submission No. 4 [(fn 617)] reflects a dispute concerning the status of Mischief Reef, Second Thomas Shoal, and Subi Reef as "low-tide elevations" within the meaning of Article 13 of the Convention [(i.e., the UNCLOS)] and is not barred from the Tribunal's consideration by any requirement of Section 1 of Part XV [of the UNCLOS]. Low-tide elevations do not generate entitlement to a territorial sea, exclusive economic zone, or continental shelf. This is not a dispute concerning sovereignty over the features, notwithstanding any possible question concerning whether low-tide elevations may be subject to a claim of territorial sovereignty. Nor is this a dispute concerning sea boundary delimitation: the status of a feature as a "low-tide elevation," "island," or a "rock" relates to the entitlement to maritime zones generated by that feature, not to the delimitation of such entitlements in the event that they overlap. If, however, China has an entitlement to an exclusive economic zone or to a continental shelf overlapping that of the Philippines in the area of Mischief Reef, Second Thomas Shoal, or Subi Reef, [then] the Tribunal considers that the existence of overlapping entitlements may have practical considerations for the selection of the vertical datum and tidal model against which the status of the features is to be assessed. This may be particularly true if the Parties' respective data and models indicate differing results. Accordingly, subject to a caveat with respect to the possible effects of any overlapping entitlements, the Tribunal concludes that it has jurisdiction to address the matters raised in the Philippines' Submission No.4." (Permanent Court of Arbitration (2015), *PCA Case No 2013-19: Award on Jurisdiction and Admissibility*, 29 October 2015, para.401; emphasis original). Fn 23 defines 'low-tide elevation'. Although a low-tide elevation wholly or partly within a state's territorial sea may be used as a baseline for measuring that territorial sea's breadth, such a feature located beyond a country's territorial sea is denied a territorial sea of its own (text to fns 23 and 24). Fn 159 describes Section 1 of Part XV of the UNCLOS.

624 Paragraph 407 of the arbitral tribunal's Award on Jurisdiction and Admissibility argues: "The Philippines' Submission No. 10 [(fn 620)] reflects a dispute concerning China's actions that allegedly interfere with the traditional fishing activities of Philippine nations at Scarborough

In its Award dated 12th July 2016, the arbitral tribunal in the *South China Sea Arbitration* made the remainder of its findings as to its jurisdiction that it had not determined in its Award on Jurisdiction and Admissibility dated 29th October 2015, which include the following: (i) China's claims in the South China Sea do not include one to 'historic title', within the meaning of Article 298(1)(a)(i) of the UNCLOS[625], over the

Shoal. This is not a dispute concerning sovereignty or maritime boundary delimitation, nor is it barred from the Tribunal's consideration by any requirement of Section 1 of Part XV [of the UNCLOS]. The Philippines has clarified that these activities occur within the 12 nautical mile territorial sea that would be generated by Scarborough Shoal irrespective of whether the feature where considered to be a rock or island pursuant to Article 121 of the Convention [(i.e., the UNCLOS)]. The Tribunal notes that traditional fishing rights may exist even within the territorial waters of another State and considers that its jurisdiction to address this dispute is not dependent on a prior determination of sovereignty over Scarborough Shoal. Articles 297 [(fn 615)] and 298 [(fn 614)] of the Convention have no **application in the Territorial Sea and thus impose no limitation on the Tribunal's** jurisdiction. Accordingly, to the extent that the claimed rights and alleged interference occurred within the territorial sea of Scarborough Shoal, the Tribunal concludes that it has **jurisdiction to address the matters raised in the Philippines' Submission No.10."** (Permanent Court of Arbitration (2015), *PCA Case No 2013-19: Award on Jurisdiction and Admissibility*, 29 October 2015, para.407; emphasis original). Fn 159 describes Section 1 of Part XV of the UNCLOS. The first paragraph of the section entitled 'Part VIII of the UNCLOS: Regime of Islands', in Chapter 1, quotes Article 121 of the UNCLOS; Paragraphs 2 and 3 of this Article, read together with Article 3 of the UNCLOS (text to fn 2), entitle each island and rock to a territorial sea of twelve nautical miles.

625 The issue for the arbitral tribunal to determine is whether the current dispute amounts to one "involving historic … titles" within Article 298(1)(a)(i) of the UNCLOS (fn 186 and accompanying text), which, if the tribunal were to conclude in the affirmative, would put those aspects of the *South China Sea Arbitration* to which these historic title(s) applied beyond the tribunal's jurisdiction consequent to the Government of China's Declaration under Article 298(1)(a) of the UNCLOS (fn 583) – upon which that party would rely. The arbitral tribunal investigates this matter in depth: "Article 298(1)(a)(i) of the Convention [(i.e., the UNCLOS)] provides for an exception for disputes involving 'historic titles'. While the ordinary meaning of this term already implies a notion of property, the Tribunal considers that the meaning of the Convention's reference to 'historic titles' should be understood in the particular context of the evolution of the international law of the sea. … The first reference to historic title in the treaties preceding the present Convention appears in the 1958 Geneva Convention on the Territorial Sea and the Contiguous Zone, Article 12 of which [(fn 26)] addresses the delimitation of the territorial sea, but provides that "[t]he provisions of this paragraph shall not apply, however, where it is necessary by reason of historic title or other special circumstances to delimit the territorial seas of the two States in a way which is at variance with this provision. This provision was introduced by Norway, reflecting its recent experience before the International Court of Justice [in *Fisheries Case (United Kingdom v. Norway)*, in which the ICJ stated, at pages 130-131: "By "historic waters" are usually meant waters which are treated as internal waters but which would not have that character were it not for the existence of an historic title. The United Kingdom Government refers to the notion of historic titles both in respect of territorial waters and internal waters, considering such titles, in both cases, as derogations from general

international law. In its opinion Norway can justify the claim that these waters are territorial or internal on the ground that she has exercised the necessary jurisdiction over them for a long period without opposition from other States ... with the result that her jurisdiction over these waters must now be recognized although it constitutes a derogation from the rules in force. Norwegian sovereignty over these waters would constitute an exception, historic titles justifying situations which would otherwise be in conflict with international law."]. As used in Article 12 of the 1958 Convention, 'historic title' was clearly intended to have the same meaning as its uses in *Anglo-Norwegian Fisheries* [i.e., *Fisheries Case (United Kingdom v. Norway)*], namely as an area of sea claimed exceptionally as internal waters (or, possibly, as territorial sea). ... In 1962 ... the UN Secretariat produced a memorandum on historic waters, which considered the term as equivalent to historic title. [This memorandum concluded, at Paragraphs 185, 186, 188 and 189: "185. In determining whether or not a title to "historic waters" exists, there are three factors which have to be taken into consideration, namely, (i) The authority exercised over the area by the State claiming it as "historic waters"; (ii) The continuity of such exercise of authority; (iii) The attitude of foreign states. 186. First, effective exercise of sovereignty over the area by the claiming State is a necessary requirement for title to the area as "historic waters" of that State. Secondly, such exercise of sovereignty must have continued during a considerable time so as to have developed into a usage. Thirdly, the attitude of foreign States to the activities of the claiming State in the area must have been such that it can be characterized as an attitude of general toleration. ... Particularly, it would seem reasonable, in the case of a State (or States) claiming historic title to waters bordered by two or more States, to accord special importance to the attitude of other riparian State (or States). .... 188. The burden of proof of title to "historic waters" is on the State claiming such title, in the sense that, if the State is unable to prove to the satisfaction of whoever has to decide the matter that the requirements necessary for the title have been fulfilled, [then] its claim to the title will be disallowed. [I]n accordance with general procedural rules each party has the burden of proof with respect to the facts on which he relies. ... 189. The legal status of "historic waters," i.e., the question whether they are to be considered as internal waters or as part of the territorial sea, would in principle depend on whether the sovereignty exercised in the particular case over the area by the claiming State and forming a basis for the claim, was sovereignty as over internal waters or sovereignty as over the territorial sea. [T]he sovereignty to be acquired should be commensurate with the sovereignty actually exercised." (United Nations (1962), Juridical Regime of Historic waters including historic bays – Study prepared by the Secretariat: Document A/CN.4/143 (New York: United Nations), 25).] ... The term 'historic rights' is general in nature and can describe any rights that a State may possess that would not normally arise under the general rules of international law, absent particular historical circumstances. Historic rights may include sovereignty, but may equally include more limited rights, such as fishing rights or rights of access, that fall well short of a claim of sovereignty. 'Historic title', in contrast, is used specifically to refer to historic sovereignty to land or maritime areas. 'Historic waters' is simply a term for historic title over maritime areas, typically exercised either as a claim to internal waters or as a claim to the territorial sea ... . [A] 'historic bay' is simply a bay in which a State claims historic waters. [T]his usage was understood by the drafters of the Convention and ... the reference to 'historic titles' in Article 298(1)(a)(i) of the Convention [(text to fn 186)] is accordingly a reference to claims of sovereignty over maritime areas derived from historical circumstances. This accords with the only other direct usage of the term, in Article 15 of the Convention [(fn 26 and accompanying text)], where historical sovereignty would understandably bear on the delimitation of the territorial sea. Other "historic rights," in contrast, are nowhere mentioned in the Convention, and the Tribunal sees nothing to suggest that Article 298(1)(a)(i) [of the UNCLOS] was intended to also exclude jurisdiction over a broad and unspecified category of possible claims to historic rights falling short of sovereignty. [T]his terminological distinction … exists also in Chinese[;] in its public statements, China has invoked its "historic rights" (li shi xing quan li, or 历史性权利) in the South China Sea, rather than historic title (li shi xing suo you quan, or 历史性所有权), as that term appears in the official Chinese text of the Convention. … China's usage has not been entirely consistent [–] the English version of China's Note Verbale of 6 July 2011 [from the Chinese Embassy in Manila to the Department of Foreign Affairs of the Philippines, No. (11) PG-202] … refers to "waters of which China has historic titles including sovereign rights and jurisdiction." This instance is at odds with the vast majority of China's statements [–] it more likely represents an error in translation or an instance of imprecise drafting, rather than a claim by China to sovereignty over the entirety of the South China Sea. [Whilst] the absence of a claim to historic title [may not] be inferred from China's use of the broader and less-specific term, as historic title constitutes one form of historic right, … China's conduct … is incompatible with a claim that the waters of the South China Sea constitute China's territorial sea or internal waters." (Permanent Court of Arbitration (2016), *PCA Case No 2013-19: Award*, 12 July 2016, paras.217, 221-222 and 225-228; italic emphasis original; bold emphasis added). The arbitral tribunal refers to China's conduct regarding the latter's thalassic claim, as follows: "Since 1956, China has proclaimed a series of maritime zones – a territorial sea, a contiguous zone, a continental shelf, and an exclusive economic zone – that are, at least in general terms, in line with those anticipated by the Convention [(i.e., the UNCLOS)]. Nevertheless, China's repeated invocation of rights "formed in the long historical course" and its linkage of this concept with the 'nine-dash line' [(fn 581)] indicates that China understands its rights to extend, in some form, beyond the maritime zones expressly described in the Convention. The Tribunal therefore turns to the rights that China has actually invoked in the South China Sea. Much of the area encompassed by the 'nine-dash line', however, would also fall within a claim to an exclusive economic zone or continental shelf drawn from the various features of the Spratly Islands. … [T]he mere fact that China asserts rights in the South China Sea does not indicate that China considers those rights to derive from the 'nine-dash line'. Where, however, China has asserted rights in areas beyond the maximum entitlements that could be claimed under the Convention, the Tribunal considers that such assertions indicate a claim to rights arising independently of the Convention. … In June 2012, the China National Offshore Oil Corporation … issued a notice of open blocks for petroleum exploration adjacent to the western edge of the 'nine-dash line'. The western portions of at least one of these blocks (Block BS16) lie beyond 200 nautical miles from any feature in the South China Sea claimed by China, and beyond any possible extended continental shelf. … Thus, with respect to some areas of the blocks, even assuming the maximum possible claim to entitlements that China could make under the Convention, China's authority to issue the petroleum blocks in question cannot be based solely upon entitlements derived from the Convention. [In addition], China has … objected to the Philippines' award of petroleum blocks within the 'nine-dash line' … . The area of the Philippines' petroleum blocks could be almost covered by entitlements claimed by China under the Convention, if China were understood to claim an exclusive economic zone from all high-tide features in the Spratly Islands … and from Scarborough Shoal. Despite the possibility that China's claims were based on a theory of entitlement to continental shelf rights pursuant to the Convention, the framing of China's objections [– which include 'incontrovertible Chinese sovereignty over the Spratly Islands and their adjacent waters', specified Philippine petroleum blocks being situated 'deep within the nine-dash line', and other identified Philippine petroleum blocks being located 'in the waters over which China has historic titles that include sovereign rights and jurisdiction' –] strongly indicates that China considers its rights with respect to petroleum resources to stem from historic rights.

waters of the South China Sea and, therefore, the tribunal has jurisdiction to address Philippine Submissions 1[626] and 2[627] [622], (ii) regarding Philippine Submission 15[628], there is no dispute between China and the Philippines such as would necessitate the arbitral tribunal to exercise jurisdiction [623], and (iii) the arbitral tribunal has jurisdiction to attend to the issues raised in the Philippine Submissions 1[629], 2[630], 3[631], 4[632], 5[633],

---

[I]n May 2012, [China's Ministry of Agriculture announced] a [s]ummer [ba]n on marine fishing [over part of the South China sea, which] could be almost entirely covered by entitlements claimed from the Convention, if China were understood to claim an exclusive economic zone from the very small rocks of Scarborough Shoal. However, taken together with the conclusion above about the grant of petroleum blocks and China's frequent reference to historic rights without further specification, the Tribunal concludes that China does claim rights to petroleum resources and fisheries within the 'nine-dash line' on the basis of historic rights existing independently of the Convention. ... China has unequivocally stated that it respects freedom of navigation and overflight in the South China Sea. ... Within the territorial sea, the Convention does not provide for freedom of overflight or for freedom of navigation, beyond a right of innocent passage [text to fn 32)]. Accordingly, the Tribunal considers China's commitment to respect both freedom of navigation and overflight to establish that China does not consider the sea areas within the 'nine-dash line' to be equivalent to its territorial sea or internal waters. The Tribunal also notes that China declared baselines for the territorial sea surrounding Hainan and the Paracel Islands[.] China would presumably not have done so if the waters both within and beyond 12 nautical miles of those islands already formed part of China's territorial sea (or internal waters) by virtue of a claim to historic rights through the 'nine-dash' line. [Thus,] China claims rights to the living and non-living resources within the 'nine-dash line' but (apart from the territorial sea generated by any islands) does not consider that those waters form part of its territorial sea or internal waters. ..." (Permanent Court of Arbitration (2016), *PCA Case No 2013-19: Award*, 12 July 2016, paras.207-214). The arbitral tribunal perorates so: "Having concluded that the exception to jurisdiction in Article 298(1)(a)(i) [of the UNCLOS] is limited to disputes involving historic titles [(text to fn 186)] and that China does not claim historic title to the waters of [the] South China Sea, but rather a constellation of historic rights short of title, the Tribunal holds that it has jurisdiction to consider the Philippines' Submissions No. 1 [(fn 603)] and 2 [(fn 604)]. As China has not made such a claim, the Tribunal need not consider whether there would be any limit to the application of Article 298 [of the UNCLOS] to expansive claims of historic title extending well beyond those that may have been anticipated when the Convention was concluded in 1982." (Permanent Court of Arbitration (2016), *PCA Case No 2013-19: Award*, 12 July 2016, para.229). The subsection entitled 'Optional Exceptions to the Applicability of Compulsory Procedures', in the section titled 'Part XV of the UNCLOS: Settlement of Disputes' in Chapter 1, comprises Article 298 of the UNCLOS.

[626] Fn 603 quotes Philippine Submission 1.

[627] Fn 604 quotes Philippine Submission 2.

[628] Fn 610 quotes Philippine Submission 15.

[629] Fn 603 quotes Philippine Submission 1.

[630] Fn 604 quotes Philippine Submission 2.

[631] Fn 611 quotes Philippine Submission 3.

[632] Fn 617 quotes Philippine Submission 4.

[633] Fn 605 quotes Philippine Submission 5.

6[634], 7[635], 8[636], 9[637], 10[638], 11[639], 12[640], 13[641], and 14(d)[642], and these claims are admissible [624]. On the merits of the case, the arbitral tribunal in its Award dated 12th July 2016: (i) declared that China's claims to sovereign – including historic – rights in respect of the maritime areas of the South China Sea within the nine-dash line breached the UNCLOS and were illegal to the extent that these demands exceeded the substantive and geographical limits of China's thalassic entitlements under this Convention, and that the UNCLOS superseded such rights where they were in excess of those restrictions[643] [625], (ii) found that none of the terrestrial areas of the South China Sea which were relevant to the

---

[634] Fn 618 quotes Philippine Submission 6.

[635] Fn 619 quotes Philippine Submission 7.

[636] Fn 606 quotes Philippine Submission 8.

[637] Fn 607 quotes Philippine Submission 9.

[638] Fn 620 quotes Philippine Submission 10.

[639] Fn 621 quotes Philippine Submission 11.

[640] Fn 608 quotes Philippine Submission 12.

[641] Fn 622 quotes Philippine Submission 13.

[642] The second sentence of fn 609 explains the introduction of, and quotes, Philippine Submission 14(d).

[643] The arbitral tribunal in the *South China Sea Arbitration* "concludes that *China's claim to historic rights to the living and non-living resources within the 'nine-dash line' is incompatible with the Convention [(i.e., the UNCLOS)] to the extent that it exceeds the limits of China's maritime zones as provided for by the Convention*. This is apparent in the text of the Convention which comprehensively addresses the rights of other States within the areas of the exclusive economic zone [(the subsections entitled 'The Coastal State's Jurisdiction, Rights and Duties Therein', 'Rights and Duties of Other States in the Exclusive Economic Zone', 'Artificial Islands, Installations and Structures', 'Conservation and Utilization of Living Resources', 'Migratory, Anadromous, Catadromous and Sedentary Species', 'Rights of Landlocked States as regards Exclusive Economic Zones', 'Rights of Geographically Disadvantaged States' and 'Non-Applicability and Restrictions on Transfer of these Rights', in the section titled 'Part V of the UNCLOS: Exclusive Economic Zone' in Chapter 1)] and continental shelf [the subsections entitled 'The Coastal State's Rights over the Continental Shelf', 'The Legal Status of Overlying Waters and Rights of Other States', 'Submarine Cables and Pipelines on the Continental Shelf', 'Artificial Islands, Installations and Structures; Drilling' and 'Tunnelling in the Subsoil of the Ocean Floor', in the section titled 'Part VI of the UNCLOS: Continental Shelf' in Chapter 1)] and *leaves no space for an assertion of historic rights*. ... Accordingly, upon China's accession to the Convention and its entry into force, *any historic rights that China may have had to the living and non-living resources within the 'nine-dash line were superseded, as a matter of law and as between the Philippines and China, by the limits of the maritime zones provided for by the Convention*. ... *Accession to the Convention reflects a commitment to bring incompatible claims into alignment with its provisions*, and its continued operation necessarily calls for compromise by those States with prior claims in excess of the Convention's limits (Permanent Court of Arbitration (2016), *PCA Case No 2013-19: Award*, 12 July 2016, paras.261-262; emphasis added). Fn 581 describes China's 'nine-dash line' claim.

Philippine Submissions generated entitlement to an exclusive economic zone or a continental shelf, and consequently declared Mischief Reef and Second Thomas Shoal to be within the exclusive economic zone and continental shelf of the Philippines[644] [626], and (iii) found China, by

---

[644] In the operative section of its Award dated 12th July 2016, the arbitral tribunal in the *South China Sea Arbitration* states: "1203. For the reasons set out in this Award, the Tribunal unanimously, and without any prejudice to any questions of sovereignty or maritime boundary delimitation, decides as follows: ... B. In relation to the merits of the Parties' disputes, the Tribunal: ... (3) FINDS, with respect to the status of features in the South China Sea: ... b. that Scarborough Shoal, Gaven Reef (North), McKennan Reef, Johnson Reef, Cuarteron Reef, and Fiery Cross Reef include, or in their natural condition did include, naturally formed areas of land, surrounded by water, which are above water at high tide, within the meaning of Article 121(1) of the Convention [(text to fn 152)]; c. that Subi Reef, Gaven Reef (South), Hughes Reef, Mischief Reef, and Second Thomas Shoal, are low-tide elevations, within the meaning of Article 13 of the Convention [(fn 23)]; d. that Subi Reef lies within 12 nautical miles of the high-tide feature of Sandy Cay on the reefs to the west of Thitu [and is therefore within Sandy Cay's territorial sea (text to fn 12, and the quoted passage containing fn 152)]; e. that Gaven Reef (South) lies within 12 nautical miles of the high-tide features of Gaven Reef (North) and Namyit Island [and is therefore within both the territorial sea of Gaven Reef (North) and that of Namyit Island (text to fn 12, and the quoted passage containing fn 152)]; and f. that Hughes Reef lies within 12 nautical miles of the high-tide features of McKennan Reef and Sin Cowe Island [and is therefore within both the territorial sea of McKennan Reef and that of Sin Cowe Island (text to fn 12, and the quoted passage containing fn 152)]; (4) DECLARES that, as low-tide elevations, Mischief Reef and Second Thomas Shoal do not generate entitlements to a territorial sea [(text to fn 24)], exclusive economic zone, or continental shelf [(final sentence of the quoted passage containing fn 152)] and are not features that are capable of appropriation; (5) DECLARES that, as low-tide elevations, Subi Reef, Gaven Reef (South), and Hughes Reef do not generate entitlements to a territorial sea [(text to fn 24)], exclusive economic zone, or continental shelf [(final sentence of the quoted passage containing fn 152)] and are not features that are capable of appropriation, but may be used as the baseline for measuring the breadth of the territorial sea of high-tide features situated at a distance not exceeding the breadth of the territorial sea [(text to fn 23)]; (6) DECLARES that Scarborough Shoal, Gaven Reef (North), McKennan Reef, Johnson Reef, Cuarteron Reef, and Fiery Cross Reef, in their natural condition, are rocks that cannot sustain human habitation or economic life of their own, within the meaning of Article 121(3) of the Convention [(final sentence of the quoted passage containing fn 152)] and accordingly that Scarborough Shoal, Gaven Reef (North), McKennan Reef, Johnson Reef, Cuarteron Reef, and Fiery Cross Reef generate no entitlement to an exclusive economic zone or continental shelf [(final sentence of the quoted passage containing fn 152)]; (7) FINDS with respect to the status of other features in the South China Sea: a. that none of the high-tide features in the Spratly Islands, in their natural condition, are capable of sustaining human habitation or economic life of their own within the meaning of Article 121(3) of the Convention [(final sentence of the quoted passage containing fn 152)]; b. that none of the high-tide features in the Spratly Islands generate entitlements to an exclusive economic zone or continental shelf [(final sentence of the quoted passage containing fn 152)]; and c. that therefore there is no entitlement to an exclusive economic zone or continental shelf generated by any feature claimed by China that would overlap the entitlements of the Philippines in the area of Mischief Reef and Second Thomas Shoal; and DECLARES that Mischief Reef and Second Thomas Shoal are

virtue of its behaviour in the South China Sea, including that part of the latter within the exclusive economic zone and/or continental shelf of the Philippines, to have contravened Articles 56[645], 58(3)[646], 60[647], 77[648], 80[649], 94[650], 123[651], 192[652], 194(1)[653], 194(5)[654], 197[655], 206[656], 279[657], 296[658] and 300[659] of the UNCLOS [627].

---

within the exclusive economic zone and continental shelf of the Philippines;" (Permanent Court of Arbitration (2016), *PCA Case No 2013-19: Award*, 12 July 2016, para.1203(B)(3)-(7); emphasis original).

[645] The subsection entitled 'The Coastal State's Jurisdiction, Rights and Duties Therein', in the section titled 'Part V of the UNCLOS: Exclusive Economic Zone' in Chapter 1, comprises Article 56 of the UNCLOS.

[646] The final sentence of the subsection entitled 'Rights and Duties of Other States in the Exclusive Economic Zone', in the section titled 'Part V of the UNCLOS: Exclusive Economic Zone' in Chapter 1, contains Article 58(3) of the UNCLOS.

[647] The subsection entitled 'Artificial Islands, Installations and Structures', in the section titled 'Part V of the UNCLOS: Exclusive Economic Zone' in Chapter 1, consists of Article 60 of the UNCLOS.

[648] The text to fn 129 comprises Article 77(1) of the UNCLOS. The text to fn 130 contains Article 77(2) of the UNCLOS. The text to fn 131, and the second sentence of the last paragraph of the subsection entitled 'Migratory, Anadromous, Catadromous and Sedentary Species' in the section entitled 'Part V of the UNCLOS: Exclusive Economic Zone' in Chapter 1 (to which fn 131 refers), contain Article 77(4) of the UNCLOS.

[649] The first sentence of the subsection entitled 'Artificial Islands, Installations and Structures; Drilling', in the section titled 'Part VI of the UNCLOS: Continental Shelf'' in Chapter 1, comprises Article 80 of the UNCLOS.

[650] Article 94 of the UNCLOS imposes duties specified therein upon the flag state concerning the regulation of ships on the high seas that are flying its flag. For instance, Article 94(3) of the UNCLOS declares: "Every State shall take such measures for ships flying its flag as are necessary to ensure safety at sea with regard, *inter alia*, to: (a) the construction, equipment and seaworthiness of ships; (b) the manning of ships, labour conditions and the training of crews, taking into account the applicable international instruments; (c) the use of signals, the maintenance of communications and the prevention of collisions."; emphasis original The last sentence of fn 319 defines '*inter alia*'.

[651] Paragraph 3 of the Award dated 12th July 2016 of the arbitral tribunal in the *South China Sea Arbitration* states: "The South China sea is a semi-enclosed sea in the western Pacific Ocean … ." Article 122 of the UNCLOS defines 'enclosed or semi-enclosed sea' as "a gulf, basin or sea surrounded by two or more States and connected to another sea or the ocean by a narrow outlet or consisting entirely or primarily of the territorial seas and exclusive economic zones of two or more coastal states." Article 123 of the UNCLOS requires countries that border an enclosed or semi-enclosed sea to co-operate with each other in the discharge of their obligations and the exercise of their rights under the UNCLOS, and, accordingly, to: (a) "coordinate the management, conservation, exploration and exploitation of the living resources of the sea;" (b) "coordinate the implementation of their rights and duties with respect to the protection and preservation of the marine environment;" (c) "coordinate their scientific research policies and undertake where appropriate joint programmes of scientific research in the area;" and (d) "invite, as appropriate, other interested States or international organizations to cooperate with them in furtherance of the provisions of this article."

In its interpretation of the terms of Article 121(3) of the UNCLOS[660], the arbitral tribunal held the verb to 'sustain', in association with the term 'human habitation', to mean "to provide that which is necessary to keep

---

[652] Article 192 of the UNCLOS proclaims: "States have the obligation to protect and preserve the marine environment."

[653] Article 194(1) of the UNCLOS asseverates: "States shall take, individually or jointly as appropriate, all measures consistent with this Convention [(i.e., the UNCLOS)] that are necessary to prevent, reduce and control pollution of the marine environment from any source, using for this purpose the best practicable means at their disposal and in accordance with their capabilities, and they shall endeavour to harmonize their policies in this connection."

[654] Article 194(5) of the UNCLOS avers: "The measures taken in accordance with this Part [(i.e., Part XII of the UNCLOS, which is entitled 'Protection and Preservation of the Marine Environment')] shall include those necessary to protect and preserve rare or fragile ecosystems as well as the habitat of depleted, threatened or endangered species and other forms of marine life."

[655] Article 197 of the UNCLOS declares: "States shall cooperate on a global basis and, as appropriate, on a regional basis, directly or through competent international organizations, in formulating and elaborating international rules, standards and recommended practices and procedures consistent with this Convention [(i.e., the UNCLOS)], for the protection and preservation of the marine environment, taking into account characteristic regional features."

[656] Article 206 of the UNCLOS proclaims: "When States have reasonable grounds for believing that planned activities under their jurisdiction or control may cause substantial pollution of or significant and harmful changes to the marine environment, they shall, as far as practicable, assess the potential effects of such activities on the marine environment and shall communicate reports of the results of such assessments in the manner provided in article 205 [of the UNCLOS]." Article 205 of the UNCLOS asseverates: "States shall publish reports of the results obtained pursuant to article 204 [of the UNCLOS] or provide such reports at appropriate intervals to the competent international organizations, which should make them available to all States." Article 204 of the UNCLOS avers: "1. States shall, consistent with the rights of other States, endeavour, as far as practicable, directly or through the competent international organizations, to observe, measure, evaluate and analyse, by recognized scientific methods, the risks or effects of pollution of the marine environment. 2. In particular, States shall keep under surveillance the effects of any activities which they permit or in which they engage in order to determine whether these activities are likely to pollute the marine environment."

[657] The first sentence of the subsection entitled 'Disputes are to be Settled by Peaceful Means of the Parties' Choice', in the section titled 'Part XV of the UNCLOS: Settlement of Disputes' in Chapter 1, comprises Article 279 of the UNCLOS.

[658] The subsection entitled 'Compulsory Procedures: Finality and Binding Force of Decisions', in the section titled 'Part XV of the UNCLOS: Settlement of Disputes' in Chapter 1, consists of Article 296 of the UNCLOS.

[659] Article 300 of the UNCLOS declares: "States Parties shall fulfil in good faith the obligations assumed under this Convention [(i.e., the UNCLOS)] and shall exercise the rights, jurisdiction and freedoms recognized in this Convention in a manner which would not constitute an abuse of right." Fn 192 defines 'States Parties'.

[660] The last sentence of the quoted passage containing fn 152 states Article 121(3) of the UNCLOS.

humans alive and healthy over a continuous period of time, according to a proper standard" [628]. Whilst the use of the word 'or' between the phrases 'human habitation' and 'economic life' in Article 121(3) of the UNCLOS indicates that a high-tide feature would need to be "able to sustain *either* human habitation *or* an economic life of its own"[661] in order to be granted an exclusive economic zone and continental shelf [629], it is submitted that both 'sustained human habitation' – requiring such a feature to be competent "to support, maintain, and provide food, drink and shelter to some humans to enable them to reside there permanently or habitually over an extended period of time" [630], and 'sustained economic activity of its own' – requiring the high-tide feature together with its territorial sea to be able to support an independent, long-term economic life [631], are difficult to demonstrate in respect of any islet. Having held each of Scarborough Shoal [632], Johnson Reef [633], Cuarteron Reef [634], Fiery Cross Reef [635], Gaven Reef (North) [636] and McKennan Reef [637] to be a 'rock' for the purposes of Article 121(3) to the UNCLOS[662] – and, therefore, to be accompanied by a territorial sea but neither by an economic zone nor a continental shelf [638], the Tribunal proceeded to analyze the high-tide features of Itu Aba (Island), Thitu (Island), West York (Island), Spratly Island, South-West Cay, and North-East Cay against the criteria in that Paragraph of the Convention – together with "the other, less significant high-tide features in the Spratly Islands, which are even less capable of sustaining economic life" [639] – concluding "that none of the high-tide features in the Spratly Islands are capable of sustaining human habitation or an economic life of their own[, and so] the effect of Article 121(3) [of the UNCLOS] is that such features shall have no exclusive economic zone or continental shelf" [640]. On this latter group of high-tide features[663], the arbitral tribunal made, *inter alia*[664], the following comments.

---

[661] Emphasis added.

[662] The final sentence of the quoted passage containing fn 152 comprises Article 121(3) of the UNCLOS.

[663] 'This latter group of high-tide features' comprises Itu Aba, Thitu, West York, Spratly Island, South-West Cay, North-East Cay and 'the other less significant high-tide features in the Spratly Islands'.

On the basis of the evidence in the record, it appears to the Tribunal that the principal high-tide features in the Spratly [I]slands are capable of enabling the survival of small groups of people. There is historical evidence of potable[665] water, although of varying quality, that could be combined with rainwater collection and storage. There is also naturally occurring vegetation capable of providing shelter and the possibility of at least limited agriculture to supplement the food resources of the surrounding waters. The record indicates that small numbers of fishermen, mainly from Hainan [i.e., China, of which Hainan is a constituent island], have historically been present on Itu Aba and other more significant features and appear to have survived principally on the basis of the resources at hand (notwithstanding the references to annual deliveries of rice and other sundries) [641].

The principal features of the Spratly Islands are not barren rocks or sand cays, devoid of fresh water, that can be dismissed as uninhabitable on the basis of their physical characteristics alone. [Nevertheless], the features are not obviously habitable, and their capacity even to enable human survival appears to be distinctly limited. In these circumstances, ... the physical characteristics of the features do not definitively indicate the capacity of the features. Accordingly, the Tribunal [must] consider the historical evidence of human habitation and economic life on the Spratly Islands and the implications of such evidence for the natural capacity of the features [642].

In addition to the presence of fishermen noted above, Itu Aba and South-West Cay were the site of Japanese mining and fishing activities in the 1920s and 1930s. The Spratlys were also the site of the ... activities of Thomas Cloma and his associates in the 1950s[666]. More recently, many

---

[664] The last sentence of fn 319 defines '*inter alia*'.

[665] The final sentence of fn 548 defines 'potable'.

[666] The Kingdom of Colonia St John's website states: "In the period between 1947 and 1950, the fishing boats belonging to Tomas Cloma, a Philippine citizen ... , made a number of visits to the Spratly group of islands in search for better fishing grounds. Cloma considered establishing an ice plant and cannery on Itu Aba, the largest island of the group (approximately 2 square miles in area), and was planning the exploitation of guano. [1955:] Five years after Cloma's initial visits to the Spratlys ... [t]he Philippine Armed forces sent an amphibian bomber on a patrol mission over the Spratly group of islands. The patrol took aerial photos of the islands, but they showed no settlements. A view of Itu Aba, however, showed the remains of a wharf and some ruined buildings. [Morton] Meads ... explained that the buildings on Itu Aba were the remnants of a Japanese submarine base built there during the war. ... [Philippine] Vice-President Carlos P. Garcia ... recommended to

President [Ramon] Magsaysay that the Philippines lay claim to the group. The Nationalist Chinese (Taiwanese) Government made clear that it would contest such a move 'because the islands formed part of their territory'. The matter progressed no further for a while and the public interest in the affair waned. [1956:] It was ignited again the following year when Cloma laid claim to a territory in the South China Sea, apparently including part or whole of the Spratly group. Cloma and his associates decided to send an expedition to the territory he claimed. … Cloma [informed Garcia] that 40 Philippine citizens were undertaking survey and occupation work "in a territory in the China Sea outside the Philippine waters and not within the jurisdiction of any country" and that the said territory was being claimed by him and his associates to which effect due notice had been posted on each of the surveyed and occupied islands, to be subsequently published in the press and sent to the representatives of foreign governments. … Vice-President Garcia received the Nationalist Chinese (Taiwanese) Ambassador who informed him that the islands [claimed by Cloma, which Cloma had] renamed Freedomland were well known and belonged to Nationalist China. Garcia replied that he would call a conference of Government agencies to discuss the matter. … The communist Chinese Kwan Ming Daily said that the Freedomland islands, together with the Spratlys, were in fact Nansha Islands which had been Chinese since the times before Magellan. The South Vietnamese Government in Saigon issued a communiqué stating that the Spratlys and the Paracels [i.e., the Paracel Islands, which are in the South China Sea – north of the Spratly Islands] had always been part of Vietnam and had been recognised as such in the San Francisco Peace Conference of September 1951. … Cloma [appealed] to the UN "through the friendly agency of the Philippines and the spiritual guidance of the Vatican" to create an arbitrating body composed of friendly powers which would decide on the status of Freedomland, and to undertake trusteeship over Freedomland under the administration and the guidance of the US[A] until the question of ownership is finally resolved. A Nationalist Chinese patrol … visited [the] Spratlys … . The same day, another Cloma expedition set out to bring provisions to the twenty nine men left there by the May expedition … . Arriving at Itu Aba, the expedition found that the markers they had put up in March had been removed and that the Nationalist Chinese had added their own sign onto an old Japanese marker, also painting a sign on one of the ruined concrete buildings. The French Charge d'Affairs in Manila informed Juan M. Arreglado, the legal counsellor to the Department of Foreign Affairs [of the Philippines], that the Spratlys belonged to France by virtue of an occupation effected in 1932-1933. France had ceded the Paracels to Vietnam, he said, but not the Spratlys. His statement seemed to be supported by the fact that a marker found on Itu Aba bore the words "Ile de France, April 25, 1933." The ruins there were believed to ha[ve] been a French fertilizer factory and not (as Meads had originally said) a Japanese submarine base. Vice President Garcia responded by saying that … he had warned Cloma not to do anything that could have political repercussions of any kind. The same day, a South Vietnam Legation spokesman said that the Spratlys were officially incorporated in the Vietnamese province of Baria in 1929. When the French officially took possession in 1930, they notified the US[A], China, the Philippines and the Netherlands [(i) which, in 1956, retained Netherlands New Guinea – although the Netherlands' former colony the Dutch East Indies had become the newly-independent state of Indonesia, (ii) but which, in 1930, possessed the Dutch East Indies – which *then* included the territory that survived the commencement of Indonesian independence as Netherlands New Guinea, i.e., the western part of New Guinea that is *now* (but was not in 1956) the easternmost section of Indonesia]. Only Japan protested but officially renounced its claim in the Peace treaty of 1952. Consequently, the French transfer of sovereignty included both the Spratlys and the Paracels. The Department of Foreign Affairs received confidential reports that the Dutch Government was about to stake its own claim over the disputed islands, with the backing of the UK. The same day, Cloma [contacted the Ministry of Foreign Affairs of of the features have been transformed by substantial construction efforts and are now the site of installations hosting significant numbers of personnel, generally of a governmental nature. The first question for the Tribunal is whether any of this activity constitutes "human habitation" or an "economic life of its own" for the purposes of Article 121(3) [of the UNCLOS]. The second is whether there is evidence to suggest that the historical record of human activity on the Spratly Islands is not proof of the natural capacity of the features [643].

---

the Philippines], stating that two small islands near Spratly Island, not previously included in the map of Freedomland, had been discovered. .... Cloma ... made plans for organizing a government for Freedomland. Cloma presented a paper to the Secretary of Foreign Affairs [of the Philippines] announcing the establishment of a separate Government for the Archipelago of Freedomland. ... Freedomland adopted the laws of the Philippines. ... As the first act of the new Government, Cloma formally delivered the Nationalist Chinese flag removed from Itu Aba to the Nationalist Chinese Embassy in Manila. ... Cloma wrote to the Chinese Ambassador in Manila, expressing concern about reports that the Nationlist Government had granted some private businessmen the authority to undertake mining surveys. Surveys of the natural resources of Freedomland had already been done by Cloma, and surface mining of phosphates had been in progress ... with 4000 tonnes standing ready for shipment to New Zealand and Japanese buyers. [1959:] Cloma learned that some Taiwanese merchants were selling phosphates[,] which had come from Freedomland[,] in Japan. ... [1960:] Cloma initiated agreements with a Hong Kong company for the exploitation of Freedomland's resources ... . [1971:] [Philippine] President [Ferdinand] Marcos issued and read a press statement concerning Freedomland, saying that his Foreign Office had requested the Nationalist Chinese Government to withdraw its garrison from Itu Aba ... which ... belonged to the Allied war booty [i.e., from the Second World War of 1939-1945] and no one was permitted to introduce troops to it without the consent of the Allies. In the same statement, President Marcos ... said that he had taken steps to protect Freedomland and that the Philippines were in occupation and control of the islands of Pagasa, Lawak and Patag. ... Following this statement, the Governments of Great Britain and the Netherlands announced the abandonment of their rights as trustees over [the] Spratly Islands. [T]wo Congressmen ... filed a bill [in the Philippine Congress] appropriating [PHP] 1 million for the development of Freedomland[,] which the Philippines was now claiming. .... [1972:] ... Cloma constituted an Advisory Council for the Government of Freedomland. ... [1974:] ... Cloma and the Supreme Council of Freedomland drafted a new Constitution, changing the country's status to Principality. ... The new Constitution encouraged the colonization of the territory by people from around the world. ... Cloma was alarmed at the deterioriation of the political system in the Philippines. ... He announced his resignation as Head of State [of Freedomland] ... . He asked the Supreme Council [of Freedomland] to change the name of the country to Colonia, and to elevate its status to the 'Kingdom of Colonia'. That done, Cloma retired and resigned from the Supreme Council and as Head of State in favour of Prince John de Mariveles. ... A new Constitution was approved for the kingdom, the Secretariat in Manila closed and the new seat of the Government-in-exile established in Labuan, Sabah (part of Malaysia). ..." (Kingdom of Colonia St John (2019), "The History of the Kingdom of Colonia St John," accessed December 23, 2019, <http://www.colonia.asia/history%20-%20the%20history%20of%20the%20kingdom%20of%20colonia%20st%20john.htm>).

(a) Historical Human Habitation of the Features of the Spratly Islands[667]

[T]he criterion of human habitation is not met by the temporary inhabitation of the Spratly Islands by fishermen, even for extended periods. [T]he Tribunal considers human habitation to entail the non-transient inhabitation of a feature by a stable community of people for whom the feature constitutes a home and on which they can remain. This standard is not met by the historical presence of fishermen that appears in the record before the Tribunal. [T]he very fact that the fishermen are consistently recorded as being "from Hainan," or elsewhere, is evidence … that they do not represent the natural population of the Spratlys. Nowhere is there any reference to the fishermen "of Itu Aba," "of Thitu," or "of North Danger Reef," nor is there any suggestion that the fishermen were accompanied by their families. Nor do any of the descriptions of conditions on the features suggest the creation of the shelter and facilities that the Tribunal would expect for a population intending to reside permanently among the islands. Rather, the record indicates a pattern of temporary residence on the features for economic purposes, with the fishermen remitting their profits, and ultimately returning, to the mainland [644].

The same conclusion holds true with respect to Japanese commercial activities on Itu Aba and South-West Cay. A crew of Formosan [i.e., Taiwanese] labourers, brought to the Spratlys to mine guano or capture sea turtles, is inherently transient in nature: their objective was to extract the economic resources of the Spratlys for the benefit of the population of Formosa [i.e., Taiwan, which was formerly a colony of Japan] to which they would return. It was not to make a new life for themselves on the islands. … The temporary presence of these persons on the features for a few short years does not suffice to establish a settled community within the meaning of "human habitation" in Article 121(3) [of the UNCLOS] [645].

[T]he Tribunal does not consider that the military or other government personnel presently stationed on the features in the Spratly Islands by one or another of the littoral States suffice to constitute "human habitation" for the purposes of Article 121(3) [of the UNCLOS]. These groups are heavily dependent on outside supply … . [Such]

667 Emphasis original.

personnel are deployed to the Spratly Islands in an effort to support the various claims to sovereignty that have been advanced. There is no evidence that they choose to inhabit there of their own volition, nor can it be expected that any would remain if the official need for their presence were to dissipate. Even where the current human presence in the Spratly Islands includes civilians, as is the case on at least Thitu and (very recently) Itu Aba, the Tribunal considers that their presence there is motivated by official considerations and would not have occurred, but for the disputed claims to sovereignty over these features [646].

The Tribunal sees no indication that anything fairly resembling a stable human community has ever been formed on the Spratly Islands. Rather, the islands have been a temporary refuge and base of operations for fishermen and a transient residence for labourers engaged in mining and fishing. The introduction of the exclusive economic zone [by the UNCLOS[668]] was not intended to grant extensive maritime entitlements to small features whose historical contribution to human settlement is as slight as that. Nor was the exclusive economic zone intended to encourage States to establish artificial populations in the hope of making expansive claims, precisely what has now occurred in the South China Sea. On the contrary, Article 121(3) [of the UNCLOS] was intended to prevent such developments and to forestall a provocative and counterproductive effort to manufacture entitlements [647].

The Tribunal sees no evidence that would suggest that the historical absence of human habitation on the Spratly Islands is the product of intervening forces or otherwise does not reflect the limited capacity of the features themselves. Accordingly, the Tribunal concludes that Itu Aba, West York, Spratly Island, South-West Cay, and North-East Cay are not capable of sustaining human habitation within the meaning of Article 121(3) [of the UNCLOS]. The Tribunal ... reaches the same conclusion with respect to, the other, less significant high-tide features in the Spratly Islands, which are even less capable of sustaining human habitation ... [648].

---

[668] The phrase 'exclusive economic zone' was first used at UNCLOS III (fn 12), of which the UNCLOS was the end product (first sentence of the second paragraph of the section entitled 'Introduction', in Chapter 1).

(b) Historical Economic Life of Their Own of the Features of the Spratly Islands[669]

[A]ll of the economic activity in the Spratly Islands that appears in the historical record has been essentially extractive in nature (*i.e.*[670], mining for guano, collecting shells, and fishing), aimed … at utilising the resources of the Spratlys for the benefit of the populations of Hainan, Formosa, Japan, the Philippines, Viet Nam, or elsewhere. [T]o constitute the economic life of the feature, economic activity must be oriented around the feature itself and not be focused solely on the surrounding territorial sea or entirely dependent on external resources. [E]xtractive economic activity, without the presence of a stable local community, necessarily falls short of constituting the economic life of the feature [649].

Applying this standard, the history of extractive economic activity does not constitute for the features of the Spratly Islands, evidence of an economic life of their own. … [650].

Having declared all the high-tide features within the Spratly Islands to be rocks that cannot sustain human habitation or economic life of their own within the meaning of Article 121(3) of the UNCLOS[671], the arbitral tribunal in the *South China Sea Arbitration* concluded that there were no overlapping entitlements between China and the Philippines with regard to each country's exclusive economic zone and continental shelf, and, therefore, no need to delimit any boundaries. Consequently, the Government of China's Declaration that utilized the exception in Article 298(1)(a) of the UNCLOS[672] to the comprehensive scope of the jurisdiction of any arbitral tribunal constituted in accordance with Annex VII to the UNCLOS[673], which was subsequently invoked by China[674], was

---

[669] Emphasis original.

[670] Emphasis original.

[671] The last sentence of the quoted passage containing fn 152 states Article 121(3) of the UNCLOS.

[672] The section below entitled 'Article 298(1)(a) of the UNCLOS' considers the working of Article 298(1)(a) of the UNCLOS.

[673] Fn 583 quotes China's Declaration of 25th August 2006 under Article 298 of the UNCLOS (optional exceptions to the applicability of Section 2 of Part XV of the UNCLOS). The subsection entitled 'Optional Exceptions to the Applicability of Compulsory Procedures', in the section titled 'Part XV of the UNCLOS: Settlement of Disputes' in Chapter 1, contains

inapplicable to the *South China Sea Arbitration*. Therefore, the tribunal was legally able to address whether the low-tide elevations[675] of Mischief Reef and Second Thomas Shoal[676] fell within the exclusive economic zone and/or the continental shelf of the Philippines – as Philippine Submission 5 requested[677].

> [T]he Philippines' Submission No. 5 does not itself call for the Tribunal to decide a dispute concerning sea boundary delimitation ... . [N]othing in the Convention [(i.e., the UNCLOS)] prevents a Tribunal from recognising the existence of an exclusive economic zone or continental shelf, or of addressing the legal consequence of such zones, in an area where the entitlements of the State claiming an exclusive economic zone or continental shelf are not overlapped by the entitlements of any other State. Doing so does not implicate the delimitation of maritime boundaries or the exclusion from jurisdiction in Article 298(1)(a)(i) [of the UNCLOS][678] [651]. ...
>
> The Tribunal has already held ... that there is no legal basis for any Chinese historic rights, or sovereign rights and jurisdiction beyond those provided for in the Convention, in the waters of the South China Sea encompassed by the 'nine-dash line'[679]. The Tribunal sees no evidence that, prior to the Convention, China ever established a historic right to the exclusive use of the living and non-living resources of the waters of the South China Sea ... . In any event, any such right would have been superseded by the adoption of the Convention[680] and the legal creation of the exclusive economic zone[681]. The 'nine-dash line'[682] thus cannot

---

Article 298 of the UNCLOS. Fn 163 describes Sections 2 and 3 of Part XV of the UNCLOS.

674 Text to fn 592.

675 Fn 23 defines 'low-tide elevation'.

676 Fn 683.

677 Fn 605 quotes Philippine Submission 5.

678 The heading '(a)(i)' in the first sentence of the subsection entitled 'Optional Exceptions to the Applicability of Compulsory Procedures' in the section titled 'Part XV of the UNCLOS: Settlement of Disputes' in Chapter 1, together with the first sentence of fn 188, comprises Article 298(1)(a)(i) of the UNCLOS.

679 Fn 643 and accompanying text.

680 Fn 679.

681 Fn 668 and accompanying text.

provide a basis for any entitlement by China to maritime zones in the area of Mischief Reef or Second Thomas Shoal[683] that would overlap the entitlement of the Philippines to an exclusive economic zone and continental shelf generated from baselines on the island of Palawan[684] [652].

The Tribunal has now held … that Mischief Reef and Second Thomas Shoal are low-tide elevations and, as such, generate no entitlement to maritime zones of their own[685]. The Tribunal has also now held (see paragraph 626 above[686]) that neither Itu Aba nor any other high-tide feature in the Spratly Islands, is a fully entitled island for the purposes of Article 121 of the Convention[687]. As such, pursuant to the operation of Article 121(3) of the Convention[688], these features are legally considered to be "rocks" and to generate no exclusive economic zone or continental shelf. The Tribunal also notes that there is no maritime feature that is above water at high tide in its natural condition and that is located within 12 nautical miles of either Mischief Reef or Thomas Shoal[689] [653].

---

682 Fn 581 describes China's 'nine dash line' claim.

683 The arbitral tribunal in the *South China Sea Arbitration* held in its Award dated 12th July 2016 that Mischief Reef and Second Thomas Shoal are low-tide elevations, which, as such, are entitled to neither a territorial sea, nor an exclusive economic zone, nor a continental shelf (fn 644).

684 The last sentence of the second paragraph of the subsection entitled 'The Exclusive Economic Zone', in the section titled 'Part V of the UNCLOS: Exclusive Economic Zone' in Chapter 1, indicates how the exclusive economic zone is determined and from which baselines it is generated. The subsection entitled 'Definition of the Continental Shelf', in the section titled 'Part VI of the UNCLOS: Continental Shelf' in Chapter 1, describes how the outer limit of the continental shelf is ascertained – and specifies from which baselines it is measured.

685 Fn 644.

686 The last clause (i.e., from the word 'concluding') of the penultimate sentence of the ninth paragraph of the current subsection (i.e., that entitled 'Example Arbitration Case – The South China Sea Arbitration') comprises Paragraph 626 of the Award dated 12th July 2016 of the arbitral tribunal in the *South China Sea Arbitration*.

687 The first paragraph of the section entitled 'Part VIII of the UNCLOS: Regime of Islands', in Chapter 1, quotes Article 121 of the UNCLOS.

688 The final sentence of the quoted passage containing fn 152 – this passage being the paragraph to which fn 687 refers – states Article 121(3) of the UNCLOS.

689 Whilst the low-water line on a low-tide elevation that is located partly within the territorial sea of the mainland or an island may be used as the baseline for measuring the breadth of that sea, a low-tide elevation is refused its own territorial sea if it is entirely situated beyond the territorial sea of any high-tide feature (text to fns 23 and 24). Fn 23 defines 'low-tide elevation'. As no high-tide feature is located within twelve nautical miles of either Mischief Reef or Thomas Shoal – this distance being the maximum breadth of the territorial sea that may be claimed, as measured from baselines that are determined in conformity with the

From these conclusions, it follows that there exists no legal basis for any entitlement by China to maritime zones in the area of Mischief Reef or Second Thomas Shoal. Accordingly, there is no situation of overlapping entitlements that would call for the application of Articles 15[690], 74[691], or 83[692] [of the UNCLOS] to delimit the overlap. Because no delimitation is required – or, indeed, even possible – there is no possible basis for the application of the exception to jurisdiction in Article 298(1)(a)(i) [of the UNCLOS][693] [654]. ...

[T]he Tribunal concludes that Mischief Reef and Second Thomas Shoal are both low-tide elevations that generate no maritime zones of their own. The Tribunal also concludes that none of the high-tide features in the Spratly Islands are capable of sustaining human habitation or an economic life of their own within the meaning of those terms in Article 121(3) of the Convention. All of the high-tide features in the Spratly Islands are therefore legally rocks for [the] purposes of Article 121(3) [of the UNCLOS] and do not generate entitlements to an exclusive economic zone or continental shelf. There is, accordingly, no possible entitlement by China to any maritime zone in the area of either Mischief Reef or Second Thomas Shoal and no jurisdictional obstacle to the Tribunal's consideration of the Philippines' Submission No. 5[694] [655].

With respect to the Philippines' Submission No. 5, the Tribunal concludes that both Mischief Reef and Second Thomas Shoal are located within 200 nautical miles of the Philippines' coast on the island of Palawan and are located in an area that is not overlapped by the entitlements generated by any maritime feature claimed by China. It follows, therefore, that, as between the Philippines and China, Mischief

---

UNCLOS (first sentence of the subsection entitled 'The Limits of the Territorial Sea and the Concept of the Baseline', in the section titled 'Part II of the UNCLOS: Territorial Sea and Contiguous Zone' in Chapter 1), neither of these low-tide elevations may be used by states attempting to assert sovereignty over one or more of the high-tide features in the Spratly Islands to extend territorial sea of those claimed feature(s).

[690] The subsection entitled 'Delimitation of the Territorial Sea between States', in the section titled 'Part II of the UNCLOS: Territorial Sea and Contiguous Zone' in Chapter 1, contains Article 15 of the UNCLOS.

[691] The subsection entitled 'Delimitation of the Exclusive Economic Zone between States' in the section titled 'Part V of the UNCLOS: 'Part V of the UNCLOS: Exclusive Economic Zone', comprises Article 74 of the UNCLOS.

[692] The subsection entitled 'Delimitation of the Continental Shelf between States' in the section titled 'Part VI of the UNCLOS: Continental Shelf', consists of Article 83 of the UNCLOS.

[693] Fn 678.

[694] Fn 605 quotes Philippine Submission 5.

Reef and Second Thomas Shoal form part of the exclusive economic zone and continental shelf of the Philippines[695] [656].

Analysis

The two Awards granted by the Annex VII arbitral tribunal in the *South China Sea Arbitration*, and the reasoning on which they are based, taken together comprise a first-class piece of politico-legal thinking. The arbitral tribunal excludes from the jurisdictional exception in Article 298(1)(a) of the UNCLOS, which China has utilized in its Declaration of 25th August 2006[696], the rights and sovereignty claimed by the Government of China over the maritime area within its nine-dash line, by finding that only an absolute sovereign claim to this territory as Chinese internal waters or territorial sea would render it within the 'historic titles' head of this exception. Consequently, a judgment as to the validity of the Chinese claim over the thalassic areas of the nine-dash line falls within the arbitral tribunal's jurisdiction. The tribunal then proceeds to find that the part of this claim that extends beyond the rights conferred on coastal states by the UNCLOS within their own maritime zones, the high seas, and, especially, the maritime zones of other littoral countries – in particular the Philippines, is incompatible with the UNCLOS and, therefore, in breach of international law. Accession to the UNCLOS means acceptance of the rights conferred, and duties imposed, by this Convention on the acceding state, and a consequent renunciation of historic rights that exceed those which the UNCLOS confers on its States Parties[697]. Thus, the tribunal finds China to be in breach of several provisions of the Convention, both within

[695] The exclusive economic zone extends to a distance of no more than 200 nautical miles from the baselines from which the territorial sea's breadth is measured (as the final sentence of the second paragraph of the subsection entitled 'The Exclusive Economic Zone', in the section titled 'Part V of the UNCLOS: Exclusive Economic Zone' in Chapter 1, specifies), and the continental shelf extends to a distance of at least 200 nautical miles from these baselines (as the subsection entitled 'Definition of the Continental Shelf', in the section titled 'Part VI of the UNCLOS: Continental Shelf' in Chapter 1, explains). Therefore, Mischief Reef and Second Thomas Shoal, by virtue of being less than 200 nautical miles from the baselines on the long north-west coast of Palawan from which the width of the territorial sea of the Philippines is measured, is part of the exclusive economic zone and continental shelf of the Philippines.

[696] Fn 583 contains this Declaration.

[697] Fn 192 defines 'States Parties'.

the Philippine exclusive economic zone and/or continental shelf and on the high seas. This minimization of the scope of the historic rights of littoral states is coupled with a findings of a high threshold for a high-tide feature to be classified as an 'island' rather than a 'rock' under Article 121 of the UNCLOS[698], which attempts to stem the tendency of coastal countries to claim sovereignty over high-tide features in the high seas in order to assert an exclusive economic zone and a continental shelf around those features over which they can then apply 'rights' which are accorded by the relevant part of the UNCLOS – such as to build artificial islands in accordance with Article 60(1)(a) of the UNCLOS in the claimed exclusive economic zone[699] encircling each of these high-tide features, and in observance of Article 80 of the UNCLOS in its claimed continental shelf[700]. Then, based on an exploration of their physical characteristics and accumulated records relating to activities formerly pursued there, the arbitral tribunal finds that the high-tide features to which it applies Article 121 of the UNCLOS – including all those in the Spratly Islands, fail to demonstrate the capacity to "sustain human habitation or economic life" in Paragraph 3 of that Article[701], which results in the tribunal classifying these features as 'rocks' as defined within that Paragraph – and thereby denying every one of them its own exclusive economic zone and continental shelf. This technique enabled the tribunal in the *South China Sea Arbitration* to uphold the exclusive economic zone and continental shelf of the Philippines without risk of having to entertain rival maritime claims from China via the Spratly Islands. As no boundary delimitation of either territorial sea, or exclusive economic zone, or continental shelf, was required between competing

---

[698] The first paragraph of the section entitled 'Part VIII of the UNCLOS: Regime of Islands', in Chapter 1, quotes Article 121 of the UNCLOS.

[699] The first sentence of the first paragraph of the subsection entitled 'Artificial Islands, Installations and Structures', in the section titled 'Part V of the UNCLOS: Exclusive Economic Zone' in Chapter 1, comprises Article 60(1) of the UNCLOS.

[700] The first sentence of the section titled 'Part VI of the UNCLOS: Continental Shelf' in Chapter 1, consists of Article 80 of the UNCLOS.

[701] The final sentence of the quoted passage containing fn 152 states Article 121(3) of the UNCLOS.

states under Articles 15[702], 74[703] and 83[704] of the UNCLOS, respectively, the Government of China was unable to prevail concerning its attempt to avoid the jurisdiction of the arbitral tribunal using its Declaration under Article 298 of the UNCLOS[705] on the ground that its dispute with the Philippines concerned "the interpretation or application of [A]rticles 15, 74 or 83 [of the UNCLOS] relating to sea boundary delimitations"[706]. More than being a victory for the Philippines, however, as the press at the time tended to report[707], the arbitral tribunal's findings in the *South China Sea Arbitration*, are a rigorous defence of the rights conferred, and obligations imposed, by the UNCLOS on all its States Parties. By reading the derogations in Article 298(1)(a)(i) of the UNCLOS concerning "the interpretation or application of [A]rticles … relating to sea boundary delimitations"[708] and "historic … titles[709]" narrowly, and by construing the phrase "Rocks which cannot sustain human habitation or economic life of their own" in Article 121(3) of the UNCLOS[710] broadly, such that all the high-tide features that the applicant State asks it to classify it designates as 'rocks' rather than 'islands' – which results in these being granted a

[702] The subsection entitled 'Delimitation of the Territorial Sea between States', in the section titled 'Part II of the UNCLOS: Territorial Sea and Contiguous Zone' in Chapter 1, comprises Article 15 of the UNCLOS.

[703] The subsection entitled 'Delimitation of the Exclusive Economic Zone between States' in the section titled 'Part V of the UNCLOS: 'Part V of the UNCLOS: Exclusive Economic Zone', consists of Article 74 of the UNCLOS.

[704] The subsection entitled 'Delimitation of the Continental Shelf between States' in the section titled 'Part VI of the UNCLOS: Continental Shelf', contains Article 83 of the UNCLOS.

[705] Fn 583 comprises this Declaration.

[706] Article 298(1)(a)(i) of the UNCLOS contains this quoted phrase, which is found in the first sentence of the subsection entitled 'Optional Exceptions to the Applicability of Compulsory Procedures', in the section titled 'Part V of the UNCLOS: Settlement of Disputes' in Chapter 1.

[707] For instance, *The Guardian* stated "The judgment by an international tribunal in The Hague came down overwhelmingly in favour of the claims made by the Philippines and is likely to increase global diplomatic pressure on Beijing to scale back military expansion in the area. By depriving certain outcrops of territorial-generating status, the ruling from the permanent court of arbitration effectively punches holes in China's all-encompassing "nine-dash" line that stretches deep into the South China Sea." (Phillips, T., Holmes, O, and Bowcott, O. (2016), Beijing rejects tribunal's ruling in South China Sea case, *The Guardian*, Tuesday 12 July 2016, accessed December 25, 2019, <https://www.theguardian.com/world/2016/jul/12/philippines-wins-south-china-sea-case-against-china>).

[708] Fn 706.

[709] Fn 706.

[710] Fn 701.

territorial sea but denied both an exclusive economic zone and a continental shelf, the arbitral tribunal facilitates the normal process of delimiting the maritime boundaries of the littoral states of the South China Sea and enables it, as the adjucatory body in this dispute, to rule on the merits of the case with regard to alleged infractions of the UNCLOS. The narrow interpretation of derogations/exceptions to fundamental treaties by the judicial authorities is long-settled in European Union law, especially in relation to derogations that permit restrictions to free movement within the European Union's internal market[711]. The approach of the Court of Justice of the European Union, and its predecessor the European Court of Justice, in respect of the internal market (and its forerunner the common market) is to remove obstacles to the free movement of goods, persons, services and capital between Member States of the European Union (and of its precursors the European Community and (before this) the European

---

[711] For example, with regard to: (i) *the freedom of establishment*, in 1974 the European Court of Justice stated: "Having regard to the fundamental character of freedom of establishment and the rule on equal treatment with nationals in the system of the Treaty [establishing the European Economic Community], the exceptions allowed by the first paragraph of Article 55 [of the Treaty] cannot be given a scope which would exceed the objective for which this exemption clause was inserted." (Case 2/74, *Jean Reyners v. Belgian State* [1974], ECR 631, para.43); (ii) *the free movement of services*, in 1991 the European Court of Justice declared: "[T]he rules relating to the freedom to provide services preclude national rules which have such discriminatory effects unless those rules fall within the derogating provision contained in Article 56 of the Treaty [establishing the European Economic Community] to which Article 66 [of the Treaty] refers. It follows from Article 56 [of the Treaty], which must be interpreted strictly, that discriminatory rules may be justified on grounds of public policy, public security or public health." (Case C-260/89, *Elliniki Radiophonia Tiléorassi Anonimi Etairia and Panellinia Omospondia Syllogon Prossopikou v. Dimotiki Étairia Plifoforissis, Sotirios Kouvelas, Nicolaos Avdellas and Others* [1991], ECR I-2925, para.24); (iii) *the free movement of capital*, in 2000 the European Court of Justice proclaimed: "The question which arises is therefore whether Article 73d(1)(b) of the Treaty [establishing the European Community], which provides that Article 73b thereof is without prejudice to the right of Member States [of the European Community] to take any measures which are justified on grounds of public policy or public security, permits national legislation, such as that at issue in the main proceedings, which merely requires prior authorisation for direct foreign investments which are such as to represent a threat to public policy or public security. It should be observed, first, that while Member States are still, in principle, free to determine the requirements of public policy and public security in the light of their national needs, those grounds must, in the Community context and, in particular, as derogations from the fundamental principle of free movement of capital, be interpreted strictly, so that their scope cannot be determined unilaterally by each Member State without any control by the Community institutions ... ." (Case C-54/99, *Association Église de Scientologie de Paris and Scientology International Reserves Trust v. The Prime Minister* [2000], ECR I-1335, paras.16-17).

Economic Community), in order to aid the establishment of the internal market (or the common market) for which the relevant, effective Treaty provided or provides[712]. Is it possible to identify an analogous reason relating to the UNCLOS for the ICJ, the ITLOS and arbitral tribunals to narrowly interpret the exceptions in Article 298(1) of the UNCLOS as the establishment of the internal market provides for the Court of Justice of the European Union to strictly interpret derogations that relate to the freedom of movement of goods, persons, services and capital? Inspection of the Preamble to the UNCLOS[713] reveals the following recitals that may be relevant.

> *The States Parties to this Convention,*
>
> *Prompted* by the desire to settle, in a spirit of mutual understanding and cooperation, all issues relating to the law of the sea and aware of the historic significance of this Convention as an important contribution to the maintenance of peace, justice and progress for all peoples of the world, …

---

[712] The Treaty establishing the European Economic Community stated: "*Le marché commun est [(d'être)] progressivement établi au cours d'une période de transition de douze années.* [i.e., The common market is (to be) established gradually over a transition period of twelve years.] *La période de transition est divisée en trois étapes, de quatre années chacune …* [i.e., The transition period is divided into three steps, of four years each …] (*Traité instituant la Communauté Économique Européenne* (1957), Article 8(1); emphasis added). The Treaty establishing the European Community declared: "The [European] Community shall adopt measures with the aim of progressively establishing the internal market over a period expiring on 31 December 1992 … . The internal market shall comprise an area without internal frontiers in which the free movement of goods, persons, services and capital is ensured in accordance with the provisions of this Treaty. (Treaty Establishing the European Community (1992), *Official Journal of the European Communities 1992*, C 224/1, 31 August 1992, Article 7a). The Treaty on the Functioning of the European Union proclaims: "The [European] Union shall adopt measures with the aim of establishing or ensuring the functioning of the internal market, in accordance with the relevant provisions of the Treaties [i.e., the Treaty on European Union and the Treaty on the Functioning of the European Union]. The internal market shall comprise an area without internal frontiers in which the free movement of goods, persons, services and capital is ensured in accordance with the provision of the Treaties." (Treaty on the Functioning of the European Union (2016), *Official Journal of the European Union 2016*, C 202/47, 7 June 2016, Article 26(1)-(2)).

[713] The preamble and annexes to an international treaty are part of "the context for the purpose of the interpretation of [the] treaty" (United Nations (1969), "Vienna Convention on the Law of Treaties," Article 31(2)).

> *Recognizing* the desirability of establishing through this Convention, with due regard for the sovereignty of all States, a legal order for the seas and oceans which will facilitate international communication, and will promote the peaceful uses of the seas and oceans … ,
>
> *Bearing in mind* that the achievement of these goals will contribute to the realization of a just and equitable economic order … ,
>
> *Believing* that the codification and progressive development of the law of the sea achieved in this Convention will contribute to the strengthening of peace, security, cooperation and friendly relations among all nations in conformity with the principles of justice and equal rights … ,
>
> *Affirming* that matters not regulated by this Convention continue to be governed by the rules and principles of general international law, …[714] [657].

From a perspective of the harmonization of *national* rules and practice relating to the sea being a net benefit to all, the intent contained in these recitals might be distilled thus: 'Within the framework of the rules and principles of international law and acknowledging the sovereignty of all states, the UNCLOS provides a progressive legal order for the oceans and seas which will further their peaceful use and facilitate global communication, thereby helping to realize a just, equitable economic order and contribute to the strengthening of peace, justice, progress, security, co-operation and equal rights amongst all nations and peoples.' Whilst not as firm an expression of international integration as the wish to establish the internal market is of European integration, the above intent is nevertheless consistent with the gradual establishment of a worldwide system for the law of the sea to which countries are expected to conform. In this light, it would be reasonable to expect the ICJ, the ITLOS and arbitral tribunals to provide a narrow interpretation of the exceptions that Article 298 of the UNCLOS provides, unless the circumstances of the particular dispute indicate otherwise. Dr. Treves[715] has addressed this matter in part on a note posted on the UN's Audiovisual Library of International Law – but this

[714] Emphasis original.
[715] Fn 519 provides information concerning Dr. Treves.

comment will have preceded the arbitral tribunal's Awards in the *South China Sea Arbitration*[716].

> ... The Convention [(i.e., the UNCLOS)] – differently from other codification conventions – has put its application and interpretation under the jurisdiction of international judges and arbitrators. Compulsory jurisdiction either of the International Tribunal for the Law of the Sea, of the International Court of Justice or of arbitral tribunals, is the rule, although with important limitations and exceptions. Cases submitted to adjudication on the basis of the Convention since 1994 prove that, although slowly, States are considering submission to judicial or arbitral settlement of their disputes as something normal in international maritime relations, not as a hostile act. ... The Convention prefers stability to adaptability. ... Flexibility is entrusted to the interpretations judicial and arbitral bodies may adopt while settling disputes. ... [658]

Two points emerge from Dr. Treves' remark. First, the discretion granted to the ICJ, the ITLOS, or an arbitral tribunal (as appropriate in accordance with Article 287 of the ITLOS) may be used to minimize the scope of derogations from the UNCLOS. Second, his reference to the submission to compulsory modes of dispute resolution concerning the interpretation or application of the UNCLOS as being considered normal in

---

[716] Whilst the arbitral tribunal's Awards in the *South China Sea Arbitration* are dated 29th October 2015 and 12th July 2016, Dr. Treves stated that the UNCLOS was "presently binding for *154* States, as well as the *European Community* (as of 24 July 2008)" (United Nations Audiovisual Library of International Law (2019), "United Nations Convention on the Law of the Sea: Introductory Note By Tullio Treves," accessed December 26, 2019, <https://legal.un.org/avl/ha/uncls/uncls.html>; emphasis added). At the time of writing, there are 157 Signatories to the UNCLOS and 168 Parties to this Convention (United Nations Treaty Collection (2019), "Chapter XXI Law of the Sea: 6. United Nations Convention on the Law of the Sea," accessed December 26, 2019, <https://treaties.un.org/Pages/ViewDetailsIII.aspx?src=TREATY&mtdsg_no=XXI-6&chapter=21&Temp=mtdsg3&clang=_en>). When the Treaty on Lisbon entered into force on 1st December 2009, the European Community was superseded by the European Union – the Treaty establishing the European Community was renamed the Treaty on the Functioning of the European Union and, throughout this Treaty (subject to two exceptions): (i) the words 'Community' and 'European Community' were replaced by the word 'Union', and (ii) the phrase 'European Communities' was replaced by the expression 'European Union' (Treaty of Lisbon amending the Treaty on European Union and the Treaty establishing the European Community (2007), *Official Journal of the European Union 2007*, C 306/1, 17 December 2017, Articles 2(1) and 2(2)(a); EUR-Lex (2019), "Glossary of summaries: Treaties," accessed December 26, 2019, <https://eur-lex.europa.eu/summary/glossary/ treaties.html>).

global maritime relations rather than a hostile act, reinforces the approach taken by the Government of the Philippines in commencing an arbitration under Annex VII to the UNCLOS against China (i.e., the *South China Sea Arbitration*) – which the Government of China seemed to regard as a hostile act, as evidenced by its refusal to either participate in the arbitral proceedings or to implement the necessary corrections as required by the tribunal's Award dated 12th July 2016. Whilst the arbitral tribunal in the *South China Sea Arbitration* found China to be in breach of several provisions of the UNCLOS, China may not be the only littoral state of the South China Sea that is currently contravening this Convention – and the Government of China might, therefore, consider the aforementioned arbitral tribunal to be have discriminated against that country. Such would be an understandable inference from the perspective of the Government of China. Notwithstanding this, the arbitral tribunal's findings in the *South China Sea Arbitration* are, as stated above, a rigorous defence of the rights conferred, and obligations imposed, by the UNCLOS on all its States Parties. Therefore, the tribunal is very likely to have been impartial in its deliberations. At present, high-tide features and/or low-tide elevations in the Spratly Islands are occupied by the military of China (including, for instance, Cuarteron Reef, Fiery Cross Reef and Mischief Reef), Malaysia (including, for example, Investigator Shoal, Mariveles Reef and Swallow Reef), the Philippines (including, for instance, North-East Cay, Second Thomas Shoal and Thitu), Taiwan (comprising Itu Aba and Zhongzhou Reef), and Vietnam (including, for example, Sin Cowe Island, South-West Cay and Spratly Island)[717]. This situation does not appear to be a recipe for peace and co-operation in the South China Sea, despite ongoing bilateral dialogues between these countries[718]. In *Essays on International Law*, I

---

[717] Wikipedia (2019), "Spratly Islands," accessed December 26, 2019, <https://en.wikipedia.org/wiki/Spratly_Islands>.

[718] For instance, on Friday 26th July 2019, Xinhua News Agency wrote: "China and the Philippines have reached important consensus on bilateral ties, the South China Sea issue and regional cooperation and development during the 22nd diplomatic consultation between the two countries, a Foreign Ministry spokesperson said on Friday. Spokesperson Hua Chunying told a routine news briefing that this consultation, held on Tuesday in Manila, is the first diplomatic consultation after the relationship between the two countries has been upgraded to a relationship of comprehensive strategic cooperation. The two sides agreed to

wrote: "Even in the 21st century, countries have ignored provisions of the latter [i.e., international law] – including 4 of the 5 permanent members of the United Nations Security Council on at least one occasion," observing that, whilst the UK and the USA had "withdraw[n] their troops from Iraq" – thereby ending the unlawful invasion of that country, China and Russia "continue[d] to breach international law by stationing armed forces on their occupied territories" [659]. In order to uphold the validity of the worldwide socio-legal order, it is crucial that the Permanent Members of the UNSC abide by international law – thereby setting a good example to the governments of all Member States of the UN. Thus, although the Governments of China, Malaysia, the Philippines, Taiwan and Vietnam are each stationing their troops on high-tide features and low-tide elevations of the Spratly Islands, the Government of China – as that of a Permanent Member of the UNSC – should start the process of peaceful withdrawal of armed forces from the area by recalling all the Chinese troops that are presently located on and around the Spratly Islands to China. This would follow the good example that the Governments of the UK and the USA set in 2011 by withdrawing their military personnel from Iraq to their respective home countries[719]. It would then be possible for a resolution to be moved at the UNSC which required all the armed forces of any nation which remained in the disputed region to be moved away from the Spratly Islands and their territorial seas.

---

adhere to the direction of good-neighborly friendship. ... The two sides agreed to adhere to the direction of maintaining peace and stability in the South China Sea. They believe that the current situation in the South China Sea is generally stable thanks to the joint efforts of China and the Philippines and other regional countries. China and the Philippines agreed to hold the Fifth Meeting of the Bilateral Consultation Mechanism (BCM) on the South China Sea as soon as possible to jointly control the maritime situation and push forward joint development. Both countries will continue to work together to promote the consultation on a Code of Conduct (COC) in the South China Sea. ..." (Xinhua News Agency (2019), "China, Philippines reach important consensus through diplomatic consultation," accessed December 26, 2019, <http://www.xinhuanet.com/english/2019-07/26/c_138261164.htm>).

[719] The UK and the USA participated in the invasion of Iraq in 2003; both withdrew their armed forces from the last-mentioned country by the end of 2011 (Baber, G. (2017), *Essays on International Law* (Newcastle-upon-Tyne: Cambridge Scholars Publishing), 314).

The Value of Arbitration under Annex VII to the UNCLOS

Article 5 of Annex VII to the UNCLOS provides for the arbitral tribunal to decide upon its own procedure, unless the disputants agree otherwise[720]. The flexibility that this provision offers to the tribunal enables it to tailor the arbitral procedure to its perception of what the dispute before it involves – which, due to the more formal proceedings before the ICJ and in front of the ITLOS, is less possible for these latter adjucatory bodies to do than for such an arbitral tribunal. For the *South China Sea Arbitration*, settlement by arbitration under Annex VII to the UNCLOS was the most suitable of the compulsory procedures for the resolution of disputes concerning the interpretation or the application of the UNCLOS that Article 287 of the Convention offers to its States Parties – because the other alternatives available for this particular case[721], i.e., legal proceedings at the ICJ or the ITLOS, offer more a more formalized procedure than arbitration under Annex VII to the UNCLOS – which may have limited the judges from determining optimally this politically-sensitive case. Recalling the ICJ's determination of *Land, Island and Maritime Frontier Dispute (El Salvador/Honduras: Nicaragua intervening)*,[722] the Court was procedurally well-equipped to consider the revisitation of one of its determinations in that case in the subsequent proceedings of *Application for Revision of the Judgment of 11 September 1992 in the Case concerning the* Land, Island and Maritime Frontier Dispute (El Salvador/Honduras: Nicaragua intervening) *(El Salvador v. Honduras)* by the provisions of Articles 61 of the Statute of the ICJ and 99 of the ICJ's Rules of Court.[723] It is submitted that, if it had been possible to

[720] Fn 196 quotes Article 5 of Annex VII to the UNCLOS.

[721] As the subject matter for the South China Sea Arbitration was mostly outside the four categories of dispute that may be submitted to the special arbitral procedure for which Annex VIII to the UNCLOS provides (Article 1 of Annex VIII to the UNCLOS, which fn 197 specifies), this alternative for settling the dispute would not have been available to the parties to the *South China Sea Arbitration*.

[722] The subsection entitled 'Example ICJ Case – El Salvador/Honduras: Nicaragua intervening', in the section above titled 'The International Court of Justice', considers *Land, Island and Maritime Frontier Dispute (El Salvador/Honduras: Nicaragua intervening)*.

[723] The antepenultimate paragraph of the subsection entitled 'A Summary of Jurisdictional and Procedural Aspects of the ICJ', in the section above titled 'The International Court of Justice', includes Paragraphs 1, 2, 4 and 5 of Article 61 of the Statute of the ICJ, and all five Paragraphs of Article 99 of the ICJ's Rules of Court.

authorize an arbitral tribunal constituted under Annex VII to the UNCLOS to adjudicate on the inland (as well as the coastal) aspects of *Land, Island and Maritime Frontier Dispute (El Salvador/Honduras: Nicaragua intervening)*[724], then the lack of appropriate procedural rules therein to govern this complex but fairly conventional dispute would likely to have led to a less satisfactory outcome than that which the ICJ accomplished.

ARTICLE 298(1)(A) OF THE UNCLOS

Subject to conditions stated therein[725], Article 298(1)(a) of the UNCLOS empowers a state to declare in writing that it does not accept compulsory dispute resolution by the ICJ, the ITLOS and/or arbitration under Annex VII (and/or Annex VIII) to the UNCLOS[726], in respect of disputes concerning interstate boundary delimitation of the territorial sea[727], the exclusive economic zone[728] or the continental shelf[729], or with

[724] Notwithstanding the fact that the substance of the dispute in *Land, Island and Maritime Frontier Dispute (El Salvador/Honduras: Nicaragua intervening)* was only partly within the ambit of the UNCLOS, it would have been impossible to institute an arbitration under Annex VII to the UNCLOS for this case, as the date of its initiation – 11th December 1986 (text to fn 288) – preceded the date on which the UNCLOS entered into force – 16th November 1994 (fns 240 and 571).

[725] Fns 188, 189 and 190 contain the conditions that Clauses (i), (ii) and (iii), respectively, of Article 298(1)(a) of the UNCLOS lay down with regard to the operation of a written declaration that a state has made under that Subparagraph.

[726] Article 287(1) of the UNCLOS specifies these four means for the settlement of disputes concerning the interpretation or application of the UNCLOS. The first sentence of the subsection entitled 'Compulsory Procedures: Choice of Procedure', in the section titled 'Part XV of the UNCLOS: Settlement of Disputes' in Chapter 1, states Article 287(1) of the UNCLOS.

[727] i.e., disputes regarding the interpretation or application of Article 15 of the UNCLOS, which the Convention labels 'Delimitation of the territorial sea between States with opposite or adjacent coasts'. The subsection entitled 'Delimitation of the Territorial Sea between States', in the section titled 'Part II of the UNCLOS: Territorial Sea and Contiguous Zone' in Chapter 1, consists of Article 15 of the UNCLOS.

[728] i.e., disputes concerning the interpretation or application of Article 74 of the UNCLOS, which the Convention designates 'Delimitation of the exclusive economic zone between States with opposite or adjacent coasts'. The subsection entitled 'Delimitation of the Exclusive Economic Zone between States', in the section titled 'Part V of the UNCLOS: Exclusive Economic Zone' in Chapter 1, contains the provisions of Article 74 of the UNCLOS.

[729] i.e., disputes regarding the interpretation or application of Article 83 of the UNCLOS, which the Convention names 'Delimitation of the continental shelf between States with opposite or

regard to "historic bays or titles"[730]. Notwithstanding the interpretation of this provision which the arbitral tribunal in the *South China Sea Arbitration* has used[731], it is worth (re)visiting key points of the UN Secretariat's memorandum on historic waters[732].

> ... [W]hile "historic bays" present the classic example of historic title to maritime areas, ... a historic title may exist also to other waters than bays, such as straits or archipelagos, or in general to all those waters which can form part of the maritime domain of a State [660]. ...
>
> In determining whether or not a title to "historic waters" exists, there are three factors which have to be taken into consideration, namely, (i) The authority exercised over the area by the State claiming it as "historic waters"; (ii) The continuity of such exercise of authority; (iii) The attitude of foreign States [661].
>
> First, effective exercise of sovereignty over the area by the claiming State is a necessary requirement for title to the area as "historic waters" of that State. Second, such exercise of sovereignty must have continued during a considerable time so as to have developed into a usage. Thirdly, the attitude of foreign States to the activities of the claiming State in the area must have been such that it can be characterized as an attitude of general toleration. ... [662]

In *Fisheries Case (United Kingdom v. Norway)*[733], all three of these conditions existed along the north-west coast of Norway, which enabled the ICJ to confirm that specified waters beyond the edge of the mainland were to be classified as historic waters of Norway, i.e., waters over which

---

adjacent coasts'. The subsection entitled 'Delimitation of the Continental Shelf between States', in the section titled 'Part VI of the UNCLOS: Continental Shelf' in Chapter 1, comprises the provisions of Article 83 of the UNCLOS.

730 The first sentence of the subsection entitled 'Optional Exceptions to the Applicability of Compulsory Procedures' – up to but not including point (b), in the section titled in 'Part XV of the UNCLOS: Settlement of Disputes' in Chapter 1, together with the first sentence of fn 188, the first sentence of fn 189, and fn 190, constitute Article 298(1)(a) of the UNCLOS.

731 The subsection entitled 'Example Arbitration Case – The South China Sea Arbitration', in the section above titled 'International Arbitrations' considers in depth how the arbitral tribunal has interpreted China's written declaration under Article 298(1)(a) of the UNCLOS and, in particular, the tribunal's view of the meaning of the phrase 'historic titles' (fn 625).

732 Fn 625 quotes from Paragraphs 185, 186, 188 and 189 of this memorandum.

733 Judgment of December 18th 1951, *I.C.J. Reports 1951*, 116-144.

that country possessed an historic title[734]. Whilst the 'historic bays or titles' exception is noteworthy, it is the derogation in Article 298(1)(a)(i) of the UNCLOS that excludes interpretation or application of those provisions of the Convention which regulate the delimitation of maritime boundaries between states, i.e., Articles 15, 74 and 83 of the UNCLOS, that countries who do not wish to submit their disputes to a compulsory process of dispute resolution are likely to invoke in order to assert that the matter in question is beyond the jurisdiction of the court or tribunal that is asked to adjudicate upon it. Even though Article 298 of the UNCLOS provides a major optional exception from the jurisdiction of the ICJ, the ITLOS, any arbitral tribunal constituted under Annex VII to the UNCLOS and any special arbitral tribunal formed under Annex VIII to the UNCLOS, in the form of exclusion of the interpretation or application of Articles 15, 74 and 83 of the UNCLOS, it nevertheless attempts to ensure that disputes involving the delimitation of thalassic boundaries between states *are* satisfactorily resolved, by: (i) requiring a state that has made a declaration under Article 298(1)(a)(i) of the UNCLOS to submit the dispute to conciliation under Section 2 of Annex V to the UNCLOS[735], if this is requested by any disputant after no agreement has been reached between

---

[734] The ICJ notes: "The coastal zone concerned in the dispute … lies north of latitude 66° 28.8' N., … and includes the coast of the mainland of Norway and all the islands, islets, rocks and reefs, known by the name of the "skjaergaard" (literally, rock rampart), together with all Norwegian internal and territorial waters. The coast of the mainland … is of a very distinctive configuration. Very broken along its whole length, it constantly opens out into indentations often penetrating for great distances inland … . To the west, the land configuration stretches out into the sea: the large and small islands, mountainous in character, the islets, rocks and reefs, some always above water, others emerging only at low tide, are in truth but an extension of the Norwegian mainland. … Within the "skjaergaard," almost every island has its large and its small bays; countless arms of the sea, straits, channels and mere waterways serve as a means of communication for the local population which inhabits the islands as it does the mainland. The coast of the mainland does not constitute, as it does in practically all other countries, a clear dividing line between land and sea. What matters, what really constitutes the Norwegian coast line, is the outer line of the "skjaergaard." … Along the coast are situated comparatively shallow banks, veritable under-water terraces which constitute fishing grounds where fish are particularly abundant; these grounds were known to Norwegian fishermen and exploited by them from time immemorial. … In these barren regions the inhabitants of the coastal zone derive their livelihood essentially from fishing." (International Court of Justice (1951), *Fisheries Case (United Kingdom v. Norway)*, Judgment of December 18th 1951, *I.C.J. Reports 1951*, 116-144, 127-128).

[735] Fn 175 contains the provisions of Section 2 of Annex V to the UNCLOS.

the parties in their negotiations[736],(ii) requiring the disputants to attempt to negotiate an agreement that is founded on the report of the conciliation commission that conducted the particular conciliation under Annex V to the UNCLOS[737] between these parties concerning this dispute[738], (iii) requiring the parties to mutually consent to submitting their dispute to compulsory adjudication by the ICJ, the ITLOS or an arbitral tribunal constituted under Annex VII (or Annex VIII) to the UNCLOS unless they agree elsewise, if the negotiations in point (ii) do not give rise to an agreement between the disputants[739], (iv) disapplying Article 298(1)(a) of the UNCLOS from disputes regarding maritime boundaries that are to be resolved in conformity with a multilateral or bilateral agreement that is binding upon the states which are parties to it[740], (v) empowering a State Party[741] to the UNCLOS to rescind a declaration that it has made under Paragraph 1 therein[742], and (vi) permitting that State Party to submit a

---

[736] Fn 188 and accompanying text.

[737] Although the conciliation is commenced under Section 2 of Annex V to the UNCLOS (text to fn 735), that Section provides for the Articles 2-10 of Section 1 of Annex V to the UNCLOS to govern the conciliation procedure (point (v) in fn 175). Fn 157 quotes the provisions of Section 1 of Annex V to the UNCLOS, abridging Articles 2, 3, 4, 7(1) and 8 therein.

[738] Fn 189.

[739] Fn 189. This point is important in restricting the evasive scope of the government of any coastal state that wishes to avoid compulsory adjudication of its country's claims concerning territorial sea, exclusive economic zone and/or continental shelf versus those of neighbouring coastal countries, to cases in which the other disputant(s) *agree not* to submit the question over the maritime boundaries at issue to the ICJ, the ITLOS, or an arbitral tribunal established under Annex VII (or Annex VIII) to the UNCLOS, in instances in which negotiation, conciliation and/or mediation in respect of the differing national positions as to the location of those boundaries have not brought about a solution that is acceptable to all affected parties.

[740] Fn 190.

[741] Fn 192 defines 'States Parties'.

[742] i.e., Article 298(1) of the UNCLOS, which includes all the three heads of optional exceptions (Articles 298(1)(a), 298(1)(b) and 298(1)(c) of the UNCLOS) that a state may choose to include in any written declaration which it makes to disapply compulsory adjudication of the eligible disputes by the ICJ, the ITLOS, an arbitral tribunal constituted under Article VII to the UNCLOS and/or a special arbitral tribunal formed under Article VIII to the UNCLOS. Fn 730 locates Article 298(1)(a) of the UNCLOS. The text to fn 191 comprises Article 298(1)(b) of the UNCLOS. Point (c) of the first sentence of the subsection entitled 'Optional Exceptions to the Applicability of Compulsory Procedures', in the section titled 'Part XV of the UNCLOS: Settlement of Disputes' in Chapter 1, contains Article 298(1)(c) of the UNCLOS.

dispute which this declaration (if that country has not revoked it) excludes to any procedure which the UNCLOS specifies[743].

Table 2.1. List of states for which a Declaration under Article 298(1) of the UNCLOS is in force[744]

State	Article 298(1)(a)	Article 298(1)(b)	Article 298(1)(c)
Algeria	√ (i.e., in force)	√	√
Angola	√ Exclusion applies to Annex VII arbitral tribunals only		
Argentina	√	√	√
Australia	√		
Belarus[745]	√	√	√
Cabo Verde		√	
Canada	√	√	√
Chile	√	√	√
China	√	√	√
Cuba	√ Exclusion applies to the ICJ only	√ Exclusion applies to the ICJ only	√ Exclusion applies to the ICJ only
The Democratic Republic of the Congo	√ Exclusion applies to Annex VII arbitral tribunals only		

743 Article 298(2) of the UNCLOS contains points (v) and (vi) in current sentence in the text. The first clause in the penultimate sentence of the subsection entitled 'Optional Exceptions to the Applicability of Compulsory Procedures', in the section titled 'Part XV of the UNCLOS: Settlement of Disputes' in Chapter 1, contains Article 298(2) of the UNCLOS.

744 The data for Table 2.1 are taken from the following source: United Nations Treaty Collection (2019), "Chapter XXI Law of the Sea: 6. United Nations Convention on the Law of the Sea," accessed December 28, 2019, <https://treaties.un.org/Pages/ViewDetailsIII.aspx?src=TREATY&mtdsg_no=XXI-6&chapter=21&Temp=mtdsg3&clang=_en>.

745 When the Byelorussian Soviet Socialist Republic signed the UNCLOS on 10th December 1982, its Declaration under Article 298(1) of the UNCLOS excluded all three categories of dispute described therein; when this Soviet Socialist Republic's successor – the independent state named the Republic of Belarus – ratified the UNCLOS on 30th August 2006, the latter's Declaration under Article 298(1) of the UNCLOS reaffirmed the previous Declaration's exclusion of the classes of dispute listed in Paragraphs (b) and (c) of that Article, but did not mention the categories of dispute specified in Article 298(1)(a) of the UNCLOS (United Nations Treaty Collection (2019), "Chapter XXI Law of the Sea: 6. United Nations Convention on the Law of the Sea," accessed December 28, 2019, <https://treaties.un.org/Pages/ViewDetailsIII.aspx?src=TREATY&mtdsg_no=XXI-6&chapter=21&Temp=mtdsg3&clang=_en>). It is submitted that, in the absence of a written revocation of the Byelorussian Soviet Socialist Republic's Declaration – or of that part of it excluding the classes of dispute specified in Article 298(1)(a) of the UNCLOS, Belarus continues to apply that Subparagraph.

State	Article 298(1)(a)	Article 298(1)(b)	Article 298(1)(c)
Denmark	√ Exclusion applies to Annex VII arbitral tribunals only	√ Exclusion applies to Annex VII arbitral tribunals only	√ Exclusion applies to Annex VII arbitral tribunals only
Ecuador	√	√	√
Egypt	√	√	√
Equatorial Guinea	√		
France	√	√	√
Gabon	√		
Greece	√	√	√
Guinea-Bissau	√ Exclusion applies to the ICJ only	√ Exclusion applies to the ICJ only	√ Exclusion applies to the ICJ only
Iceland	√ Exclusion only covers interpretation of Article 83 of the UNCLOS		
Italy	√		
Kenya	√		
Malaysia	√		
Mexico	√	√	
Montenegro	√		
Nicaragua	√ Exclusion does not apply to the ICJ	√ Exclusion does not apply to the ICJ	√ Exclusion does not apply to the ICJ
Norway	√ Exclusion applies to Annex VII arbitral tribunals only	√ Exclusion applies to Annex VII arbitral tribunals only	√ Exclusion applies to Annex VII arbitral tribunals only
Palau	√		
Portugal	√	√	√
The Republic of Korea	√	√	√
Russia	√	√	√
Saudi Arabia	√	√	
Singapore	√		
Slovenia[746]	√	√	√

[746] Slovenia's Declaration under Article 298(1) of the UNCLOS expressly excludes arbitration under Annex VII to the UNCLOS; notwithstanding this, its Declaration under *Article 287(1)* of the UNCLOS *selects arbitration under Article VII to the UNCLOS* as the forum for resolving disputes regarding the interpretation or application of the Convention (United Nations Treaty Collection (2019), "Chapter XXI Law of the Sea: 6. United Nations Convention on the Law of the Sea," accessed December 28, 2019, <https://treaties.un.org/Pages/ViewDetailsIII.aspx?src=TREATY&mtdsg_no=XXI-6&chapter=21&Temp=mtdsg3&clang=_en>). Therefore, it is submitted that Slovenia wishes to exclude *even* its favoured method of Annex VII arbitration from adjudicating disputes that fall within the scope of Article 298(1) of the UNCLOS – i.e., Slovenia *also* wishes, by implication, to exclude its less-preferable means of compulsory adjudication from the list that Article

Table 2.1. (Continued)

State	Article 298(1)(a)	Article 298(1)(b)	Article 298(1)(c)
Spain	√		
Thailand	√	√	√
Togo		√	√
Trinidad & Tobago	√		
Tunisia	√	√	√
Ukraine	√	√	√
The UK		√	√
Uruguay		√	

Table 2.1 shows that 42 states have filed a Declaration under Article 298(1) of the UNCLOS with the Secretary-General of the UN[747]. 38, 28 and 24 of these countries have excluded, wholly or partly, the classes of dispute listed in Subparagraphs (a), (b) and (c) of that Paragraph, respectively. These numbers indicate that states tend to be more concerned about the risk of unfavourable, binding decisions being imposed on them by international adjudicators regarding delimitation of their maritime boundaries versus their coastal neighbours, than they are about such judgments in respect of military and law enforcement activities and, especially, those involving the UNSC. Of the seven countries that have submitted declarations to the Secretary-General which exclude at least one but less than all four of the means of compulsory dispute-settlement procedures that Article 287(1) of the UNCLOS specifies, i.e., the ITLOS, the ICJ, an arbitral tribunal constituted in compliance with Annex VII to the UNCLOS and a special arbitral tribunal formed in observance of Annex VIII to the UNCLOS, only one (i.e., Nicaragua) excludes the ITLOS and Annex VIII special arbitral tribunals, two (i.e., Cuba and Guinea-Bissau) exclude the ICJ, and five (i.e., Angola, the Democratic Republic of the Congo, Denmark, Nicaragua and Norway) exclude Annex

287(1) of the UNCLOS provides, i.e., the ICJ, the ITLOS, and special arbitration under Annex VIII to the UNCLOS.

747 Article 298(6) of the UNCLOS states: "Declarations and notices of withdrawal of declarations under this article [i.e., Article 298 of the UNCLOS] shall be deposited with the Secretary-General of the United Nations, who shall transmit copies thereof to the States Parties." Fn 192 defines 'States Parties'.

VII arbitral tribunals. It is opined that Nicaragua's endorsement of the ICJ may have been a vote of confidence in the Judgment of the Chamber of the Court in *Land, Island and Maritime Frontier Dispute (El Salvador/ Honduras: Nicaragua intervening)*[748], as this state made its Declarations under Article 287(1) and 298(1) of the UNCLOS on ratifying the Convention – an event that took place a few years after the date of this Judgment[749]. It is submitted that Honduras, which ratified the UNCLOS just over a year after that date, may also have been satisfied with the ICJ's Judgment in *Land, Island and Maritime Frontier Dispute (El Salvador/ Honduras: Nicaragua intervening)*, as this country, in its Declaration under Article 287(1) of the UNCLOS dated 18th June 2002, selected the ICJ as its preferred forum for compulsory adjudication in respect of the interpretation and application of the UNCLOS[750].

---

[748] Judgment of 11 September 1992, *I.C.J. Reports 1992*, 351-618. The subsection entitled 'Example ICJ Case – El Salvador/Honduras: Nicaragua intervening', in the section above titled 'The International Court of Justice', discusses *Land, Island and Maritime Frontier Dispute (El Salvador/Honduras: Nicaragua intervening)* as an exemplar of how the ICJ conducts the cases that are submitted to it.

[749] The date of the Judgment of the Chamber of the ICJ in *Land, Island and Maritime Frontier Dispute (El Salvador/Honduras: Nicaragua intervening)* is 11th September 1992 (fn 748). The date of Nicaragua's ratification of the UNCLOS is 3rd May 2000; upon its ratification of the UNCLOS, Nicaragua stated, *inter alia*: "In accordance with article 287, paragraph 1, of the Convention, Nicaragua hereby declares that it accepts only recourse to the International Court of Justice as a means for the settlement of disputes concerning the interpretation or application of the Convention. Nicaragua hereby declares that it accepts only recourse to the International Court of Justice as a means for the settlement of the categories of disputes set forth in subparagraphs (a), (b) and (c) of paragraph 1 of article 298 of the Convention." (United Nations Treaty Collection (2019), "Chapter XXI Law of the Sea: 6. United Nations Convention on the Law of the Sea," accessed December 28, 2019, <https://treaties.un.org/Pages/ViewDetailsIII.aspx?src=TREATY&mtdsg_no=XXI-6&chapter=21&Temp=mtdsg3&clang=_en>). The final sentence of fn 319 defines '*inter alia*'.

[750] Honduras ratified the UNCLOS on 5th October 1993; its Declaration under Article 287(1) of the UNCLOS reads as follows: "18 June 2002 *Declaration under article 287:* In accordance with article 287, paragraph 1, of the United Nations Convention on the Law of the Sea, the State of Honduras chooses the International Court of Justice as the means for the settlement of disputes of any kind concerning the interpretation or application of the said Convention. Notwithstanding the foregoing, the State of Honduras reserves the possibility of considering any other means of peaceful settlement, including the International Tribunal for the Law of the Sea, as agreed on a case-by-case basis." (United Nations Treaty Collection (2019), "Chapter XXI Law of the Sea: 6. United Nations Convention on the Law of the Sea," accessed December 28, 2019, <https://treaties.un.org/Pages/ViewDetailsIII.aspx?src=TREATY&mtdsg_no=XXI-6&chapter=21&Temp=mtdsg3&clang=_en>; emphasis original).

Finally, although it is difficult to provide any plausible reasons why four states that have each submitted to the Secretary-General of the UN a Declaration under Article 298(1) of the UNCLOS, only excluded arbitration under Annex VII to the UNCLOS in respect of some (i.e., Angola and the Democratic Republic of the Congo, which are adjacent coastal states) or all (i.e., Denmark and Norway, which are neighbouring maritime countries) of the classes of dispute listed in that Paragraph, it is noteworthy that Norway also chose the ICJ as its favoured adjudicatory forum under Article 287(1) of the UNCLOS[751]. It is possible that the Government of Norway considered that subsequent determinations of the ICJ might be similarly favourable to its country's interests as the Court's earlier Judgment in *Fisheries Case (United Kingdom v. Norway)*[752] had been, because the ICJ might tend to follow its previous decisions more closely than other fora would – especially arbitral tribunals. Notwithstanding this, the UK – which was the losing disputant in *Fisheries Case (United Kingdom v. Norway)*, selected the ICJ as its preferred means of compulsory adjudication under Article 287(1) of the UNCLOS, as well[753]. It can only be surmised that, at the date of this Declaration[754], the

[751] Norway's Declarations under Articles 287(1) and 298(1) of the UNCLOS are as follows: "*Declaration pursuant to article 287 of the Convention:* "The Government of the Kingdom of Norway declares pursuant to article 287 of the Convention that it chooses the International Court of Justice for the settlement of disputes concerning the interpretation or application of the Convention." *Declaration pursuant to article 298 of the Convention:* "The Government of the Kingdom of Norway declares pursuant to article 298 of the Convention that it does not accept an arbitral tribunal constituted in accordance with Annex VII [to the UNCLOS] of any of the categories of disputes mentioned in article 298 [of the UNCLOS]."" (United Nations Treaty Collection (2019), "Chapter XXI Law of the Sea: 6. United Nations Convention on the Law of the Sea," accessed December 28, 2019, <https://treaties.un.org/Pages/ViewDetailsIII.aspx?src=TREATY&mtdsg_no=XXI-6&chapter=21&Temp=mtdsg3&clang=_en>; emphasis original).

[752] Judgment of December 18th 1951, *I.C.J. Reports 1951*, 116-144.

[753] The UK's Declaration under Article 287(1) of the UNCLOS is dated 12th January 1998; it proclaims: "In accordance with article 287, paragraph 1, of the [UNCLOS], the Kingdom of Great Britain and Northern Ireland chooses the International Court of Justice for the settlement of disputes concerning the interpretation or application of the Convention [(i.e., the UNCLOS)]. The International Tribunal for the Law of the Sea is a new institution, which the United King[do]m hopes will make an important contribution to the peaceful settlement of disputes concerning the law of the sea. In addition to those cases where the Convention itself provides for the compulsory jurisdiction of the Tribunal, the United Kingdom remains ready to consider the submission of disputes to the Tribunal as may be agreed on a case-by-case basis." (United Nations Treaty Collection (2019), "Chapter XXI

UK remained taken aback more by the Award dated 14th March 1978 of the arbitral tribunal in *Delimitation of the Continental Shelf between the United Kingdom of Great Britain and Northern Ireland, and the French Republic*[755] than it was in respect of the ICJ's Judgment of 18th December 1951 in *Fisheries Case (United Kingdom v. Norway)*[756]. Nevertheless, Table 2.1 specifies that the UK's Declaration under Article 298(1) of the UNCLOS covers the categories of dispute in Subparagraphs (b) and (c) of that Paragraph, but not those in Subparagraph (a)[757]. Thus, regarding the delimitation of maritime boundaries between the UK and its neighbouring states, by the early years of the present century[758] the Government of the UK appeared to be confident that both the ICJ and any arbitral tribunal constituted in accordance with Annex VII to the UNCLOS would fairly consider its country's territorial interests, thereby sensibly minimizing impressions that those earlier decisions might have made.

CONCLUSION

This chapter considers how cases concerning the law of the sea are organized before the ICJ, the ITLOS and an international arbitral tribunal – in particular one that is constituted under Article VII to the UNCLOS. The conduct of proceedings before the ICJ and the ITLOS are considered, with

---

Law of the Sea: 6. United Nations Convention on the Law of the Sea," accessed December 28, 2019, <https://treaties.un.org/Pages/ViewDetailsIII.aspx?src=TREATY&mtdsg_n o=XXI-6&chapter=21&Temp=mtdsg3&clang=_en>).

[754] i.e., on 12th January 1998 (fn 753).

[755] Fn 572. Chapter 3 discusses aspects of *Delimitation of the Continental Shelf between the United Kingdom of Great Britain and Northern Ireland, and the French Republic*.

[756] Fn 752. Chapter 3 considers *Fisheries Case (United Kingdom v. Norway)*.

[757] The UK's Declaration under Article 298(1) of the UNCLOS is dated 7th April 2003; it asseverates: "[T]he United Kingdom of Great Britain and Northern Ireland does not accept any of the procedures provided for in section 2 of Part XV of the Convention [(i.e., the UNCLOS)] with respect to the categories of disputes referred to in paragraph 1(b) and (c) of article 298." (United Nations Treaty Collection (2019), "Chapter XXI Law of the Sea: 6. United Nations Convention on the Law of the Sea," accessed December 28, 2019, <https://treaties.un.org/Pages/ViewDetailsIII.aspx?src=TREATY&mtdsg_no=XXI-6&chapter=21&Temp=mtdsg3&clang=_en>).

[758] i.e., when the UK made its Declaration under Article 298(1) of the UNCLOS – which was on 7th April 2003 (fn 757).

procedural rules of the latter being compared with equivalent provisions of the former. The rules of the ITLOS[759], which was established much later than the ICJ[760], are similar to, and, in some aspects the same as, the regulations of the ICJ – although there are a few instances in which the former differ substantially from the latter. The fact that proceedings before the ITLOS are, in large part, modelled upon those at the ICJ, endorses the latter's handling of the cases which come before it. The current chapter illustrates each set of proceedings with the aid of a case, which is also included for arbitration conducted under Annex VII to the UNCLOS. As an arbitral tribunal that is formed under Annex VII to the UNCLOS is to decide upon its own procedure unless the disputants agree otherwise[761] [663], the tribunal is provided with the opportunity to show the necessary flexibility to manage the dispute on which it has been asked to adjudicate. In the example provided, i.e., the *South China Sea Arbitration*, the tribunal successfully demonstrated the necessary adaptability by refusing to allow the lack of co-operation from one of the parties to affect its thoroughness in ascertaining provisions of the UNCLOS that had been infringed.

A state which deposits with the Secretary-General of the UN a Declaration under Article 298(1) of the UNCLOS[762], may, *inter alia*[763], indicate therein that it does not accept that the ICJ, the ITLOS, an arbitral tribunal constituted under Article VII to the UNCLOS and/or a special arbitral tribunal established under Article VIII to the UNCLOS, may adjudicate disputes regarding the application of Articles 15, 74 or 83 of the UNCLOS – which regulate delimitation of the boundary of the territorial sea, exclusive economic zone and continental shelf, respectively, between

---

[759] Fn 372 and its accompanying text summarize the timeline for the initialization of the ITLOS.

[760] The UN Charter founds the ICJ (first sentence of the first paragraph of the subsection entitled 'A Summary of Jurisdictional and Procedural Aspects of the ICJ', in the section above titled 'The International Court of Justice'). Article 7(1) of the UN Charter states: "There are established as principal organs of the United Nations: a General Assembly, a Security Council, an Economic and Social Council, a Trusteeship Council, *an International Court of Justice* and a Secretariat." (emphasis added). The UN Charter was signed on 26th June 1945, and entered into force on 24th October 1945 (United Nations (2019), "Charter of the United Nations," accessed December 29, 2019, <https://www.un.org/en/charter-united-nations/>).

[761] Fn 196 quotes Article 5 of Annex VII to the UNCLOS, from which this clause is drawn, and summarizes Annex VII to the UNCLOS.

[762] Fn 747.

[763] The last sentence of fn 319 defines '*inter alia*'.

countries with opposite or adjacent coasts, or those that involve historic titles or bays; this is an optional exception under Article 298(1)(a) of the UNCLOS from the applicability of Section 2 of Part XV of the UNCLOS, which is subject to the conditions which that Subparagraph contains[764]. Table 2.1 shows that, of the 42 countries that have filed a Declaration under Article 298(1) of the UNCLOS with the Secretary-General, 38 of these have excluded, wholly or partly, the categories of dispute listed in Subparagraph (a) of that Paragraph. This substantial number and high percentage[765] of states that have chosen to exclude or restrict compulsory adjudication (under Section 2 of Part XV of the UNCLOS) of disputes concerning interstate maritime delimitation, together with the lower figure and proportion of countries which have opted to rule out or limit these fora to settle disputes falling into Subparagraphs (b)[766] and (c)[767] of Article 298(1) of the UNCLOS, indicates that states tend to be cautious about agreeing to submit disputes regarding the delimitation of their territorial sea, exclusive economic zone and/or continental shelf to adjucatory procedures for which the UNCLOS provides that impose a binding decision on them.

---

[764] The subsection entitled 'Optional Exceptions to the Applicability of Compulsory Procedures', in the section titled 'Part XV of the UNCLOS: Settlement of Disputes' in Chapter 1, and the section above in the present chapter entitled 'Article 298(1)(a) of the UNCLOS', specifies the contents, and investigates the workings, respectively, of Article 298(1)(a) of the UNCLOS.

[765] (38/42) * 100% = 90% of the states that have deposited a Declaration under Article 298(1) of the UNCLOS with the Secretary-General of the United Nations have included in that Declaration the categories of dispute that Article 298(1)(a) of the UNCLOS lists.

[766] Of the 42 states that have deposited a Declaration under Article 298(1) of the UNCLOS with the Secretary-General of the United Nations, 28 have excluded, wholly or partly, the classes of dispute specified in Subparagraph (b) of that Paragraph from the fora for which Section 2 of Part XV of the UNCLOS provides (Table 2.1). Thus, (28/42) * 100% = 67% of these 42 countries have included in this Declaration disputes falling within Article 298(1)(b) of the UNCLOS.

[767] Of the 42 states that have filed a Declaration under Article 298(1) of the UNCLOS with the Secretary-General of the United Nations, 28 have excluded, wholly or partly, the type of dispute identified in Subparagraph (c) of that Paragraph from the fora for which Section 2 of Part XV of the UNCLOS provides (Table 2.1). Hence, (24/42) * 100% = 57% of those 42 countries have included in that Declaration disputes falling within Article 298(1)(c) of the UNCLOS.

Chapter 3 explores selected cases before the ICJ, the ITLOS and international arbitral tribunals which have involved matters concerning thalassic baselines and/or the delimitation of maritime boundaries. It concludes themes that this monograph pursues.

Chapter 3

BASELINES AND BOUNDARY DELIMITATION

ABSTRACT

Fisheries Case (United Kingdom v. Norway) is a dispute settled by the ICJ in 1951, which developed the Law of the Sea in relation to baselines for the delimitation of the territorial sea. *Delimitation of the Continental Shelf between the United Kingdom of Great Britain and Northern Ireland, and the French Republic* is a case adjudicated by an *ad hoc* arbitral tribunal in 1977 and 1978 that was challenged with delimiting a boundary in the western part of the English Channel. *Delimitation of the maritime boundary between Ghana and Côte D'Ivoire in the Atlantic Ocean (Ghana/Côte D'Ivoire)* is a dispute submitted to the ITLOS, which in its Judgment of 2017 delimited the boundary between Côte D'Ivoire and Ghana pursuant to their stalled negotiations. Each provides a good example of different aspects of the area of baselines and maritime boundary delimitation. Further developments of the Law of the Sea are anticipated, including in this topic, turning into the 2020s.

Keywords: arbitration, baseline, boundary, delimitation, ICJ, ITLOS, maritime

In *Fisheries Case (United Kingdom v. Norway)*[768], the ICJ held by ten votes to two that the method that Norway used to delimit its fisheries zone by virtue of the Norwegian Royal Decree of July 12th 1935 is compatible with, and by eight votes to four that the baselines which this Decree fixed are in accordance with, international law [664]. The Decree provided for straight baselines to be drawn northward from the latitude of 66° 28.8' North between fixed points on the mainland, islands and rocks[769], to which the lines of delimitation of the Norwegian fisheries zone ran parallel; the zone for which this Decree provided was the area that Norway considered to be her territorial sea [665]. The ICJ holds that, as the skjaergaard[770] – which borders the mainland of Norway to the west – makes up a whole with this mainland, the outer low-water line[771] of the skjaergaard must be taken into consideration in drawing the baselines to delimit the Norwegian territorial sea [666]. In its Memorial, the UK proposed the method of the *trace parallèle* to effect the low-water mark rule for the delineation of the baselines over the territory in question, which comprises drawing the outer limit of the strip of territorial waters by following the Norwegian coast; however, where a coast is deeply indented and chopped into – as is that of Eastern Finnmark, or where it is adjacent to an archipelago – such as the skjaergaard along the western part of the coast at issue, the baseline becomes independent of the low-water line and is only able to be determined by a geometrical construction [667]. In its Reply, the UK abandoned the *trace parallèle* and proposed the arcs of circles method[772] to

---

[768] Judgment of December 18th 1951, *I.C.J. Reports 1951*, 116-144.

[769] Fn 734 describes the coastal zone in Norway that is the subject of this dispute, which is known as the 'skjaergaard'.

[770] Fn 769.

[771] The normal baseline for measuring the breadth of the territorial sea under both the CTSCZ and the UNCLOS is the low-water line along the coast (fn 4 and accompanying text). The ICJ's Judgment in *Fisheries Case (United Kingdom v. Norway)* predated (fn 768) both the CTSCZ and the UNCLOS, which entered into force on 10th September 1964 and 16th November 1994 (fns 240 and 571), respectively; the CHS, the CCS and the CFCLRHS came into effect on 30th September 1962, 10th June 1964 and 20th March 1966, respectively (United Nations Audiovisual Library of International Law (2019), "1958 Geneva Conventions on the Law of the Sea: Introductory Note By Tullio Treves," accessed December 30, 2019, <https://legal.un.org/avl/ha/gclos/gclos.html>).

[772] The arcs of circle method involves drawing a continuous series of intersecting arcs from points on the coastline; the radius of each arc is equal to the breadth of the territorial sea that the relevant coastal state is claiming (Hartig, R.L. (1972), Remarks Concerning the

effect the low-water mark rule for the drawing of the requisite baselines; the ICJ put this method to one side, observing that it was not legally obligatory and that Counsel for the Government of the UK admitted this in his oral reply [668]. The ICJ favoured the method of straight baselines in respect of delimitation of the territorial sea from the outer low-water line of the skjaergaard – a position which became the law in the Article 4(1) of the CTSCZ and, later[773], Article 7(1) of the UNCLOS[774], stating the following.

> [I]n order to apply [t]he principle that the belt of territorial waters must follow the general direction of the coast[775] … , several States have deemed it necessary to follow the straight base-lines method[;] they have not encountered objections of principle by other States. This method consists of selecting appropriate points on the low-water mark and drawing straight lines between them. This has been done, not only in the case of well-defined bays, but also in cases of minor curvatures of the coast line where it was solely a question of giving a simpler form to the belt of territorial waters. It has been contended, on behalf of the United Kingdom, that Norway may draw straight lines only across bays. The Court is unable to share this view. If the belt of territorial waters must follow the outer line of the "skjaergaard," and if the method of straight base-lines must be admitted in certain cases, [then] there is no valid reason to draw them only across bays, as in Eastern Finnmark, and not also to draw them between islands, islets and rocks, across the sea areas separating them, even when such areas do not fall within the conception of a bay. It is sufficient that they should be situated between the island formations of the "skaergaard," *inter fauces terrarum*[776] [669].

Recently Published State Department Charts, *in* United States Congress: Senate Committee on Commerce – *Ninety-Second Congress: Second Session on Provisional U.S. Charts Delimiting Alaskan Territorial Boundaries, May 15, 1972, Serial No. 92-69* (Washington, D.C.: United States Government Printing Office), 168-172, 168).

773 First clause of the second sentence of fn 771.

774 Fn 7 and accompanying text.

775 Article 4(2) of the CTSCZ and, subsequently (fn 773), Article 7(3) of the UNCLOS, incorporated this principle (fn 8 and accompanying text).

776 Emphasis original. The phrase '*inter fauces terrarum*' means "[b]etween the jaws of the lands[, i.e., n]early enclosed or surrounded by dry land" (Oxford Reference (2019), "*Inter fauces terrarium,*" accessed December 30, 2019, <https://www.oxfordreference.com/view/10.1093/acref/9780195369380.001.0001/acref-9780195369380-e-1031>).

The ICJ held that the ten-mile rule for the closing lines of bays – i.e., if the distance between the low-water marks of a bay's natural entrance points is 10 miles[777] or less, then a closing line may be drawn between these marks, and the waters therein are deemed to be internal waters – "ha[d] not acquired the authority of a general rule of international law"[778], even though some states had applied it in their treaties and national law and certain arbitral awards had applied it [670]. The Court restated[779] that the skjaergaard makes up a whole with the Norwegian mainland, and held that the waters between the baselines of the strip of territorial waters of Norway and this mainland to be internal waters – including the waters which the navigational route known as the Indreleia[780] followed; thus, the ICJ found that the Government of Norway, in setting the baselines for the delimitation of the Norwegian fisheries zone by the Norwegian Royal Decree of July 12th 1935, had not breached international law [671]. The ICJ reasoned as follows.

> It does not at all follow that, in the absence of rules having the technically precise character alleged by the United Kingdom Government, the delimitation undertaken by the Norwegian Government in 1935 is not subject to certain principles which make it possible to judge as to its validity under international law. ... In this connection,

---

[777] A 'mile' may mean a nautical mile or, alternatively, a statute mile (fn 19). In *Fisheries Case (United Kingdom v. Norway)*, a 'mile' unquestionably means a *nautical* mile – as indicated by the phrase "ten sea miles" on page 131 therein (International Court of Justice (1951), *Fisheries Case (United Kingdom v. Norway)*, Judgment of December 18th 1951, *I.C.J. Reports 1951*, 116-144, 131).

[778] Enshrined in Article 10(4) of the UNCLOS, the current rule of international law is a 'twenty-four nautical mile rule for the closing-lines of bays', i.e., if the distance between the low-water marks of a bay's natural entrance points is 24 nautical miles or less, then a closing line may be drawn between these marks, and the waters therein are deemed to be internal waters (text to fn 19).

[779] The ICJ made this statement at page 128 of its Judgment in *Fisheries Case (United Kingdom v. Norway)* (text to fn 771).

[780] 'Indreleia' is the name of a marine channel in the Nord-Trøndelag region of Norway (Geographic.org (2019), "Geographical Names – Indreleia: Norway," accessed December 31, 2019, <https://geographic.org/geographic_names/name.php?uni=286538&fid=44 11&c=norway>). Later in its Judgment in *Fisheries Case (United Kingdom v. Norway)*, the ICJ stated: "Since the Court has found that the waters of the Indreleia are internal waters, the waters of the Vestfjord, as indeed the waters of all other Norwegian fjords, can only be regarded as internal waters." (International Court of Justice (1951), *Fisheries Case (United Kingdom v. Norway)*, Judgment of December 18th 1951, *I.C.J. Reports 1951*, 116-144, 142).

certain basis considerations inherent in the nature of the territorial sea, bring to light certain criteria which, though not entirely precise, can provide courts with an adequate basis for their decisions, which can be adapted to the diverse facts in question. Among these considerations, some reference must be made to the close dependence of the territorial sea upon the land domain. It is the land which confers upon the coastal State a right to the waters off its coasts. It follows that while such a State must be allowed the latitude necessary in order to be able to adapt its delimitation to practical needs and local requirements, the drawing of base-lines must not depart to any appreciable extent from the general direction of the coast[781]. Another fundamental consideration, of particular importance in this case, is the … close relationship existing between certain sea areas and the land formations which divide or surround them. The real question raised in the choice of base-lines is in effect whether certain sea areas lying within these lines are sufficiently closely linked to the land domain to be subject to the regime of internal waters[782]. This idea, which is at the basis of the determination of the rules relating to bays[783], should be liberally applied in the case of a coast, the geographical configuration of which is as unusual as that of Norway. Finally, there is one consideration … the scope of which extends beyond purely geographical factors: that of certain economic interests peculiar to a region, the reality and importance of which are clearly evidenced by a long usage. Norway puts forward the 1935 Decree [i.e., the Norwegian Royal Decree of July 12th 1935] as the application of a traditional system of delimitation, a system which she claims to be in complete conformity with international law. The Norwegian Government has referred in this connection to an historic title, the meaning of which was made clear by Counsel for Norway at the sitting on October 12th, 1951: "The Norwegian Government does not rely upon history to justify exceptional rights, to

---

[781] Article 4(2) of the CTSCZ and, subsequently (fn 773), Article 7(3) of the UNCLOS, included this consideration (fn 8 and accompanying text). The text to fn 775 also makes this point in respect of the principle that the strip of territorial waters must follow the general direction of the coast.

[782] Article 4(2) of the CTSCZ and, subsequently (fn 773), Article 7(3) of the UNCLOS, incorporated this consideration (fn 8 and accompanying text), *in addition to* the concern to which the text to fn 781 refers.

[783] These rules developed to become Paragraphs 4 and 5 of Article 7 of the CTSCZ, which were later (fn 773) adopted as Paragraphs 4 and 5 of Article 10 of the UNCLOS (fns 19-20 accompanying text).

> claim areas of sea which the general law would deny; it invokes history, together with other factors, to justify the way in which it applies the general law." This conception of an historic title[784] is in consonance with the Norwegian Government's understanding of the general rules of international law. In its view, these rules of international law take into account the diversity of facts and, therefore, concede that the drawing of base-lines must be adapted to the special conditions obtaining in different regions. In its view, the system of delimitation applied in 1935 [i.e., by the Norwegian Royal Decree of July 12th 1935], a system characterized by the use of straight lines, does not therefore infringe the general law; it is an adaptation rendered necessary by local conditions [672].

The ICJ found the Norwegian system of maritime boundary delimitation to have been "consistently applied by the Norwegian authorities", and to have "encountered no opposition on the part of other States" [673]. As it considered that "the few uncertainties or contradictions, real or apparent, which the United Kingdom Government claims to have discovered in Norwegian practice ... may be easily understood in the light of the variety of the facts and conditions prevailing in the long period which has elapsed since 1812 [i.e., from the moment at which the Norwegian Royal Decree of February 22nd 1812[785] was introduced], and that, therefore, little importance need be attached to these, it held that "the Norwegian authorities applied their system of delimitation consistently and uninterruptedly from 1869 [i.e., from the point at which the Norwegian Royal Decree of October 16th 1869 was passed[786]] until the time when the dispute arose" [674]. The ICJ refused to accept the claim of the Government of the UK that it was unaware of the Norwegian system of maritime boundary delimitation, and that, consequently, this arrangement "lacked the notoriety essential to provide the basis of an historic title enforceable against it," because the Government of the UK "could not have

[784] Fn 625 considers the meaning of the term 'historic title' as interpreted by the arbitral tribunal constituted under Annex VII to the UNCLOS to adjudicate the *South China Sea Arbitration*.

[785] The Norwegian Royal Decree of July 12th 1935 relies upon the Norwegian Royal Decrees of February 22nd 1812, October 16th 1869, January 5th 1881 and September 9th 1889 (the International Court of Justice (1951), *Fisheries Case (United Kingdom v. Norway)*, Judgment of December 18th 1951, *I.C.J. Reports 1951*, 116-144, 125).

[786] Fn 785.

been ignorant of the [Norwegian Royal] Decree of [October 16th] 1869 which had at once provoked a request for explanations by the French Government[, n]or, knowing of it, could it have been under any misapprehension as to the significance of its terms, which clearly described it as constituting the application of a system" [675].

> The Court notes that in respect of a situation which could only be strengthened with the passage of time, the United Kingdom Government refrained from formulating reservations. The notoriety of the facts, the general toleration of the international community, Great Britain's position in the North Sea, her own interest in question, and her prolonged abstention would in any case warrant Norway's enforcement of her system against the United Kingdom. The Court is thus led to conclude that the method of straight lines, established in the Norwegian system, was imposed by the peculiar geography of the Norwegian coast; that even before the dispute arose, this method had been consolidated by a constant and sufficiently long practice, in the face of which the attitude of governments bears witness to the fact that they did not consider it to be contrary to international law [676].

Finally, the ICJ ascertains and holds that the set of baselines that the Norwegian Royal Decree of July 12th 1935 sets out is in accordance with the Norwegian system of drawing straight baselines which follow the general direction of the coast, and that these baselines do, in fact, follow that direction, stating the following.

> The schedule appended to the [Norwegian Royal] Decree of July 12th, 1935, indicates the fixed points between which the straight base-lines are drawn. The Court notes that these lines were the result of a careful study initiated by the Norwegian authorities as far back as 1911. The base-lines recommended by the Foreign Affairs Committee of the Storting[787] for the delimitation of the fisheries zone and adopted and

[787] The website of the Norwegian Parliament states: "The Storting is the Norwegian Parliament. It is the supreme arena for political debate and decision-making in the Kingdom of Norway." (Stortinget (2019), "The Storting," accessed December 31, 2019, <https://www.stortinget.no/en/In-English/About-the-Storting/>).

made public for the first time by the Decree of July 12th, 1935, are the same as those which the so-called Territorial Waters Boundary Commissions, successively appointed on June 29th, 1911, and July 12th, 1912, had drawn in 1912 for Finnmark and in 1913 for Nordland and Troms. The Court further notes that the 1911 and 1912 Commissions advocated these lines and in so doing constantly referred, as the 1935 Decree itself did, to the traditional system of delimitation adopted by earlier acts and more particularly by the [Norwegian Royal] Decrees of 1812, 1869 and 1889[788]. In the absence of convincing evidence to the contrary, the Court cannot readily find that the lines adopted in these circumstances by the 1935 Decree are not in accordance with the traditional Norwegian system. ... [Notwithstanding this, t]he United Kingdom Government contends that certain lines do not follow the general direction of the coast, or do not follow it sufficiently closely, or that they do not respect the natural connection existing between certain sea areas and the land formations separating or surrounding them. ... The United Kingdom Government has directed its criticism more particularly against two sectors, the delimitation of which they represented as extreme cases of deviation from the general direction of the coast: the sector of Svaerholthavet (between base-points 11 and 12) and that of Lopphavet (between base-points 20 and 21). ... The base-line between points 11 and 12, which is 38.6 sea miles in length, delimits the waters of the Svaerholt lying between Cape Nordkyn and the North Cape. The United Kingdom Government denies that the basin so delimited has the character of a bay. ... In its opinion, the calculation of the basin's penetration inland must stop at the tip of the Svaerholt peninsula [, which yields] a penetration inland [of] 11.5 sea miles, as against 38.6 miles of breadth at the entrance ... . The Court is unable to share this view. It considers that the basin in question must be contemplated in the light of all the geographical factors involved. The fact that a peninsula juts out and forms two wide fjords, the Laksefjord and the Porsangerfjord, cannot deprive the basin of the character of a bay. It is the distances between the disputed base-line and the most inland point of these fjords, 50 and 75 sea miles respectively, which must be taken into account in appreciating the proportion between the penetration inland and the width at the mouth. The Court concludes that Svaerholthavet has the character of a bay. ... The base-line [between

---

[788] Fn 785.

base-points 20 and 21, which the Norwegian Royal Decree of July 12th 1935 uses to delimit the Lopphavet basin] has been challenged [by the Government of the United Kingdom] on the ground that it does not respect the general direction of the coast. … [T]o properly apply the rule, regard must be had for the relation between the deviation complained of and what … must be regarded as the *general*[789] direction of the coast. … [T]he divergence between th[is] base-line and the land formations is not such that it is a distortion of the general direction of the Norwegian coast. Even if it were considered that in the sector under review the deviation was too pronounced, … the Norwegian Government has relied upon an historic title clearly referable to the waters of Lopphavet, namely, the exclusive privilege to fish and hunt whales granted at the end of the 17th century to Lt.-Commander Erich Lorch under a number of licences which show, *inter alia*[790], that the water situated in the vicinity of the sunken rock of Gjesbaaen or Gjesboene and the fishing grounds pertaining thereto were regarded as falling exclusively within Norwegian sovereignty. … These ancient concessions tend to confirm that the Norwegian Government's contention that the fisheries zone reserved before 1812 [i.e., prior to the introduction the Norwegian Royal Decree of February 22nd 1812] was in fact much extensive than the one delimited in 1935 [by the Norwegian Royal Decree of July 12th 1935]. … The Court considers that … the historical data produced in support of this contention by the Norwegian Government lend some weight to the idea of the survival of traditional rights reserved to the inhabitants of the Kingdom [of Norway] over fishing grounds included in the 1935 delimitation, particularly in the case of Lopphavet. Such rights, founded on the vital needs of the population and attested by very ancient and peaceful usage, may legitimately be taken into account in drawing a line which, moreover, appears to the Court to have been kept within the bounds of what is moderate and reasonable [677].

Whilst the *rationes decidendi*[791] of *Fisheries Case (United Kingdom v. Norway)* have inspired aspects of the CTSCZ and the UNCLOS, in

---

789 Emphasis original.

790 Emphasis original. The final sentence of fn 319 defines '*inter alia*'.

791 Fn 367 defines '*ratio decidendi*'. There are several reasons which, together, form the basis for the ICJ's decisions in *Fisheries Case (United Kingdom v. Norway)*, as to: (i) the legality of

particular provisions therein concerning straight baselines, bays and historic title, arguably more important still is the way that the ICJ crafts a favourable result for the inhabitants of north-west Norway, who heavily rely on local sources of fish for their living. History, physical geography and Norwegian rules as to drawing baselines for the delimitation of Norway's territorial sea combine to enable the Court to declare the straight baselines used in the Norwegian Royal Decree of July 12th 1935 to be compatible with international law. The main difficulty with the approach of the Court in this case and its outcome, is that these may potentially encourage claims from coastal states concerning especially their internal waters and/or their territorial sea which stretch the meaning of provisions of the UNCLOS to more than would have been intended by those of its drafters that wished to enact a straightforward delimitation of maritime zones. One benefit of the approach to baselines and maritime delimitation that the 1935 Decree uses, and which the ICJ upheld in *Fisheries Case (United Kingdom v. Norway)*, is that it creates a precedent that clarifies and simplifies the process for generating baselines and zones over complex coastal terrain, which, whilst favouring the coastal state (i.e., Norway), is only mildly disadvantageous to its neighbouring countries. Consequently, it is unlikely that the substance of the decision will be challenged by the UK, Russia or any other regional state in the forseeable future.

The *Delimitation of the Continental Shelf between the United Kingdom of Great Britain and Northern Ireland, and the French Republic* comprises two arbitral awards, dated 30th June 1977[792] and 14th March 1978[793]. The first of these decisions was based upon an arbitration agreement signed in Paris in 1975, which constituted an *ad hoc*[794] arbitral tribunal comprising

---

the method that the Norwegian Royal Decree of July 12th 1935 uses to delimit its fisheries zone, and (ii) the baselines which this Decree draws – hence the use of the plural form of the phrase '*ratio decidendi*': '*rationes decidendi*'.

[792] United Nations (2006), *Delimitation of the Continental Shelf between the United Kingdom of Great Britain and Northern Ireland, and the French Republic*, Decision of 30 June 1977, *Reports of International Arbitral Awards*, 3-270, 3.

[793] United Nations (2006), *Delimitation of the Continental Shelf between the United Kingdom of Great Britain and Northern Ireland, and the French Republic*, Decision of 14 March 1978, *Reports of International Arbitral Awards*, 271-413, 271.

[794] Fn 207 defines '*ad hoc*'.

five arbitrators[795], which it named a Court of Arbitration[796]. Article 2 of the Arbitration Agreement specified the jurisdiction of the Court of Arbitration, as follows.

> 1. The Court [of Arbitration] is requested to decide, in accordance with the rules of international law applicable in the matter as between the Parties [i.e., the Government of the United Kingdom of Great Britain and Northern Ireland, and the Government of the French Republic], the following question: What is the course of the boundary (or boundaries) between the portions of the continental shelf appertaining to the United Kingdom and the Channel Islands and to the French Republic, respectively, westward of 30 minutes west of the Greenwich Meridian as far as the 1,000 metre isobath? 2. The choice of the 1,000 metre isobath is without prejudice to the position of either Government concerning the outer limit of the continental shelf [678].

The second decision, i.e., that dated 14th March 1978, was the result of arbitral proceedings before the same arbitral tribunal (i.e., the Court of Arbitration), which were commenced after the Government of the United

---

795 Article 1(1) of the Arbitration Agreement designated the arbitrators as Sir Humphrey Waldock – whom the Government of the United Kingdom nominated, Mr. Paul Reuter – whom the Government of France nominated, and Messrs. Herbert Briggs, Erik Castren (fn 796), and Endre Ustor (United Nations (2006), *Delimitation of the Continental Shelf between the United Kingdom of Great Britain and Northern Ireland, and the French Republic*, Decision of 30 June 1977, *Reports of International Arbitral Awards*, 3-270, 5). On 6th April 1976, the Government of France, in observance of Article 1(2) of the Arbitration Agreement, appointed Mr. André Gros to succeed Mr. Paul Reuter, who resigned for health reasons (United Nations (2006), *Delimitation of the Continental Shelf between the United Kingdom of Great Britain and Northern Ireland, and the French Republic*, Decision of 30 June 1977, *Reports of International Arbitral Awards*, 3-270, 7). Article 1(2) of the Arbitration Agreement states: "Should the President or any other Member of the Court [of Arbitration] be or become unable to act, the vacancy shall be filled by a new Member appointed by the Government which nominated the Member to be replaced in the case of the two Members nominated by the United Kingdom and French Government, or by agreement between the two Governments in the case of the President or the remaining to Members[.]" (United Nations (2006), *Delimitation of the Continental Shelf between the United Kingdom of Great Britain and Northern Ireland, and the French Republic*, Decision of 30 June 1977, *Reports of International Arbitral Awards*, 3-270, 5).

796 Article 1(1) of the Arbitration Agreement appointed Mr. Erik Castren as the President of the Court of Arbitration (United Nations (2006), *Delimitation of the Continental Shelf between the United Kingdom of Great Britain and Northern Ireland, and the French Republic*, Decision of 30 June 1977, *Reports of International Arbitral Awards*, 3-270, 5).

Kingdom, by an Application to the Court of Arbitration dated 17th October 1977, invoked Article 10(2) of the Arbitration Agreement, in order to attain clarification on two aspects of the Court of Arbitration's first decision – i.e., that dated 30th June 1977, which the Court of Arbitration had delivered on 18th July 1977[797] [679]. The beginning of this Application reads as follows.

---

[797] Article 10(2) of the Arbitration Agreement declares: "Either Party may, *within three months of the rendering of the decision*, refer to the Court [of Arbitration] any dispute between the Parties [i.e., the Government of the United Kingdom of Great Britain and Northern Ireland, and the Government of the French Republic] as to the meaning and scope of the decision." (United Nations (2006), *Delimitation of the Continental Shelf between the United Kingdom of Great Britain and Northern Ireland, and the French Republic*, Decision of 30 June 1977, *Reports of International Arbitral Awards*, 3-270, 7; emphasis added). As the Court of Arbitration had delivered its first decision (i.e., that dated 30th June 1997) on *18th July 1977*, and seeing that the Government of the United Kingdom's Application to the Court of Arbitration pursuant to Article 10(2) of the Arbitration Agreement was dated *17th October 1977*, this Application was *just* submitted within the valid time period. The Court of Arbitration clarified this unequivocally in the *third* paragraph of its decision dated 14th March 1978, in response to the objection that the Government of France filed with the former, which the *second* paragraph of this decision summarizes, that the Government of the United Kingdom's Application was inadmissible because it was out of time – based on the wording of Article 10(2) of the Arbitration Agreement in the French version of the Agreement: "2. The French Government, in alleging that the Application is out of time, invokes the provision in paragraph 2 of the Article [i.e., Article 10 of the Arbitration Agreement] which allows reference of a dispute regarding interpretation of the Decision only "dans les trois mois suivant la décision prise," and it points to the fact that the Court's Decision is expressly dated 30 June 1977 whereas the Application was filed only on 17 October 1977. … 3. This objection appears to the Court of Arbitration to be wholly unfounded. Article 10, paragraph 2, confers upon either Party the right, within the period which it specifies, to refer to the Court any dispute between them as to the meaning and scope of the decision. Such a right can have no reality or object otherwise than in relation to a decision the purport of which has been made known to the Parties. Consequently, when in the French text of the Agreement the paragraph provides that the right may be exercised "dans les trois mois suivant la décision prise," it is logical to suppose that by these words the Parties intended that the three-months' period should begin to run from the date when the decision was taken vis-à- vis the Parties, that is, the date when it was handed down to the Parties. That such was indeed the intention of the Parties is confirmed by the wording of the English text of the paragraph, which speaks expressly of reference to the Court "within three months of the *rendering* of the decision." The natural meaning of "rendering" in the context of Article 10 [of the Arbitration Agreement] is, in the opinion of the Court, the handing down or delivering of the decision to the Parties; and that this is the meaning with which it is used in Article 10 is corroborated by the fact that the word "render" unmistakably has this meaning in the very next Article of the Agreement [(i.e., Article 11(1) of the Arbitration Agreement, which proclaims: "A Party wishing to carry out, at any time before the Court [of Arbitration] has rendered its decision on the question specified in Article 2 [of the Arbitration Agreement – which the immediately-preceding quoted passage in the text contains], any activity in a portion of what it considers to be its continental shelf within the area submitted to arbitration shall, subject to the remaining provisions of this

APPLICATION TO THE COURT OF ARBITRATION PURSUANT TO THE PROVISIONS OF ARTICLE 10, PARAGRAPH 2, OF THE ARBITRATION AGREEMENT OF 10 JULY 1975

1. In accordance with the provisions of Article 10, paragraph 2, of the Arbitration Agreement between the Government of the United Kingdom and the Government of the French Republic signed in Paris on 10 July 1975 ("the Arbitration Agreement"), the United Kingdom wish hereby to refer to the Court of Arbitration two questions relating to the meaning, or alternatively the scope, of the Court's Decision of 30 July 1977, which are in dispute between the Parties, namely: (*1*) the techniques and methods employed for drawing on the boundary-line chart the 12-mile enclave boundary to the north and west of the Channel Islands; (*2*) the techniques and methods employed for drawing on the boundary-line chart the portion of the boundary west of point "M" out to the 1,000-metre isobath.

2. The reasons justifying this application are set out below. ...[798] [680].

The following extract from this Application provides some of the reasoning relating to the query concerning the Channel Islands.

8. In paragraph 202 of its Decision [of 30 June 1977], the Court [of Arbitration] "decides that this boundary (sc the enclave boundary north and west of the Channel Islands) shall be drawn at a distance of 12 nautical miles from the established baselines of the territorial sea of the Channel Islands"[799][.] In the United Kingdom's submission , this is the definitive decision of the Court upon this issue.

Article [i.e., Paragraphs 2-6 of Article 11 of the Arbitration Agreement] obtain the prior consent of the other Party.")]. Since the meaning expressed in the English text of Article 10 paragraph 2, is also the meaning indicated by common sense and fairness, the Court of Arbitration must conclude that the English text accurately expresses the intention of the Parties regarding the date for the commencement of the three-month period." (United Nations (2006), *Delimitation of the Continental Shelf between the United Kingdom of Great Britain and Northern Ireland, and the French Republic*, Decision of 14 March 1978, *Reports of International Arbitral Awards*, 271-413, 285-286; emphasis original).

[798] Emphasis original.

[799] Paragraph 202 of the Court of Arbitration's Decision of 30 June 1977 states: "The second part of the solution is to delimit a second boundary establishing, vis-à-vis the Channel Islands,

9. The relevant section of the boundary is subsequently described, in paragraph 203 of the Court's Decision and the *dispositif*, as arcs of circles of the 12-mile radius[800], and the co-ordinates of the points of intersection of these arcs with the mid-Channel median line and with one another ... are listed. ... The Technical Report [of the technical expert appointed by the Court] contains a listing of the basepoints which have been used for determining the relevant arcs of circles, the co-ordinates defining each of which are also listed, and these listings are reproduced in paragraph 203 and the *dispositif* of the Court's Decision [of 30 June 1977].

10. Unfortunately, however, the basepoints so listed comprise only an incomplete selection of the relevant points on the established baselines from which the territorial sea of the Channel Islands has consistently been measured by the United Kingdom. Accordingly, the boundary line in this part of the arbitration area as traced on the boundary-line chart and as defined in the Decision [of 30 June 1977] does not correspond in all respects to a true 12-mile limit north and west of the Channel Islands and does not, for example, correspond accurately to the established 12-mile fishery limit maintained and enforced in this area pursuant to the relevant legislation of the United Kingdom and the Channel Islands. ...

11. ... [T]he appropriate basepoints for determining the 12-mile limit north and west of the Channel Islands should also include the following ... . All of these points are, in the wording used in paragraph 202 of the Court's Decision [of 30 June 1977], points on "the established baselines

the southern limit of the continental shelf held by the Court [of Arbitration] to be appurtenant to the French Republic in this region to the south of the mid-Channel median line. This second boundary must not ... be so drawn as to allow the continental shelf of the French Republic to encroach upon the established 12-mile fishery zone of the Channel Islands. The Court therefore further decides that this boundary shall be drawn at a distance of 12 nautical miles from the established baselines of the territorial sea of the Channel Islands. The effect will be to accord to the French Republic a substantial band of continental shelf in mid-Channel which is continuous with its continental shelf to the east and west of the Channel Islands region; and at the same time to leave to the Channel Islands, to their north and to their west, a zone of seabed and subsoil extending 12 nautical miles from the baselines of the two Bailiwicks [(of Guernsey and Jersey)]. The result, so far as the Channel Islands are concerned, is to enclose them in an enclave formed, to their north and west, by the boundary of the 12-mile zone just described by the Court and, to their east, south and south-east by the boundary between them and the coasts of Normandy and Brittany ... ." (United Nations (2006), *Delimitation of the Continental Shelf between the United Kingdom of Great Britain and Northern Ireland, and the French Republic*, Decision of 30 June 1977, *Reports of International Arbitral Awards*, 3-270, 95).

[800] Fn 772 describes the arcs of circle method for drawing baselines to determine the breadth of the territorial sea.

> of the territorial sea of the Channel Islands" [(fn 32)]: "established," because they have consistently used by the United Kingdom, without protest by France or other States, for the delimitation of the existing 3-mile territorial sea of the Channel Islands and for the delimitation of the 6-mile and 12-mile belts provided for in the London Fisheries Convention of 1964; and, on the territorial sea baseline, because they represent in every case, either points on the low-water line along the coast, or alternatively low-tide elevations lying well within the 3-mile territorial sea of the Channel Islands, and are therefore proper to be used as part of the baseline from which the territorial sea is measured in accordance with the applicable rules of international law. It follows … that the omission of the base points is inconsistent with the practice followed in defining the course of other parts of the boundary lines, and cannot be reconciled with paragraph 202 of the Court's Decision [of 30 June 1977 (fn 32)][801] [681].

The Court of Arbitration, in its Decision of 14 March 1978, agreed with the point in the Application of the United Kingdom dated 17th October 1977 in relation to the baselines to the north and west of the Channel Islands that the base-points used in this location in its Decision of 30th June 1977 were not totally in accord with its intentions in Paragraph 202 of that latter Decision[802], and corrected this by substituting for those a list of base-points appended to this Application. In Subparagraph 4 of the operative part of its Decision of 14 March 1978, i.e., Paragraph 114, the Court of Arbitration stated the following.

> 114. For these reasons,
>
> THE COURT OF ARBITRATION, in regard to the questions raised by the Application filed by the United Kingdom on 17 October 1977 under Article 10, paragraph 2, of the Arbitration Agreement,
>
> Decides unanimously that: …

[801] Emphasis original.

[802] Fn 799 quotes Paragraph 202 of the Court of Arbitration's Decision of 30 June 1977 in *Delimitation of the Continental Shelf between the United Kingdom of Great Britain and Northern Ireland, and the French Republic*, Decision of 14 March 1978, *Reports of International Arbitral Awards*.

(4) In relation to the boundary to the north and west of the Channel Islands,

a. the course of the boundary for this region defined in paragraph 2 of the *dispositif* of the Decision of 30 June 1977 is not a correct application of the express findings of the Court in paragraph 202 of that Decision regarding the principles to be applied in delimiting the said boundary;

b. paragraph 202 of the Decision of 30 June 1977 expresses the intention of the Court, and the definition of the boundary line to the north and west of the Channel Islands shall, therefore, now be rectified so as to follow the line composed of segments of arcs of circles of a 12-mile radius, drawn from the base-points A to M on the baselines of the Bailiwick of Guernsey listed in Appendix A.4 to the Application … and joining the 12 points of intersection of these arcs of circles also listed in that Appendix. …[803] [682]

The above excerpts from the two decisions in *Delimitation of the Continental Shelf between the United Kingdom of Great Britain and Northern Ireland, and the French Republic* show how difficult it is, both politically and technically, to arrive at optimal decisions concerning the delimitation of maritime boundaries between neighbouring coastal states. The Government of the United Kingdom was unhappy about the first decision of the arbitral tribunal in relation to the delimitation of the territorial sea of the Channel Islands on their north and west sides, and submitted, only just in the requisite time as stated in the arbitration agreement, a list of base-points that it considered to be more correctly aligned with the tribunal's expressed intentions in respect of the delimitation of the boundary in question than those base-points used by the tribunal. The Government of France attempted to prevent the United Kingdom's application for revision from being accepted for consideration by the arbitral tribunal, by claiming on a fairly weak basis that this application was out of time and should therefore be rejected. As the arbitration agreement had been previously agreed between the Governments of the United Kingdom and France, one might have expected

---

[803] Emphasis original.

a commitment from both Governments as to the award(s) granted by the arbitral tribunal. It is submitted that this incentive for disputants is lacking from arbitrations that are commenced under Annex VII to the UNCLOS[804], unless both parties have chosen this method of dispute resolution in a Declaration made pursuant to Article 287(1) of the UNCLOS[805].

In *Delimitation of the maritime boundary between Ghana and Côte D'Ivoire in the Atlantic Ocean (Ghana/Côte D'Ivoire)*[806], a Special Chamber of the ITLOS was formed in January 2015 to adjudicate the dispute, and was dissolved after it delivered its decision in September 2017[807]. The operative part of the Special Chamber's Judgment, i.e., Paragraph 660, was reached unanimously, and is as follows.

> 660. For these reasons,
> THE SPECIAL CHAMBER
> (1) Unanimously,
> *Finds* that it has jurisdiction to delimit the maritime boundary between the Parties in the territorial sea, in the exclusive economic zone and on the continental shelf, both within and beyond 200 nm [nautical miles].
> (2) Unanimously,
> *Finds* that there is no tacit agreement between the Parties to delimit their territorial sea, exclusive economic zone and continental shelf both within and beyond 200 nm, and *rejects* Ghana's claim that Côte d'Ivoire is estopped from objecting to the "customary equidistance boundary."
> (3) Unanimously,
> *Decides* that the single maritime boundary for the territorial sea, the exclusive economic zone and the continental shelf within and beyond 200 nm starts at … and is defined by turning points A, B, C, D, E, F with the following coordinates and connected by geodetic[808] lines: … [.] From

---

[804] Fn 196 summarizes Annex VII to the UNCLOS.

[805] The first sentence of the subsection entitled 'Compulsory Procedures: Choice of Procedure', in the section titled 'Part XV of the UNCLOS: Settlement of Disputes' in Chapter 1, comprises Article 287(1) of the UNCLOS.

[806] Case No. 23. Judgment of 23 September 2017, *ITLOS Reports 2017*, 4.

[807] Fn 389 and accompanying text.

[808] 'Geodetic' means "of or relating to geodesy, especially as applied to land surveying" (Pearsall, J. (editor) (1998), *The New Oxford Dictionary of English* (Oxford: Oxford University Press), 767). 'Geodesy' is "the branch of mathematics dealing with the shape

turning point F, the single maritime boundary continues as a geodetic line starting at an azimuth[809] of … until it reaches the outer limits of the continental shelf.

(4) Unanimously,

Finds that it has jurisdiction to decide on the claim of Côte d'Ivoire against Ghana on the alleged international responsibility of Ghana.

(5) Unanimously,

Finds that Ghana did not violate the sovereign rights of Côte d'Ivoire.

(6) Unanimously,

Finds that Ghana did not violate article 83, paragraphs 1 and 3, of the Convention [(i.e., the UNCLOS)][810].

(7) Unanimously,

Finds that Ghana did not violate the provisional measures prescribed by the Special Chamber in its Order of 25 April 2015[811]. [683]

Article 83 of the UNCLOS concerns the delimitation of the continental shelf between states with opposite or adjacent coasts. Côte d'Ivoire's claim that Ghana was in breach of Article 83(1) of the UNCLOS, was based on its belief that Ghana had acted in the disputed area of the boundary unilaterally, had been inflexible in negotiations with Côte d'Ivoire, and had intentionally shut down all routes to an adjudicatory settlement in the dispute between the two countries [684]. Ghana responded that these allegations are not supported by facts, stating that its activities had been carried out openly and with the co-operation of Côte d'Ivoire [685]. The Special Chamber commented that the obligation under Article 83(1) of the Convention for countries with opposite or adjacent coasts to reach an agreement on the delimitation of the continental shelf, entailed negotiations

---

and area of the earth or large portions of it" (Pearsall, J. (editor) (1998), *The New Oxford Dictionary of English*, 767).

809 An 'azimuth' is "the horizonal direction of a celestial object from the observer, expressed as the angular distance from the north or south point of the horizon to the point at which a vertical circle passing through the object intersects with the horizon" (Pearsall, J. (editor) (1998), *The New Oxford Dictionary of English*, 119).

810 The text to fn 146 comprises Article 83(1) of the UNCLOS. The second sentence of fn 145 specifies Article 83(3) of the UNCLOS.

811 Emphasis original.

in order to accomplish this delimitation, which required a duty to negotiate in good faith – an obligation of behaviour; therefore, a transgression of this duty could not be founded solely upon the non-accomplishment of one of the state's expectations from the negotiations [686]. The Special Chamber considered that Côte d'Ivoire had not demonstrated that Ghana lacked good faith in the six-year negotiations over the delimitation to the two countries' maritime boundary; for instance, the fact that Ghana had initially rejected the avenue for a binding settlement was not at variance with the duty to negotiate in good faith, as Côte d'Ivoire claimed, because Article 298 of the UNCLOS[812] expressly allowed States Parties to exclude specified categories of dispute from compulsory procedures [687]. Thus, Ghana did not contravene Article 83(1) of the UNCLOS [688]. In proceeding to find that Ghana did not infringe Article 83(3) of the UNCLOS, the Special Chamber noted that Côte d'Ivoire and Ghana disagreed on the interpretation of this Paragraph and as to whether it applied in the circumstances at issue – and, accordingly, interpreted Article 83(3) of the UNCLOS [689].

Of the three cases described above, the ICJ determined the first, an arbitral tribunal adjudicated the second, and the ITLOS decided the third. Although there is overlap between them – for instance delimitation of the territorial sea is an aspect that is common to all three, they are decidedly different in their emphasis and in the time at which they came before the court or arbitral tribunal to be heard. The first preceded the adoption in 1958 of the Geneva Conventions, i.e., the CCS, the CFCLRHS, the CHS and the CTSCZ. Both decisions of the arbitral tribunal hearing the second case took place after the Geneva Conventions came into effect in the 1960s[813] but before the UNCLOS was adopted in 1982. Both the Order concerning the requested provisional measures and the hearing in the third case took place in the current decade, i.e., the 2010s, which will turn into the 2020s just 45 minutes after the time at which these words are being written; this moment is substantially after the UNCLOS came into effect in

[812] The subsection entitled 'Optional Exceptions to the Applicability of Compulsory Procedures', in the section titled 'Part XV of the UNCLOS: Settlement of Disputes' in Chapter 1, contains Article 298 of the UNCLOS.

[813] Fn 771.

1994. Thus, the Law of the Sea – including those aspects of it concerning baselines and boundary delimitation, is a dynamic, evolving subject, which is likely to see many more developments, even in the constructive and comprehensive Convention that is the UNCLOS. The ITLOS is likely to increase its workload over the new decade, especially as its judges become more specialized and experienced in the subject. The ICJ will continue to provide stability in its Judgments, and the arbitral tribunals constituted under Articles VII and VIII of the UNCLOS flexibility.

REFERENCES

[1] United Nations (1982). "United Nations Convention on the Law of the Sea," *United Nations Treaty Series* Registration Number 31363, Article 320.

[2] United Nations Treaty Collection (2019). "Chapter XXI Law of the Sea: 6. United Nations Convention on the Law of the Sea," Accessed July 17, 2019. https://treaties.un.org/Pages/ViewDetailsIII.aspx?src=TREATY&mtdsg_no=XXI6&chapter=21&Temp=mtdsg3&clang=_en.

[3] United Nations (1982). "United Nations Convention on the Law of the Sea," Article 311(1).

[4] Continental Shelf Programme (2019). "Background to UNCLOS." Accessed July 17, 2019. http://www.continentalshelf.org/about/1143.aspx.

[5] United Nations (1982). "United Nations Convention on the Law of the Sea," Article 89.

[6] United Nations (1982). "United Nations Convention on the Law of the Sea," Article 86.

[7] United Nations (1982). "United Nations Convention on the Law of the Sea," Article 1(1).

[8] United Nations (1982). "United Nations Convention on the Law of the Sea," Article 136.

[9] United Nations (1982). "United Nations Convention on the Law of the Sea," Article 2(3).

[10] United Nations (1982). "United Nations Convention on the Law of the Sea," Article 2(1).

[11] United Nations (1982). "United Nations Convention on the Law of the Sea," Article 2(2).

[12] United Nations (1982). "United Nations Convention on the Law of the Sea," Article 3.

[13] United Nations (1982). "United Nations Convention on the Law of the Sea," Article 4.

[14] United Nations (1982). "United Nations Convention on the Law of the Sea," Article 5.

[15] United Nations (1982). "United Nations Convention on the Law of the Sea," Article 121(2).

[16] United Nations (1982). "United Nations Convention on the Law of the Sea," Article 6.

[17] United Nations (1982). "United Nations Convention on the Law of the Sea," Article 7(1).

[18] United Nations (1982). "United Nations Convention on the Law of the Sea," Article 7(3).

[19] United Nations (1982). "United Nations Convention on the Law of the Sea," Article 7(2).

[20] United Nations (1982). "United Nations Convention on the Law of the Sea," Article 7(4).

[21] United Nations (1982). "United Nations Convention on the Law of the Sea," Article 7(5).

[22] United Nations (1982). "United Nations Convention on the Law of the Sea," Article 7(6).

[23] United Nations (1982). "United Nations Convention on the Law of the Sea," Article 8(1).

[24] United Nations (1982). "United Nations Convention on the Law of the Sea," Article 8(2).

[25] United Nations (1982). "United Nations Convention on the Law of the Sea," Article 9.

[26] United Nations (1982). "United Nations Convention on the Law of the Sea," Article 10(1).

[27] United Nations (1982). "United Nations Convention on the Law of the Sea," Article 10(6).

[28] United Nations (1982). "United Nations Convention on the Law of the Sea," Article 10(2).

[29] United Nations (1982). "United Nations Convention on the Law of the Sea," Article 10(4).

[30] United Nations (1982). "United Nations Convention on the Law of the Sea," Article 10(5).

[31] United Nations (1982). "United Nations Convention on the Law of the Sea," Article 11.

[32] United Nations (1982). "United Nations Convention on the Law of the Sea," Article 12.

[33] United Nations (1982). "United Nations Convention on the Law of the Sea," Article 13(1).

[34] United Nations (1982). "United Nations Convention on the Law of the Sea," Article 13(2).

[35] United Nations (1982). "United Nations Convention on the Law of the Sea," Article 14.

[36] United Nations (1982). "United Nations Convention on the Law of the Sea," Article 15.

[37] United Nations (1982). "United Nations Convention on the Law of the Sea," Article 16(1).

[38] United Nations (1982). "United Nations Convention on the Law of the Sea," Article 17.

[39] United Nations (1982). "United Nations Convention on the Law of the Sea," Article 18(1)(a).

[40] United Nations (1982). "United Nations Convention on the Law of the Sea," Article 18(1)(b).

[41] United Nations (1982). "United Nations Convention on the Law of the Sea," Article 18(2).

[42] United Nations (1982). "United Nations Convention on the Law of the Sea," Article 19(1).

[43] United Nations (1982). "United Nations Convention on the Law of the Sea," Article 19(2)(a).

[44] United Nations (1982). "United Nations Convention on the Law of the Sea," Article 19(2)(b).

[45] United Nations (1982). "United Nations Convention on the Law of the Sea," Article 19(2)(c).

[46] United Nations (1982). "United Nations Convention on the Law of the Sea," Article 19(2)(d).

[47] United Nations (1982). "United Nations Convention on the Law of the Sea," Article 19(2)(e).

[48] United Nations (1982). "United Nations Convention on the Law of the Sea," Article 19(2)(f).

[49] United Nations (1982). "United Nations Convention on the Law of the Sea," Article 19(2)(g).

[50] United Nations (1982). "United Nations Convention on the Law of the Sea," Article 19(2)(h).

[51] United Nations (1982). "United Nations Convention on the Law of the Sea," Article 19(2)(i).

[52] United Nations (1982). "United Nations Convention on the Law of the Sea," Article 19(2)(j).

[53] United Nations (1982). "United Nations Convention on the Law of the Sea," Article 19(2)(k).

[54] United Nations (1982). "United Nations Convention on the Law of the Sea," Article 19(2)(l).

[55] United Nations (1982). "United Nations Convention on the Law of the Sea," Article 20.

[56] United Nations (1982). "United Nations Convention on the Law of the Sea," Article 23.

[57] United Nations (1982). "United Nations Convention on the Law of the Sea," Article 21(1)(a).

[58] United Nations (1982). "United Nations Convention on the Law of the Sea," Article 21(1)(b).

[59] United Nations (1982). "United Nations Convention on the Law of the Sea," Article 21(1)(c).
[60] United Nations (1982). "United Nations Convention on the Law of the Sea," Article 21(1)(d).
[61] United Nations (1982). "United Nations Convention on the Law of the Sea," Article 21(1)(e).
[62] United Nations (1982). "United Nations Convention on the Law of the Sea," Article 21(1)(f).
[63] United Nations (1982). "United Nations Convention on the Law of the Sea," Article 21(1)(g).
[64] United Nations (1982). "United Nations Convention on the Law of the Sea," Article 21(1)(h).
[65] United Nations (1982). "United Nations Convention on the Law of the Sea," Article 21(2).
[66] United Nations (1982). "United Nations Convention on the Law of the Sea," Article 21(3).
[67] United Nations (1982). "United Nations Convention on the Law of the Sea," Article 21(4).
[68] United Nations (1982). "United Nations Convention on the Law of the Sea," Article 22(1).
[69] United Nations (1982). "United Nations Convention on the Law of the Sea," Article 22(2).
[70] United Nations (1982). "United Nations Convention on the Law of the Sea," Article 22(3)(a).
[71] United Nations (1982). "United Nations Convention on the Law of the Sea," Article 22(3)(b).
[72] United Nations (1982). "United Nations Convention on the Law of the Sea," Article 22(3)(c).
[73] United Nations (1982). "United Nations Convention on the Law of the Sea," Article 22(3)(d).
[74] United Nations (1982). "United Nations Convention on the Law of the Sea," Article 22(4).
[75] United Nations (1982). "United Nations Convention on the Law of the Sea," Article 25(1).

[76] United Nations (1982). "United Nations Convention on the Law of the Sea," Article 25(2).

[77] United Nations (1982). "United Nations Convention on the Law of the Sea," Article 25(3).

[78] United Nations (1982). "United Nations Convention on the Law of the Sea," Article 24(1).

[79] United Nations (1982). "United Nations Convention on the Law of the Sea," Article 24(1)(a).

[80] United Nations (1982). "United Nations Convention on the Law of the Sea," Article 24(1)(b).

[81] United Nations (1982). "United Nations Convention on the Law of the Sea," Article 24(2).

[82] United Nations (1982). "United Nations Convention on the Law of the Sea," Article 26(1).

[83] United Nations (1982). "United Nations Convention on the Law of the Sea," Article 26(2).

[84] United Nations (1982). "United Nations Convention on the Law of the Sea," Article 27(1)(a).

[85] United Nations (1982). "United Nations Convention on the Law of the Sea," Article 27(1)(b).

[86] United Nations (1982). "United Nations Convention on the Law of the Sea," Article 27(1)(c).

[87] United Nations (1982). "United Nations Convention on the Law of the Sea," Article 27(1)(d).

[88] United Nations (1982). "United Nations Convention on the Law of the Sea," Article 27(2).

[89] United Nations (1982). "United Nations Convention on the Law of the Sea," Article 27(5).

[90] United Nations (1982). "United Nations Convention on the Law of the Sea," Article 28(1).

[91] United Nations (1982). "United Nations Convention on the Law of the Sea," Article 28(2).

[92] United Nations (1982). "United Nations Convention on the Law of the Sea," Article 28(3).

[93] United Nations (1982). "United Nations Convention on the Law of the Sea," Article 30.

[94] United Nations (1982). "United Nations Convention on the Law of the Sea," Article 31.

[95] United Nations (1982). "United Nations Convention on the Law of the Sea," Article 33(1)(a).

[96] United Nations (1982). "United Nations Convention on the Law of the Sea," Article 33(1)(b).

[97] United Nations (1982). "United Nations Convention on the Law of the Sea," Article 33(2).

[98] Amerasinghe, C. (1974). The Problem of Archipelagoes in the International Law of the Sea, *The International and Comparative Law Quarterly*, 23(3), 539-575, 539.

[99] Brock, J. (1966). Archipelago Concept of Limits of Territorial Seas, *Naval War College Review*, 19(4), 34-97, 55.

[100] United Nations (1982). "United Nations Convention on the Law of the Sea," Article 46(b).

[101] United Nations (1982). "United Nations Convention on the Law of the Sea," Article 46(a).

[102] United Nations (1982). "United Nations Convention on the Law of the Sea," Article 47(1).

[103] United Nations (1982). "United Nations Convention on the Law of the Sea," Article 47(2).

[104] United Nations (1982). "United Nations Convention on the Law of the Sea," Article 47(3).

[105] United Nations (1982). "United Nations Convention on the Law of the Sea," Article 47(4).

[106] United Nations (1982). "United Nations Convention on the Law of the Sea," Article 47(5).

[107] United Nations (1982). "United Nations Convention on the Law of the Sea," Article 47(6).

[108] United Nations (1982). "United Nations Convention on the Law of the Sea," Article 47(8).

[109] United Nations (1982). "United Nations Convention on the Law of the Sea," Article 50.

[110] United Nations (1982). "United Nations Convention on the Law of the Sea," Article 48.

[111] United Nations (1982). "United Nations Convention on the Law of the Sea," Article 49(1).

[112] United Nations (1982). "United Nations Convention on the Law of the Sea," Article 49(2).

[113] United Nations (1982). "United Nations Convention on the Law of the Sea," Article 49(3).

[114] United Nations (1982). "United Nations Convention on the Law of the Sea," Article 49(4).

[115] United Nations (1982). "United Nations Convention on the Law of the Sea," Article 51(1).

[116] United Nations (1982). "United Nations Convention on the Law of the Sea," Article 51(2).

[117] United Nations (1982). "United Nations Convention on the Law of the Sea," Article 52(1).

[118] United Nations (1982). "United Nations Convention on the Law of the Sea," Article 52(2).

[119] United Nations (1982). "United Nations Convention on the Law of the Sea," Article 53(1).

[120] United Nations (1982). "United Nations Convention on the Law of the Sea," Article 53(2).

[121] United Nations (1982). "United Nations Convention on the Law of the Sea," Article 53(3).

[122] United Nations (1982). "United Nations Convention on the Law of the Sea," Article 53(4).

[123] United Nations (1982). "United Nations Convention on the Law of the Sea," Article 53(5).

[124] United Nations (1982). "United Nations Convention on the Law of the Sea," Article 53(6).

[125] United Nations (1982). "United Nations Convention on the Law of the Sea," Article 53(7).

[126] United Nations (1982). "United Nations Convention on the Law of the Sea," Article 53(8).
[127] United Nations (1982). "United Nations Convention on the Law of the Sea," Article 53(9).
[128] United Nations (1982). "United Nations Convention on the Law of the Sea," Article 55.
[129] United Nations (1982). "United Nations Convention on the Law of the Sea," Article 57.
[130] United Nations (1982). "United Nations Convention on the Law of the Sea," Article 56(1)(a).
[131] United Nations (1982). "United Nations Convention on the Law of the Sea," Article 56(1)(b)(i).
[132] United Nations (1982). "United Nations Convention on the Law of the Sea," Article 56(1)(b)(ii).
[133] United Nations (1982). "United Nations Convention on the Law of the Sea," Article 56(1)(b)(iii).
[134] United Nations (1982). "United Nations Convention on the Law of the Sea," Article 56(1)(c).
[135] United Nations (1982). "United Nations Convention on the Law of the Sea," Article 56(2).
[136] United Nations (1982). "United Nations Convention on the Law of the Sea," Article 56(3).
[137] United Nations (1982). "United Nations Convention on the Law of the Sea," Articles 58(1) and 87(1)(a)-(c).
[138] United Nations (1982). "United Nations Convention on the Law of the Sea," Article 58(2).
[139] United Nations (1982). "United Nations Convention on the Law of the Sea," Article 58(3).
[140] United Nations (1982). "United Nations Convention on the Law of the Sea," Article 59.
[141] United Nations (1982). "United Nations Convention on the Law of the Sea," Article 60(1)(a).
[142] United Nations (1982). "United Nations Convention on the Law of the Sea," Article 60(1)(b).

[143] United Nations (1982). "United Nations Convention on the Law of the Sea," Article 60(1)(c).

[144] United Nations (1982). "United Nations Convention on the Law of the Sea," Article 60(2).

[145] United Nations (1982). "United Nations Convention on the Law of the Sea," Article 60(3).

[146] United Nations (1982). "United Nations Convention on the Law of the Sea," Article 60(4).

[147] United Nations (1982). "United Nations Convention on the Law of the Sea," Article 60(5).

[148] United Nations (1982). "United Nations Convention on the Law of the Sea," Article 60(6).

[149] United Nations (1982). "United Nations Convention on the Law of the Sea," Article 60(7).

[150] United Nations (1982). "United Nations Convention on the Law of the Sea," Article 60(8).

[151] United Nations (1982). "United Nations Convention on the Law of the Sea," Article 61(1).

[152] United Nations (1982). "United Nations Convention on the Law of the Sea," Article 61(2).

[153] United Nations (1982). "United Nations Convention on the Law of the Sea," Article 61(3).

[154] United Nations (1982). "United Nations Convention on the Law of the Sea," Article 61(4).

[155] United Nations (1982). "United Nations Convention on the Law of the Sea," Article 61(5).

[156] United Nations (1982). "United Nations Convention on the Law of the Sea," Article 62(1).

[157] United Nations (1982). "United Nations Convention on the Law of the Sea," Article 62(2).

[158] United Nations (1982). "United Nations Convention on the Law of the Sea," Article 62(3).

[159] United Nations (1982). "United Nations Convention on the Law of the Sea," Article 62(4).

[160] United Nations (1982). "United Nations Convention on the Law of the Sea," Article 62(4)(a).
[161] United Nations (1982). "United Nations Convention on the Law of the Sea," Article 62(4)(b).
[162] United Nations (1982). "United Nations Convention on the Law of the Sea," Article 62(4)(c).
[163] United Nations (1982). "United Nations Convention on the Law of the Sea," Article 62(4)(d).
[164] United Nations (1982). "United Nations Convention on the Law of the Sea," Article 62(4)(e).
[165] United Nations (1982). "United Nations Convention on the Law of the Sea," Article 62(4)(f).
[166] United Nations (1982). "United Nations Convention on the Law of the Sea," Article 62(4)(g).
[167] United Nations (1982). "United Nations Convention on the Law of the Sea," Article 62(4)(h).
[168] United Nations (1982). "United Nations Convention on the Law of the Sea," Article 62(4)(i).
[169] United Nations (1982). "United Nations Convention on the Law of the Sea," Article 62(4)(j).
[170] United Nations (1982). "United Nations Convention on the Law of the Sea," Article 62(4)(k).
[171] United Nations (1982). "United Nations Convention on the Law of the Sea," Article 64(1).
[172] United Nations (1982). "United Nations Convention on the Law of the Sea," Article 65.
[173] United Nations (1982). "United Nations Convention on the Law of the Sea," Article 66(1).
[174] United Nations (1982). "United Nations Convention on the Law of the Sea," Article 66(2).
[175] United Nations (1982). "United Nations Convention on the Law of the Sea," Article 66(3)(a).
[176] United Nations (1982). "United Nations Convention on the Law of the Sea," Article 66(3)(b).

[177] United Nations (1982). "United Nations Convention on the Law of the Sea," Article 66(3)(c).

[178] United Nations (1982). "United Nations Convention on the Law of the Sea," Article 66(3)(d).

[179] United Nations (1982). "United Nations Convention on the Law of the Sea," Article 66(4).

[180] United Nations (1982). "United Nations Convention on the Law of the Sea," Article 67(1).

[181] United Nations (1982). "United Nations Convention on the Law of the Sea," Article 67(2).

[182] United Nations (1982). "United Nations Convention on the Law of the Sea," Article 67(3).

[183] United Nations (1982). "United Nations Convention on the Law of the Sea," Article 68.

[184] United Nations (1982). "United Nations Convention on the Law of the Sea," Article 77(4).

[185] United Nations (1982). "United Nations Convention on the Law of the Sea," Article 69(1).

[186] United Nations (1982). "United Nations Convention on the Law of the Sea," Article 69(2)(a).

[187] United Nations (1982). "United Nations Convention on the Law of the Sea," Article 69(2)(b).

[188] United Nations (1982). "United Nations Convention on the Law of the Sea," Article 69(2)(c).

[189] United Nations (1982). "United Nations Convention on the Law of the Sea," Article 69(2)(d).

[190] United Nations (1982). "United Nations Convention on the Law of the Sea," Article 69(3).

[191] United Nations (1982). "United Nations Convention on the Law of the Sea," Article 69(4).

[192] United Nations (1982). "United Nations Convention on the Law of the Sea," Article 70(2).

[193] United Nations (1982). "United Nations Convention on the Law of the Sea," Article 70(1).

[194] United Nations (1982). "United Nations Convention on the Law of the Sea," Article 70(3).
[195] United Nations (1982). "United Nations Convention on the Law of the Sea," Article 70(3)(a).
[196] United Nations (1982). "United Nations Convention on the Law of the Sea," Article 70(3)(b).
[197] United Nations (1982). "United Nations Convention on the Law of the Sea," Article 70(3)(c).
[198] United Nations (1982). "United Nations Convention on the Law of the Sea," Article 70(3)(d).
[199] United Nations (1982). "United Nations Convention on the Law of the Sea," Article 70(4).
[200] United Nations (1982). "United Nations Convention on the Law of the Sea," Article 70(5).
[201] United Nations (1982). "United Nations Convention on the Law of the Sea," Article 71.
[202] United Nations (1982). "United Nations Convention on the Law of the Sea," Article 72(1).
[203] United Nations (1982). "United Nations Convention on the Law of the Sea," Article 73(1).
[204] United Nations (1982). "United Nations Convention on the Law of the Sea," Article 73(3).
[205] United Nations (1982). "United Nations Convention on the Law of the Sea," Article 73(4).
[206] United Nations (1982). "United Nations Convention on the Law of the Sea," Article 74(1).
[207] United Nations (1982). "United Nations Convention on the Law of the Sea," Article 74(2).
[208] United Nations (1982). "United Nations Convention on the Law of the Sea," Article 74(4).
[209] United Nations (1982). "United Nations Convention on the Law of the Sea," Article 75(1).
[210] United Nations (1982). "United Nations Convention on the Law of the Sea," Article 76(1).

[211] United Nations (1982). "United Nations Convention on the Law of the Sea," Article 76(2).
[212] United Nations (1982). "United Nations Convention on the Law of the Sea," Article 76(4)(a).
[213] United Nations (1982). "United Nations Convention on the Law of the Sea," Article 76(7).
[214] United Nations (1982). "United Nations Convention on the Law of the Sea," Article 76(4)(b).
[215] United Nations (1982). "United Nations Convention on the Law of the Sea," Article 76(5).
[216] Commission on the Limits of the Continental Shelf (1999). Scientific and Technical Guidelines of the Commission on the Limits of the Continental Shelf: Adopted by the Commission on 13 May 1999 at its fifth session (New York: Commission on the Limits of the Continental Shelf), para.4.1.2.
[217] United Nations (1982). "United Nations Convention on the Law of the Sea," Article 76(6).
[218] United Nations (1982). "United Nations Convention on the Law of the Sea," Article 76(8).
[219] Commission on the Limits of the Continental Shelf (1999). Scientific and Technical Guidelines of the Commission on the Limits of the Continental Shelf: Adopted by the Commission on 13 May 1999 at its fifth session, paras.9.1.3-9.1.6.
[220] United Nations (1982). "United Nations Convention on the Law of the Sea," Article 77(1).
[221] United Nations (1982). "United Nations Convention on the Law of the Sea," Article 77(2).
[222] United Nations (1982). "United Nations Convention on the Law of the Sea," Article 78(1).
[223] United Nations (1982). "United Nations Convention on the Law of the Sea," Article 78(2).
[224] United Nations (1982). "United Nations Convention on the Law of the Sea," Article 79(1).

[225] United Nations (1982). "United Nations Convention on the Law of the Sea," Article 79(2).

[226] United Nations (1982). "United Nations Convention on the Law of the Sea," Article 79(3).

[227] United Nations (1982). "United Nations Convention on the Law of the Sea," Article 79(4).

[228] United Nations (1982). "United Nations Convention on the Law of the Sea," Article 79(5).

[229] United Nations (1982). "United Nations Convention on the Law of the Sea," Article 80.

[230] United Nations (1982). "United Nations Convention on the Law of the Sea," Article 81.

[231] United Nations (1982). "United Nations Convention on the Law of the Sea," Article 82(1).

[232] United Nations (1982). "United Nations Convention on the Law of the Sea," Article 82(2).

[233] United Nations (1982). "United Nations Convention on the Law of the Sea," Article 82(3).

[234] United Nations (1982). "United Nations Convention on the Law of the Sea," Articles 82(4) and 1(2).

[235] United Nations (1982). "United Nations Convention on the Law of the Sea," Article 83(1).

[236] United Nations (1982). "United Nations Convention on the Law of the Sea," Article 83(2).

[237] United Nations (1982). "United Nations Convention on the Law of the Sea," Article 83(4).

[238] United Nations (1982). "United Nations Convention on the Law of the Sea," Article 84(1).

[239] United Nations (1982). "United Nations Convention on the Law of the Sea," Article 85.

[240] United Nations (1982). "United Nations Convention on the Law of the Sea," Article 121(1).

[241] United Nations (1982). "United Nations Convention on the Law of the Sea," Article 121(2).

[242] United Nations (1982). "United Nations Convention on the Law of the Sea," Article 121(3).

[243] United Nations Office for Ocean Affairs and the Law of the Sea (1988). The Law of the Sea: Régime of Islands Legislative History of Part VIII (Article 121) of the United Nations Convention on the Law of the Sea (New York: United Nations), para.3.

[244] United Nations Office for Ocean Affairs and the Law of the Sea (1988). The Law of the Sea: Régime of Islands Legislative History of Part VIII (Article 121) of the United Nations Convention on the Law of the Sea, para.4.

[245] United Nations Office for Ocean Affairs and the Law of the Sea (1988). The Law of the Sea: Régime of Islands Legislative History of Part VIII (Article 121) of the United Nations Convention on the Law of the Sea, para.5.

[246] United Nations (1982). "United Nations Convention on the Law of the Sea," Article 279.

[247] United Nations (1945). "Charter of the United Nations," *United Nations Treaty Series* Registration Number N/A, Article 2(3).

[248] United Nations (1945). "Charter of the United Nations," Article 33(1).

[249] United Nations (1982). "United Nations Convention on the Law of the Sea," Article 280.

[250] United Nations (1982). "United Nations Convention on the Law of the Sea," Article 281.

[251] United Nations (1982). "United Nations Convention on the Law of the Sea," Article 282.

[252] United Nations (1982). "United Nations Convention on the Law of the Sea," Article 283(1).

[253] United Nations (1982). "United Nations Convention on the Law of the Sea," Article 283(2).

[254] United Nations (1982). "United Nations Convention on the Law of the Sea," Article 284(1).

[255] United Nations (1982). "United Nations Convention on the Law of the Sea," Article 284(2).

[256] United Nations (1982). "United Nations Convention on the Law of the Sea," Article 284(3).
[257] United Nations (1982). "United Nations Convention on the Law of the Sea," Article 285.
[258] United Nations (1982). "United Nations Convention on the Law of the Sea," Article 286.
[259] United Nations (1982). "United Nations Convention on the Law of the Sea," Article 299(1).
[260] United Nations (1982). "United Nations Convention on the Law of the Sea," Article 299(2).
[261] United Nations (1982). "United Nations Convention on the Law of the Sea," Article 297(2)(a).
[262] United Nations (1982). "United Nations Convention on the Law of the Sea," Article 297(1)(a).
[263] United Nations (1982). "United Nations Convention on the Law of the Sea," Article 297(1)(b).
[264] United Nations (1982). "United Nations Convention on the Law of the Sea," Article 297(1)(c).
[265] United Nations (1982). "United Nations Convention on the Law of the Sea," Article 297(3)(a).
[266] United Nations (1982). "United Nations Convention on the Law of the Sea," Article 297(3)(b).
[267] United Nations (1982). "United Nations Convention on the Law of the Sea," Article 297(3)(c).
[268] United Nations (1982). "United Nations Convention on the Law of the Sea," Article 298(1)(a)(i).
[269] United Nations (1982). "United Nations Convention on the Law of the Sea," Article 298(1)(b).
[270] United Nations (1982). "United Nations Convention on the Law of the Sea," Article 298(1)(c).
[271] United Nations (1982). "United Nations Convention on the Law of the Sea," Article 298(2).
[272] United Nations (1982). "United Nations Convention on the Law of the Sea," Article 298(3).

[273] United Nations (1982). "United Nations Convention on the Law of the Sea," Article 298(4).

[274] United Nations (1982). "United Nations Convention on the Law of the Sea," Article 287(1).

[275] United Nations (1982). "United Nations Convention on the Law of the Sea," Article 287(3).

[276] United Nations (1982). "United Nations Convention on the Law of the Sea," Article 287(4).

[277] United Nations (1982). "United Nations Convention on the Law of the Sea," Article 287(5).

[278] United Nations (1982). "United Nations Convention on the Law of the Sea," Article 287(6).

[279] United Nations (1982). "United Nations Convention on the Law of the Sea," Article 287(7).

[280] United Nations (1982). "United Nations Convention on the Law of the Sea," Article 287(8).

[281] United Nations (1982). "United Nations Convention on the Law of the Sea," Article 288(1).

[282] United Nations (1982). "United Nations Convention on the Law of the Sea," Article 288(2).

[283] United Nations (1982). "United Nations Convention on the Law of the Sea," Article 288(3).

[284] United Nations (1982). "United Nations Convention on the Law of the Sea," Article 296(1).

[285] United Nations (1982). "United Nations Convention on the Law of the Sea," Article 296(2).

[286] United Nations (1982). "United Nations Convention on the Law of the Sea," Article 295.

[287] United Nations (1982). "United Nations Convention on the Law of the Sea," Article 294(1).

[288] United Nations (1982). "United Nations Convention on the Law of the Sea," Article 294(2).

[289] United Nations (1982). "United Nations Convention on the Law of the Sea," Article 289.

[290] United Nations (1982). "United Nations Convention on the Law of the Sea," Article 293(1).

[291] United Nations (1982). "United Nations Convention on the Law of the Sea," Article 291(1).

[292] United Nations (1982). "United Nations Convention on the Law of the Sea," Article 291(2).

[293] United Nations (1982). "United Nations Convention on the Law of the Sea," Article 290(1).

[294] United Nations (1982). "United Nations Convention on the Law of the Sea," Article 290(2).

[295] United Nations (1982). "United Nations Convention on the Law of the Sea," Article 290(3).

[296] United Nations (1982). "United Nations Convention on the Law of the Sea," Article 290(4).

[297] United Nations (1982). "United Nations Convention on the Law of the Sea," Article 290(6).

[298] United Nations (1982). "United Nations Convention on the Law of the Sea," Article 292(1).

[299] United Nations (1982). "United Nations Convention on the Law of the Sea," Article 292(2).

[300] United Nations (1982). "United Nations Convention on the Law of the Sea," Article 292(3).

[301] United Nations (1982). "United Nations Convention on the Law of the Sea," Article 292(4).

[302] United Nations (1958). "Convention on Fishing and Conservation of the Living Resources of the High Seas," *United Nations Treaty Series* Registration Number 8164, Article 9(1).

[303] United Nations (1982). "United Nations Convention on the Law of the Sea," Article 287(1)(a).

[304] United Nations (1982). "United Nations Convention on the Law of the Sea," Annex IX, Article 7(3).

[305] United Nations (1945). "Statute of the International Court of Justice," *United Nations Treaty Series* Registration Number N/A, Article 59.

[306] United Nations (1945). “Charter of the United Nations,” Article 7(1).

[307] United Nations (1945). “Charter of the United Nations,” Article 33(2).

[308] United Nations (1945). “Charter of the United Nations,” Article 36(1).

[309] United Nations (1945). “Charter of the United Nations,” Article 36(3).

[310] United Nations (1945). “Charter of the United Nations,” Article 92.

[311] United Nations (1945). “Charter of the United Nations,” Article 93(1).

[312] United Nations (1945). “Charter of the United Nations,” Article 94(1).

[313] United Nations (1945). “Statute of the International Court of Justice,” Articles 2 and 3.

[314] United Nations (1945). “Statute of the International Court of Justice,” Article 4(1).

[315] United Nations (1945). “Statute of the International Court of Justice,” Article 9.

[316] United Nations (1945). “Statute of the International Court of Justice,” Article 13(1).

[317] United Nations (1945). “Statute of the International Court of Justice,” Article 16(1).

[318] United Nations (1945). “Statute of the International Court of Justice,” Article 17(1).

[319] United Nations (1945). “Statute of the International Court of Justice,” Article 23(1).

[320] United Nations (1945). “Statute of the International Court of Justice,” Article 34(1).

[321] United Nations (1945). “Statute of the International Court of Justice,” Article 36(1).

[322] United Nations (1945). “Statute of the International Court of Justice,” Article 36(2)(a).

[323] United Nations (1945). "Statute of the International Court of Justice," Article 36(2)(b).
[324] United Nations (1945). "Statute of the International Court of Justice," Article 36(2)(c).
[325] United Nations (1945). "Statute of the International Court of Justice," Article 36(2)(d).
[326] United Nations (1945). "Statute of the International Court of Justice," Article 36(3).
[327] United Nations (1945). "Statute of the International Court of Justice," Article 36(4).
[328] United Nations (1945). "Statute of the International Court of Justice," Article 38(1).
[329] United Nations (1945). "Statute of the International Court of Justice," Article 39(1).
[330] United Nations (1945). "Statute of the International Court of Justice," Article 39(2).
[331] United Nations (1945). "Statute of the International Court of Justice," Article 40(1).
[332] United Nations (1945). "Statute of the International Court of Justice," Article 40(2).
[333] United Nations (1945). "Statute of the International Court of Justice," Article 40(3).
[334] United Nations (1945). "Statute of the International Court of Justice," Article 42(1).
[335] United Nations (1945). "Statute of the International Court of Justice," Article 42(2).
[336] United Nations (1945). "Statute of the International Court of Justice," Article 43(1).
[337] United Nations (1945). "Statute of the International Court of Justice," Article 43(2).
[338] United Nations (1945). "Statute of the International Court of Justice," Article 43(3).
[339] United Nations (1945). "Statute of the International Court of Justice," Article 43(4).

[340] United Nations (1945). "Statute of the International Court of Justice," Article 43(5).

[341] International Court of Justice (2019). Rules of Court (1978) adopted on 14 April 1978 and entered into force on 1 July 1978 – amended to 21 October 2019 (The Hague: International Court of Justice), Article 54(1).

[342] International Court of Justice (2019). Rules of Court (1978) adopted on 14 April 1978 and entered into force on 1 July 1978 – amended to 21 October 2019, Article 56(1)-(2).

[343] International Court of Justice (2019). Rules of Court (1978) adopted on 14 April 1978 and entered into force on 1 July 1978 – amended to 21 October 2019, Article 57.

[344] International Court of Justice (2019). Rules of Court (1978) adopted on 14 April 1978 and entered into force on 1 July 1978 – amended to 21 October 2019, Article 58(1).

[345] International Court of Justice (2019). Rules of Court (1978) adopted on 14 April 1978 and entered into force on 1 July 1978 – amended to 21 October 2019, Article 58(2).

[346] United Nations (1945). "Statute of the International Court of Justice," Article 45.

[347] United Nations (1945). "Statute of the International Court of Justice," Article 46.

[348] International Court of Justice (2019). Rules of Court (1978) adopted on 14 April 1978 and entered into force on 1 July 1978 – amended to 21 October 2019, Article 59.

[349] United Nations (1945). "Statute of the International Court of Justice," Article 47(2).

[350] United Nations (1945). "Statute of the International Court of Justice," Article 48.

[351] United Nations (1945). "Statute of the International Court of Justice," Article 49.

[352] International Court of Justice (2019). Rules of Court (1978) adopted on 14 April 1978 and entered into force on 1 July 1978 – amended to 21 October 2019, Article 60(1).

[353] International Court of Justice (2019). Rules of Court (1978) adopted on 14 April 1978 and entered into force on 1 July 1978 – amended to 21 October 2019, Article 60(2).
[354] International Court of Justice (2019). Rules of Court (1978) adopted on 14 April 1978 and entered into force on 1 July 1978 – amended to 21 October 2019, Article 61(1).
[355] International Court of Justice (2019). Rules of Court (1978) adopted on 14 April 1978 and entered into force on 1 July 1978 – amended to 21 October 2019, Article 61(2).
[356] International Court of Justice (2019). Rules of Court (1978) adopted on 14 April 1978 and entered into force on 1 July 1978 – amended to 21 October 2019, Article 61(4).
[357] International Court of Justice (2019). Rules of Court (1978) adopted on 14 April 1978 and entered into force on 1 July 1978 – amended to 21 October 2019, Article 62(1).
[358] United Nations (1945). "Statute of the International Court of Justice," Article 50.
[359] International Court of Justice (2019). Rules of Court (1978) adopted on 14 April 1978 and entered into force on 1 July 1978 – amended to 21 October 2019, Articles 63(1) and 57.
[360] International Court of Justice (2019). Rules of Court (1978) adopted on 14 April 1978 and entered into force on 1 July 1978 – amended to 21 October 2019, Article 63(1).
[361] International Court of Justice (2019). Rules of Court (1978) adopted on 14 April 1978 and entered into force on 1 July 1978 – amended to 21 October 2019, Article 65.
[362] United Nations (1945). "Statute of the International Court of Justice," Article 52.
[363] United Nations (1945). "Statute of the International Court of Justice," Article 53(1).
[364] United Nations (1945). "Statute of the International Court of Justice," Article 53(2).
[365] United Nations (1945). "Statute of the International Court of Justice," Article 54(1).

[366] International Court of Justice (2019). Rules of Court (1978) adopted on 14 April 1978 and entered into force on 1 July 1978 – amended to 21 October 2019, Articles 72, 61(2), 61(4) and 62.

[367] International Court of Justice (2019). Rules of Court (1978) adopted on 14 April 1978 and entered into force on 1 July 1978 – amended to 21 October 2019, Article 72.

[368] United Nations (1945). "Statute of the International Court of Justice," Article 54(2).

[369] United Nations (1945). "Statute of the International Court of Justice," Article 54(3).

[370] United Nations (1945). "Statute of the International Court of Justice," Article 55(1).

[371] United Nations (1945). "Statute of the International Court of Justice," Article 56(1).

[372] United Nations (1945). "Statute of the International Court of Justice," Article 57.

[373] United Nations (1945). "Statute of the International Court of Justice," Article 58.

[374] International Court of Justice (2019). Rules of Court (1978) adopted on 14 April 1978 and entered into force on 1 July 1978 – amended to 21 October 2019, Article 94(2).

[375] United Nations (1945). "Statute of the International Court of Justice," Article 60.

[376] United Nations (1945). "Statute of the International Court of Justice," Article 56(2).

[377] International Court of Justice (2019). Rules of Court (1978) adopted on 14 April 1978 and entered into force on 1 July 1978 – amended to 21 October 2019, Article 95(1).

[378] International Court of Justice (2019). Rules of Court (1978) adopted on 14 April 1978 and entered into force on 1 July 1978 – amended to 21 October 2019, Article 96.

[379] United Nations (1945). "Statute of the International Court of Justice," Article 61(1).

[380] International Court of Justice (2019). Rules of Court (1978) adopted on 14 April 1978 and entered into force on 1 July 1978 – amended to 21 October 2019, Article 99(1).

[381] International Court of Justice (2019). Rules of Court (1978) adopted on 14 April 1978 and entered into force on 1 July 1978 – amended to 21 October 2019, Article 99(2).

[382] International Court of Justice (2019). Rules of Court (1978) adopted on 14 April 1978 and entered into force on 1 July 1978 – amended to 21 October 2019, Article 99(4).

[383] International Court of Justice (2019). Rules of Court (1978) adopted on 14 April 1978 and entered into force on 1 July 1978 – amended to 21 October 2019, Article 99(5).

[384] United Nations (1945). "Statute of the International Court of Justice," Article 61(2).

[385] United Nations (1945). "Statute of the International Court of Justice," Article 61(4).

[386] United Nations (1945). "Statute of the International Court of Justice," Article 61(5).

[387] International Court of Justice (2019). Rules of Court (1978) adopted on 14 April 1978 and entered into force on 1 July 1978 – amended to 21 October 2019, Article 100(2).

[388] United Nations (1945). "Statute of the International Court of Justice," Article 62(1).

[389] United Nations (1945). "Statute of the International Court of Justice," Article 62(2).

[390] International Court of Justice (2019). Rules of Court (1978) adopted on 14 April 1978 and entered into force on 1 July 1978 – amended to 21 October 2019, Article 81(2).

[391] International Court of Justice (2019). Rules of Court (1978) adopted on 14 April 1978 and entered into force on 1 July 1978 – amended to 21 October 2019, Article 81(2)(a).

[392] International Court of Justice (2019). Rules of Court (1978) adopted on 14 April 1978 and entered into force on 1 July 1978 – amended to 21 October 2019, Article 81(2)(b).

[393] International Court of Justice (2019). Rules of Court (1978) adopted on 14 April 1978 and entered into force on 1 July 1978 – amended to 21 October 2019, Article 81(2)(c).

[394] International Court of Justice (2019). Rules of Court (1978) adopted on 14 April 1978 and entered into force on 1 July 1978 – amended to 21 October 2019, Article 81(3).

[395] United Nations (1945). "Statute of the International Court of Justice," Article 63(1).

[396] United Nations (1945). "Statute of the International Court of Justice," Article 63(2).

[397] International Court of Justice (2019). Rules of Court (1978) adopted on 14 April 1978 and entered into force on 1 July 1978 – amended to 21 October 2019, Article 82(2).

[398] International Court of Justice (2019). Rules of Court (1978) adopted on 14 April 1978 and entered into force on 1 July 1978 – amended to 21 October 2019, Article 82(2)(a).

[399] International Court of Justice (2019). Rules of Court (1978) adopted on 14 April 1978 and entered into force on 1 July 1978 – amended to 21 October 2019, Article 82(2)(b).

[400] International Court of Justice (2019). Rules of Court (1978) adopted on 14 April 1978 and entered into force on 1 July 1978 – amended to 21 October 2019, Article 82(2)(c).

[401] International Court of Justice (2019). Rules of Court (1978) adopted on 14 April 1978 and entered into force on 1 July 1978 – amended to 21 October 2019, Article 82(2)(d).

[402] International Court of Justice (1992). *Land, Island and Maritime Frontier Dispute (El Salvador/Honduras: Nicaragua intervening)*, Judgment of 11 September 1992, *I.C.J. Reports 1992*, 351-618, 356.

[403] International Court of Justice (1990). *Land, Island and Maritime Frontier Dispute (El Salvador/Honduras), Application to Intervene*, Judgment of 13 September 1990, *I.C.J. Reports 1990*, 92-137, 94.

[404] International Court of Justice (1990). *Land, Island and Maritime Frontier Dispute (El Salvador/Honduras), Application to Intervene*, Judgment of 13 September 1990, *I.C.J. Reports 1990*, 92-137, 98.

[405] International Court of Justice (1992). *Land, Island and Maritime Frontier Dispute (El Salvador/Honduras: Nicaragua intervening)*, Judgment of 11 September 1992, *I.C.J. Reports 1992*, 351-618, 353.

[406] International Court of Justice (1990). *Land, Island and Maritime Frontier Dispute (El Salvador/Honduras), Application to Intervene*, Judgment of 13 September 1990, *I.C.J. Reports 1990*, 92-137, 98 and 93.

[407] International Court of Justice (1990). *Land, Island and Maritime Frontier Dispute (El Salvador/Honduras), Application to Intervene*, Judgment of 13 September 1990, *I.C.J. Reports 1990*, 92-137, 107.

[408] International Court of Justice (1990). *Land, Island and Maritime Frontier Dispute (El Salvador/Honduras), Application to Intervene*, Judgment of 13 September 1990, *I.C.J. Reports 1990*, 92-137, 112.

[409] International Court of Justice (1990). *Land, Island and Maritime Frontier Dispute (El Salvador/Honduras), Application to Intervene*, Judgment of 13 September 1990, *I.C.J. Reports 1990*, 92-137, 109-110.

[410] International Court of Justice (1990). *Land, Island and Maritime Frontier Dispute (El Salvador/Honduras), Application to Intervene*, Judgment of 13 September 1990, *I.C.J. Reports 1990*, 92-137, 113.

[411] International Court of Justice (1990). *Land, Island and Maritime Frontier Dispute (El Salvador/Honduras), Application to Intervene*, Judgment of 13 September 1990, *I.C.J. Reports 1990*, 92-137, 116.

[412] International Court of Justice (1990). *Land, Island and Maritime Frontier Dispute (El Salvador/Honduras), Application to Intervene*, Judgment of 13 September 1990, *I.C.J. Reports 1990*, 92-137, 117.

[413] International Court of Justice (1990). *Land, Island and Maritime Frontier Dispute (El Salvador/Honduras), Application to Intervene*, Judgment of 13 September 1990, *I.C.J. Reports 1990*, 92-137, 116-117.

[414] International Court of Justice (1990). *Land, Island and Maritime Frontier Dispute (El Salvador/Honduras), Application to Intervene*, Judgment of 13 September 1990, *I.C.J. Reports 1990*, 92-137, 117-118.

[415] International Court of Justice (1990). *Land, Island and Maritime Frontier Dispute (El Salvador/Honduras), Application to Intervene*, Judgment of 13 September 1990, *I.C.J. Reports 1990*, 92-137, 119.

[416] International Court of Justice (1990). *Land, Island and Maritime Frontier Dispute (El Salvador/Honduras), Application to Intervene*, Judgment of 13 September 1990, *I.C.J. Reports 1990*, 92-137, 121.

[417] International Court of Justice (1990). *Land, Island and Maritime Frontier Dispute (El Salvador/Honduras), Application to Intervene*, Judgment of 13 September 1990, *I.C.J. Reports 1990*, 92-137, 124-125.

[418] International Court of Justice (1990). *Land, Island and Maritime Frontier Dispute (El Salvador/Honduras), Application to Intervene*, Judgment of 13 September 1990, *I.C.J. Reports 1990*, 92-137, 126.

[419] International Court of Justice (1990). *Land, Island and Maritime Frontier Dispute (El Salvador/Honduras), Application to Intervene*, Judgment of 13 September 1990, *I.C.J. Reports 1990*, 92-137, 128.

[420] International Court of Justice (1990). *Land, Island and Maritime Frontier Dispute (El Salvador/Honduras), Application to Intervene*, Judgment of 13 September 1990, *I.C.J. Reports 1990*, 92-137, 128 and 137.

[421] International Court of Justice (1990). *Land, Island and Maritime Frontier Dispute (El Salvador/Honduras), Application to Intervene*, Judgment of 13 September 1990, *I.C.J. Reports 1990*, 92-137, 108-109 and 128.

[422] International Court of Justice (1990). *Land, Island and Maritime Frontier Dispute (El Salvador/Honduras), Application to Intervene*, Judgment of 13 September 1990, *I.C.J. Reports 1990*, 92-137, 130.

[423] International Court of Justice (1990). *Land, Island and Maritime Frontier Dispute (El Salvador/Honduras), Application to Intervene*, Judgment of 13 September 1990, *I.C.J. Reports 1990*, 92-137, 131.

[424] International Court of Justice (1990). *Land, Island and Maritime Frontier Dispute (El Salvador/Honduras), Application to Intervene*, Judgment of 13 September 1990, *I.C.J. Reports 1990*, 92-137, 109 and 132.

[425] International Court of Justice (1990). *Land, Island and Maritime Frontier Dispute (El Salvador/Honduras), Application to Intervene*, Judgment of 13 September 1990, *I.C.J. Reports 1990*, 92-137, 132.

[426] International Court of Justice (1990). *Land, Island and Maritime Frontier Dispute (El Salvador/Honduras), Application to Intervene*, Judgment of 13 September 1990, *I.C.J. Reports 1990*, 92-137, 133.

[427] International Court of Justice (1990). *Land, Island and Maritime Frontier Dispute (El Salvador/Honduras), Application to Intervene*, Judgment of 13 September 1990, *I.C.J. Reports 1990*, 92-137, 134-135.

[428] International Court of Justice (1990). *Land, Island and Maritime Frontier Dispute (El Salvador/Honduras), Application to Intervene*, Judgment of 13 September 1990, *I.C.J. Reports 1990*, 92-137, 100 and 135-136.

[429] International Court of Justice (1990). *Land, Island and Maritime Frontier Dispute (El Salvador/Honduras), Application to Intervene*, Judgment of 13 September 1990, *I.C.J. Reports 1990*, 136.

[430] International Court of Justice (1990). *Land, Island and Maritime Frontier Dispute (El Salvador/Honduras), Application to Intervene*, Judgment of 13 September 1990, *I.C.J. Reports 1990*, 137.

[431] International Court of Justice (1992). *Land, Island and Maritime Frontier Dispute (El Salvador/Honduras: Nicaragua intervening)*, Judgment of 11 September 1992, *I.C.J. Reports 1992*, 351-618, 609.

[432] International Court of Justice (1992). *Land, Island and Maritime Frontier Dispute (El Salvador/Honduras: Nicaragua intervening)*, Judgment of 11 September 1992, *I.C.J. Reports 1992*, 351-618, 609-610.

[433] International Court of Justice (1992). *Land, Island and Maritime Frontier Dispute (El Salvador/Honduras: Nicaragua intervening)*, Judgment of 11 September 1992, *I.C.J. Reports 1992*, 351-618, 610.

[434] International Court of Justice (1992). *Land, Island and Maritime Frontier Dispute (El Salvador/Honduras), Application to Intervene*, Declaration of Judge Oda, *I.C.J. Reports 1992*, 619-620, 619.

[435] International Court of Justice (1992). *Land, Island and Maritime Frontier Dispute (El Salvador/Honduras), Application to Intervene*, Declaration of Judge Oda, *I.C.J. Reports 1992*, 619-620, 619-620.

[436] International Court of Justice (1992). *Land, Island and Maritime Frontier Dispute (El Salvador/Honduras), Application to Intervene*, Declaration of Judge Oda, *I.C.J. Reports 1992*, 619-620, 620.

[437] International Court of Justice (1992). *Land, Island and Maritime Frontier Dispute (El Salvador/Honduras: Nicaragua intervening)*, Separate Opinion of Judge Torres Bernárdes, *I.C.J. Reports 1992*, 629-731, 730-731.

[438] International Court of Justice (2003). Application for Revision of the Judgment of 11 September 1992 in the Case concerning the Land, Island and Maritime Frontier Dispute (El Salvador/Honduras: Nicaragua intervening) (El Salvador v. Honduras: Summary of the Judgment delivered by the Chamber on Thursday 18 December 2003, Summary 2003/5, 18 December 2003 (The Hague: International Court of Justice), 1.

[439] International Court of Justice (2003). *Application for Revision of the Judgment of 11 September 1992 in the Case concerning the* Land, Island and Maritime Frontier Dispute (El Salvador/Honduras: Nicaragua intervening) *(El Salvador v. Honduras)*, Judgment of 18 December 2003, *I.C.J. Reports 2003*, 392-412, 397-398.

[440] International Court of Justice (2003). *Application for Revision of the Judgment of 11 September 1992 in the Case concerning the* Land, Island and Maritime Frontier Dispute (El Salvador/Honduras: Nicaragua intervening) *(El Salvador v. Honduras)*, Judgment of 18 December 2003, *I.C.J. Reports 2003*, 392-412, 401-402.

[441] International Court of Justice (2003). *Application for Revision of the Judgment of 11 September 1992 in the Case concerning the* Land, Island and Maritime Frontier Dispute (El Salvador/Honduras: Nicaragua intervening) *(El Salvador v. Honduras)*, Judgment of 18 December 2003, *I.C.J. Reports 2003*, 392-412, 402.

[442] International Court of Justice (2003). *Application for Revision of the Judgment of 11 September 1992 in the Case concerning the* Land,

Island and Maritime Frontier Dispute (El Salvador/Honduras: Nicaragua intervening) *(El Salvador v. Honduras)*, Judgment of 18 December 2003, *I.C.J. Reports 2003*, 392-412, 406-407.

[443] International Court of Justice (2003). *Application for Revision of the Judgment of 11 September 1992 in the Case concerning the* Land, Island and Maritime Frontier Dispute (El Salvador/Honduras: Nicaragua intervening) *(El Salvador v. Honduras)*, Judgment of 18 December 2003, *I.C.J. Reports 2003*, 392-412, 400.

[444] International Court of Justice (2003). *Application for Revision of the Judgment of 11 July 1996 in the Case concerning* Application of the Convention on the Prevention and Punishment of the Crime of Genocide (Bosnia and Herzegovina v. Yugoslavia), Preliminary Objections *(Yugoslavia v. Bosnia and Herzegovina)*, Judgment of 3 February 2003, *I.C.J. Reports 2003*, 7-30, 12.

[445] International Court of Justice (2003). *Application for Revision of the Judgment of 11 September 1992 in the Case concerning the* Land, Island and Maritime Frontier Dispute (El Salvador/Honduras: Nicaragua intervening) *(El Salvador v. Honduras)*, Judgment of 18 December 2003, *I.C.J. Reports 2003*, 392-412, 411.

[446] United Nations (1982). "United Nations Convention on the Law of the Sea," Annex VI, Article 33(1).

[447] United Nations (1982). "United Nations Convention on the Law of the Sea," Annex VI, Article 33(2).

[448] United Nations (1982). "United Nations Convention on the Law of the Sea," Annex VI, Article 1(1).

[449] International Tribunal for the Law of the Sea (2019). "General Information." Accessed November 10, 2019. https://www.itlos.org/general-information/.

[450] United Nations (1982). "United Nations Convention on the Law of the Sea," Annex VI, Articles 21 and 20(1).

[451] United Nations (1982). "United Nations Convention on the Law of the Sea," Annex VI, Article 21.

[452] United Nations (1982). "United Nations Convention on the Law of the Sea," Annex VI, Article 22.

[453] United Nations (1982). "United Nations Convention on the Law of the Sea," Article 187.
[454] United Nations (1982). "United Nations Convention on the Law of the Sea," Annex VI, Article 2(1).
[455] United Nations (1982). "United Nations Convention on the Law of the Sea," Annex VI, Article 2(2).
[456] United Nations (1982). "United Nations Convention on the Law of the Sea," Annex VI, Article 3(2).
[457] United Nations (1982). "United Nations Convention on the Law of the Sea," Annex VI, Article 3(1).
[458] United Nations (1982). "United Nations Convention on the Law of the Sea," Annex VI, Article 4(1).
[459] United Nations (1982). "United Nations Convention on the Law of the Sea," Annex VI, Article 4(2).
[460] United Nations (1982). "United Nations Convention on the Law of the Sea," Annex VI, Article 4(4).
[461] United Nations (1982). "United Nations Convention on the Law of the Sea," Annex VI, Article 5(1).
[462] United Nations (1982). "United Nations Convention on the Law of the Sea," Annex VI, Article 7(1).
[463] United Nations (1982). "United Nations Convention on the Law of the Sea," Annex VI, Article 7(2).
[464] United Nations (1982). "United Nations Convention on the Law of the Sea," Annex VI, Article 8(1).
[465] United Nations (1982). "United Nations Convention on the Law of the Sea," Annex VI, Article 13(1).
[466] United Nations (1982). "United Nations Convention on the Law of the Sea," Annex VI, Articles 13(3), 14 and 15(2).
[467] United Nations (1982). "United Nations Convention on the Law of the Sea," Annex VI, Article 15(1).
[468]] International Tribunal for the Law of the Sea (2009). Rules of the Tribunal adopted on 28 October 1997 – amended to 25 September 2018 (ITLOS/8, 17 March 2009) (Hamburg: International Tribunal for the Law of the Sea), Article 29(1).

[469] International Tribunal for the Law of the Sea (2009). Rules of the Tribunal adopted on 28 October 1997 – amended to 25 September 2018 (ITLOS/8, 17 March 2009), Article 29(2).

[470] International Tribunal for the Law of the Sea (2009). Rules of the Tribunal adopted on 28 October 1997 – amended to 25 September 2018 (ITLOS/8, 17 March 2009), Article 29(3).

[471] International Tribunal for the Law of the Sea (2019). "Chambers." Accessed November 13, 2019. https://www.itlos.org/en/the-tribunal/chambers/.

[472] United Nations (1982). "United Nations Convention on the Law of the Sea," Annex VI, Article 15(2).

[473]] International Tribunal for the Law of the Sea (2009). Rules of the Tribunal adopted on 28 October 1997 – amended to 25 September 2018 (ITLOS/8, 17 March 2009), Article 30(1).

[474] International Tribunal for the Law of the Sea (2009). Rules of the Tribunal adopted on 28 October 1997 – amended to 25 September 2018 (ITLOS/8, 17 March 2009), Article 30(2).

[475] International Tribunal for the Law of the Sea (2009). Rules of the Tribunal adopted on 28 October 1997 – amended to 25 September 2018 (ITLOS/8, 17 March 2009), Article 30(3).

[476] International Tribunal for the Law of the Sea (2009). Rules of the Tribunal adopted on 28 October 1997 – amended to 25 September 2018 (ITLOS/8, 17 March 2009), Article 30(4).

[477] International Tribunal for the Law of the Sea (2019). "President Jin-Hyun Paik." Accessed November 13, 2019. https://www.itlos.org/the-tribunal/members/president-jin-hyun-paik/.

[478] International Tribunal for the Law of the Sea (2017). Press Release: Dispute concerning delimitation of the maritime boundary between Ghana and Côte D'Ivoire – Special Chamber delivers its judgment on 23 September 2017 (ITLOS/Press 264, 23 September 2017) (Hamburg: International Tribunal for the Law of the Sea), 1.

[479] International Tribunal for the Law of the Sea (2017). *Delimitation of the maritime boundary between Ghana and Côte D'Ivoire in the*

Atlantic Ocean (Ghana/Côte D'Ivoire), Judgment of 23 September 2017, *ITLOS Reports 2017*, 4, para.7.

[480] United Nations (1982). "United Nations Convention on the Law of the Sea," Annex VI, Article 15(3).

[481] International Tribunal for the Law of the Sea (2009). Rules of the Tribunal adopted on 28 October 1997 – amended to 25 September 2018 (ITLOS/8, 17 March 2009), Article 28(2).

[482] International Tribunal for the Law of the Sea (2009). Rules of the Tribunal adopted on 28 October 1997 – amended to 25 September 2018 (ITLOS/8, 17 March 2009), Article 28(3).

[483] International Tribunal for the Law of the Sea (2009). Rules of the Tribunal adopted on 28 October 1997 – amended to 25 September 2018 (ITLOS/8, 17 March 2009), Article 28(4).

[484] International Tribunal for the Law of the Sea (2009). Rules of the Tribunal adopted on 28 October 1997 – amended to 25 September 2018 (ITLOS/8, 17 March 2009), Article 28(5).

[485] International Tribunal for the Law of the Sea (2009). Rules of the Tribunal adopted on 28 October 1997 – amended to 25 September 2018 (ITLOS/8, 17 March 2009), Article 28(6).

[486] United Nations (1982). "United Nations Convention on the Law of the Sea," Annex VI, Article 17(2).

[487] United Nations (1982). "United Nations Convention on the Law of the Sea," Annex VI, Article 17(3).

[488] International Tribunal for the Law of the Sea (2009). Rules of the Tribunal adopted on 28 October 1997 – amended to 25 September 2018 (ITLOS/8, 17 March 2009), Article 43.

[489] United Nations (1982). "United Nations Convention on the Law of the Sea," Annex VI, Article 24(1).

[490] United Nations (1982). "United Nations Convention on the Law of the Sea," Annex VI, Article 24(2).

[491] United Nations (1982). "United Nations Convention on the Law of the Sea," Annex VI, Article 24(3).

[492] United Nations (1982). "United Nations Convention on the Law of the Sea," Annex VI, Article 25(1).

[493] United Nations (1982). "United Nations Convention on the Law of the Sea," Annex VI, Article 26(1).

[494] United Nations (1982). "United Nations Convention on the Law of the Sea," Annex VI, Article 26(2).

[495] International Tribunal for the Law of the Sea (2009). Rules of the Tribunal adopted on 28 October 1997 – amended to 25 September 2018 (ITLOS/8, 17 March 2009), Article 74.

[496] International Tribunal for the Law of the Sea (2009). Rules of the Tribunal adopted on 28 October 1997 – amended to 25 September 2018 (ITLOS/8, 17 March 2009), Article 58.

[497] United Nations (1982). "United Nations Convention on the Law of the Sea," Annex VI, Article 27.

[498] International Tribunal for the Law of the Sea (2009). Rules of the Tribunal adopted on 28 October 1997 – amended to 25 September 2018 (ITLOS/8, 17 March 2009), Article 59(1).

[499] International Tribunal for the Law of the Sea (2009). Rules of the Tribunal adopted on 28 October 1997 – amended to 25 September 2018 (ITLOS/8, 17 March 2009), Article 62(4).

[500] International Tribunal for the Law of the Sea (2009). Rules of the Tribunal adopted on 28 October 1997 – amended to 25 September 2018 (ITLOS/8, 17 March 2009), Article 66.

[501] International Tribunal for the Law of the Sea (2009). Rules of the Tribunal adopted on 28 October 1997 – amended to 25 September 2018 (ITLOS/8, 17 March 2009), Article 67(2).

[502] International Tribunal for the Law of the Sea (2009). Rules of the Tribunal adopted on 28 October 1997 – amended to 25 September 2018 (ITLOS/8, 17 March 2009), Article 68.

[503] International Tribunal for the Law of the Sea (2009). Rules of the Tribunal adopted on 28 October 1997 – amended to 25 September 2018 (ITLOS/8, 17 March 2009), Articles 69(1) and 69(3).

[504] International Tribunal for the Law of the Sea (2009). Rules of the Tribunal adopted on 28 October 1997 – amended to 25 September 2018 (ITLOS/8, 17 March 2009), Article 71(1)-(2).

[505] International Tribunal for the Law of the Sea (2009). Rules of the Tribunal adopted on 28 October 1997 – amended to 25 September 2018 (ITLOS/8, 17 March 2009), Article 72.

[506] International Tribunal for the Law of the Sea (2009). Rules of the Tribunal adopted on 28 October 1997 – amended to 25 September 2018 (ITLOS/8, 17 March 2009), Article 73(1).

[507] International Tribunal for the Law of the Sea (2009). Rules of the Tribunal adopted on 28 October 1997 – amended to 25 September 2018 (ITLOS/8, 17 March 2009), Article 73(2).

[508] International Tribunal for the Law of the Sea (2009). Rules of the Tribunal adopted on 28 October 1997 – amended to 25 September 2018 (ITLOS/8, 17 March 2009), Article 75(1).

[509] International Tribunal for the Law of the Sea (2009). Rules of the Tribunal adopted on 28 October 1997 – amended to 25 September 2018 (ITLOS/8, 17 March 2009), Article 75(2).

[510] International Tribunal for the Law of the Sea (2009). Rules of the Tribunal adopted on 28 October 1997 – amended to 25 September 2018 (ITLOS/8, 17 March 2009), Article 76(1).

[511] International Tribunal for the Law of the Sea (2009). Rules of the Tribunal adopted on 28 October 1997 – amended to 25 September 2018 (ITLOS/8, 17 March 2009), Article 76(2).

[512] International Tribunal for the Law of the Sea (2009). Rules of the Tribunal adopted on 28 October 1997 – amended to 25 September 2018 (ITLOS/8, 17 March 2009), Article 76(4).

[513] International Tribunal for the Law of the Sea (2009). Rules of the Tribunal adopted on 28 October 1997 – amended to 25 September 2018 (ITLOS/8, 17 March 2009), Article 77(1).

[514] International Tribunal for the Law of the Sea (2009). Rules of the Tribunal adopted on 28 October 1997 – amended to 25 September 2018 (ITLOS/8, 17 March 2009), Articles 78(1) and 72.

[515] International Tribunal for the Law of the Sea (2009). Rules of the Tribunal adopted on 28 October 1997 – amended to 25 September 2018 (ITLOS/8, 17 March 2009), Article 78(1).

[516] International Tribunal for the Law of the Sea (2009). Rules of the Tribunal adopted on 28 October 1997 – amended to 25 September 2018 (ITLOS/8, 17 March 2009), Article 80.

[517] International Tribunal for the Law of the Sea (2009). Rules of the Tribunal adopted on 28 October 1997 – amended to 25 September 2018 (ITLOS/8, 17 March 2009), Article 84(1).

[518] International Tribunal for the Law of the Sea (2009). Rules of the Tribunal adopted on 28 October 1997 – amended to 25 September 2018 (ITLOS/8, 17 March 2009), Article 85(1).

[519] International Tribunal for the Law of the Sea (2009). Rules of the Tribunal adopted on 28 October 1997 – amended to 25 September 2018 (ITLOS/8, 17 March 2009), Article 86(1).

[520] United Nations (1982). "United Nations Convention on the Law of the Sea," Annex VI, Article 28.

[521] United Nations (1982). "United Nations Convention on the Law of the Sea," Annex VI, Article 29(1).

[522] International Tribunal for the Law of the Sea (2009). Rules of the Tribunal adopted on 28 October 1997 – amended to 25 September 2018 (ITLOS/8, 17 March 2009), Article 88(1).

[523] International Tribunal for the Law of the Sea (2009). Rules of the Tribunal adopted on 28 October 1997 – amended to 25 September 2018 (ITLOS/8, 17 March 2009), Article 88(2).

[524] United Nations (1982). "United Nations Convention on the Law of the Sea," Annex VI, Article 30.

[525] International Tribunal for the Law of the Sea (2009). Rules of the Tribunal adopted on 28 October 1997 – amended to 25 September 2018 (ITLOS/8, 17 March 2009), Article 125(1)(b).

[526] International Tribunal for the Law of the Sea (2009). Rules of the Tribunal adopted on 28 October 1997 – amended to 25 September 2018 (ITLOS/8, 17 March 2009), Article 125(1)(a).

[527] International Tribunal for the Law of the Sea (2009). Rules of the Tribunal adopted on 28 October 1997 – amended to 25 September 2018 (ITLOS/8, 17 March 2009), Article 125(1)(c).

[528] International Tribunal for the Law of the Sea (2009). Rules of the Tribunal adopted on 28 October 1997 – amended to 25 September 2018 (ITLOS/8, 17 March 2009), Article 125(1)(d).

[529] International Tribunal for the Law of the Sea (2009). Rules of the Tribunal adopted on 28 October 1997 – amended to 25 September 2018 (ITLOS/8, 17 March 2009), Article 125(1)(e).

[530] International Tribunal for the Law of the Sea (2009). Rules of the Tribunal adopted on 28 October 1997 – amended to 25 September 2018 (ITLOS/8, 17 March 2009), Article 125(1)(f).

[531] International Tribunal for the Law of the Sea (2009). Rules of the Tribunal adopted on 28 October 1997 – amended to 25 September 2018 (ITLOS/8, 17 March 2009), Article 125(1)(g).

[532] International Tribunal for the Law of the Sea (2009). Rules of the Tribunal adopted on 28 October 1997 – amended to 25 September 2018 (ITLOS/8, 17 March 2009), Article 125(1)(h).

[533] United Nations (1982). "United Nations Convention on the Law of the Sea," Annex VI, Article 30(1).

[534] International Tribunal for the Law of the Sea (2009). Rules of the Tribunal adopted on 28 October 1997 – amended to 25 September 2018 (ITLOS/8, 17 March 2009), Article 125(1)(i).

[535] International Tribunal for the Law of the Sea (2009). Rules of the Tribunal adopted on 28 October 1997 – amended to 25 September 2018 (ITLOS/8, 17 March 2009), Article 125(1)(j).

[536] International Tribunal for the Law of the Sea (2009). Rules of the Tribunal adopted on 28 October 1997 – amended to 25 September 2018 (ITLOS/8, 17 March 2009), Article 125(1)(k).

[537] International Tribunal for the Law of the Sea (2009). Rules of the Tribunal adopted on 28 October 1997 – amended to 25 September 2018 (ITLOS/8, 17 March 2009), Article 125(1)(l).

[538] International Tribunal for the Law of the Sea (2009). Rules of the Tribunal adopted on 28 October 1997 – amended to 25 September 2018 (ITLOS/8, 17 March 2009), Article 125(1)(m).

[539] United Nations (1982). "United Nations Convention on the Law of the Sea," Annex VI, Article 30(3).

[540] United Nations (1982). "United Nations Convention on the Law of the Sea," Annex VI, Article 30(4).
[541] International Tribunal for the Law of the Sea (2009). Rules of the Tribunal adopted on 28 October 1997 – amended to 25 September 2018 (ITLOS/8, 17 March 2009), Article 124(2).
[542] International Tribunal for the Law of the Sea (2009). Rules of the Tribunal adopted on 28 October 1997 – amended to 25 September 2018 (ITLOS/8, 17 March 2009), Article 127(1).
[543] International Tribunal for the Law of the Sea (2009). Rules of the Tribunal adopted on 28 October 1997 – amended to 25 September 2018 (ITLOS/8, 17 March 2009), Article 127(2).
[544] International Tribunal for the Law of the Sea (2009). Rules of the Tribunal adopted on 28 October 1997 – amended to 25 September 2018 (ITLOS/8, 17 March 2009), Article 128(1).
[545] International Tribunal for the Law of the Sea (2009). Rules of the Tribunal adopted on 28 October 1997 – amended to 25 September 2018 (ITLOS/8, 17 March 2009), Article 128(2).
[546] International Tribunal for the Law of the Sea (2009). Rules of the Tribunal adopted on 28 October 1997 – amended to 25 September 2018 (ITLOS/8, 17 March 2009), Article 128(5).
[547] International Tribunal for the Law of the Sea (2009). Rules of the Tribunal adopted on 28 October 1997 – amended to 25 September 2018 (ITLOS/8, 17 March 2009), Article 128(4).
[548] International Tribunal for the Law of the Sea (2009). Rules of the Tribunal adopted on 28 October 1997 – amended to 25 September 2018 (ITLOS/8, 17 March 2009), Article 129(3).
[549] United Nations (1982). "United Nations Convention on the Law of the Sea," Annex VI, Article 31(1).
[550] United Nations (1982). "United Nations Convention on the Law of the Sea," Annex VI, Article 31(2).
[551] United Nations (1982). "United Nations Convention on the Law of the Sea," Annex VI, Article 31(3).

[552] International Tribunal for the Law of the Sea (2009). Rules of the Tribunal adopted on 28 October 1997 – amended to 25 September 2018 (ITLOS/8, 17 March 2009), Article 99(2).

[553] International Tribunal for the Law of the Sea (2009). Rules of the Tribunal adopted on 28 October 1997 – amended to 25 September 2018 (ITLOS/8, 17 March 2009), Article 99(2)(a).

[554] International Tribunal for the Law of the Sea (2009). Rules of the Tribunal adopted on 28 October 1997 – amended to 25 September 2018 (ITLOS/8, 17 March 2009), Article 99(2)(b).

[555] International Tribunal for the Law of the Sea (2009). Rules of the Tribunal adopted on 28 October 1997 – amended to 25 September 2018 (ITLOS/8, 17 March 2009), Article 99(4).

[556] International Tribunal for the Law of the Sea (2009). Rules of the Tribunal adopted on 28 October 1997 – amended to 25 September 2018 (ITLOS/8, 17 March 2009), Article 99(3).

[557] United Nations (1982). "United Nations Convention on the Law of the Sea," Annex VI, Article 32(1).

[558] United Nations (1982). "United Nations Convention on the Law of the Sea," Annex VI, Article 32(2).

[559] United Nations (1982). "United Nations Convention on the Law of the Sea," Annex VI, Article 32(3).

[560] International Tribunal for the Law of the Sea (2009). Rules of the Tribunal adopted on 28 October 1997 – amended to 25 September 2018 (ITLOS/8, 17 March 2009), Article 100(2).

[561] International Tribunal for the Law of the Sea (2009). Rules of the Tribunal adopted on 28 October 1997 – amended to 25 September 2018 (ITLOS/8, 17 March 2009), Article 100(2)(a).

[562] International Tribunal for the Law of the Sea (2009). Rules of the Tribunal adopted on 28 October 1997 – amended to 25 September 2018 (ITLOS/8, 17 March 2009), Article 100(2)(b).

[563] International Tribunal for the Law of the Sea (2009). Rules of the Tribunal adopted on 28 October 1997 – amended to 25 September 2018 (ITLOS/8, 17 March 2009), Article 100(2)(c).

[564] International Tribunal for the Law of the Sea (2009). Rules of the Tribunal adopted on 28 October 1997 – amended to 25 September 2018 (ITLOS/8, 17 March 2009), Article 107.

[565] International Tribunal for the Law of the Sea (2009). Rules of the Tribunal adopted on 28 October 1997 – amended to 25 September 2018 (ITLOS/8, 17 March 2009), Article 108(1).

[566] International Tribunal for the Law of the Sea (2009). Rules of the Tribunal adopted on 28 October 1997 – amended to 25 September 2018 (ITLOS/8, 17 March 2009), Article 108(3).

[567] International Tribunal for the Law of the Sea (2009). Rules of the Tribunal adopted on 28 October 1997 – amended to 25 September 2018 (ITLOS/8, 17 March 2009), Article 108(4).

[568] International Tribunal for the Law of the Sea (2019). *The M/V "Norstar" Case (Panama v. Italy)*, Judgment of 10 April 2019, *ITLOS Reports 2019*, nyp, paras.1 and 69.

[569] International Tribunal for the Law of the Sea (2019). *The M/V "Norstar" Case (Panama v. Italy)*, Judgment of 10 April 2019, *ITLOS Reports 2019*, nyp, para.5.

[570] International Tribunal for the Law of the Sea (2019). *The M/V "Norstar" Case (Panama v. Italy)*, Judgment of 10 April 2019, *ITLOS Reports 2019*, nyp, para.6.

[571] International Tribunal for the Law of the Sea (2019). *The M/V "Norstar" Case (Panama v. Italy)*, Judgment of 10 April 2019, *ITLOS Reports 2019*, nyp, para.9.

[572] International Tribunal for the Law of the Sea (2019). *The M/V "Norstar" Case (Panama v. Italy)*, Judgment of 10 April 2019, *ITLOS Reports 2019*, nyp, para.12.

[573] International Tribunal for the Law of the Sea (2019). *The M/V "Norstar" Case (Panama v. Italy)*, Judgment of 10 April 2019, *ITLOS Reports 2019*, nyp, para.14.

[574] International Tribunal for the Law of the Sea (2019). *The M/V "Norstar" Case (Panama v. Italy)*, Judgment of 10 April 2019, *ITLOS Reports 2019*, nyp, paras.14-16.

[575] International Tribunal for the Law of the Sea (2019). *The M/V "Norstar" Case (Panama v. Italy)*, Judgment of 10 April 2019, *ITLOS Reports 2019*, nyp, para.17.

[576] International Tribunal for the Law of the Sea (2019). *The M/V "Norstar" Case (Panama v. Italy)*, Judgment of 10 April 2019, *ITLOS Reports 2019*, nyp, para.19.

[577] International Tribunal for the Law of the Sea (2019). *The M/V "Norstar" Case (Panama v. Italy)*, Judgment of 10 April 2019, *ITLOS Reports 2019*, nyp, para.21.

[578] International Tribunal for the Law of the Sea (2019). *The M/V "Norstar" Case (Panama v. Italy)*, Judgment of 10 April 2019, *ITLOS Reports 2019*, nyp, para.22.

[579] International Tribunal for the Law of the Sea (2019). *The M/V "Norstar" Case (Panama v. Italy)*, Judgment of 10 April 2019, *ITLOS Reports 2019*, nyp, para.23.

[580] International Tribunal for the Law of the Sea (2019). *The M/V "Norstar" Case (Panama v. Italy)*, Judgment of 10 April 2019, *ITLOS Reports 2019*, nyp, para.24.

[581] International Tribunal for the Law of the Sea (2019). *The M/V "Norstar" Case (Panama v. Italy)*, Judgment of 10 April 2019, *ITLOS Reports 2019*, nyp, para.32.

[582] International Tribunal for the Law of the Sea (2019). *The M/V "Norstar" Case (Panama v. Italy)*, Judgment of 10 April 2019, *ITLOS Reports 2019*, nyp, para.33.

[583] International Tribunal for the Law of the Sea (2019). *The M/V "Norstar" Case (Panama v. Italy)*, Judgment of 10 April 2019, *ITLOS Reports 2019*, nyp, para.34.

[584] International Tribunal for the Law of the Sea (2019). *The M/V "Norstar" Case (Panama v. Italy)*, Judgment of 10 April 2019, *ITLOS Reports 2019*, nyp, paras.35-36.

[585] International Tribunal for the Law of the Sea (2019). *The M/V "Norstar" Case (Panama v. Italy)*, Judgment of 10 April 2019, *ITLOS Reports 2019*, nyp, para.37.

[586] International Tribunal for the Law of the Sea (2019). *The M/V "Norstar" Case (Panama v. Italy)*, Judgment of 10 April 2019, *ITLOS Reports 2019*, nyp, para.38.

[587] International Tribunal for the Law of the Sea (2019). *The M/V "Norstar" Case (Panama v. Italy)*, Judgment of 10 April 2019, *ITLOS Reports 2019*, nyp, para.39.

[588] International Tribunal for the Law of the Sea (2019). *The M/V "Norstar" Case (Panama v. Italy)*, Judgment of 10 April 2019, *ITLOS Reports 2019*, nyp, para.40.

[589] International Tribunal for the Law of the Sea (2019). *The M/V "Norstar" Case (Panama v. Italy)*, Judgment of 10 April 2019, *ITLOS Reports 2019*, nyp, para.43.

[590] International Tribunal for the Law of the Sea (2019). *The M/V "Norstar" Case (Panama v. Italy)*, Judgment of 10 April 2019, *ITLOS Reports 2019*, nyp, para.44.

[591] International Tribunal for the Law of the Sea (2019). *The M/V "Norstar" Case (Panama v. Italy)*, Judgment of 10 April 2019, *ITLOS Reports 2019*, nyp, para.50.

[592] International Tribunal for the Law of the Sea (2019). *The M/V "Norstar" Case (Panama v. Italy)*, Judgment of 10 April 2019, *ITLOS Reports 2019*, nyp, para.51.

[593] International Tribunal for the Law of the Sea (2019). *The M/V "Norstar" Case (Panama v. Italy)*, Judgment of 10 April 2019, *ITLOS Reports 2019*, nyp, para.52.

[594] International Tribunal for the Law of the Sea (2019). *The M/V "Norstar" Case (Panama v. Italy)*, Judgment of 10 April 2019, *ITLOS Reports 2019*, nyp, para.53.

[595] International Tribunal for the Law of the Sea (2019). *The M/V "Norstar" Case (Panama v. Italy)*, Judgment of 10 April 2019, *ITLOS Reports 2019*, nyp, para.61.

[596] International Tribunal for the Law of the Sea (2019). *The M/V "Norstar" Case (Panama v. Italy)*, Judgment of 10 April 2019, *ITLOS Reports 2019*, nyp, para.54.

[597] International Tribunal for the Law of the Sea (2019). *The M/V "Norstar" Case (Panama v. Italy)*, Judgment of 10 April 2019, *ITLOS Reports 2019*, nyp, para.55.

[598] International Tribunal for the Law of the Sea (2019). *The M/V "Norstar" Case (Panama v. Italy)*, Judgment of 10 April 2019, *ITLOS Reports 2019*, nyp, para.56.

[599] International Tribunal for the Law of the Sea (2019). *The M/V "Norstar" Case (Panama v. Italy)*, Judgment of 10 April 2019, *ITLOS Reports 2019*, nyp, para.57.

[600] International Tribunal for the Law of the Sea (2019). *The M/V "Norstar" Case (Panama v. Italy)*, Judgment of 10 April 2019, *ITLOS Reports 2019*, nyp, para.59.

[601] International Tribunal for the Law of the Sea (2019). *The M/V "Norstar" Case (Panama v. Italy)*, Judgment of 10 April 2019, *ITLOS Reports 2019*, nyp, para.62.

[602] International Tribunal for the Law of the Sea (2019). *The M/V "Norstar" Case (Panama v. Italy)*, Judgment of 10 April 2019, *ITLOS Reports 2019*, nyp, postface.

[603] International Tribunal for the Law of the Sea (2019). "Case No. 25." Accessed December 10, 2019. https://www.itlos.org/cases/list-of-cases/case-no-25/.

[604] United Nations (1982). "United Nations Convention on the Law of the Sea," Article 287(1)(c).

[605] United Nations (1982). "United Nations Convention on the Law of the Sea," Article 287(1)(d).

[606] United Nations (1982). "United Nations Convention on the Law of the Sea," Annex VII, Article 11.

[607] Permanent Court of Arbitration (2015). *PCA Case No 2013-19 in the matter of an arbitration before an arbitral tribunal constituted under Annex VII to the 1982 United Nations Convention on the Law of the Sea between the Republic of the Philippines and the People's Republic of China: Award on Jurisdiction and Admissibility*, 29 October 2015, The Hague: Permanent Court of Arbitration, para.26.

[608] Official Gazette of the Government of the Philippines (2013). Statement: The Secretary of Foreign Affairs on the UNCLOS Arbitral Proceedings against China, January 22, 2013.

[609] Permanent Court of Arbitration (2015). *PCA Case No 2013-19: Award on Jurisdiction and Admissibility*, 29 October 2015, para.27.

[610] Ministry of Foreign Affairs of the People's Republic of China (2014). Position Paper of the Government of the People's Republic of China on the Matter of Jurisdiction in the South China Sea Arbitration Initiated by the Republic of the Philippines, 7 December 2014, para.1.

[611] Ministry of Foreign Affairs of the People's Republic of China (2014). Position Paper of the Government of the People's Republic of China on the Matter of Jurisdiction in the South China Sea Arbitration Initiated by the Republic of the Philippines, 7 December 2014, para.3.

[612] Permanent Court of Arbitration (2015). *PCA Case No 2013-19: Award on Jurisdiction and Admissibility*, 29 October 2015, para.413(A).

[613] Permanent Court of Arbitration (2015). *PCA Case No 2013-19: Award on Jurisdiction and Admissibility*, 29 October 2015, para.413(B).

[614] Permanent Court of Arbitration (2015). *PCA Case No 2013-19: Award on Jurisdiction and Admissibility*, 29 October 2015, paras.413(C) and 26.

[615] Permanent Court of Arbitration (2015). *PCA Case No 2013-19: Award on Jurisdiction and Admissibility*, 29 October 2015, para.413(D).

[616] Permanent Court of Arbitration (2015). *PCA Case No 2013-19: Award on Jurisdiction and Admissibility*, 29 October 2015, para.413(E).

[617] Permanent Court of Arbitration (2015). *PCA Case No 2013-19: Award on Jurisdiction and Admissibility*, 29 October 2015, para.413(F).

[618] Permanent Court of Arbitration (2015). *PCA Case No 2013-19: Award on Jurisdiction and Admissibility*, 29 October 2015, para.413(G).

[619] Permanent Court of Arbitration (2015). *PCA Case No 2013-19: Award on Jurisdiction and Admissibility*, 29 October 2015, para.413(H).

[620] Permanent Court of Arbitration (2015). *PCA Case No 2013-19: Award on Jurisdiction and Admissibility*, 29 October 2015, para.413(I).

[621] Government of the Republic of the Philippines (2014). Arbitration under Annex VII of the United Nations Convention on the Law of the Sea (Republic of the Philippines v. People's Republic of China): Memorial of the Philippines Volume 1, 30 March 2014, para.400.

[622] Permanent Court of Arbitration (2016). *PCA Case No 2013-19 in the matter of an arbitration before an arbitral tribunal constituted under Annex VII to the 1982 United Nations Convention on the Law of the Sea between the Republic of the Philippines and the People's Republic of China: Award*, 12 July 2016 (The Hague: Permanent Court of Arbitration), para.1203(A)(1).

[623] Permanent Court of Arbitration (2016). *PCA Case No 2013-19: Award*, 12 July 2016, para.1203(A)(8).

[624] Permanent Court of Arbitration (2016). *PCA Case No 2013-19: Award*, 12 July 2016, para.1203(A)(7).

[625] Permanent Court of Arbitration (2016). *PCA Case No 2013-19: Award*, 12 July 2016, para.1203(B)(2).

[626] Permanent Court of Arbitration (2016). *PCA Case No 2013-19: Award*, 12 July 2016, para.1203(B)(3)-(7).

[627] Permanent Court of Arbitration (2016). *PCA Case No 2013-19: Award*, 12 July 2016, para.1203(B)(8)-(10) and (12)-(16).

[628] Permanent Court of Arbitration (2016). *PCA Case No 2013-19: Award*, 12 July 2016, para.487.

[629] Permanent Court of Arbitration (2016). *PCA Case No 2013-19: Award*, 12 July 2016, para.504(d).

[630] Permanent Court of Arbitration (2016). *PCA Case No 2013-19: Award*, 12 July 2016, para.490.
[631] Permanent Court of Arbitration (2016). *PCA Case No 2013-19: Award*, 12 July 2016, paras.499-500 and 502-503.
[632] Permanent Court of Arbitration (2016). *PCA Case No 2013-19: Award*, 12 July 2016, para.554.
[633] Permanent Court of Arbitration (2016). *PCA Case No 2013-19: Award*, 12 July 2016, para.557.
[634] Permanent Court of Arbitration (2016). *PCA Case No 2013-19: Award*, 12 July 2016, para.560.
[635] Permanent Court of Arbitration (2016). *PCA Case No 2013-19: Award*, 12 July 2016, para.563.
[636] Permanent Court of Arbitration (2016). *PCA Case No 2013-19: Award*, 12 July 2016, para.566.
[637] Permanent Court of Arbitration (2016). *PCA Case No 2013-19: Award*, 12 July 2016, para.569.
[638] United Nations (1982). "United Nations Convention on the Law of the Sea," Article 121(2)-(3).
[639] Permanent Court of Arbitration (2016). *PCA Case No 2013-19: Award*, 12 July 2016, para.625.
[640] Permanent Court of Arbitration (2016). *PCA Case No 2013-19: Award*, 12 July 2016, para.626.
[641] Permanent Court of Arbitration (2016). *PCA Case No 2013-19: Award*, 12 July 2016, para.615.
[642] Permanent Court of Arbitration (2016). *PCA Case No 2013-19: Award*, 12 July 2016, para.616.
[643] Permanent Court of Arbitration (2016). *PCA Case No 2013-19: Award*, 12 July 2016, para.617.
[644] Permanent Court of Arbitration (2016). *PCA Case No 2013-19: Award*, 12 July 2016, para.618.
[645] Permanent Court of Arbitration (2016). *PCA Case No 2013-19: Award*, 12 July 2016, para.619.
[646] Permanent Court of Arbitration (2016). *PCA Case No 2013-19: Award*, 12 July 2016, para.620.

[647] Permanent Court of Arbitration (2016). *PCA Case No 2013-19: Award*, 12 July 2016, para.621.

[648] Permanent Court of Arbitration (2016). *PCA Case No 2013-19: Award*, 12 July 2016, para.622.

[649] Permanent Court of Arbitration (2016). *PCA Case No 2013-19: Award*, 12 July 2016, para.623.

[650] Permanent Court of Arbitration (2016). *PCA Case No 2013-19: Award*, 12 July 2016, para.624.

[651] Permanent Court of Arbitration (2016). *PCA Case No 2013-19: Award*, 12 July 2016, para.629.

[652] Permanent Court of Arbitration (2016). *PCA Case No 2013-19: Award*, 12 July 2016, para.631.

[653] Permanent Court of Arbitration (2016). *PCA Case No 2013-19: Award*, 12 July 2016, para.632.

[654] Permanent Court of Arbitration (2016). *PCA Case No 2013-19: Award*, 12 July 2016, para.633.

[655] Permanent Court of Arbitration (2016). *PCA Case No 2013-19: Award*, 12 July 2016, para.646.

[656] Permanent Court of Arbitration (2016). *PCA Case No 2013-19: Award*, 12 July 2016, para.647.

[657] United Nations (1982). "United Nations Convention on the Law of the Sea," Preamble.

[658] United Nations Audiovisual Library of International Law (2019). "United Nations Convention on the Law of the Sea: Introductory Note By Tullio Treves." Accessed December 26, 2019. https://legal.un.org/avl/ha/uncls/uncls.html.

[659] Baber, G. (2017). *Essays on International Law* (Newcastle-upon-Tyne: Cambridge Scholars Publishing), 314.

[660] United Nations (1962). Juridical Regime of Historic waters including historic bays – Study prepared by the Secretariat: Document A/CN.4/143 (New York: United Nations), para.183.

[661] United Nations (1962). Juridical Regime of Historic waters including historic bays – Study prepared by the Secretariat, para.185.

[662] United Nations (1962). Juridical Regime of Historic waters including historic bays – Study prepared by the Secretariat, para.186.

[663] United Nations (1982). "United Nations Convention on the Law of the Sea," Annex VII, Article 5.

[664] International Court of Justice (1951). *Fisheries Case (United Kingdom v. Norway)*, Judgment of December 18th 1951, *I.C.J. Reports 1951*, 116-144, 143.

[665] International Court of Justice (1951). *Fisheries Case (United Kingdom v. Norway)*, Judgment of December 18th 1951, *I.C.J. Reports 1951*, 116-144, 125.

[666] International Court of Justice (1951). *Fisheries Case (United Kingdom v. Norway)*, Judgment of December 18th 1951, *I.C.J. Reports 1951*, 116-144, 128.

[667] International Court of Justice (1951). *Fisheries Case (United Kingdom v. Norway)*, Judgment of December 18th 1951, *I.C.J. Reports 1951*, 116-144, 128-129.

[668] International Court of Justice (1951). *Fisheries Case (United Kingdom v. Norway)*, Judgment of December 18th 1951, *I.C.J. Reports 1951*, 116-144, 129.

[669] International Court of Justice (1951). *Fisheries Case (United Kingdom v. Norway)*, Judgment of December 18th 1951, *I.C.J. Reports 1951*, 116-144, 129-130.

[670] International Court of Justice (1951). *Fisheries Case (United Kingdom v. Norway)*, Judgment of December 18th 1951, *I.C.J. Reports 1951*, 116-144, 131.

[671] International Court of Justice (1951). *Fisheries Case (United Kingdom v. Norway)*, Judgment of December 18th 1951, *I.C.J. Reports 1951*, 116-144, 132.

[672] International Court of Justice (1951). *Fisheries Case (United Kingdom v. Norway)*, Judgment of December 18th 1951, *I.C.J. Reports 1951*, 116-144, 132-133.

[673] International Court of Justice (1951). *Fisheries Case (United Kingdom v. Norway)*, Judgment of December 18th 1951, *I.C.J. Reports 1951*, 116-144, 136-137.

[674] International Court of Justice (1951). *Fisheries Case (United Kingdom v. Norway)*, Judgment of December 18th 1951, *I.C.J. Reports 1951*, 116-144, 138.

[675] International Court of Justice (1951). *Fisheries Case (United Kingdom v. Norway)*, Judgment of December 18th 1951, *I.C.J. Reports 1951*, 116-144, 138-139.

[676] International Court of Justice (1951). *Fisheries Case (United Kingdom v. Norway)*, Judgment of December 18th 1951, *I.C.J. Reports 1951*, 116-144, 139.

[677] International Court of Justice (1951). *Fisheries Case (United Kingdom v. Norway)*, Judgment of December 18th 1951, *I.C.J. Reports 1951*, 116-144, 140-142.

[678] United Nations (2006). *Delimitation of the Continental Shelf between the United Kingdom of Great Britain and Northern Ireland, and the French Republic*, Decision of 30 June 1977, *Reports of International Arbitral Awards*, 3-270, 5.

[679] United Nations (2006). *Delimitation of the Continental Shelf between the United Kingdom of Great Britain and Northern Ireland, and the French Republic*, Decision of 14 March 1978, *Reports of International Arbitral Awards*, 271-413, 272 and 275.

[680] United Nations (2006). *Delimitation of the Continental Shelf between the United Kingdom of Great Britain and Northern Ireland, and the French Republic*, Decision of 14 March 1978, *Reports of International Arbitral Awards*, 271-413, 275.

[681] United Nations (2006). *Delimitation of the Continental Shelf between the United Kingdom of Great Britain and Northern Ireland, and the French Republic*, Decision of 14 March 1978, *Reports of International Arbitral Awards*, 271-413, 276-277.

[682] United Nations (2006). *Delimitation of the Continental Shelf between the United Kingdom of Great Britain and Northern Ireland,*

and the French Republic, Decision of 14 March 1978, *Reports of International Arbitral Awards*, 271-413, 329-330.

[683] International Tribunal for the Law of the Sea (2017). *Delimitation of the maritime boundary between Ghana and Côte D'Ivoire in the Atlantic Ocean (Ghana/Côte D'Ivoire)*, Judgment of 23 September 2017, *ITLOS Reports 2017*, 4, para.660.

[684] International Tribunal for the Law of the Sea (2017). *Delimitation of the maritime boundary between Ghana and Côte D'Ivoire in the Atlantic Ocean (Ghana/Côte D'Ivoire)*, Judgment of 23 September 2017, *ITLOS Reports 2017*, 4, para.599.

[685] International Tribunal for the Law of the Sea (2017). *Delimitation of the maritime boundary between Ghana and Côte D'Ivoire in the Atlantic Ocean (Ghana/Côte D'Ivoire)*, Judgment of 23 September 2017, *ITLOS Reports 2017*, 4, paras.601-602.

[686] International Tribunal for the Law of the Sea (2017). *Delimitation of the maritime boundary between Ghana and Côte D'Ivoire in the Atlantic Ocean (Ghana/Côte D'Ivoire)*, Judgment of 23 September 2017, *ITLOS Reports 2017*, 4, para.604.

[687] International Tribunal for the Law of the Sea (2017). *Delimitation of the maritime boundary between Ghana and Côte D'Ivoire in the Atlantic Ocean (Ghana/Côte D'Ivoire)*, Judgment of 23 September 2017, *ITLOS Reports 2017*, 4, paras.604-605.

[688] International Tribunal for the Law of the Sea (2017). *Delimitation of the maritime boundary between Ghana and Côte D'Ivoire in the Atlantic Ocean (Ghana/Côte D'Ivoire)*, Judgment of 23 September 2017, *ITLOS Reports 2017*, 4, paras.605 and 660(6).

[689] International Tribunal for the Law of the Sea (2017). *Delimitation of the maritime boundary between Ghana and Côte D'Ivoire in the Atlantic Ocean (Ghana/Côte D'Ivoire)*, Judgment of 23 September 2017, *ITLOS Reports 2017*, 4, paras.624, 630, 634 and 660(6).

BIBLIOGRAPHY

Amerasinghe, C. (1974). The Problem of Archipelagoes in the International Law of the Sea, *The International and Comparative Law Quarterly*, 23(3), 539-575.

Association of Southeast Asian Nations (2019). "*ASEAN Member States*." Accessed December 16, 2019. https://asean.org/asean/asean-member-states/.

Association of Southeast Asian Nations/Government of the People's Republic of China (2012). Declaration on the Conduct of Parties in the South China Sea. *Phnom Penh*, 4th November 2012.

Baber, G. (2017). *Essays on International Law*. Newcastle-upon-Tyne: Cambridge Scholars Publishing.

Berkeley Law University of California (2019). "*Judge Tullio Treves*." Accessed December 26, 2019. https://www.law.berkeley.edu/wp-content/uploads/2015/04/treves-bio.pdf.

Bluebird Marine Systems (2019). "*Vladimir Golitsyn*." Accessed December 5, 2019. http://www.bluebird-electric.net/oceanography/Global_Ocean_Commisioners/Vladimir_Golitsyn.htm.

Brock, J. (1966). Archipelago Concept of Limits of Territorial Seas, *Naval War College Review*, 19(4), 34-97.

Case 2/74. *Jean Reyners v. Belgian State* [1974] ECR 631.

Case C-260/89. *Elliniki Radiophonia Tiléorassi Anonimi Etairia and Panellinia Omospondia Syllogon Prossopikou v. Dimotiki Étairia*

Plifoforissis, Sotirios Kouvelas, Nicolaos Avdellas and Others [1991] ECR I-2925.

Case C-54/99. *Association Église de Scientologie de Paris and Scientology International Reserves Trust v. The Prime Minister* [2000] ECR I-1335.

Central American Court of Justice (1917). *El Salvador v. Nicaragua*, Judgment of 9 March 1917, *American Journal of International Law*, 11(3), 674-730.

Commission on the Limits of the Continental Shelf (1999). *Scientific and Technical Guidelines of the Commission on the Limits of the Continental Shelf*: Adopted by the Commission on 13 May 1999 at its fifth session. New York: Commission on the Limits of the Continental Shelf.

Consiglio Nazionale delle Ricerche (2019). "*Tullio Treves*." Accessed December 26, 2019. https://www.cnr.it/sigla/genericdownload/CV%20Tullio_Treves%20Prot.0000321%20del%2025.09.18.pdf?nodeRef=f0253ea3-10b0-4440-9cab-ff8859d6d142;1.0.

Continental Shelf Programme (2019). "*Background to UNCLOS*." Accessed July 17 and 20, 2019. http://www.continentalshelf.org/about/1143.aspx.

Curtis, Mallet-Prevost, Colt & Mosle LLP (2019). "*Tullio Treves Consultant*." Accessed December 26, 2019. https://www.curtis.com/our-people/tullio-treves/experience.

EUR-Lex (2019). "*Glossary of summaries: Treaties*." Accessed December 26, 2019. https://eur-lex.europa.eu/summary/glossary/treaties.html.

Geographic.org (2019). "*Geographical Names – Indreleia: Norway*." Accessed December 31, 2019. https://geographic.org/geographic_names/name.php?uni=286538&fid=4411&c=norway.

GNS Science (2019). "*The Foot of the Continental Slope*." Accessed August 25, 2019. https://www.gns.cri.nz/static/unclos/footslope.html.

Government of the People's Republic of China (1992). *Law on the Territorial Sea and the Contiguous Zone of 25 February 1992*.

Government of the Republic of the Philippines (2014). Arbitration under Annex VII of the United Nations Convention on the Law of the Sea

(Republic of the Philippines v. People's Republic of China): *Memorial of the Philippines Volume 1*, 30 March 2014.

Hartig, R. L. (1972). Remarks Concerning the Recently Published State Department Charts, *in* United States Congress: Senate Committee on Commerce – *Ninety-Second Congress: Second Session on Provisional U.S. Charts Delimiting Alaskan Territorial Boundaries, May 15, 1972, Serial No. 92-69*. Washington, D.C.: United States Government Printing Office. 168-172.

International Court of Justice (1951). *Fisheries Case (United Kingdom v. Norway)*, Judgment of December 18th 1951, *I.C.J. Reports 1951*, 116-144.

International Court of Justice (1974). *Nuclear Tests (Australia v. France)*, Judgment of 20 December 1974, *I.C.J. Reports 1974*, 253-274.

International Court of Justice (1981). *Continental Shelf (Tunisia/Libyan Arab Jamahiriya), Application to Intervene*, Judgment of 14 April 1981, *I.C.J. Reports 1981*, 3-21.

International Court of Justice (1984). *Continental Shelf (Libyan Arab Jamahiriya/Malta), Application to Intervene*, Judgment of 21 March 1984, *I.C.J. Reports 1984*, 3-30.

International Court of Justice (1986). *Frontier Dispute (Burkina Faso/Mali)*, Judgment of 22 December 1986, *I.C.J. Reports 1986*, 554-651.

International Court of Justice (1990a). *Land, Island and Maritime Frontier Dispute (El Salvador/Honduras), Application to Intervene*, Judgment of 13 September 1990, *I.C.J. Reports 1990*, 92-137.

International Court of Justice (1990b). *Land, Island and Maritime Frontier Dispute (El Salvador/Honduras), Application to Intervene*, Separate Opinion of Judge Oda, *I.C.J. Reports 1990*, 138-144.

International Court of Justice (1992a). *Land, Island and Maritime Frontier Dispute (El Salvador/Honduras), Application to Intervene*, Declaration of Judge Oda, *I.C.J. Reports 1992*, 619-620.

International Court of Justice (1992b). *Land, Island and Maritime Frontier Dispute (El Salvador/Honduras: Nicaragua intervening)*, Judgment of 11 September 1992, *I.C.J. Reports 1992*, 351-618.

International Court of Justice (1992c). *Land, Island and Maritime Frontier Dispute (El Salvador/Honduras: Nicaragua intervening)*, Separate Opinion of Judge Torres Bernárdes, *I.C.J. Reports 1992*, 629-731.

International Court of Justice (1998a). *Land and Maritime Boundary between Cameroon and Nigeria, Preliminary Objections*, Judgment of 11 June 1998, *I.C.J. Reports 1998*, 275-327.

International Court of Justice (1998b). Special Agreement for Submission to the International Court of Justice of the Dispute between Indonesia and Malaysia concerning Sovereignty over Pulau Ligitan and Pulau Sipadan – jointly notified to the Court on 2 November 1998: 1998 General List No. 102. The Hague: International Court of Justice.

International Court of Justice (2002). *Land and Maritime Boundary between Cameroon and Nigeria (Cameroon v. Nigeria: Equatorial Guinea intervening)*, Judgment of 10 October 2002, *I.C.J. Reports 2002*, 303-458.

International Court of Justice (2003a). *Application for Revision of the Judgment of 11 July 1996 in the Case concerning* Application of the Convention on the Prevention and Punishment of the Crime of Genocide (Bosnia and Herzegovina v. Yugoslavia), Preliminary Objections *(Yugoslavia v. Bosnia and Herzegovina)*, Judgment of 3 February 2003, *I.C.J. Reports 2003*, 7-30.

International Court of Justice (2003b). *Application for Revision of the Judgment of 11 September 1992 in the Case concerning the Land, Island and Maritime Frontier Dispute* (El Salvador/Honduras: Nicaragua intervening) *(El Salvador v. Honduras)*, Dissenting Opinion of Judge Paolillo, *I.C.J. Reports 2003*, 413-426.

International Court of Justice (2003c). *Application for Revision of the Judgment of 11 September 1992 in the Case concerning the Land, Island and Maritime Frontier Dispute* (El Salvador/Honduras: Nicaragua intervening) *(El Salvador v. Honduras)*, Judgment of 18 December 2003, *I.C.J. Reports 2003*, 392-412.

International Court of Justice (2003d). *Application for Revision of the Judgment of 11 September 1992 in the Case concerning the Land, Island and Maritime Frontier Dispute* (El Salvador/Honduras:

Nicaragua intervening) (El Salvador v. Honduras: Summary of the Judgment delivered by the Chamber on Thursday 18 December 2003, Summary 2003/5, 18 December 2003. The Hague: International Court of Justice.

International Court of Justice (2005). Rules of Court (1978) adopted on 14 April 1978 and entered into force on 1 July 1978 – amended to 29 September 2005. The Hague: International Court of Justice.

International Court of Justice (2019a). "*All Judges ad hoc.*" Accessed October 18, 2019, and November 5, 2019. https://www.icj-cij.org/en/all-judges-ad-hoc.

International Court of Justice (2019b). "*All Members.*" Accessed October 18, 2019, and November 5, 2019. https://www.icj-cij.org/en/all-mem bers.

International Court of Justice (2019c). "*Basis of the Court's jurisdiction.*" Accessed October 6, 2019. https://www.icj-cij.org/en/basis-of-jurisdiction.

International Court of Justice (2019d). "*Chambers and Committees.*" Accessed November 15, 2019. https://www.icj-cij.org/en/chambers-and-committees.

International Court of Justice (2019e). "*Current Members.*" Accessed October 4, 2019, and November 15, 2019. https://www.icj-cij.org/en/current-members.

International Court of Justice (2019f). "*Declarations recognizing the jurisdiction of the Court as compulsory.*" Accessed October 5, 2019. https://www.icj-cij.org/en/declarations.

International Court of Justice (2019g). "*Declarations recognizing the jurisdiction of the Court as compulsory: Ireland.*" Accessed October 5, 2019. https://www.icj-cij.org/en/declarations/ie.

International Court of Justice (2019h). "*How the Court Works.*" Accessed October 6, 2019. https://www.icj-cij.org/en/how-the-court-works.

International Court of Justice (2019i). "*Judges ad hoc.*" Accessed October 18, 2019. https://www.icj-cij.org/en/judges-ad-hoc.

International Court of Justice (2019j). "*Presidency.*" Accessed October 9, 2019. https://www.icj-cij.org/en/presidency.

International Court of Justice (2019k). Press Release Unofficial No. 2019/22: 22 May 2019, Mr. Philippe Gautier elected Registrar of the International Court of Justice. The Hague, International Court of Justice.

International Court of Justice (2019l). Rules of Court (1978) adopted on 14 April 1978 and entered into force on 1 July 1978 – amended to 21 October 2019. The Hague: International Court of Justice.

International Tribunal for the Law of the Sea (2006). *Guidelines Concerning the Preparation and Presentation of Cases before the Tribunal* (ITLOS/9, 14 November 2006). Hamburg: International Tribunal for the Law of the Sea.

International Tribunal for the Law of the Sea (2009). *Rules of the Tribunal* adopted on 28 October 1997 – amended to 25 September 2018 (ITLOS/8, 17 March 2009). Hamburg: International Tribunal for the Law of the Sea.

International Tribunal for the Law of the Sea (2012). *Delimitation of the maritime boundary in the Bay of Bengal (Bangladesh/Myanmar)*, Judgment of 14 March 2012, *ITLOS Reports 2012*, 4.

International Tribunal for the Law of the Sea (2016a), Order: The M/V "Norstar" Case (*Panama v. Italy*) (Case No. 25, Order 2016/6, 29 November 2019). Hamburg: International Tribunal for the Law of the Sea.

International Tribunal for the Law of the Sea (2016b). *The M/V "Norstar" Case (Panama v. Italy), Preliminary Objections*, Judgment of 4 November 2016, *ITLOS Report 2016*, 44.

International Tribunal for the Law of the Sea (2016c), Written Preliminary Objections under Article 294, Paragraph 3, of the United Nations Convention on the Law of the Sea: The M/V "Norstar" Case (*Panama v. Italy*) (Case No. 25, 10 March 2016). Hamburg: International Tribunal for the Law of the Sea.

International Tribunal for the Law of the Sea (2017a). *Delimitation of the maritime boundary between Ghana and Côte D'Ivoire in the Atlantic Ocean (Ghana/Côte D'Ivoire)*, Judgment of 23 September 2017, *ITLOS Reports 2017*, 4.

International Tribunal for the Law of the Sea (2017b), Order: The M/V "Norstar" Case (*Panama v. Italy*) (Case No. 25, Order 2017/1, 15 November 2017). Hamburg: International Tribunal for the Law of the Sea.

International Tribunal for the Law of the Sea (2017c). Press Release: Dispute concerning delimitation of the maritime boundary between Ghana and Côte D'Ivoire – Special Chamber delivers its judgment on 23 September 2017 (ITLOS/Press 264, 23 September 2017). Hamburg: International Tribunal for the Law of the Sea.

International Tribunal for the Law of the Sea (2018), Order: The M/V "Norstar" Case (*Panama v. Italy*) (Case No. 25, Order 2018/1, 20 July 2018). Hamburg: International Tribunal for the Law of the Sea.

International Tribunal for the Law of the Sea (2019a). "*Case No. 25*." Accessed December 7 and 10, 2019. https://www.itlos.org/cases/list-of-cases/case-no-25/.

International Tribunal for the Law of the Sea (2019b). "*Case No. 25 Preliminary Objections*." Accessed December 6, 2019. https://ww w.itl os.org/en/cases/list-of-cases/case-no-25/case-no-25-preliminary-objec tions/.

International Tribunal for the Law of the Sea (2019c). "*Chambers*." Accessed November 13 and 14, 2019. https://www.itlos.org/en/the-tribunal/chambers/.

International Tribunal for the Law of the Sea (2019d). E-mail from Ms. Julia Ritter, Press Officer at the ITLOS, to Dr. Graeme Baber, 16th November 2019.

International Tribunal for the Law of the Sea (2019e). "*General Information*." Accessed November 10, 2019. https://www.itlos.org/gen eral-information/.

International Tribunal for the Law of the Sea (2019f). "*Judge Elsa Kelly*." Accessed November 14, 2019. https://www.itlos.org/the-tribunal/mem bers/judge-elsa-kelly/.

International Tribunal for the Law of the Sea (2019g). "*Judge Jean-Pierre Cot*." Accessed November 14, 2019. https://www.itlos.org/the-tribuna l/members/judge-jean-pierre-cot/.

International Tribunal for the Law of the Sea (2019h). "*Judge Liesbeth Lijnzaad.*" Accessed November 14, 2019. https://www.itlos.org/the-tribunal/members/judge-liesbeth-lijnzaad/.

International Tribunal for the Law of the Sea (2019i). "*Judge Roman A. Kolodkin.*" Accessed November 14, 2019. https://www.itlos.org/the-tribunal/members/judge-roman-a-kolodkin/.

International Tribunal for the Law of the Sea (2019j). "*Judges ad hoc.*" Accessed November 15, 2019, and December 5, 2019. https://www.itlos.org/the-tribunal/judges-ad-hoc/.

International Tribunal for the Law of the Sea (2019k). "*Judge Tafsir Malick Ndiaye.*" Accessed November 14, 2019. https://www.itlos.org/the-tribunal/members/judge-tafsir-malick-ndiaye/.

International Tribunal for the Law of the Sea (2019l). "*Members.*" Accessed November 11, 2019. https://www.itlos.org/the-tribunal/members/.

International Tribunal for the Law of the Sea (2019m). Order: Constitution of Chamber for the dispute concerning delimitation of the maritime boundary between Mauritius and Maldives in the Indian Ocean (Mauritius/Maldives) (Case No. 28, Order 2019/4, 27 September 2019). Hamburg: International Tribunal for the Law of the Sea.

International Tribunal for the Law of the Sea (2019n). Order: Request for the prescription of provisional measures regarding the M/T "*San Padre Pio*" Case (Switzerland v. Nigeria) (Case No. 27, 6 July 2019). Hamburg: International Tribunal for the Law of the Sea.

International Tribunal for the Law of the Sea (2019o). "*President Jin-Hyun Paik.*" Accessed November 13, 2019, and December 5, 2019. https://www.itlos.org/the-tribunal/members/president-jin-hyun-paik/.

International Tribunal for the Law of the Sea (2019p). "*Publications.*" Accessed December 6, 2019. https://www.itlos.org/publications/.

International Tribunal for the Law of the Sea (2019q). *The M/V "Norstar" Case (Panama v. Italy)*, Judgment of 10 April 2019, *ITLOS Reports 2019*, nyp.

International Tribunal for the Law of the Sea (2019r). "*The Registrar.*" Accessed November 13, 2019. https://www.itlos.org/the-registry/the-registrar/the-registrar/.

International Tribunal for the Law of the Sea (2019s). "*Vice-President David Joseph Attard*". Accessed November 14, 2019. https://www.itlos.org/the-tribunal/members/vice-president-david-jose ph-attard/.

Kingdom of Colonia St John (2019). "*The History of the Kingdom of Colonia St John.*" Accessed December 23, 2019. http://www.colonia.asia/history%20-%20the%20history%20of%20the%20kingdom%20of%20colonia%20st%20john.htm.

Kohen, M.G., and Hébié, M. (2011). Territory, Acquisition. *Max Planck Encyclopedia of Public International Law.*

McFarlane, G. (1984). *The Layman's Dictionary of English Law*. London: Waterlow Publishers Limited.

Merriam-Webster (2019a). "*arguendo* adverb." Accessed December 16, 2019. https://www.merriam-webster.com/legal/arguendo.

Merriam-Webster (2019b). "*note verbale* noun." Accessed December 5, 2019. https://www.merriam-webster.com/dictionary/note%20verbale.

Merriam-Webster (2019c). "*proprio motu* adverb." Accessed September 23, 2019. https://www.merriam-webster.com/dictionary/proprio%20motu.

Merriam-Webster (2019d). "*res inter alios acta* noun." Accessed October 25, 2019. https://www.merriam-webster.com/legal/res%20inter%20alios%20acta.

Ministry of Foreign Affairs of the People's Republic of China (2014). *Position Paper of the Government of the People's Republic of China on the Matter of Jurisdiction in the South China Sea Arbitration Initiated by the Republic of the Philippines,* 7 December 2014.

Official Gazette of the Government of the Philippines (2013). Statement: *The Secretary of Foreign Affairs on the UNCLOS Arbitral Proceedings against China*, January 22, 2013.

Organization for Economic Co-operation and Development (2019). "*Glossary of Statistical Terms: Exclusive Economic Zone (EEZ).*"

Accessed July 20, 2019. https://stats.oecd.org/glossary/detail.asp?ID=884.

Oxford Reference (2019a). "*In concreto.*" Accessed October 20, 2019. Https://www.oxfordreference.com/view/10.1093/acref/9780195369380.001.0001/acref-9780195369380-e-897.

Oxford Reference (2019b). "*Inter fauces terrarium.*" Accessed December 30, 2019. https://www.oxfordreference.com/view/10.1093/acref/9780195369380.001.0001/acref-9780195369380-e-1031.

Pearsall, J. (editor) (1998). *The New Oxford Dictionary of English*. Oxford: Oxford University Press.

Permanent Court of Arbitration (2015). *PCA Case No 2013-19 in the matter of an arbitration before an arbitral tribunal constituted under Annex VII to the 1982 United Nations Convention on the Law of the Sea between the Republic of the Philippines and the People's Republic of China: Award on Jurisdiction and Admissibility*, 29 October 2015. The Hague: Permanent Court of Arbitration.

Permanent Court of Arbitration (2016). *PCA Case No 2013-19 in the matter of an arbitration before an arbitral tribunal constituted under Annex VII to the 1982 United Nations Convention on the Law of the Sea between the Republic of the Philippines and the People's Republic of China: Award*, 12 July 2016. The Hague: Permanent Court of Arbitration.

Permanent Court of Arbitration (2019a). "*About us.*" Accessed December 15, 2019. https://pca-cpa.org/en/about/.

Permanent Court of Arbitration (2019b). "*Contracting Parties.*" Accessed December 15, 2019. https://pca-cpa.org/en/about/introduction/contracting-parties/.

Permanent Court of Arbitration (2019c). "*Documents and Resources: PCA Rules & Conventions.*" Accessed December 15, 2019. https://pca-cpa.org/en/documents/pca-conventions-and-rules/pca-founding-conventions-and-internal-rules/.

Permanent Mission of the People's Republic of China to the United Nations (2009a). *Note verbale* to Mr. Ban Ki-moon, Secretary-General of the United Nations, CML/17/2009, New York, 7th May 2009.

Permanent Mission of the People's Republic of China to the United Nations (2009b). *Note verbale* to Mr. Ban Ki-moon, Secretary-General of the United Nations, CML/18/2009, New York, 7th May 2009.

Philippine Embassy in Madrid (2019). "*Albert F. Del Rosario*." Accessed December 16, 2019. https://www.philembassymadrid.com/albert-f-del-rosario.

Phillips, T., Holmes, O, and Bowcott, O. (2016). Beijing rejects tribunal's ruling in South China Sea case. *The Guardian*, Tuesday 12 July 2016. Accessed December 25, 2019. https://www.theguardian.co m/world/2016/jul/12/philippines-wins-south-china-sea-case-against-china.

Rotterdam Mainport University 1of Applied Sciences (2015). *Maritime Symposium: Bunkering at sea* – March 12th 2015. Rotterdam: Rotterdam Mainport University of Applied Sciences.

Royal Museums Greenwich (2019). "*What is a nautical mile?*" Accessed July 19, 2019. https://www.rmg.co.uk/discover/explore/nautical-mile-0.

South China Morning Post (2019). *Former Philippine diplomat Albert Del Rosario, who criticized China, back in Manila after Hong Kong deportation.* https://www.scmp.com/week-asia/politics/article/3015470/philippines-del-rosario-held-hong-kong-airport-after-anti-china.

Stortinget (2019). "*The Storting*." Accessed December 31, 2019. https://www.stortinget.no/en/In-English/About-the-Storting/.

Symmons, C. (1995). Some Problems Relating to the Definition of Insular Formations in International Law – Islands and Low-Tide Elevations, *University of Durham Maritime Briefing*, 1(5).

Traité instituant la Communauté Économique Européenne (1957).

Treaty Establishing the European Community (1992). *Official Journal of the European Communities 1992*, C 224/1, 31 August 1992.

Treaty of Lisbon amending the Treaty on European Union and the Treaty establishing the European Community (2007). *Official Journal of the European Union 2007*, C 306/1, 17 December 2007.

Treaty on the Functioning of the European Union (2016). *Official Journal of the European Union 2016*, C 202/47, 7 June 2016.

United Nations (1945). "Charter of the United Nations," *United Nations Treaty Series* Registration Number N/A.

United Nations (1945). "Statute of the International Court of Justice," *United Nations Treaty Series* Registration Number N/A.

United Nations (1958). "Convention on Fishing and Conservation of the Living Resources of the High Seas," *United Nations Treaty Series* Registration Number 8164.

United Nations (1958). "Convention on the Continental Shelf," *United Nations Treaty Series* Registration Number 7302.

United Nations (1958). "Convention on the Territorial Sea and the Contiguous Zone," *United Nations Treaty Series* Registration Number 7477.

United Nations (1962). Juridical Regime of Historic waters including historic bays – Study prepared by the Secretariat: Document A/CN.4/143. New York: United Nations.

United Nations (1969). "Vienna Convention on the Law of Treaties," *United Nations Treaty Series* Registration Number 18232.

United Nations (1982). "United Nations Convention on the Law of the Sea," *United Nations Treaty Series* Registration Number 31363.

United Nations (2006a). *Delimitation of the Continental Shelf between the United Kingdom of Great Britain and Northern Ireland, and the French Republic*, Decision of 30 June 1977, *Reports of International Arbitral Awards*, 3-270.

United Nations (2006b). *Delimitation of the Continental Shelf between the United Kingdom of Great Britain and Northern Ireland, and the French Republic*, Decision of 14 March 1978, *Reports of International Arbitral Awards*, 271-413.

United Nations (2019a). "*Charter of the United Nations*." Accessed December 29, 2019. https://www.un.org/en/charter-united-nations/.

United Nations (2019b). "*Department for General Assembly and Conference Management: United Nations Regional Groups of Member States*." Accessed November 11, 2019. https://www.un.org/depts/DGACM/RegionalGroups.shtml.

United Nations Audiovisual Library of International Law (2019a). "*1958 Geneva Conventions on the Law of the Sea: Introductory Note by Tullio Treves*." Accessed December 30, 2019. https://legal.un.org/a vl/ha/gclos/gclos.html.

United Nations Audiovisual Library of International Law (2019b). "*United Nations Convention on the Law of the Sea: Introductory Note by Tullio Treves*." Accessed December 26, 2019. https://legal.un.org/avl/ha/un cls/uncls.html.

United Nations Office for Ocean Affairs and the Law of the Sea (1988). The Law of the Sea: Régime of Islands Legislative History of Part VIII (Article 121) of the United Nations Convention on the Law of the Sea. New York: United Nations.

United Nations Treaty Collection (2019). "*Chapter XXI Law of the Sea: 6. United Nations Convention on the Law of the Sea*." Accessed July 17, 2019, and December 15, 16, 26 and 28, 2019. https://treaties.un.org/P ages/ViewDetailsIII.aspx?src=TREATY&mtdsg_no=XXI-6&chapter=21&Temp=mtdsg3&clang=_en.

University of Ottawa (2019). "*JuriGlobe: World Legal Systems Research Group – Alphabetical Index of the Political Entities and Corresponding Legal Systems.*" Accessed October 4, 2019, and November 11, 2019. http://www.juriglobe.ca/eng/sys-juri/index-alph a.php.

Walker, G. (2005). Defining Terms in the 1982 Law of the Sea Convention IV: The Last Round of Definitions Proposed By the International Law Association (American Branch) Law of the Sea Committee, *California Western International Law Journal*, 36(1), 133-183.

Walker, G. (editor) (2012). *Definitions for the Law of the Sea: Terms Not Defined by the 1982 Convention*. Leiden: Martinus Nijhoff Publishers.

Wikipedia (2019). "*Spratly Islands*." Accessed December 26, 2019. https://en.wikipedia.org/wiki/Spratly_Islands.

Xinhua News Agency (2019). "*China, Philippines reach important consensus through diplomatic consultation*." Accessed December 26, 2019. http://www.xinhuanet.com/english/2019-07/26/c_13826 1164.htm.

About the Author

Graeme Baber

Graeme Baber is a jurist and a legal researcher, specializing in financial law and international law. His previous monographs are *The Impact of Legislation and Regulation on the Freedom of Movement of Capital in Estonia, Poland and Latvia* (Cambridge Scholars Publishing, 2010), *The Free Movement of Capital and Financial Services: An Exposition?* (Cambridge Scholars Publishing, 2014), *The European Union and the Global Financial Crisis: A View from 2016* (Nova Science Publishers, 2016), *Essays on International Law* (Cambridge Scholars Publishing, 2017), *International Financial Law: Quo Vadis?* (Nova Science Publishers, 2017), *Preferential Trade Agreements and International Law* (Routledge, 2018), and *The United Nations System: A Synopsis* (Cambridge Scholars Publishing, 2019). Graeme has published many papers. He is also an experienced teacher of university students.

INDEX

A

B

C

D

E

J

L

M

P

R

S

T

U